BEYOND THE SUNSET

MERCER UNIVERSITY PRESS

Endowed by

TOM WATSON BROWN
and
THE WATSON-BROWN FOUNDATION, INC.

BEYOND THE SUNSET

The Melungeon Outdoor Drama, 1969–1976

Wayne Winkler

MERCER UNIVERSITY PRESS

Macon, Georgia

1979   2019

40 Years of Publishing Excellence

MUP/ P589

© 2019 by Mercer University Press
Published by Mercer University Press
1501 Mercer University Drive
Macon, Georgia 31207
All rights reserved

9 8 7 6 5 4 3 2 1

Books published by Mercer University Press are printed on acid-free paper
that meets the requirements of the American National Standard for
Information Sciences—Permanence of Paper for Printed Library Materials.

Printed and bound in the United States.

This book is set in Adobe Garamond Pro

Cover/jacket design by Burt&Burt

ISBN   978-0-88146-718-5
Cataloging-in-Publication Data is available from the Library of Congress

CONTENTS

For Claire and Josef

1

"NOTHING WE DO EVER WORKS"

A rooster crowing somewhere on Newman's Ridge woke Claude with a start. *I must have dozed off for just a minute*, he thought. It couldn't have been for very long; it was still dark in the hollow behind the school. As he looked up the hill behind him, however, Claude could see a faint glow of daylight. The other men were stirring. Some had stretched out on the log benches and taken a nap, but it seemed like the rooster had awakened them as well.

Claude and the others had spent the entire night guarding the newly built amphitheater behind the elementary school. Of course, they'd been certain there was no bomb. *Almost* certain—*but you cain't never tell*, as the old folks said. If someone really wanted to blow up the amphitheater, it's doubtful they'd talk about it. On the other hand, some people were pretty worked up about the idea of the outdoor drama—like the man who'd sold the little pieces of land adjoining the school property. Claude had negotiated that transaction when the committee said they needed it for the amphitheater. Claude hadn't been completely honest about what the amphitheater was going to be used for, and the man wasn't happy about it when he found out. Maybe he was the one who started the rumor about a bomb. Maybe it was someone else who opposed the whole project. *There were plenty of those—people who complained about anything anyone tried to do to make things better*, Claude thought ruefully. *We've got people here who would be against the second coming of Jesus.* Probably it was just one of those rumors that seems to come out of nowhere but spreads like wildfire through dry grass. In any event, nothing had happened, so that was one less thing to worry about.

The weather wasn't going to be a problem, either. It was going to be a hot day again, with the temperature topping out in the upper 80s, but at least there was no rain in the forecast. The rows of log benches set into the terraced ground of the amphitheater were still in shadow and covered with a light film of dew, but there was now enough daylight for Claude to see that there wasn't a cloud in the sky, nothing to keep people away.

As he poured the last lukewarm cup of coffee from a thermos, Claude Collins stood and stretched. He was just a little taller than average height, with a coppery tint to his skin and thick, slightly wavy dark hair. His eyes, red and swollen from staying awake most of the night, lacked their usual twinkle behind his black horn-rimmed glasses. As looked out over the amphitheater with satisfaction, he smiled his usual lopsided grin and thought, *We've gotten it done!*

Everyone had worked hard getting this place ready. None of them had the slightest idea how to build an amphitheater; most of them had never even seen one. Somebody had sent them some plans, but most of the men who were responsible for building the amphitheater didn't know how to read plans and blueprints. They could build a barn or even a house without plans, but some of them couldn't even read their own names. They were good men, smart men, but education wasn't a priority for a lot of families in the county.

Mr. Welton had been surprised, to say the least, when he showed up a couple of weeks earlier with the student actors from Carson-Newman College and found that the amphitheater wasn't completed. But the local men had gotten a good start on it, and a lot of necessary work had been completed. They had leveled the area at the bottom of the hill where the stage would be, dug a drainage ditch, and terraced the hillside for the log benches. They had everything they needed to finish—the split logs that would serve as seats, the gravel for the aisles, the lumber for the stage, the backdrop, the concession stand, and the ticket booth. They had a few lights, and more had been ordered. Everyone pitched in once Mr. Welton told them what needed to be done, and the students joined in with the VISTA workers and the Happy Pappies, Kyle Greene's men from Operation Mainstream, to get the amphitheater built. There were still a few little things left to do, but they had all day to finish before the people began arriving—*if* they arrived.

That was the worry that was still on Claude's mind as he absent-mindedly scratched at the stubble on his cheeks. He'd spent almost all his forty-two years living in Hancock County, not counting his Army time or the brief time he'd spent living in Ellicott City, Maryland, on the western edge of Baltimore. But even there, a colony of folks from Hancock County, people who'd moved there to find work, made it feel like home. He knew how people in Hancock County felt about things, how they reacted to new ideas.

He had to admit, a lot had been accomplished in the last few years, more than he would have expected. But this idea to stage an outdoor drama—about *this* subject—made Claude wonder if they hadn't bitten off more than they could chew. A lot of people didn't like the idea, that was certain. But the college professors who did that economic study had been right; this story was the only thing Hancock County had that might inspire people to make that white-knuckle trip across Clinch Mountain to come to Sneedville and leave some money behind.

Selling the idea to the rest of the people in the county was the trickiest part, and they hadn't been entirely successful. A lot of people still never said *that* word, the word they used for the folks who lived on the Ridge and in the valley on the other side of it. Claude never heard it, anyway. The Reverend Leonard and the teachers at the Presbyterian mission school never said it. *Maybe they should have*, Claude thought. *Then maybe I'd have known why I caught so much hell when I graduated from the mission school after eighth grade.* He and the other boys from the Ridge were picked on a lot when they started attending the public high school. They'd thought it was because they were poor, and had old, worn-out clothes—but lots of the other kids were poor, too. No, it was something else—something that was whispered but never spoken out loud.

Then that article came out in the *Saturday Evening Post* back in 1947, Claude's first year of college down in Knoxville. Everyone in the county seemed angry and embarrassed to have the whole world reading about Hancock County and the people who lived there. Folks said one local girl had even dropped out of the teacher's college in Johnson City because she was embarrassed to be from Hancock County, where *those* people lived. *I never even knew I was one of* those *people*, Claude remembered. *And mother said never to name that word any more.* It was something everyone seemed ashamed of. And now they were about to put on a play and tell the world? Invite everyone to come in and hear about it? *It's a gamble, that's for sure.*

Then there was the widespread feeling in the county that *nothing we do ever works*. Except for the few people who were involved with this project from the start, most people in the county probably shared that feeling. If Claude were completely honest with himself, he'd have to admit that a big part of him agreed. But the world was changing. In a few weeks, a man would walk on the moon. If America could accomplish that, Hancock County could certainly stage an outdoor drama. Couldn't they?

As the sun came up over Sneedville on that Thursday, the day before Independence Day, 1969, Claude Collins had more butterflies in his stomach than the actors who would take the stage that evening. Putting on an outdoor drama was one thing. Putting on a drama about the Melungeons was something else entirely.

Claude finished his coffee, stretched again, and wondered if he'd have time for a nap before everything got started. There was still a lot to do before the premiere of *Walk Toward the Sunset*.

HIGHWAY 31

All Charlie Turner wanted was a road. Not even a new road. Just to fix up the one they had. Was that too much to ask?

Charles Turner was the mayor of Sneedville, the county seat of Hancock County and a tiny town wedged between the Clinch River and Newman's Ridge. Sneedville's central feature was the courthouse; it was surrounded by a low wall where men sat, rolled cigarettes, gossiped, and watched the little bit of traffic along Main Street. The other government buildings in Sneedville were the U.S. Post Office, a red-brick building a couple of blocks east of the courthouse on Main Street, and the Hancock County Jail, a hundred-year-old, two-story wooden structure one block west and south of the courthouse, on aptly named Jail Street. An elementary school and a high school were also within the town limits.

Local businesses clustered near the courthouse included a drugstore, owned and operated by Charlie Turner; a department store and a Cash n' Tote variety store, both belonging to Charlie's brother, Alvin York "Sonny" Turner; a hardware store; a tiny movie theater; a small grocery; a five-room motel over a beauty parlor; a restaurant and diner; a gas station; and a funeral home. These and a few other businesses handled most of the everyday needs of the people of Sneedville. For anything else, a person had to drive to Morristown.

Since taking office in 1961, Turner had been trying to get the state—or the federal government—or *somebody*—to improve the road to Morristown. Morristown was only twenty-three miles from Sneedville, but the trip from Sneedville to Morristown was mostly along State Highway 31. Highway 31 ran between Sneedville and Mooresburg; at Mooresburg, you had to turn right to go west on U.S. 11-W. Then, at Bean Station, a left turn led south on U.S. 25-E into Morristown.

Morristown was where the jobs were. Most of the people in Hancock County who worked at a job—that is, made a living by means other than farming—held jobs in Morristown, working in one of the small factories, lumberyards, or in one of the other mostly blue-collar jobs to be found there. Morristown had just over 20,000 people, with another 19,000 or so living in surrounding Hamblen County. Only 874 people lived in Sneedville; there were only 6,719 people in all of Hancock County. Without Morristown, there would be practically no work for the people of Hancock County.

The problem was the road. Highway 31 went over Clinch Mountain, which was technically a long ridge, incorporating several summits. The southernmost end of Clinch Mountain was Signal Point Peak, at the junction of Knox, Union, and Granger counties. Running from southwest to northeast, Clinch Mountain stretched 150 miles, all the way to its northernmost point, Garden Mountain, near Burke's Garden in southwest Virginia. It wasn't particularly high, as mountains go—it reached 4,689 feet at one point—but there were only two natural gaps on the whole thing—and both of those gaps were on the Virginia end of the mountain.

Leaving Sneedville on the southwest side of town, you crossed the Clinch River. Charlie remembered when there wasn't even a bridge; you crossed the river on a sort of raft/barge that ferried you across. Then you drove along the south bank of the river for a few miles before 31 turned south toward Clinch Mountain. Once you got through Luther—which consisted mainly of a store that once had a post office—and the zinc mine at Flat Gap, you started climbing the mountain just past Treadway. It was a steep, twisty road, full of hairpin turns but without much in the way of guardrails that might keep a car from plunging off the side of the mountain. You probably wouldn't go very far before a tree or a rock kept your car from going all the way to the bottom, but you were unlikely to be in any kind of shape to climb back up the steep mountainside to the road. Unless someone saw you go over the side, you might be stuck in the wreckage of your car for, well, days, or maybe weeks.

The people who drove Highway 31 every day knew every twist and turn of the road. In good weather, they had no problem negotiating the route, day or night. But a half-inch of snow changed the situation considerably. Snow didn't fall often in northeast Tennessee, but you could count on at least three or four good snows in winter. And the mountain was high enough that snow stuck on the road near the top, even if it didn't stick down below. If the road became icy, or even slick from heavy rains, Clinch Mountain was a forbidding obstacle to even the most experienced drivers. It could guarantee that the last few moments of your life would be exciting indeed.

Because of Clinch Mountain and State Highway 31, employers in Morristown were reluctant to hire people from Sneedville or Hancock County. Oh, they were good workers, all right—good people. But if the weather turned bad, even just a little bit bad, most of those good people weren't going to risk the drive to show up at work. A good snow could keep them away from work for a week, maybe more, depending on when the state road crews finally got 31 clear enough to drive.

It helped if you told a prospective employer that, if you got the job, you were planning to move to Morristown, but it wasn't only jobs that drew people out of Hancock County. Living in Morristown meant you could shop for groceries in a real supermarket instead of one of the dozens of tiny country stores that served Hancock County. You could go to a movie once in a while—a *current* movie, not like the ones at the Sneedville theater. You could take your wife to a nice restaurant. And your kids could go to a better school, one that could pay for better teachers and give your kids a better chance of learning a trade or even going to college. In Morristown, you could make a better life for yourself and for your family.

Charlie Turner was well acquainted with the desire to move somewhere with more opportunity. Years later, he would tell a reporter from up north, "My whole [high school] graduation class left. But I just said, 'I'll be darned if I'll do that. I'll just run for mayor and see what I can do.'"[1] But when he was just starting out, he taught in a one-room schoolhouse on Newman's Ridge.[2] Later, he opened a drugstore. He wasn't a pharmacist, like most people who open small-town drugstores, but he still did well. One bit of drugstore business Turner could handle was developing photographs; he was a skilled photographer and had won several awards. Eventually, he ran for mayor of Sneedville. Hancock County was almost totally Republican, but Charlie was a Democrat and the only Democrat in his family. Still, he won the election—and the one after that. And the one after that. Charlie Turner stayed in Sneedville on his own terms and made it work. But he knew how unusual his decision was. There was a saying among former Hancock County residents: "A lot of smart people come out of Hancock County—and the smarter they are, the quicker they come out of there." Most people as smart and ambitious as Charlie Turner got out of Hancock County, sooner or later.

The folks who left Hancock County for Morristown weren't really *gone*—not really. They were still connected. The ones who lived in Morristown or nearby referred to Hancock County as "Overhome," as in "Are you going over home this weekend?" Mama and Daddy still lived there on the old family farm. Brothers and sisters, aunts and uncles, cousins and old friends—they were still "Overhome," and you could be there for a visit in less than an hour, most days.

---

[1] Magnussen, "Appalachia scrapes bottom of pork barrel," 17-B.
[2] Glenn, "The Melungeons have left, but their heritage remains," 21.

Some of those who moved to Morristown were still very involved in life "Over-home"; some still attended the church where they'd gone to Sunday school and been baptized. Some were even involved in Hancock County government. The ties binding them to Hancock County might have stretched a little, but they weren't broken. But when folks moved to Morristown, they reduced the population and the tax base of the county and made it harder to provide services to the ones who remained.

Many people moved farther away than Morristown. A whole colony of transplanted Hancock Countians lived in or near Baltimore, drawn away during World War II by good-paying jobs at shipyards and defense plants. Even more had moved north, to Indiana, Ohio, and Michigan, taking factory jobs with union paychecks, making more money than was possible even in Morristown. They still came home sometimes, most of them, maybe two or three times a year, when the kids got a vacation from school. They'd load up the family car and head down home. Interstate I-75, the "Hillbilly Highway," was slowly being built across Kentucky, and nearly every time these transplanted Hancock Countians came home, a little more of the trip was made on a four-lane divided road.

The transplants were different after they'd been up north a while. They had different attitudes; some of them had stopped going to church or were going to a different kind of church from the one they'd grown up in. They'd become more cosmopolitan, and the folks at home sometimes felt that the transplants looked down on them a bit. Their kids had Midwestern accents, and they enthralled their country cousins with tales of life in the big city. And, as time went on and the kids got older and busier, these families made the trip back home less often. Pretty soon, they came back home only for funerals. They weren't part of the county anymore. They were gone.

By 1969, Hancock County had fewer people that it had in 1869. The population had peaked in 1940; census figures for that year showed 11,231 souls living in the county. The 1960 census counted only 7,757, a population loss of almost 31 percent in twenty years. Since 1960, Charlie guessed, at least a thousand more had left the county. The birth rate couldn't keep up with the number of people leaving for better opportunities elsewhere.

As mayor of Sneedville, Charlie Turner had helped attract some new jobs to the county seat. The voters had almost unanimously approved a bond issue to develop an industrial park, one that would be occupied by Electric Motors & Specialties, Inc., from Garrett near Fort Wayne, Indiana.[3] Senator Albert Gore

---

[3] "Hancock Votes 98.6 'For the Bonds,'" 2.

had helped the county land a $98,000 grant from the federal Economic Development Administration to further develop the property. That would bring as many as 135 new jobs into the county—eventually.[4]

Despite that growth, there was talk that the New Jersey Zinc Company's mine at Flat Gap would cut back operations. It hadn't helped matters when 150 men—nearly the entire workforce—walked off the job a couple of years earlier to protest the one-day suspension of two men for what the company called "failure to obey orders." It was seen as a wildcat strike, a violation of the contract between the company and the Steelworkers Union.[5] It got settled quickly enough, but the unavoidable truth was that, sooner or later, a mining operation would extract all the raw material it is economically feasible to get, and the mine would shut down. That day was coming soon at Flat Gap, and that would eliminate more jobs than Electric Motors was going to bring in. Despite all the work of Charlie Turner and others in the county, Hancock County was going to wind up with a net loss of jobs.

Improving Highway 31 was crucial; that road was a lifeline for Hancock County. If the road weren't so dangerous, people could commute to work in Morristown and remain in Hancock County.

There were really only four ways in and out of Hancock County—well, five, if you counted State Highway 66. But that stretch of 66 was narrow and even more crooked than Highway 31. Locals often said that the turns were so tight on 66 that you could kiss your own ass on some of them. Like Highway 31, it crossed Clinch Mountain, joining U.S. 11-W at Rogersville. The preferred route to Rogersville was to take State Highway 33 east out of Sneedville, where it met U.S. 70 at Kyles Ford on the Clinch River. Crossing the river on the old highway bridge, U.S. 70 went over Clinch Mountain to reach 11-W at Rogersville on the other side. There were a few jobs to be had in Rogersville, the county seat of Hawkins County and the second-oldest town in Tennessee, but Morristown was closer, bigger, and had more opportunities.

Highway 33 ran through the center of Sneedville, and if you went west instead of east, you could follow 33 as it turned just before the Clinch River bridge. For a few miles, Highway 33 paralleled the river and Highway 31 on the opposite bank and eventually connected with U.S. 25-E, just south of Tazewell, about twenty-eight miles from Sneedville. Charlie Turner couldn't help feeling a little bitter when he thought about Tazewell. Tazewell had received federal aid

---

[4] "EDA Approves $98,000 Grant," 1.
[5] Montgomery, "Early Settlement of 'Walkout' Seen," 1.

Sneedville couldn't get; Tazewell had received the highway funding Charlie had been pestering everyone from Nashville to Washington, D.C., to get.

The only other highway out of Sneedville was State Highway 63, which began at the courthouse and went north, across Newman's Ridge, then took a southeasterly turn, winding up at U.S. 25-E near Harrogate and Cumberland Gap. You could turn right from 63 onto Mulberry Road, which crossed the state line into Lee County, Virginia, and eventually connected with U.S. Highway 70, which went north to Jonesville—a town not much bigger than Sneedville, with the same lack of jobs.

None of these highways were as important to Sneedville and Hancock County as State Highway 31. And try as he might, Charlie Turner hadn't been able to get that road improved. But now—*now* he could see a chance. If no one would build a road for people going *out* of Sneedville, maybe they would build a road for people coming *in*.

Like everyone else, Turner had his doubts about the idea of an outdoor drama. Still, those two professors from Carson-Newman College had studied the county's economic situation and told county leaders that their best chance of economic development was tourism, and their best chance of developing tourism was with an outdoor drama.

Outdoor dramas were popular and attracted tourists, even to small towns like Boone, North Carolina. They'd been staging *Horn in the West* in Boone since 1952; it was the third-oldest outdoor drama in the nation. But Boone was a college town, home of Appalachian State University, and had a direct highway connection to Winston-Salem and Interstate I-40. *Trail of the Lonesome Pine*, performed in Big Stone Gap, forty-five miles from Sneedville, was the longest running outdoor drama in the Commonwealth of Virginia. Big Stone Gap was just off U.S. 23, a major highway that ran from Jacksonville, Florida, to Mackinaw City, Michigan. *Unto These Hills* was staged in Cherokee, North Carolina, on the Qualla Boundary Indian Reservation on the eastern edge of the Great Smoky Mountains National Park, and the park drew millions of visitors each year.

Sneedville wasn't close to anything—no major highways or tourist attractions. Turner and the other local leaders were counting on their outdoor drama to entice tourists across Clinch Mountain into a town that lacked any of the usual amenities for tourists, like restaurants or motels. Oh, sure, the Green Top Inn on Main Street in Sneedville served good food—very good food, as a matter of fact—but the exterior of the restaurant looked rough, and the interior wasn't much better. And the Town Motel—well, that was just five little rooms over the beauty parlor on Main Street. Up to now, that had been plenty; not many folks came to Sneedville needing a motel room. But if the tourists came, the restaurants and motels might follow. That was the hope, anyway.

Charlie Turner and the other leaders in Hancock County were counting on the subject of the play to attract tourists, but it was the subject of the play that had been so controversial. Melungeons weren't a topic people in Hancock County were used to talking about. Even the word "Melungeon" was not usually spoken in public. And no one in the county wanted to be identified as a Melungeon. Everyone had been upset when that *Saturday Evening Post* article came out. The Melungeons were Hancock County's dirty little secret.

Times were changing, though, and people were starting to see Melungeons in a different light. Those articles by Louise Davis in the *Nashville Tennessean* hadn't been as negative as the *Post* article. Several other more-or-less positive articles had been published in various newspapers and magazines, and that new novel by Jesse Stuart, *Daughter of the Legend*, was very sympathetic to the Melungeons. People were curious about the Melungeons. And, as the Reverend Connor had pointed out, if Hancock County didn't take advantage of that curiosity, some other place would, and would reap the benefits. If the Melungeons were Hancock County's best shot at attracting tourists, then the people of Sneedville were going to give it a try—even if hardly anyone in the county admitted to being a Melungeon.

As Thursday, 3 July 1969, dawned in Sneedville, Charlie Turner had a lot of work to do. It was going to be an historic Independence Day weekend. For the first time, tourists were going to arrive in Sneedville, Tennessee.

3

THOSE PEOPLE

A Malungeon isn't a nigger, and he isn't an Indian, and he isn't a white man. God only knows what he is.

—Unnamed Tennessee legislator, circa 1890[1]

Whites left them alone because they were so wild and devil-fired and queer and witchy. If a man was fool enough to go into Melungeon country and if he come back without being shot, he was just sure to wizzen and perish away with some ailment nobody could name. Folks said terrible things went on back yonder, blood-drinking and devil worship and carryings on that would freeze a good Christian's spine-bone.

—Folklore collected by James Aswell, 1940[2]

Hancock County, Tennessee, was known—so far as it was known at all—for only two things: being one of the poorest counties in America and being the home of the Melungeons. Just a few years earlier, the people of Hancock County would have been more likely to put on a play celebrating their poverty than willingly publicize the Melungeons.

Hancock County, named for Declaration of Independence signer John Hancock, is in the northeastern corner of Tennessee, seventy miles or so northeast of Knoxville, and is adjacent to the border with Virginia. Formed in 1845 from a portion of Hawkins County, it lies within the "ridge and valley" portion of the Appalachian Mountains, an area characterized by long, even ridges and long, continuous valleys between them. The two dominant ridges in the county are Clinch Mountain on the southern edge and Powell Mountain on its northern border. Powell Mountain separates the two main rivers that flow through Hancock County, the Clinch River and the smaller, shorter Powell River. The only incorporated town in the county is the county seat, Sneedville, named after Knoxville attorney John Sneed, who defended the county from lawsuits by residents who objected to the county's incorporation.

---

[1] Dromgoole, "The Malungeons," 472.
[2] Aswell, *God Bless the Devil*, 207–208.

It's a poor county. Aside from some fertile river bottom areas, most of the land is ill-suited for agriculture. As such, it attracted few settlers; only 5,660 people were reported in the county's first census in 1850. With few natural resources, the county has neither a railroad nor a major highway running through it.

The Melungeons were a mixed-ethnic population first documented in the Clinch River region of northeast Tennessee and southwest Virginia in the early nineteenth century. Hancock County seemed to have the highest concentration of Melungeon residents, and since the 1840s, journalists have been coming to this remote area to learn about these mysterious people.

Most residents figured the Melungeons were, in the words of one historian, a mixture of "runaway slaves, renegade Indians, and poor white trash."[3] No one seemed to know from where they came, but most of the white folks of the area wished the Melungeons had stayed there.

The few scholars who took note of them prior to the 1960s generally agreed that the Melungeons had a mixture of African, Native American, and European ancestry. However, no one was certain of their origins, not even the Melungeons themselves, and that mystery tended to attract newspaper and magazine writers.

The mystery even extended to the name of this group. No one knew what the word "Melungeon" meant, or how that term came to be applied to these people. The most common explanation was that the word originated with the French *mélange*, meaning "mixture," but no one could say how or when the term came to be used for this particular group of people. In Hancock County and the surrounding counties of northeast Tennessee and southwest Virginia, "Melungeon" had more than one meaning. As a Hancock County resident told anthropologist Anthony Cavender, a Melungeon was someone who "has got nigger blood in 'em."[4] "Melungeon" also had connotations beyond ethnicity; the term also meant shiftless, untrustworthy, ignorant, and dirty. It wasn't just about who your ancestors were; it was also about your place in society—and it wasn't a good place. "Melungeon" was an insult, an epithet, a name that might earn the person who used it a punch in the face.

It wasn't a word anyone used to describe themselves. "Melungeon" was an exonym, a common name used only outside the place, group, or linguistic community in question. It was *not* a term used by the people whom it described. Geographer Edward Price wrote in 1951, "There is no group of people who call

---

[3] Gallegos interview.

[4] Cavender, "The Melungeons of Upper East Tennessee," 32.

themselves Melungeons or who would recognize themselves as thus separated from the rest of the country population."[5]

Because Melungeons were defined by people outside the group, there was often disagreement among those outsiders as to whether a particular individual did or did not fit that definition. For the most part, family names were considered the most reliable indicator of Melungeon ancestry. Names such as Collins, Gibson, Bunch, Miser, Bowlin, and a few others are accepted by most who are familiar with the Melungeons as core group surnames; there are other surnames that are accepted as "Melungeon names" by some and not by others. And, of course, marriages between Melungeons and non-Melungeons introduced many more surnames to the Melungeon mix.

Unlike most ethnic groups worldwide, the Melungeons have no distinct cultural difference that sets them apart from their neighbors, no historic language other than English, no traditional folklore, no unique customs, foods, or holidays. This has caused some anthropologists to question the Melungeons' existence as a distinct population. While many Indian tribes require a certain level of ancestry, or "blood quantum," for membership, there was no objective means of determining whether someone was a Melungeon, nor could anyone quantify their ancestry by saying something like, "I'm one-quarter Melungeon." You were a Melungeon if your neighbors said you were a Melungeon, and there were no half-measures.

This held true not only for the Melungeons, but for many other similar groups that lived primarily in the southeastern United States. In the mid-twentieth century, William Gilbert, a researcher for the Library of Congress, identified nearly 200 similar groups with uncertain racial backgrounds. Most of them lived in the southeastern United States, but some could be found along the eastern seaboard in places like New Jersey and New York. Gilbert described these groups as "racial islands...complex mixtures in varying degrees of white, Indian, and Negro blood...mixed outcasts from both the white and Negro castes of America." He compiled information on the ten largest of these groups. Besides the Melungeons, Gilbert listed,

> • Brass Ankles and allied groups in South Carolina, including Red Bones, Red Legs, Turks, Marlboro Blues, and others
> • Cajans and Creoles of Alabama and Mississippi (not to be confused with the Cajuns and Creoles of Louisiana, whose background is more or less known)

---

[5] Price, "The Melungeons," 258.

- Croatans of Virginia, North Carolina, and South Carolina
- Guineas of West Virginia and Maryland
- Issues of Amherst and Rockingham Counties in Virginia
- Jackson Whites of New York and New Jersey
- Moors and Nanticokes of Delaware and New Jersey
- Red Bones of Louisiana
- Wesorts of southern Maryland

Gilbert writes, "These small local groups seem to develop especially where environmental circumstances such as forbidding swamps or inaccessible and barren mountain country favor their growth." He noted that "the vast majority cannot possibly hope to pass as 'white' under the present social system." Nor did he see any evidence that they were being absorbed into the black community.[6]

The Melungeons occupied a racial no-man's land, somewhere between black and white—not a good place to be in Jim Crow America. The people in these groups might vehemently deny African ancestry, might refuse to send their children to the segregated Negro schools, but their efforts did them no good; they were kept apart just like black people. Whites generally considered them the result of the lust of long-ago white men for black women—and maybe even the lust of white women for black men. Nothing had changed much; lots of counties in the South had places where white men made furtive trips to visit black women. The groups identified by Gilbert, however, seemed to have originated in an earlier time and had been around long enough to be identified by colloquial names like "Brass Ankles" or "Melungeons." They could claim Indian ancestry all they wanted; local whites weren't buying it. When the parents refused to send their children to school with black children, local school districts sometimes set up separate schools for them. Other school districts didn't care whether these kids went to school or not, but they damn sure weren't going to school with white kids.

Researcher Calvin Beale coined the term "tri-racial isolates" to describe these communities. He visited various places, talked with people, and made observations, which he described in 1957:

> In general all local informants will agree that the mixed population is partly white. (Blue eyes are commonly in evidence to validate this.) The white informant will insist that the mixed-blood people are partly Negro. Perhaps he will agree that they are partly Indian, perhaps not. The mixed blood individual will insist—with vehemence, if necessary—that there is no Negro ancestry

---

[6] Gilbert, "Memorandum," 438.

in his family (although he may not make this claim for all other families in the settlement) but that he is partly Indian. In a minority of communities unmistakable elements of Indian culture have been found. Presence of Negro ancestry may or may not be evident in some families from the occurrence of Negro hair forms or facial features. If evident, it tends to jeopardize claims of the group to non-Negro status. In sum, the groups described are with few exceptions considered only of white and Indian descent by their members but are regarded to be partly Negro by neighboring whites or Negroes.[7]

In his 1963 book *Almost White*, Brewton Berry had two generalized observations about the mixed-ethnic communities:

First, *they are determined not to be Negroes*. This is more than a wish with them—it is an obsession—and always has been. They vehemently deny that they have any strain of Negro ancestry (though they often suspect, and say, that certain others in their group have been touched with the tar brush). They are bitter in their prejudice against Negroes, and will disown one of their number who takes up with them. The stranger among them who implies, by word or gesture, that they are Negroes or mulattoes runs the risk of bodily harm...

Second, *they detest the epithets others have applied to them*...each locality has its own pet name for the hybrid population, and never is it complimentary—nor meant to be.[8]

These "hybrid populations" had a valid and sensible reason to "vehemently deny that they have any strain of Negro ancestry." The United States has a shameful history of mistreating African Americans. It has never been advantageous for an individual or a group to be perceived as "black" by white America. If whites had any question or doubt concerning the presumed African ancestry of a group such as the Melungeons, that group would be foolish indeed not to make the most of those questions and deny such ancestry. And if some ancestry *other* than African could be claimed—and if a significant number of whites believed that claim—the group in question might avoid a great many of the restrictions imposed on African Americans.

Most of the mixed-ethnic groups listed by Gilbert had stories about their origins that downplayed, or outright denied, the African component of their ancestry. Sometimes these stories and theories originated with the mixed-ethnic group itself, but quite often whites were the originators and purveyors of those

---

[7] Beale, "American Triracial Isolates," 188.
[8] Berry, *Almost White*, 32.

theories. Since whites had the final say-so about who was or wasn't "white," this could be very advantageous for the group.

No group seemed to have as many different theories about their origins— or such widespread dissemination of those theories through the press—as the Melungeons. Most of these theories involved what researcher Darlene Wilson called a "male offshore other"[9]—individuals or groups from some far-off land who arrived on the North American continent, usually through some romantic or historically significant means, to couple with Native American women and produce Melungeon offspring. As a result, the Melungeons have always been the object of curiosity and fascination for a great number of whites; more importantly, the Melungeons managed, in varying degrees, to avoid most of the penalties and indignities to which African Americans were subjected.

Some of the origin claims made on behalf of the Melungeons are plausible; others are clearly laughable. One can easily find works, both in print and online, that either promote or disparage the various theories that have been put forth about the Melungeons. Thus, the Melungeons have remained the object of speculation and study, and the "mystery" surrounding them has been prominent in their history and affected how they have been perceived by the larger, Caucasian-dominated society.

Most of that society definitely did not consider the Melungeons "white," especially in the nineteenth century. Under the original Tennessee constitution, adopted when Tennessee gained statehood in 1796, all free males had the right to vote, but when the constitution was re-written in 1834, the vote was restricted to free *white* males. Immediately, a question arose: Were the Melungeons "white enough" to qualify for citizenship?

William Gannaway Brownlow, a prominent Whig politician and later the Reconstruction-era governor of Tennessee, believed the Melungeons did not qualify as "white" at all. In his newspaper, *Brownlow's Whig*, he wrote in 1840 of "an impudent Malungeon…a scoundrel who is half Negro and half Indian" who dared to speak in opposition to a prominent Whig at a political meeting. In the same article, Brownlow referred to the "impudent Malungeon" as "the big Democratic Negro."[10]

Participating in the political process would prove hazardous for the "impudent Malungeons." In late 1845, several individuals were arrested and charged with illegally voting "by reason of color" in the August 1845 gubernatorial race

---

[9] Vande Brake, *Through the Back Door*, 21.

[10] "NEGRO SPEAKING," *Brownlow's Whig* (Jonesborough, TN) 7 October 1840, 3. Various writers in the nineteenth and early twentieth centuries employed different spellings of the word, including "Melungin" and "Malungeon." Today, "Melungeon" is the accepted spelling.

between Democrat Andrew Johnson (later the seventeenth president of the United States) and the aforementioned William Brownlow, representing the Whig Party. These defendants were indicted by a grand jury in Rogersville, the county seat of Hawkins County. (Newly formed Hancock County had not yet established a court system.) Vardemon Collins, one of the defendants, was one of the earliest settlers in what became Hancock County; he owned two hundred acres of land and what has been described as a "hotel and mineral springs resort" in Blackwater Valley, between Powell Mountain and Newman's Ridge.[11] In addition to other defendants with the surname Collins (Solomon, Ezekiel, Levi, Andrew, and Wyatt Collins), Zachariah Minor, his brother Lewis, and Vardemon Collins's son-in-law, Timothy Williams, were also indicted.[12]

Prosecuting the case was District Attorney General Thomas A. R. Nelson. John Netherland, a prominent attorney and Whig politician from Rogersville, defended some of the accused Melungeons in trials that took place over the next three years.

In the case of Vardemon Collins, existing records show that on 25 May 1847, Attorney General Nelson entered a *nolle prosequi*, which signifies a prosecutor's decision to voluntarily discontinue criminal charges. Hawkins County Archivist Jack Goins speculates that Nelson may have declined to prosecute because Vardy—then eighty-three years old—was ill, or possibly because Vardy paid a fine. Vardy's son-in-law, Timothy Williams, may also have paid a fine.[13]

After several delays, the trial of Wyatt Collins began on Saturday, 29 January 1848. Decades later, J. H. Newman of Hancock County corresponded with a reporter for the *Louisville Courier-Journal* about the trial.[14]

They were indicted for illegal voting when this country was Hawkins [C]ounty, and had their trial in Rogersville, and this was over forty years ago, probably fifty years ago, and in the trial Hon. Thomas A. R. Nelson, the Attorney General, who prosecuted them for illegal voting put the one on trial

---

[11] Goins, "Newman's Ridge Goins Families."
[12] Goins, "History of the Melungeons."
[13] Goins, *Melungeons and Other Pioneer Families*, 44.
[14] Jack Goins questions the identity of the person who provided this information to the *Louisville Courier-Journal*. He writes, "I am always suspicious of the old Newspaper Reporters; they sometimes stretch the truth to its ultimate limits. One of the reasons I was suspicious of this article was because I didn't remember any Newman's [*sic*] in the old records, so after I read this article I decided to see what area of Hawkins County J. H. Newman lived. And was not surprised when I could not locate him in any records of Hawkins and Hancock County during this 1830–1900 time period. He did not live in Hancock County as the records below will show. Who was this mysterious person interviewed by the reporter for the Courier Journal?" ("First Melungeon Community").

whose skin indicated he could easily convict, as being of African descent. He was old Wyatt Collins. The charge against them all was that they were of African descent and had not passed the third generation and were not entitled to vote. Col. John Netherland defended the Malungeons, and when old Wyatt Collins was put to the jury, Netherland admitted that his client voted as charged, but the only evidence that the Attorney General had was the color and features of old Wyatt, who stood erect six feet high, high cheek bones, hair straight as a horse's tail. Attorney General Nelson told the jury to look at him and judge whether or not he was a negro of African descent and had not passed the third generation. Now Mr. Netherland, for the defense stated: I make protest of this old man as to whether he is a negro or not, and I want to show his hair, hands, and feet. "Now, Wyatt," said Netherland, "I will show your features against Mr. Nelson's who is prosecuting you, and I want you to show your naked foot beside Mr. Nelson's." So Wyatt sat down and pulled his moccasin off and showed his naked feet (but Mr. Nelson would not show with him), and his feet and general features were as delicate and nice as a lady's and presented to the jury the very opposite of the African features. Then it was that the Portuguese race was brought in—the jury found a verdict of not guilty, and all the other cases took the same course. Mr. Nelson asked Mr. Netherland what race of people he called his clients. Mr. Netherland answered Portuguese; then it was, and not until then, the name of Portuguese was given these people.[15]

"Portuguese" was considered an "exotic" ethnicity by the English, Scots-Irish, and German residents of northeast Tennessee. Few records of the trial have survived, so we don't know how Netherland knew of their ancestry. It is possible that the defendants told him their ancestors were Portuguese. It is also possible that Netherland made it up. In any event, the claim worked. After the jury acquitted Wyatt Collins, Nelson entered a *nolle prosequi* declaration for the other Collins defendants. On the same day, a different jury acquitted Zachariah Minor, and the prosecution dropped its case against Lewis Minor.[16]

Decades later, Dr. Swan Burnette wrote, "The matter was finally carried before a jury and the question decided by an examination of the feet. One, I believe, was found to be sufficiently flat-footed to deprive him of a right of suffrage. The others, four or five in number, were considered as having sufficient white blood to allow them a vote." As J. H. Newman indicated to the *Courier-Journal* reporter, if the defendants were three generations removed from a Negro ancestor, Tennessee law considered them "white"—or at least "white enough."[17]

---

[15] "The Malungeons," 15.
[16] Goins, *Melungeons and Other Pioneer Families*, 44–46.
[17] Ibid.; Burnett, "A Note on the Melungeons," 347.

Netherland did not claim Indian ancestry for his clients, even though decades later Newman would describe Wyatt Collins as having "high cheek bones [and] hair straight as a horse's tail" and referred to the moccasins on Collins's feet.[18] A prominent Hancock County attorney, Lewis Jarvis, who knew many of the old Melungeons from the early 1800s, described them as "friendly Indians who came with the whites as they moved west."[19] But both of those descriptions came many decades after the voting trials. At the time of those trials, there was no evidence presented of any Indian ancestry, nor was there any advantage to claiming such an ancestry.

The 1830 census of Hawkins County listed some four hundred residents, most with Melungeon surnames, as "free persons of color"; had they been Indians, the census would have listed them as such. Netherland had no basis to claim that his clients were Indian, and for him to have done so would have done them no good at all. Indians were not white, not citizens, and not eligible to vote; in fact, the Indian Removal Act of 1830 required Indians living in the southeastern United States to move west of the Mississippi River. A claim of Indian ancestry might well have gotten the Melungeons banished from Tennessee.

A claim of Portuguese ancestry, however, served Netherland's cause well. The Portuguese, though often dark-skinned, were European and Christian. Though many Portuguese had African ancestry dating back to the Moorish invasion of the Iberian Peninsula eleven centuries earlier, that ancestry was far enough removed to satisfy Tennessee's "third generation" standard.

The illegal-voting trials of the Melungeons are likely what drew an anonymous writer to Hancock County. His account of that visit was published in several Southern newspapers as early as 1847; it appeared in *Littell's Living Age* in March 1849 under the title "The Melungens." The author clearly indicates that he believes the Melungeons had Portuguese ancestry as well as more recent African and Indian ancestors:

> The legend of their history, which they carefully preserve, is this. A great many years ago, these mountains were settled by a society of Portuguese Adventurers, men and women—who came from the long-shore parts of Virginia, that they might be freed from the restraints and drawbacks imposed on them by any form of government. These people made themselves friendly with the Indians and freed, as they were from every kind of social government, they uprooted all conventional forms of society and lived in a delightful Utopia of their own creation, trampling on the marriage relation, despising all

---

[18] "The Malungeons," *Courier-Journal*, 15.

[19] Lewis M. Jarvis, "The Melungeons," *Hancock County Times*, 17 April 1903, 1. Transcribed in William Grohse Papers, Archives of Appalachia, East Tennessee State University.

forms of religion, and subsisting upon corn (the only possible product of the soil) and wild game of the woods. These intermixed with the Indians, and subsequently their descendants (after the advances of the whites into this part of the state) with the negros [*sic*] and the whites, thus forming the present race of Melungens.[20]

Writers in the twentieth century would often claim that the Melungeons were in northeast Tennessee when the first white settlers arrived at the end of the eighteenth century—a belief fostered by a letter to a Nashville newspaper which will be examined shortly. But the author of the *Littell's Living Age* article clearly states that the Melungeons migrated to the Tennessee mountains from eastern Virginia. Jack Goins of Rogersville spent many years in the late twentieth and early twenty-first century researching Melungeon families and demonstrated, through tax rolls, deeds, and other documents, that many of the Melungeon families did indeed come from eastern Virginia.

The *Littell's* author goes on to speak of "Old Vardy," who was clearly Vardemon Collins:

> [W]e stopped at 'Old Vardy's', the hostelrie of the vicinage. Old Vardy is the 'chief cook and bottle-washer' of the Melungens, and is really a very clever fellow: but his hotel savors strongly of that peculiar perfume that one may find in the sleeping-rooms of our negro servants, especially on a close, warm, summer evening.[21]

Many have assumed that Vardy Collins was the source of information for this article. Several modern amateur researchers (and the term "amateur" is meant only to indicate they are not academics associated with any college, university, or research group; many of these researchers are as skilled as any academic) use this article to bolster their claim that the Melungeons were indeed Portuguese and claimed such ancestry as early as the 1840s.

But there are reasons to question that premise. None of the information about the origins of the Melungeons was directly attributed to "Old Vardy," and it seems highly unlikely that Vardy provided the information. Vardemon Collins didn't live to be an old man by carelessly giving information to strangers. We don't know the date of the author's visit to Hancock County, but the visit was likely inspired by news of the illegal voting arrests, and the information that the

---

[20] "The Melungens," *Littell's Living Age*, 618. (The compiler of this volume adds a note at the beginning of the article that says "We are sorry to have lost the name of the southern paper from which this is taken.")

[21] Ibid.

Melungeons' ancestors were "Portuguese adventurers" who "intermixed with Indians, and…with the negros" would have contradicted Netherland's claims and possibly jeopardized the defendants. For that reason, John Netherland seems unlikely to have been the sole source of that information. The most likely explanation is that the writer combined information obtained from non-Melungeon residents of the area, as well as from contemporary news accounts of the trials, which may have included Netherland's argument about Portuguese ancestry.

An argument similar to Netherland's was introduced in what became known as "The Celebrated Melungeon Trial" of 1872. Lewis Shepard, a prominent judge, recalled in his 1915 memoirs a case he took when he was a young attorney in Chattanooga. Martha Simmerman, then fifteen years old, was the heir to her late father's sizable estate. But family members argued that Martha's mother, Jemima Bolton, was a Negro, and that the marriage of her parents was thus illegal, making Martha illegitimate and ineligible to inherit the estate. Their attorneys produced several local Negroes who testified that the Boltons were Negroes as well, that the child's mother and aunt had kinky hair, and that "the whole bunch of them had kinky hair, just like a mulatto Negro."

Martha Simmerman had been sent away to Illinois after her mother died and her father became mentally unstable. Unbeknownst to the opposing attorneys, however, Lewis Shepard had arranged to bring the girl to Chattanooga. Martha gave a deposition and pinned a lock of her hair to the document. The hair was coal black, perfectly straight, and almost four feet long.

Shepard then argued that the Boltons were Melungeons:

> In truth, these people belonged to a peculiar race, which settled in East Tennessee at an early day and, in the vernacular of the country, they were known as "Melungeons," and were not even remotely allied to Negroes. It was proven by tradition among these people that they were descendants of the ancient Carthagenians [sic]; they were Phoenicians, who, after Carthage was conquered by the Romans, and became a Roman province, emigrated across the straits of Gibraltar, and settled in Portugal, and from thence came the distinguished Venetian general, Othello, whom Shakespeare made immortal in his celebrated play, "The Moor of Venice."

Shepard also claimed that the Melungeons were misnamed.

> The term "Melungeon" is an East Tennessee provincialism; it was coined by the people of that country to apply to these people. It is derived from the French word "mélange," meaning a mixture or medley, and has gotten into the modern dictionaries. It was applied to these people because it was at first supposed that they were of mixed blood—part white and part negro. This name is a misnomer, because it has been conclusively proven that they are not

mixed with negro blood, but are pure-blooded Carthagenians, as much as was Hannibal and the Moor of Venice and other pure-blooded descendants of the ancient Phoenicians.

Lewis Shepard might say that his claim that the Melungeons were "pure-blooded Carthagenians" had been "conclusively proven," but he offered no proof and cited no source other than "it was proven by tradition." There is no record that anyone had ever made this claim prior to this particular case—which, by the way, he won. The court ruled that Martha Simmerman was not a Negro, and that she was the rightful heir to her father's estate.[22]

Many researchers believe that Shepard based his claim on the argument given by John Netherland in his defense of the Hawkins County Melungeons charged with illegal voting. No official record of Netherland's defense survives today, but it is likely Shepard knew of the case; he may even have had access to records from those trials. Shepard never said that he made the claim of Portuguese, Carthaginian, and Phoenician ancestry because it suited his case, but in his memoirs he came close. "Our Southern high-bred people," he wrote, "will never tolerate on equal terms any person who is even remotely tainted with negro blood, but they do not make the same objection to other brown or dark-skinned people, like the Spanish, the Cubans, the Italians, etc."[23]

Virginia Easley Demarce, the former president of the National Genealogical Society who wrote about Melungeons and other mixed-ethnic groups, was skeptical of their claims of Portuguese ancestry. She says "Portuguese" was a common euphemism in the southeastern United States, meant to deflect the legal and social disadvantages of African ancestry.[24] Another researcher, C. S. Everett, concurs:

> Readers need to be aware of the fact that throughout much of the nineteenth century and well into the early twentieth, "Portuguese," like the frequently heard "Cherokee Indian Princess," was regularly nothing other than a euphemism for mixed African-American heritage. In fact, that is precisely the way "Portuguese" has been understood by generations of black Americans. "Portuguese" and "Indian Princess" were contrived defense mechanisms employed by both light- and dark-pigmented individuals of partial African heritage to hide or disguise racial identity in an oppressive social climate where skin color essentially determined one's legal status. The majority of claims to Portuguese heritage in the South emanate from the 1840s and 1850s, and reemerge in

---

[22] Shepard, *Memoirs of Judge Lewis Shepard*, 88.
[23] Ibid.
[24] DeMarce interview.

the 1880s, probably as a response to increasing institutional inequality, segregation, and Jim Crow legislation. It is no coincidence that Portuguese claims arose in that historical context.[25]

No doubt, by the latter half of the nineteenth century, some Melungeons themselves would claim to be of Portuguese ancestry. Why not? Well-educated white men like John Netherland and Lewis Shepard said they were Portuguese, descended from ancient Phoenicians and Carthaginians. If being Portuguese kept the Melungeons from being treated as African Americans were treated, they weren't going to argue with that designation.

The Melungeons showed no evidence of Portuguese ancestry—no traces of the Portuguese language, no adherence to the Catholic faith, no remnants whatsoever of Portuguese customs and traditions. If time and distance had erased those cultural artifacts, how would the Melungeons have even known of their Portuguese ancestry? Given the widespread use of the term "Portuguese" as a euphemism to hide African ancestry among not only Melungeons, but among many dark-skinned people in the American South, the validity of that claim by, or on behalf of, the Melungeons seems highly suspect.[26]

Over the years, other theories of origin would be suggested by outsiders, not by the Melungeons themselves. These theories included:

• Deserters from the expedition of Hernando de Soto, the Spanish explorer who explored what became the southeastern United States from Florida to the Mississippi River, intermarried with local Indians. Their descendants were the Melungeons.

• Melungeons were descended from the Lost Colony of Roanoke Island. Under the sponsorship of Sir Walter Raleigh, a colony of English men, women, and children attempted to establish a colony on Chesapeake Bay. Before proceeding to the selected location, the colonists were ordered to stop at Roanoke Island, located between the mainland of what is now North Carolina and the barrier islands of the Outer Banks. They were to pick up the remnants of an earlier English expedition that had been left there a year earlier. When they found no trace of that expedition, the master pilot Simon Fernandez refused to allow the colonists to return to the ships, insisting they establish their colony on Roanoke Island. The governor of the colony, John White, returned to England to

---

[25] Everett, "Melungeon History and Myth," 369.

[26] DNA testing in the twenty-first century has failed to settle the disputes over the question of Portuguese ancestry, but virtually every DNA test performed on an individual whose Melungeon ancestry is generally acknowledged has shown some degree of African ancestry.

explain the situation and plead for help. Due to numerous delays, including the impending threat of the Spanish Armada, White was unable to return to Roanoke Island for three years. When he returned, no trace of the colonists was found except for the word "CROATOAN" carved on a fence post, and the letters "CRO" carved into a nearby tree. White left without finding the colonists and never returned to Roanoke Island. The fate of the colonists inspires speculation to this day. The Lumbee Indians of North Carolina—once identified by neighbors with the pejorative term "Croatans" or "Cros"—claim partial descent from the Lost Colonists, and since some have speculated about a connection between the Lumbees and the Melungeons, the "Lost Colony" theory has had many proponents.

• The Melungeons were one of the Lost Tribes of Israel. A stone, known as the Bat Creek Stone, was excavated from a burial mound in Loudon County, Tennessee. The stone contained inscriptions entomologist Cyrus Thomas declared were Cherokee. (The Cherokee had a written language, developed by Sequoyah, marking one of the first times in history a pre-literate people had created an effective writing system.) In 1970, a widely publicized report stated that Semitist Cyrus H. Gordon proposed that the letters of inscription were Paleo-Hebrew of the first or second century A.D. Eventually both theories were discredited, and most researchers consider the Bat Creek Stone to be a fraud.

• The Melungeons originated among the Welsh Indians, a group of Native Americans supposedly descended from the Welsh prince Madoc, who founded a colony in North America in 1170. Aside from legends, no evidence has been presented for the existence of such a colony or its descendants.

• The Melungeons descended from sailors or pirates whose ships ran aground on the treacherous Outer Banks. These seamen found their way inland, where they intermarried with Indians.

• Later theories would include descent from Turks, Arabs, Sephardic Jews, and Siddis (an ethnic group from India and Pakistan) who somehow found their way to North America, intermarried with Native Americans, and spawned the Melungeons.

Skepticism regarding such claims was—and still is—common, and the claims further mythologized the Melungeons' origins up to the present day. The Melungeons themselves had little to do with the legends surrounding their ancestry and wished only to be left alone. Most of that mythologizing was done on the Melungeons' behalf by writers who wished to sell newspapers and magazines though it's possible that some of those writers sympathized with the Melungeons.

Will Allen Dromgoole wasn't particularly sympathetic toward the Melungeons. She (and Dromgoole *was* a she, despite the masculine name) shared with most white Americans of the late nineteenth century a revulsion toward the idea of race mixing. That revulsion would be reflected in the articles she wrote for a Nashville newspaper and a national magazine.

Dromgoole is best known today for her poem "The Bridge Builder" (still commonly read at high school commencements). She served as a clerk in the Tennessee Senate and overheard one Democratic lawmaker refer to an East Tennessee Republican as a "Melungeon." She began asking various legislators about the Melungeons. A veteran politician told her "A Malungeon isn't a nigger, and he isn't an Indian, and he isn't a white man. God only knows what he is. I should call him a Democrat, only he always votes the Republican ticket."[27] Already an accomplished writer, Dromgoole decided to write about the Melungeons. To do so, she visited Hancock County in summer 1890.

> I found here all colors—white women with white children and white husbands, Malungeon women with brown babies and white babies, and one, a young copper-colored woman with black eyes and straight Indian locks, had three black babies, negroes, at her heels and a third [*sic*] at her breast. She was not a negro. Her skin was red, a kind of reddish-yellow, as easily distinguishable from a mulatto as the white man from the negro. I saw an old colored man, black as the oft-quoted ace of spades, whose wife is a white woman. I am told, however, the law did take his case in hand, but the old negro pleaded his "Portygee" blood and was not convicted.[28]

Dromgoole wrote two articles published in the *Nashville Sunday American* in August and September 1890; the following year, she revised her earlier articles into a pair of stories for *The Arena*, a Boston-based magazine. Over the course of these four articles, Dromgoole seems to waver in her assessment of the Melungeons' racial background. "They possess many Indian traits, that of vengeance being strongly characteristic of them. They, likewise, resemble the negro in many things.... Many of the Malungeons claim to be Cherokee and Portuguese. Where they could have gotten their Portuguese blood is a mystery."[29]

By the time Dromgoole published her articles in *The Arena*, she had devised what she called "The Malungeon Tree and Its Four Branches," defining the Melungeons as a mixture of English, Native American, African, and Portuguese, and she even had an explanation for the genesis of this group:

---

[27] Dromgoole, "The Malungeons," 473.

[28] Dromgoole, "Land of the Malungeons," 15.

[29] Dromgoole, "A Strange People," 10, and "Land of the Malungeons," 15.

Somewhere in the eighteenth century, before the year 1797, there appeared in the eastern portion of Tennessee, at that time the Territory of North Carolina, two strange-looking men calling themselves "Collins" and "Gibson". They had a reddish brown complexion, long, straight, black hair, keen, black eyes, and sharp, clear-cut features. They spoke in broken English, a dialect distinct from anything ever heard in that section of the country. They claimed to have come from Virginia and many years after emigrating, themselves told the story of their past.

These two, Vardy Collins and Buck Gibson, were the head and source of the Melungeons in Tennessee. With the cunning of their Cherokee Ancestor, they planned and executed a scheme by which they were enabled to "set up for themselves" in the almost unbroken Territory of North Carolina.

Old Buck, as he was called, was disguised by a wash of some dark description, and taken to Virginia by Vardy where he was sold as a slave. He was a magnificent specimen of physical strength, and brought a fine price, a wagon and mules, a lot of goods, and three hundred dollars in money being paid to old Vardy for his "likely n-----". Once out of Richmond, Vardy turned his mule's shoes and struck out for the wilderness of North Carolina, as previously planned. Buck lost little time ridding himself of his Negro disguise, swore he was not the man bought of Collins, and followed in the wake of his fellow thief to the Territory.

The proceeds of the sale were divided and each chose his habitation; old Vardy choosing Newman's Ridge, where he was soon joined by others of his race, and so the Malungeons became a part of the inhabitants of Tennessee.[30]

Dromgoole claimed to have gleaned this information from "reliable parties" who got it from "old Vardy" himself. One might presume that the "reliable parties" who told the story to Dromgoole were not Melungeons, since she found the Melungeons not reliable at all, but "given to lying and stealing…and defiant (or worse, ignorant) of the very first principles of morality and cleanliness."[31]

At least one future writer would note inconsistencies in Dromgoole's reporting. William Worden wrote in a 1947 article in the *Saturday Evening Post*:

Several peculiarities mar the poetess' account of the dark people. One is that she changed her mind. In the *Arena* article of March, 1891, she rejected the theory that the Malungeons might be Negroid, basing her rejection on their appearance and on what she stated as a fact—that continuance of such blood would be impossible because octoroon women never have children, and Malungeon families were traceable for numerous generations. She said then

---

[30] Dromgoole, "The Malungeon Tree and Its Four Branches," 745.
[31] Dromgoole, "Land of the Malungeons," 15.

that she did not know where the Malungeons had come from or of what blood they were, although she was inclined to believe they were basically Portuguese.

Three months later, however, Miss Dromgoole signed another article on the same subject in the same magazine. But this time she had decided, among other things, that octoroon women were not necessarily barren after all. She no longer found the Malungeons interesting, friendly or pathetic. In June they were dirty, thieving, untrustworthy, decadent and not mysterious at all.[32]

Dromgoole found very little to like about the Melungeons. They were, according to her, "shiftless, idle, thieving, and defiant of all law, distillers of brandy, almost to a man... exceedingly shiftless, and in most cases filthy... They are rogues, natural, "born rogues," close, suspicious, inhospitable, untruthful; cowardly, and, to use their own words 'sneaky.'"[33] She concluded, "The most that can be said of one of them is, 'He is a Malungeon,' a synonym for all that is doubtful and mysterious—and unclean." [34]

Despite Dromgoole's obvious distaste for the Melungeons, her articles formed the basis of nearly everything written about the Melungeons for the next hundred years. One sentence in one of her *Arena* articles became the basis for one of the enduring legends about the Melungeons: she claimed that they were in what became northeast Tennessee years before the first white settlers, possibly even before the first white explorers.

After Dromgoole's first two articles were published in the *Nashville Sunday American* in August and September 1890, a letter to the *American* offered an intriguing possibility regarding the Melungeons. When Dromgoole re-worked her material for publication in *The Arena*, she incorporated the information from that letter. "When John Sevier attempted to organize the State of Franklin, there was living in the mountains of Eastern Tennessee a colony of dark-skinned, reddish-brown complexioned people, supposed to be of Moorish descent, who affiliated with neither whites nor blacks, and who called themselves Malungeons, and claimed to be of Portuguese descent."[35]

The letter to the editor in the *American* came from Dan W. Baird, the founder of the trade publication *Southern Lumberman*. There are a couple of problems with Baird's account. For one thing, the State of Franklin—a short-

[32] Worden, "Sons of the Legend," 130.
[33] Dromgoole, "The Malungeons," 471, 474.
[34] Ibid., 479.
[35] Dromgoole, "The Malungeons," 470.

lived attempt to create the fourteenth state from territory claimed by North Carolina—was formed in 1784. According to research by Jack Goins, who studied the migrations of the early Melungeon families using tax records, deeds, and other documentation, the first Melungeons did not come into the vicinity of Clinch Mountain until about 1800, the same time period as the first white settlers. In an interview published in 1903, Sneedville attorney Lewis Jarvis said,

> Some have said these people were here when the white people first explored this country. Others say they are a lost tribe of the Indians having no date of their existence here, traditionally or otherwise. All of this however, is erroneous and cannot be sustained. These people, not any of them were here at the time the first white hunting party came from Virginia and North Carolina in the year 1761—the noted Daniel Boone was at the head of one of these hunting parties and went on through Cumberland Gap…Vardy Collins, Shepherd Gibson, Benjamin Collins, Solomon Collins, Paul Bunch and the Goodmans, chiefs and the rest of them settled here about the year 1804, possibly about the year 1795, but all these men above named, who are called Melungeons, obtained land grants and muniments of title to the land they settled on and they were the friendly Indians who came with the whites as they moved west.[36]

Jarvis was born in Scott County, Virginia, in 1829 and lived most of his life in Hancock County, Tennessee.[37]

Casting further doubt on the information contained in Baird's *American* letter is the fact that no one has located a letter, journal, or other communication from John Sevier containing this information. Sevier served six two-year terms as governor of Tennessee, 1796–1801 and 1803–1809. Sevier *did* encounter Melungeons when he surveyed Hawkins County in 1802. According to his diary, on 26 November he spent the night on Blackwater Creek, on the northern side of Newman's Ridge, at the home of a man named Gibson.[38]

Despite documentary evidence showing the Melungeons were not in Tennessee earlier than the first white settlers, the idea that the Melungeons were indigenous people residing in the Clinch River region became one of the most persistent—and demonstrably false—legends surrounding them.

Indeed, the most appealing aspect of the Melungeons—at least to outsiders—is the mythology surrounding them, the legends that suggest mysterious origins involving exotic visitors from far away. The Melungeons soon

---

[36] Lewis Jarvis, "The Melungeons," *Hancock County Times*, 17 April 1903, 1; William Grohse papers, Archives of Appalachia, East Tennessee State University.

[37] Jarvis, "The Melungeons," 1.

[38] Sevier diary, Tennessee State Library and Archives, Nashville, TN, microfilm #546.

earned the nickname "Sons of the Legend." And whenever a newspaper or magazine writer happened onto the Melungeons, he or she rarely resisted newspaper editor Maxwell Scott's advice in the 1962 motion picture *The Man Who Shot Liberty Valance*: "When the legend becomes fact, print the legend."

However, the most legendary Melungeon of them all was not a son, but a daughter. Mahala Mullins was legendary during her lifetime, the subject of articles in newspapers from Philadelphia to Tacoma, and even in Mexico. According to the various legends, Mahala stood nearly seven feet tall and weighed as much as eight hundred pounds, could out-wrestle four men, lift a yearling bull over her head, and eat an entire pig for dinner. She was reputed to be a moonshiner, who made the best corn liquor anyone had ever tasted, and she sold it from a cabin that straddled the Virginia-Tennessee state line. When law enforcement agents from one state came to arrest her, she simply walked to the other side of her cabin and avoided arrest. Even if the lawmen could apprehend her, she was too large to be brought down the side of Newman's Ridge to be tried. Mahala reportedly gave birth to quadruplets when she was in her seventies and was murdered under mysterious circumstances; her thirty-three husbands carried her coffin to her grave. To get her body out of her cabin, a fireplace and chimney had to be removed because she was too large to fit through the door.

The truth was considerably less spectacular. Mahala was born in 1824 to Solomon and Gincie Collins, married Johnnie Mullins, and began raising children—at least twenty, fifteen of whom lived to adulthood. Johnnie and Mahala built a cabin on the north side of Newman's Ridge—not on the state line, but four miles inside Tennessee. The Mullins cabin was a well-known source of corn liquor, but there are indications that Mahala didn't make the whiskey herself; instead, she handled the financial end of the business. Johnnie and Mahala often took household and farm goods in exchange for their whiskey and had enough of those goods to attract Confederate raiders during the Civil War. The Rebels stole what they could carry and burned down the cabin. The cabin Mahala and Johnnie built after that had two relatively large rooms separated by an open space or "dogtrot," where cooking was done in warm weather. A large loft extended for the length of the cabin and provided sleeping room for the couple's numerous children.

At some point Mahala grew obese but was nowhere near the eight hundred pounds attributed to her in legend. Her weight was more likely closer to three hundred pounds, which was still a lot for a woman barely over five feet tall. A photograph shows her baring horribly swollen, misshapen legs, similar to the effects of elephantiasis. This certainly affected her mobility, especially as she got older. According to reliable reports, Hancock County Sheriff Washington Eads was ordered by a judge to apprehend Mahala and put an end to her moonshining. Eads reported back to the judge that Mahala was "ketchable, but not fetchable."

Stories about Mahala began to appear in newspapers, often in connection with stories about Federal efforts to eradicate the trade in illegal whiskey in east Tennessee. No one seemed overly concerned with accuracy regarding *any* stories coming out of the mountains, and reporters seemed to be trying to out-do each other when relating tales about Mahala Mullins.

After Johnnie Mullins died, Mahala was cared for by her granddaughter Hattie. One of Hattie's duties was to help Mahala onto her makeshift toilet: a galvanized washtub with a wide beam laid across it.

Mahala died on 10 September 1898 at the age of seventy-four. Her family didn't have to remove a fireplace to get her body out of the cabin. One end of the cabin did not have a fireplace, but a wood stove with a small chimney. The stove and wall boards on that side of the house were removed in order to get Mahala's body out of the cabin and into her nearby grave.

After her death, newspaper reports continued to build Mahala's legend. At least two newspapers speculated that she had been poisoned, presumably by competitors in the whiskey trade. A Kentucky newspaper reported that Mahala's body had been stolen from its grave; the same report claimed she had married a man named Johnson a week before she died.

Saundra Keyes Ivey did fieldwork for her doctoral dissertation in Hancock County in the mid-1970s and published an article titled "Aunt Mahala Mullins in Folklore, Fakelore, and Literature." She notes that those writing about Mahala tended to base their reports on previously published stories, rather than seeking out accurate information in Hancock County.

> An ambivalent attitude about the telling of Aunt Mahala anecdotes has therefore developed in Hancock County. On the one hand, there is pride in relating unique tales from the county's past, and the story of law enforcement officials reporting that Mahala was "ketchable but not fetchable" is told with gusto.... On the other hand, there is a justifiable wariness that the outsider may misrepresent the anecdote. While there is no sense of shame attached to Mahala's profession of bootlegging—a picture of her seated next to a container of whiskey with a dripping gourd in her hand was shown to me by a number of persons—there is a desire that this fact be understood on the county's terms. Most of my informants sensibly recognized that moonshining represented one of the few viable economic alternatives open to Mahala Mullins and others like her; all they ask is that outsiders share this recognition

and not use stories about Mahala to stereotype Hancock County as a moonshiner's haven.[39]

Mahala still occupies a central place in the folklore and history of Hancock County. Her cabin was occupied by several different families in the years after her death, and the last known occupants bought the cabin just after World War II. For many years, the cabin stood vacant; weeds and briars filled the yard and covered the cemetery. People hiked up to visit the cabin and often took pieces of wood or larger items for souvenirs. In 2000, the Vardy Community Historical Society bought the cabin, took it apart and carried the pieces down the mountain, and re-assembled the cabin across the road from the former Presbyterian church, which is now a museum. Visitors can tour the restored cabin and learn both the legends and the facts surrounding this remarkable woman.

At the end of the nineteenth century, missionaries came to Hancock County. A wide variety of denominations were establishing missions in southern Appalachia, not only to win converts to their respective denominations, but to "modernize" the region, to bring it into the "mainstream" of American life.

The Presbyterian Church in the United States of America (PCUSA)—also known as the Northern Presbyterian Church following a split in the denomination—was establishing missions around the world, and particularly across the southern Appalachians. Mark Banker writes, "Presbyterian missionaries entered the Southern Appalachians…in the aftermath of the Civil War as part of a broader wave of mainstream migration into the relatively isolated mountain en-claves. Where industrialists found abundant raw materials to exploit, the mis-sionaries discovered 'strange and peculiar' peoples."[40]

The Melungeons were as "strange and peculiar" as any Presbyterian could hope to meet—and the Melungeons had a particular need for educational op-portunities. They weren't permitted in the public schools in Hancock County or the surrounding counties. Even if they had been allowed to attend the public school in Sneedville, the Melungeon children of Blackwater Valley had no way to get there; there were mountain paths but no road across Newman's Ridge. The county did provide for some rudimentary education; Will Allen Dromgoole wrote of finding "one school among them, taught by an old Malungeon whose literary accomplishments amounted to a meagre knowledge of the alphabet and

[39] Ivey, "Aunt Mahala Mullins"
[40] Banker, "Missionaries and Mountain Peoples," 1–2.

the spelling of words. Yet, he was very earnest and called lustily to the 'chillering' to 'spry up' and to 'learn the book.'"[41]

Batey Collins, a grandson of Melungeon patriarch Vardemon Collins, lived on a portion of Ol' Vardy's land in Blackwater Valley, just north of Newman's Ridge. Batey was a Union Army veteran (East Tennessee was a Union stronghold in an otherwise Confederate state), had gone to war, traveled far and seen much, and wanted to bring to the valley educational opportunities, health care, and other "modern" benefits. He saw the Presbyterian missions as a way to accomplish that. Already, two itinerant Presbyterian ministers, Christopher Humble and H. P. Cory, were conducting services where and when they could in Blackwater Valley. Batey and his wife, Cynthia, offered the Presbyterians land on which to build a church and school, and in 1892 the Holston Presbytery of PCUSA decided to establish a mission in Blackwater.

Sending outsiders into rural Appalachia was not without risks. The region around Hancock County was plagued with violence associated with the liquor trade, between rival moonshiners and between moonshiners and law enforcement agents. A stranger moving into such an area would likely be suspected of being either an undercover lawman or a competing bootlegger and would probably be found dead in a ditch some morning. So the Presbyterian Women's Board of Missions appointed two women, Maggie Axtell and Annie Miller, as the first missionaries in Hancock County, hoping that women would not be suspected of having any interest in the whiskey traffic.

With lumber and labor supplied by residents of Blackwater Valley, the Presbyterians built a one-room log schoolhouse, offering for the first time to the children of the valley first through eighth-grade classes as mandated by the state of Tennessee. The Vardy Mission School, as it was called, was joined by the Vardy Presbyterian Church in 1899. In 1902, a new frame schoolhouse replaced the log structure.

Mary Rankin, a Scotts-born missionary and graduate of Columbia University, arrived at the Vardy Mission in 1910. She served as a teacher and nurse, offering vaccinations, first aid, home health visits, nutritional guidance, prenatal care, and obstetrical services to the people of the valley. In 1920, the Reverend Chester Leonard arrived with his wife, Josephine, and his parents. The mission thrived under the leadership of Rankin and Leonard. By 1929, a new three-story schoolhouse had been built with labor and materials again provided by residents of the valley. The new Vardy Community School boasted almost one hundred

---

[41] Dromgoole, "The Malungeons," 477.

windows for light and ventilation, as well as a Delco generator to provide electricity.

The curriculum offered by the school was even more impressive than the building itself. The ninety or so students at the school received individualized instruction and progressed at their own pace. Teachers at the Vardy school were required to have a master's degree, and they were paid through church funds (Leonard eventually got the county to contribute funds for the school). Classes were supplemented with slides and filmstrips, and the walls were filled with charts and other educational materials. Outside, a spacious and well-equipped playground gave the students opportunities to blow off steam while developing their physical strength.

The school's efforts were not confined to children; it also provided adult classes, visiting lecturers, who offered a welcome diversion from everyday life, and movies for entertainment. With the coming of the Vardy Community School, the Melungeons, who were not permitted in the region's public schools, wound up with a far better school than the public schools meant for whites only. Of course, whites were permitted to attend the Vardy School if they chose to do so.[42]

However, the missionaries never referred to the Melungeons' unique ethnic status; indeed, the word "Melungeon" was not used because it was considered an epithet.[43] The Reverend Leonard and the staff at the school wanted each student to progress as far as he or she was able, without any feeling of being inferior or different. Students who showed the aptitude and desire to go beyond the eighth grade had the opportunity to go on to other Presbyterian institutions such as Warren Wilson College, outside Asheville, North Carolina, where they could take high school classes and go on to college. Parents trusted Rev. Leonard; when the minister told Claude Collins's mother that Claude should go to Warren Wilson, she readily agreed to send him. Claude later recalled, "She'd have agreed if he'd said 'Europe.'"[44]

Claude's mother had reason to trust Rev. Leonard and the staff at the Vardy School. They recognized that Claude was special, a smart boy who, given the opportunity, could learn and go far. Claude, along with his parents and seven brothers and sisters, lived on Newman's Ridge. Every morning, Claude walked down from the Ridge, two miles down a rocky path that met Blackwater Road; the school was another two miles to the west. Claude wasn't a robust child, and

---

[42] Overbay, *Windows on the Past, passim.*

[43] Vande Brake, "Melungeon Literacies and 21st Century Technologies."

[44] Claude Collins interview (2002).

Nurse Rankin decided he needed milk. She arranged for various families along Claude's route to school to give Claude milk on his way to school. Every morning, Claude stopped at the home of one family or another and had two glasses of milk before continuing his journey.

As Collins summed up his experience at the Vardy School, "Vardy students had access to the finer things in life." Decades after he attended Vardy, R. C. Mullins fought back tears as he remembered the school that "cared about this little Melungeon boy," provided him with a strong moral foundation, and gave him the tools he needed to succeed in life. Miss Martha Collins, who served half a century as president of the bank in Sneedville, once told Claude Collins that when she picked up a young person walking along the road, she could tell within five minutes whether that person was a Vardy graduate. "She said, 'I can tell by their manners, by the way they talk, and the intellect they have. They're just different.'"[45]

The Vardy Community School created a sense of worth and accomplishment for its students, a feeling that they were as good as anyone and could do what others had done. This group of educated, confident Melungeons would be vital to the life of the county within a few years.

But many alumni of the Vardy School, armed with education and confidence, left Hancock County in search of better opportunities elsewhere, particularly in the industrial towns and cities of the Midwest. Leonard encouraged his students and the families of Newman's Ridge and Blackwater Valley to leave, to learn about the outside world and the opportunities to be found there. He knew that their opportunities would always be limited in Hancock County—even more limited than they were to others, because of the stigma of their Melungeon ancestry. With contacts in southern Indiana, Leonard found places for the farmers of the valley who struggled to raise meager crops out of the poor, rocky soil. Not only would they find the rich Midwestern topsoil far more conducive to successful farming, they would not face discrimination because of their Melungeon surnames.

World War II drew many people out of Hancock County. The dark complexions of some of the Melungeons raised questions at segregated military classification centers; in fact, the influx of hundreds of men from the Melungeon, Brass Ankle, Croatan, Redbone, and other mixed-ethnic communities led to calls from the Army to local draft boards, questioning whether the boards had sent inductees to the wrong camp. The draft board in Hancock County, like many others in the southeastern United States, began sending men to the classification

---

[45] Collins interview (2002); Mullins, "The Vardy School," presentation.

centers with affidavits confirming the identity and home address of the soldier-to-be, along with other information, including the affirmation that the man in question was considered white. The military, in most cases, went along with the classification given by the soldier's home county. Of course, most of these men were *not* considered white at home—at least, not white enough to be accepted in segregated schools—but most of the local draft boards chose to send their local mixed-ethnic men to war with a "white" classification. Interestingly, many draftees from Hancock County were rejected for military service because they were functionally illiterate—a problem not present among alumni of the Vardy Community School.

Many of those Hancock Countians not taken by the Army left home to find work in the shipyards and factories of Baltimore, Detroit, Los Angeles, and other industrial cities and towns across America. Some came home after the war, along with soldiers who had served in Europe or the Pacific, but many, soldiers and civilians alike, had seen the outside world and decided Hancock County simply had nothing for them. From its peak population of 11,231 in 1940, the county had lost almost 19 percent of its residents by 1950; by 1960, another 15 percent had left.

Those who remained in Hancock County were reminded of the stigma associated with Melungeons, which affected the non-Melungeons of the county as well, when the *Saturday Evening Post* ran an article which became infamous in county history. "Sons of the Legend," by William Worden, appeared in the 18 October 1947 issue.

> About the people of Newman's Ridge and Blackwater Swamp just one fact is indisputable: There are such strange people. Beyond that, fact gives way to legendary mystery, and written history is supplanted by garbled stories told a long time ago and half forgotten.[46]

Describing the people walking on Sneedville's unpaved main street or leaning against the courthouse wall, Worden wrote, "Either they have some Latin characteristics or the effect of the legend is to make the stranger think they have." He described cabins on Newman's Ridge, some without doors or floors. "Here, beyond where the roads end, in the clearings on the ridge, the dark people are at home," he wrote. "This is the Malungeon country. This is the country where no one ever uses the word 'Malungeon.'"[47]

---

[46] Worden, "Sons of the Legend," 28.
[47] Ibid., 29.

Worden went on to recycle material from Will Allen Dromgoole (identified by one interview subject as "Will Allen Damfool") and other writers. Incorporating some of the mythology surrounding their origins, he relates an account from the 1600s in which Indians told of a settlement of whites who lived "eight days'down the river," who "had houses and owned a bell which they sounded often, especially before meals, when all of them bowed their heads toward it." These, Worden speculates, may have been Melungeons. He recounts the Scots-Irish settlers who found strange, dark people already living on the rich farmland of the Clinch valley.

> [T]he other settlers apparently were unwilling to admit that they dark people were Caucasians, and the dividing line between "whites" and "Malungeons" began to be drawn—by the whites. Forty years later the division became serious. In the Tennessee Constitutional Convention of 1834, East Tennesseans succeeded in having the Malungeons officially classified as "free persons of color." This classification was equivalent to declaring them of Negro blood and preventing them from suing or even testifying in court in any case involving a Caucasian. The purpose was fairly obvious and the effect immediate. Other settlers simply moved onto what good bottom land the Malungeons had, and the dark people had no recourse except to retire with what they could take with them to the higher ridge land which no other settlers wanted and where no court cases could arise. Some may have been on Newman's Ridge previously, but now the rest climbed the slopes to live, taking with them their families, a few household possessions, some stock and a burning resentment of this and other injustices, such as the fact that their children were not welcome in the settler's schools, only in Negro schools, which they declined to attend.[48]

Worden recounts the many legends about the Melungeons, their supposed Portuguese, Phoenician, or Carthaginian ancestry, the suggestion that the Melungeons were descendants of the Lost Colony of Roanoke Island, and stories about Mahala Mullins. Another legend Worden shared is the story that sometime after the Civil War, they had found gold or silver somewhere along Newman's Ridge or in Blackwater Valley, that they minted their own currency, coins which contained more precious metal than equivalent coins minted by the U.S. government. Supposedly, a Melungeon $20 gold piece actually contained $30 worth of gold, making the Melungeons valued customers in the stores of Sneedville.[49]

---

[48] Ibid.
[49] Ibid., 128.

The article brought the Melungeon story up to the present day, with the conflicts over Melungeon children attending white schools, or Melungeon men serving with white soldiers during the World Wars. Worden concludes with an example of the evasiveness with which questions about the Melungeons were answered:

> In the small Tennessee hill towns, now and then, a dark man will talk to a stranger, tell a few incidents heard or seen on Newman's Ridge or advise him, "See ___. If anybody knows, he will." Only ___ never does. A lovely woman may even, looking straight at the visitor with gray eyes, say, "My own grandfather had some Indian blood and perhaps some Spanish. We don't know much about the family, but there is a story that some of De Soto's men..."
>
> The lady may have small hands and feet, high cheekbones, straight hair and olive skin, and a regal carriage. She may talk for some time and tell much that is written in no books, some hearsay, some the most fanciful legend. But one word she will never say. She will never say, "Malungeon."[50]

Worden's *Saturday Evening Post* article was not well-received in Hancock County. The non-Melungeon residents resented Worden's description of their county seat: "Sneedville, war-swollen to a population of about 400 persons, is the county seat of Hancock County, Tennessee, just below Virginia, in the mountains through which no principal highway runs, no railroad has tracks, and only a single, insecure telephone line with five or six connections straggles.... Nothing much ever happened in Sneedville."[51]

Many years later, a Hancock County resident talked with researcher Saundra Keyes Ivey about his objections to the article:

> Well, the pictures that he used, for example, in his article, were pictures taken of the very shabbiest, poorest huts, and he implied that they were all in Sneedville. And they referred to "the swamps of Sneedville" and the poor and all that. And there was nothing uplifting; it was all very degrading. And he implied that the Melungeons were freaks...that they were not intelligent. He didn't give them any complimentary remarks whatsoever—everything was down, down, down.

The same person told of his daughter who attended East Tennessee State Teachers College in Johnson City, some ninety miles by road from Sneedville. "[S]he went in as a freshman, and a girl remarked to her once, she said, 'Oh, you've got shoes,' you know. And, uh, maybe followed it up with some kind of

---

[50] Ibid., 133.
[51] Worden, "Sons of the Legend," 28.

remark on where she's from." Reportedly, one young woman attending East Tennessee State was so embarrassed by the article she dropped out of school permanently, unwilling to face her fellow students who might wonder if she were one of *those* people.[52]

Most of the white citizens at that time did not find the Melungeons mysterious, interesting, or something they wished the rest of the world to know about. Many saw the Melungeons as their county's dirty little secret, evidence of some rampant race mixing that went on generations before. Since many "white" Hancock Countians had kinship through blood or marriage with one or more Melungeon family groups, they were quite sensitive about any attention brought to their swarthy neighbors.

For many of the Melungeons, particularly the young alumni of the Vardy Community School, the article came as a shock. Many of them had never heard the word "Melungeon," and none thought of themselves as *being* Melungeon. Again, as Edward Price wrote in 1951, "There is no group of people who call themselves Melungeons or who would recognize themselves as thus separated from the rest of the country population."[53] By the mid-twentieth century, the term "Melungeon" was not used simply to describe one's ancestry; it was a comment on the socio-economic standing of an individual or family. The people of Hancock County seemed to have accepted Dromgoole's definition of a Melungeon: "shiftless, idle, thieving…filthy…born rogues…inhospitable, untruthful; cowardly…sneaky…a blot upon our state."[54]

The *Post* article mentioned the Vardy School: "Generally, they still avoid schools, except for the mission at Vardy, from which the Rev. Chester F. Leonard sends a few on to the University of Tennessee or to church colleges. One such college, Maryville, has records of half a dozen entered, none graduated." Worden makes no mention of any Melungeons who *did* graduate from college, and by the definition of the term "Melungeon" offered by Dromgoole and more or less adopted by the people of Hancock County, none had. Anyone who had the intelligence, ambition, and drive to complete college was not shiftless or idle, and therefore not a Melungeon. The Reverend Leonard, quoted in the article, is clearly uncomfortable talking about Melungeons, and gives a vague explanation: "Mr. Leonard, incidentally, says, 'The group is so intermingled that one cannot be sure of a typical specimen.'"[55]

---

[52] Ivey, "Oral, Printed, and Popular Culture Traditions," 371.
[53] Price, "The Melungeons," 258.
[54] Dromgoole, "The Malungeons," 471.
[55] Worden, "Sons of the Legend," 27.

Claude Collins picked up a copy of the *Post* while attending the University of Tennessee. Claude had attended high school classes at Warren Wilson College in Swannanoa, North Carolina, but had enrolled in Hancock County High School when school bus service was extended to Newman's Ridge. After serving in the Army in World War II, he enrolled at the University of Tennessee in Knoxville. He read the *Post* article on the bus ride back to Hancock County, and when he reached his home atop Newman's Ridge, he was full of questions. "I said. 'Mother, this magazine has our relatives in it; it has pictures of our people. It's about the Melungeons.' She looked at me and said, 'Claude—don't you name that word anymore.'"[56]

DruAnna Williams Overbay recalls how, at five years old, she went to the mailbox and found the *Saturday Evening Post*. She had just started attending the Vardy Community School, where her parents, Drew Williams and Alyce Horton Williams, were both teachers. As she thumbed through the magazine, she was amazed to find pictures of her neighbors and called out to other students to come and look. Her mother came out of the classroom and snatched the magazine from DruAnna's hands. That night, her mother became very upset while talking to her husband. "Why can't they leave us alone? I wish I never had to hear that word [Melungeon] again!" Alyce was the great-granddaughter of Batey Collins, who had donated land for the Vardy mission and who was himself the grandson of Vardemon Collins. "She didn't want me to know about Melungeons," Overbay says. "In my mother's family, they said we were 'Portugee,' That's what they called Portuguese."

Although her mother denied her Melungeon heritage, from that day on DruAnna knew that she was a Melungeon, a daughter of the legend, but it would be many years before she felt comfortable talking about it.[57]

By the early 1960s, it seemed as if no one would be talking about the Melungeons much longer, at least not in the present tense. The Melungeons were disappearing.

In September 1963, Louise Davis wrote a pair of articles for the *Nashville Tennessean Sunday Magazine*. The first article, "The Mystery of the Melungeons," was essentially a recap of what had been written before. The second, "Why Are They Vanishing?," predicted the eventual demise of the Melungeons.

Melungeons, like many of the other citizens of Hancock County, have broken out of the rigid trap of a region that has never had a railroad and had few highways to lift them over the fierce barrier of the mountains until recent

[56] Claude Collins interview (2002).
[57] Neal, "Melungeons explore mysterious mixed-race origins."

years. One theory is that, with more travel to outside areas, they are intermarrying with whites so frequently that their distinctive characteristics are vanishing, and the Melungeons will soon be a relic of the history books.

Davis noted, "The Melungeons who used to sit on the fence around the courthouse square in Sneedville are no longer there." A county resident told her, "They have more or less just died out. The families have just eroded." A former teacher acknowledged the role education had played in the disappearance of the Melungeons: "Once they get a college education, they seldom come back. They go to Chicago or other distant places where they can get good jobs and nobody will ever call them Melungeon."[58]

A 1964 article distributed by United Press International cited intermarriage rather than outmigration as the reason for the demise of the Melungeons. Under the headline "Melungeon Line Almost Extinct," John Gamble wrote, "It has been the mixing—and intermarriage—of Melungeon youths with the young people of Sneedville...that has brought the 'true' Melungeons to the point of extinction." He also observed that while the Melungeons still avoided contact with outsiders, they "have taken to many modern gadgets. Most all of them have television sets, and many of the farmers drive tractors."[59]

Davis was correct in citing outmigration as an important factor in the disappearance of the Melungeons. But Gamble came very close to uncovering a more existential truth about the Melungeons. What was happening was *assimilation*—the Melungeons were becoming absorbed into the larger society. The Melungeons had no defining cultural characteristics, no distinctive language or customs, no unique folklore or music or foodways. Their churches were of the same denominations as their neighbors, and there were no special Melungeon holidays. Other than their family names and—sometimes—their color, there was nothing that made the Melungeons distinguishable from their neighbors.

What was happening to the Melungeons was happening to most of the other mixed ethnic groups in the southeastern United States. The Croatans of North Carolina were the exception; they had gained state recognition as an Indian tribe in 1885, had more recently renamed themselves the Lumbee Indians, and were struggling for Federal recognition and benefits—a struggle that continues as of this writing. The Croatans/Lumbees had established an identity for themselves separate from their neighbors. The opposite was happening to the other mixed-ethnic groups listed at the beginning of this chapter; they were becoming indistinguishable from their neighbors.

---

[58] Davis, "Why Are They Vanishing?"
[59] Gamble, "Melungeon Line Almost Extinct," 9-C.

Most of these groups, like the Melungeons, had been defined largely by segregation, both legal and social. Many Melungeons who had more physically obvious African ancestry had already been absorbed into the tiny African-American community of Hancock County or had moved to places where they identified themselves as black and were accepted as such. But the majority of the Melungeons were quickly becoming "white." The old census designation of "free person of color" or "FPC" had been abandoned a century before; Melungeons defined themselves almost exclusively as "white."

The desegregation of county schools removed another defining line from around the Melungeons. The Presbyterians abandoned their mission in Vardy soon after the retirement of the Reverend Chester Leonard. The Vardy church was closed, and the Vardy School was taken over by the county (it would be closed in the early 1970s). Students who lived north of Newman's Ridge could now ride school buses on the newly built road over the mountain to attend high school in Sneedville.

Social segregation was also breaking down. As noted earlier, Martha Collins ("Miss Martha" to locals) served as a bank president—and *de facto* county leader—for fifty years. Claude Collins finished his education and returned to Hancock County to teach in the high school and later served as a school administrator. Melungeons were entering the mainstream of Hancock County life, some earning positions of power and influence, others simply working hard in pursuit of the American dream that seemed attainable for all in that prosperous post-World War II era.

Whether they moved away to make automobile batteries in Indiana or remained on the family farm to grow tobacco, the Melungeons weren't actually disappearing. They just weren't Melungeons anymore, at least not according to the traditional definitions. The word "Melungeon" was disappearing, and the concept of Melungeons as a distinct people was vanishing as well. In that sense, the newspaper articles seemed correct in predicting the eventual demise of the Melungeons.

But predictions, no matter how logical, have a way of turning out to be completely wrong. The Melungeons were about to return, and they would come back in a very big way.

4

THE WAR ON POVERTY

This administration today, here and now, declares unconditional war on poverty in America.

—President Lyndon B. Johnson
State of the Union Address, 8 January 1964

There are a lot of unfamiliar faces at the lunch counter today, Charlie Turner thought as he struggled to remember who these men in his drugstore were, and which agencies they represented. Lots of strangers had been coming into Sneedville lately, all of them trying to figure out a way to get some of President Johnson's largesse into Hancock County. LBJ had explained the goals of his War on Poverty: "Our aim is not only to relieve the symptom of poverty, but to cure it and, above all, to prevent it." If the president wanted to wage war on poverty, he couldn't find a better battlefield than Hancock County. It was the eighth poorest county in America and the only county in Tennessee with a declining population.

Appalachia had a central role in Johnson's campaign to end poverty. In April 1964, the president embarked on a publicity tour to build support for his programs and was photographed on the front porch of the Fletcher family home in Inez, Kentucky. The following month, the First Lady visited the impoverished Lick Branch School in Jackson, Kentucky, on a tour of eastern Kentucky locations. The images from these trips, featured in newspapers and magazines and broadcast on television, illustrated the poverty of central Appalachia in a way that the average American could understand viscerally. Appalachian poverty, which had seemed quaint and funny in comic strips like *Snuffy Smith* and *Li'l Abner*, was now represented by the gaunt faces of the adults who shook the president's hand and the ragamuffin children who welcomed Lady Bird Johnson to their one-room schoolhouse. A lot of Americans were shocked to discover that one-room schoolhouses still existed.

President Johnson rode a wave of public approval and a friendly Democrat-led Congress to push through a series of legislative initiatives. He assigned the late President Kennedy's brother-in-law, Sargent Shriver, to craft a bill that would be the centerpiece of the War on Poverty. On 20 August, Johnson signed the Economic Opportunity Act of 1964 into law. This act would create the Community Action Program, Job Corps, Legal Services, and Volunteers in Service to America (VISTA). Eleven days later, he signed the Food Stamp Act, which made permanent a pilot program that had been initiated in the early days of the Kennedy administration and was meant to eliminate hunger in America by giving poor people the ability to purchase food.

In April 1965, Johnson signed the Elementary and Secondary Education Act, which would provide funding for public schools, guarantee equal access to education, and establish high standards and accountability. In July, he signed the Social Security Act of 1965, which established Medicare and Medicaid.

While some Republicans were on board with these initiatives, or at least some of the programs, the more conservative GOP legislators resisted them, decrying the socialistic nature of the programs and the high cost to taxpayers. But public opinion nationwide supported the president. Many people saw LBJ's War on Poverty as an extension of President Franklin Roosevelt's New Deal, enacted during the Great Depression. America was prosperous in 1965, and most Americans felt the country could afford to alleviate poverty among those who had somehow missed out on the American dream.

Officials in traditionally Republican Appalachia were particularly excited about the Appalachian Regional Commission, created by the Appalachian Redevelopment Act, which LBJ signed into law on 9 March 1965. The Commission had its roots in the Council of Appalachian Governors, formed in 1960 by the governors of North Carolina, South Carolina, Pennsylvania, Alabama, Georgia, Kentucky, Maryland, Tennessee, Virginia, and West Virginia. Their goal was to seek federal funding for projects in the mountainous portions of their respective states. These areas lagged behind the rest of the nation in income, education, health care, and transportation.

Presidential candidate John F. Kennedy met with these governors during the 1960 campaign and saw first-hand the poverty of the region as he stumped for votes in the West Virginia primary. He promised that, if elected, he would help the Appalachian region. Further inspiration was provided by Harry Caudill's 1962 book *Night Comes to the Cumberlands: A Biography of a Depressed Area*, which brought the conditions in Appalachia—particularly eastern Kentucky—to national attention.

Kennedy formed the President's Appalachian Regional Commission in 1963 to help create and pass legislation that would put federal dollars into the region. Lyndon Johnson incorporated that effort into his War on Poverty and created an agency with four primary goals:

1) Increase job opportunities and per capita income in Appalachia to reach parity with the nation;

2) Strengthen the capacity of the people of Appalachia to compete in the global economy;

3) Develop and improve Appalachia's infrastructure to make the region economically competitive;

4) Build the Appalachian Development Highway System to reduce Appalachia's isolation.

It all sounded pretty good to Mayor Charles Turner of Sneedville, Tennessee, but it was that last item that really got to the heart of the particular problem he was trying to solve—the highway between Sneedville and Mooresburg that Hancock County workers had to drive on their way to jobs in Morristown. Employers in Morristown didn't want to hire workers who lived on the other side of Clinch Mountain because Highway 31 was too dangerous to travel in bad weather. People had to choose between having a job and staying in Hancock County, and when you have a family to feed—well, that's not really a choice at all, is it? A good highway over Clinch Mountain would keep those workers in Hancock County, paying local taxes and sending their kids to local schools. It would help stop the hemorrhage of human potential now devastating the county.

In 1965, Turner was forty-nine years old. Tall and balding, he looked a little bit like a cross between Harry Truman and Lyndon Johnson—a comparison he probably wouldn't have minded because he was a Democrat and admired both of those presidents. His friend, attorney Bruce Shine from Kingsport, Tennessee, recalls, "Everybody knew that Charlie Turner was inter-ested in doing the best for Sneedville and Hancock County, that he didn't have any ulterior motives. He was a damn good Democrat in a county that had few. And it was hard to say no to him."[1]

People in Sneedville certainly didn't say no to him when it came to electing him mayor. Hancock County was, and still is, a Republican stronghold; county Democrats could probably hold a convention in a small living room without feeling crowded. For a Democrat to be elected to anything in the county was simply remarkable. Of course, only those living within the city limits of Sneedville voted for mayor, so he didn't have to go up against the powerful county Republican machine—or machines, as it were; the county GOP was split

---

[1] Shine interview.

into two hostile factions. Turner's success, however, owed more to his own at-tributes than to the failings of his opponents. People liked and trusted him, and he genuinely wanted to improve the lives of his constituents.

Scott Collins, who served more than three decades as a court administrator in Hancock County and is currently a vice-president at Civis Bank, describes Turner as "one of the finest men the county has ever produced."

> Charles, Sonny, and the whole family, really, did well. They did things that were needed in the county. Charles Turner had the Turner Drug Store; Sonny had the department store—as a matter of fact, the department store was right where this bank sits today. We bought the building off Sonny and renovated this lot right here and made a bank of it.
>
> Because of where we live, geographically, and what we *didn't* have, he had a vision. And I'm sure he didn't know what to expect, but when he [was elected mayor], he had people that he would go to and ask, "What can you do for us?" And we were able to get a lot of economic development. We got water, sewers, the utility district. And some of them talked [Turner] into put-ting in parking meters—we had parking meters at one time, as a way of gen-erating funds to operate the city.[2]

The parking meters were inaugurated in April 1963. In addition to gener-ating revenue, they were intended to prevent folks from taking up a parking space all day. The cost wasn't much—a penny for 12 minutes, a nickel for an hour.[3] But they didn't last long; the meagre revenue they generated was far outweighed by the bad feeling they engendered among merchants and customers alike. But that idea was an anomaly. Most of Charlie Turner's ideas were well-received

He was ethical in a way that was unusual for politicians. For example, he didn't spend Election Day getting out the vote among his supporters. Not Char-lie Turner—he made sure he was on vacation in Florida on Election Day. He didn't want people in Sneedville to see him that day because, if they did, they might feel pressured to vote for him. He wanted people to vote for him, of course, but he wanted those votes to be completely voluntary; he didn't want people to vote for him because they had just seen him on the street or in the drugstore and would feel guilty about *not* voting for him. But the people of Sneedville elected him mayor—and then re-elected him, again and again—because they knew him to be an honorable man, and they knew he would do all he possibly could for

---

[2] Scott Collins interview.
[3] "Parking Meters," 2.

Sneedville and Hancock County. Decades later, Scott Collins, though himself a Republican, recognized the benefits of having a Democrat mayor.

> We had a lot of connections with Hub Walters; he was a senator from Tennessee at the time.[4] Everything that Mr. Turner would apply for, in terms of community economic development, would be approved because he happened to be the person who was elected mayor and was able to get things done, he being a Democrat, and Hub Walters being a Democrat. And the people that had the money wanted to do things. All these different organizations that were out there to help cities, Charles joined in with. He was very aggressive; he was a full-time mayor. I mean, he was out there all the time. And obviously, when you are able to get something to help infrastructure in the city, anything, whatever it might be, it was something we hadn't had before. He was such an asset to the community. Had a good city council; they all basically worked in unison on everything. I mean, I could go on and on talking about Charles Turner.[5]

Under Turner's leadership, Sneedville won first place (out of 134 communities in its population group) in the 1963 Tennessee Community Progress Program. That award was based on a community's pride, its development, and its improvement, particularly concerning its readiness for new industry. Sneedville had been eligible to compete for this award for only a year before winning it. Charlie Turner remembered that day in Nashville when the winners were to be announced. He'd gone to the meeting with several local leaders: Dr. Truett Pierce, the town's only physician; Howard Rhea, the lawyer; the Methodist minister, Luther Lawson; Judge Otis Greene; Bruce Lawson, the insurance agent; B.L. Satterfield, who owned the hardware store; and two or three others. They were having lunch, waiting to learn if they'd won, when somebody announced that President Kennedy had just been shot and killed in Dallas. The awards were postponed for a couple of weeks and the group drove back to Sneedville in shock, listening to news reports on the car radio. When it was finally announced that Sneedville won first place in their category, it seemed like good things were about to happen for the town and for the county.[6]

---

[4] Herbert "Hub" Walters, a native of Jefferson County, TN, was a former state representative and a prominent banker. In August 1963, Governor Frank Clement appointed Walters to the U.S. Senate following the death of Senator Estes Kefauver. Walters was understood to be a placeholder; Clement intended to run for the seat himself in 1964 but was unwilling to appoint himself to the seat. Clement did run for the seat but was defeated in the Democratic primary by Ross Bass, who went on to win the general election. Walters continued to be influential in Tennessee politics until his death in 1973. Walters State Community College in Morristown is named after him.

[5] Scott Collins interview.

[6] "Sneedville Wins Progress Award in State Competition," 1.

They were going to need some help to make those good things happen, and that's why Charlie Turner was frustrated with all the government people in his drugstore on that sunny afternoon in December 1965. There were two men from the Office of Economic Opportunity, the chief agency in the War on Poverty. Two more men represented the Department of Labor's Manpower Administration. Two of the new VISTA workers who had been assigned to the county sat at the lunch counter next to someone from State Planning Office. Watching over everything was a reporter from *The National Observer*. All these high-powered people were coming into town, offering money for this and money for that— Community Action Programs, adult education programs, job retraining programs, a Neighborhood Youth Corps. But they still hadn't addressed the issue closest to Charlie Turner's heart.

Speaking to the group in general, Turner said, "All these Federal programs won't help us a bit unless we get some access." It was Highway 31 again. Charlie Turner wanted someone to modernize the highway that was essential to Hancock County. "These other antipoverty programs are fine, but that road is what we want. When our people go down to Morristown to apply for work, the first thing the employer asks is if they're going to move to Morristown. The employers know, with the condition of the road we got now, that to hire a man from Sneedville means absenteeism. So our people are moving out of town."

Turner, like government officials all across Appalachia, had been elated by the creation of the Appalachian Regional Commission. Of particular interest to Turner was the news that the ARC would have $840,000,000 to spend on new roads. Turner didn't need a new road; he just needed $875,000 to straighten out the hairpin curves on Highway 31. Then he found out the ARC money wasn't necessarily going to go to the most impoverished areas, but to the areas that had a chance to develop economically. The people who made such determinations felt Sneedville didn't have that chance.

On the other hand, federal officials believed that nearby Tazewell, in Claiborne County, *did* have such potential. In 1962, the U.S. Public Health Service had threatened to close down a small garment factory in Tazewell because Tazewell had inadequate water and sewer systems. Town leaders persuaded the Area Redevelopment Administration (which was incorporated into LBJ's War on Poverty and became the Economic Development Administration) to put up a million dollars in grants and loans to build new systems.

The EDA field representative in Knoxville, Charles Pate, was thrilled with the results of that investment. "I'd heard about economic multiplier theories in school, but I never saw them act as dramatically as they did in Tazewell." Not only did EDA funding keep the garment factory open, but other businesses moved into Tazewell, bringing 700 new jobs. By 1965, the original federal investment of $1 million had generated an additional $9.5 million in public and private investment. Tazewell now boasted a small travel trailer factory, a new bank, a new school, and a new motel. And town leaders expected even more to come when Appalachian Regional Commission funding developed a new highway corridor incorporating U.S. Highway 25E to link up with the Interstate Highway system. But that was Charlie Turner's road money! He'd asked for the highway corridor come through Sneedville, giving him the good road to Morristown his town needed, but the Feds turned him down.

"They told me the development potential didn't justify the investment," Turner recalled bitterly. It's a hard thing to be told your town isn't worth investing in. If the idea behind the Appalachian Regional Commission was to alleviate poverty in the region, Turner thought, *Why not alleviate some of our poverty? Give us a chance to survive! Pretty soon there won't be anyone left here.*

Hancock County had been in decline since the end of World War II. Between 1950 and 1960, the county lost 15 percent of its population; during the same period, the combined counties of east Tennessee saw a 4.4 percent increase. The average family income in Hancock County was $1,442 per year, compared to the national average of $4,658. The per capita income was $588, the lowest in the state. Even with heavy outmigration, which ought to have alleviated unemployment somewhat, the unemployment rate in Hancock County was the highest in Tennessee: 29.7 percent. The national rate was 4.5 percent.

More than half the population of the county—56 percent—worked in agriculture, the highest percentage in the state. But farm work was often seasonal; less than 35 percent of the county worked in agriculture all year long. Only 13.5 percent of Hancock County workers were employed in white-collar jobs, the second-lowest rate in Tennessee. Manufacturing jobs employed only 9.4 percent of the county's workers; only three counties in the state had a lower rate. And, of course, nearly all of those manufacturing jobs were located *outside* the county. Almost 4 percent of the population of Hancock County had to cross Clinch Mountain on a dangerous highway every morning—and drive back over that road every evening.

Charlie Turner could rattle off those statistics from memory, along with others. Want to know about public assistance? The combined counties of east Tennessee had a rate of 26 people per 1,000 receiving some sort of public aid. In Hancock County, the rate was 97 per 1,000. How about housing? One of the best indicators of poverty is the rate of unsound or unhealthy housing. In 1965, 26 percent of the housing in the United States was classified "unsound," meaning unsound in structure or having unsound plumbing—or no plumbing at all. For

Tennessee, that figure was 43 percent. For east Tennessee, the Appalachian portion of the state, 53.5 percent of the housing was unsound. For Hancock County, it was 89 percent. Almost nine out of ten dwellings in the county were considered unsound.

Education might have gone a long way toward solving some of these problems, but in Hancock County, that was problematic as well. More than 30 percent of county residents had less than five years of education. Almost half the people over the age of twenty-five had left school after eighth grade, or even earlier. The dropout rate for high school students was high; 42 percent of the county's sixteen- and seventeen-year olds were not enrolled in school. Some of them came from families where education was often scorned: *Cousin Bill's oldest boy graduated high school and got above his raisin'. Thinks he's smarter than his daddy.* Some who had attended small one-teacher elementary schools simply weren't prepared for high school. And others dropped out because they needed to work to help support their families. Of those relatively few who graduated high school, most did not go on to college. Those who did go to college usually didn't come back to Hancock County to live.

The county school system itself was a mess, one that was out of Charlie Turner's control. Teachers received the state's minimum salary; Hancock County did not supplement teacher's pay as did most counties to some degree or another. The county's schools were run by a board of education and a superintendent, all of whom were elected, and that was an area of conflict between the two opposing Republican factions. One faction controlled the board, while the superintendent was the leader of the other faction. Each board member had the power to appoint teachers in his own district, so the granting of teaching jobs was a matter of political loyalty rather than merit. That went for all the other jobs relating to the schools as well—bus drivers, janitors, cafeteria workers, etc. Some of the members of the school board resisted the idea of school consolidation because it would mean a consolidation of political power as well, and some board members would lose influence while others gained. Still, some degree of school consolidation was underway, and several small schools were slated to be closed.

A report commissioned by the Tennessee Valley Authority's Clinch and Powell River Valley Association, along with the University of Tennessee, had been released in September 1965. It summed up some of the problems facing the county.

> Hancock County is living in a shadow of the past, experiencing few of the
> changes brought to the South by industrialization. Its citizens' material needs

are provided in one way or another, but the county is not making the technological and educational advances it should be making. Hancock Countians run their county and its government as their forefathers did, and they have kept the schools the same. The young people are not being trained to live in the world as it is. Because of the difficulty of making a living, many are leaving. Those who remain are worried about the area's future.

Some citizens have organized to make Sneedville more progressive. The mayor, recently re-elected, is one of the prime movers in this effort. Sneedville has received a federal grant for new water and sewerage systems. To demonstrate community support, since there are no city taxes, the mayor felt that the people should contribute to the development of their town, if only in a small way, so parking meters were installed. This decision has brought the mayor harsh criticism from some of the town's residents.

Sneedville is ready to accept an industry, but industry is reluctant to move into the county because of the road situation, educational deficiencies and other problems…. Why have the people not been aware of the need for progress before now? Is growth the best thing for the county or should there be adjustment in some other way? It is a situation which must be confronted realistically.[7]

Dammit, we're trying, thought Turner. *They won't fix our road because they think we're not worth it!* But as he looked at the EOE representatives, the state planner, and the VISTA workers sitting at his lunch counter, he understood that help *was* being offered. The OEO had created a Community Action Committee to attack poverty in the county, and the Manpower Administration set up classes to teach illiterate adults to read. They had discussed setting up a Neighborhood Youth Corps. And now they were talking about a different way, maybe, to get Charlie Turner's road fixed. Although Hancock County didn't qualify as a potential growth center, the Appalachian Act *did* provide funding for access roads for school consolidation. The state planner thought he might be able to make a case for the Mooresburg road to be improved under that provision, but they all knew it would probably be vetoed by the ARC as a "pork barrel" project.

These other programs—*well, they probably weren't going keep people from moving away, were they? No, probably not.* But these government men were trying to help. They were also guests in his town and in his drugstore. And Charlie Turner realized he might have hurt their feelings.

"I'm sorry to jump on you fellows about your programs," the mayor said. "They're all real fine programs. It's just that I've put my whole life into this town

---

[7] Carter, "Educational Resources and Needs in Hancock County, Tennessee," 45.

and this county, and only now they're telling me it doesn't have a chance to grow anyhow."[8]

---

[8] Wanniski, "Mayor Turner," 2.

5

A DRAMATIC PLAN

So far, no enterprising playwright has written a drama around the dark people of Hancock County.

—Louise Davis, 1963

Mayor Turner wasn't the only person working to improve Sneedville and Hancock County. There were several others in the town and in the county working to improve the county, even before LBJ declared war on poverty.

The Area Redevelopment Association was a demonstration project established by the federal government in 1961 to advance economic development in selected areas. The ARA was the forerunner of the Economic Development Administration, created by the Public Works and Economic Development Act (PWEDA) of 1965. Prior to the passage of the PWEDA, the ARA recruited leaders in Hancock County to form the Hancock County Overall Economic Development Program Association (OEDPA). This organization was tasked with creating a report that would identify needs and resources in the county and set goals. The president of the Hancock County OEDPA was Sneedville's physician, Dr. Truett Pierce. The vice-presidents were Sneedville hardware merchant B.L. Satterfield and county judge Otis Greene. Mayor Charles Turner was the treasurer, and the secretary was Robert Haston, county agent with the University of Tennessee Agricultural Extension Service.

Between November 1962 and February 1963, this organization prepared a report on conditions and problems and recommendations for projects beneficial to the county. The Hancock County OEDPA was made up of a wide cross-section of county residents, including attorney Howard Rhea; Baptist minister Rev. Carl Greene and Methodist minister Rev. Luther Lawson; John Wolfe, a farmer in Kyles Ford; insurance agent Bruce Lawson; Sneedville postmaster Shields Winkler; Cecile Turner, wife of the mayor; T. J. Harrison, principal of Hancock County High School; local teachers Claude Collins, Horace Greene, Calvin Hurley, and Lucille Reed; truck drivers John Snodgrass and Rod Willis; T. J. Turnmire of the Farmer's Co-Op; beauticians Judy and Fodell Hopkins; and many other county residents.

This organization recommended four projects, including renovation of the county courthouse, construction of a new county jail to replace the current structure built in 1860, sidewalk and curb construction in Sneedville, and construction of a new high school to replace the facility built in 1936 by the Public Works Administration. The construction of the high school had already been approved by the time the report was completed, but the decrepit county jail remained in use for many more years.[1]

Twenty-three members of the Hancock County OEDPA were also members of the Clinch and Powell River Valley Association (CPRVA), another group interested in the economic development of the region. The Clinch River is a 300-mile waterway stretching from Tazewell, Virginia, to its confluence with the Tennessee River in Kingston, Tennessee, and is the primary waterway in Hancock County. The Powell River, separated from the Clinch by Powell Mountain, rises near Indian Mountain in Wise County, Virginia, and flows 195 miles to its confluence with the Clinch River in the Norris Lake reservoir at the now-submerged town of Grantsboro. Under the auspices of the Tennessee Valley Authority's Office of Tributary Development, the CPRVA commissioned studies and reports dealing with resource development, industrial development, local planning, land uses, conservation, recreation, flood control, navigation, and transportation in the region.

The University of Tennessee Institute of Agriculture operates UT Extension, serving all ninety-five counties in the state. Supported by the U.S. Department of Agriculture, UT Extension emphasizes helping people improve their livelihood in their communities through a network of county agents. In the mid-1960s, the Extension Service (as it was then known) engaged in developing county leaders through a series of classes called Community Leadership Schools. County extension staff members received training in community organizing through their district program supervisors. The staff of each county office assessed leadership development programs already in place in each county—for example, the Hancock County Overall Economic Development Program Association, which disbanded after filing its 1963 report.

Recruiting the people involved in the Hancock County OEDPA was a priority for the local extension office; other priority recruits included the leaders of community clubs, 4-H, home demonstration clubs, churches, livestock associations, and others. The school would have a minimum of twenty participants and

[1] Hancock County Comprehensive Overall Economic Development Program Association Report.

no more than forty. Letters of invitation were sent to prospective participants in late 1966 under the letterhead of the extension service.

We are always trying to improve the community resource development program in Hancock County. We know that you would like to have the best in Tennessee.

In the past, the program has been adequate and even outstanding in some phases. However, the present problems that face community leaders in a county such as ours place leaders in a difficult position unless they receive special help.

In a recent staff conference, we discussed this need for special help. You will be pleased to know that a course on Organizational Techniques for Community Resource Development has been outlined and is ready to be offered [to] Community Leaders. The course will be supported by the Leadership Training Committee of Hancock County and directed and taught by the Agricultural Extension Agents of the University of Tennessee.

The course is divided into six sessions. The purpose of each session is enclosed. The purpose of the course is to *prepare you to serve as a more effective, confident community leader.*

What is involved on your part?

1. Return the enclosed card
2. Check the sessions you can attend
3. A willingness to try

You will notice on the enclosed card that the meetings will be held on Tuesday nights beginning promptly at 7:30 p.m. and ending not later than 9:30 p.m. Refreshments will be provided at each session.

Whether this is your first or fifteenth year as a community leader, this course is designed to benefit you. The information can be used in community groups such as Community Clubs, Home Demonstration Clubs, Resource Development Organizations, Church, P-T-A, civic clubs, and most others.

This letter is being sent to all community leaders on our mailing list. There is a limit of 40 who can attend each session. Preference will be given earliest returned cards. Get your card in early and check with other leaders to make sure they have returned enrollment cards and are assured of enrollment in the course.

Sincerely,
Robert Haston, Jr.
County Agent[2]

---

[2] County Agent Robert Haston Jr. to potential Hancock County OEDP recruits, September 1966.

There would be six sessions, each lasting two hours, for six consecutive weeks. Officers would be nominated at the first session and installed at the second and would preside over the meeting beginning with the third session.

The first meeting was held on 18 April 1967. The two instructors from the University of Tennessee Extension Service were Joe W. Brimm and Ralph McDade ("the USDA man you see on TV—Monday, Wednesday, and Friday mornings on WBIR-TV—Channel 10."[3]) Representing the Hancock County Extension Service (and assisting the instructors, who were from Knoxville and didn't know the local people in attendance) were county agent Robert Haston and Elmer Turner, a teacher who also worked with the Extension Service.

The initial meeting was intended to allow the participants to get to know the instructors and each other, to understand the objectives of the course, and to better understand the concept of community resource development.[4]

At the second meeting on 24 April, the participants nominated and elected officers for the Hancock County Resource Development Association (HCRDA). Jack Nelson, the superintendent of the Flat Gap Mine operated by the New Jersey Zinc Company, was elected president. Broten Livesay of Kyles Ford was vice-president; Geraldine Southern of Mulberry was chosen to be secretary-treasurer; Bill Grohse of Vardy would serve as reporter, and the Reverend R. B. Connor of the Sneedville Methodist Church was elected chaplain. The group also formed committees covering mileage, attendance, and refreshments, as well as the various communities within the county: Sneedville–Dry Branch; Mulberry; Kyles Ford; Flat Gap–Green-Lawson; and Vardy.[5]

These and subsequent training classes were covered by the *Hancock County Post*. John Montgomery, the publisher and editor, used his newspaper to promote improvement within the county. During spring 1967 he published columns by Bill Grohse, reporter for the RDA, under the headline "Leadership Classes Underway." Grohse was a New Yorker who had married a local girl and moved to the Vardy community, where he operated a country store. He filled his first article—and subsequent articles—with the names of attendees and their communities, showing that all parts of the county were represented. He was as much cheerleader as journalist, writing, "Did you cooperate for the betterment of your community by attending this meeting? If you didn't now is the time to make your plans to attend the next meeting.... If the people of different communities would cooperate—we could have roads, industry, and whatever our

---

[3] Grohse, "Leadership Classes Underway," 27 April 1967, 2.
[4] Ibid.
[5] Ibid.

county needs. We have one of the best counties in the United States." The article was also liberally sprinkled with Bible verses: "Prov. 1:5 'A wise man will hear, and will increase learning.' 2 Tim 2:13 'Study to shew thyself approved unto God, a workman that needeth not to be ashamed, rightly dividing the word of truth.'" Grohse concluded, "Don't say 'The other fellow can do that' because you ARE the other fellow. A good community begins with the person who reads this news item."

At the third meeting on 2 May, the committees representing each community each had one item on their respective agendas. The Flat Gap–Green-Lawson committee discussed ways to raise money for their library. Some favored bingo games as a fundraiser, but the committee voted against the idea and decided to study the matter further and report at the next meeting. The Vardy committee authorized the Reverend Arnold Johnson to use five dollars as a prize for that weekend's pony show, the money to come from whichever fund had that amount available. The Sneedville–Dry Branch committee elected a committee president, and the Kyles Ford committee voted to hold a fish fry, stipulating that the cost of the fish not exceed ten dollars.[6]

At the fourth meeting on 9 May, participants rated their respective communities as poor, fair, or good in a variety of categories, including local industry, education, local agriculture, sources of credit, local stores, public libraries, availability of doctors and dentists, garbage and trash disposal, fire control, and so on. Out of a possible high score of 96, Mulberry and Kyles Ford scored 55 each; Vardy reported a 49; Flat Gap reported a score of 50, and Sneedville scored 59.

In the *Post*, Bill Grohse prefaced his list of attendees with "Community leaders who thought enough of their communities to attend included…" In the next paragraph, he was even more pointed. "Notably absent from most of these meetings were the County Decision Makers. If you are a 'Decision Maker' for your county—Why not attend the meetings?" Clearly, most of the elected officials in the county—with the exception of Sneedville Mayor Charles Turner—had no interest in participating in meetings that would surely focus on their shortcomings and might eventually challenge their power. The class participants were not interested in maintaining the status quo and were already discussing organizing monthly meetings of the Resource Development Association when the leadership classes ended.[7]

---

[6] Ibid., 4 May 1967, 9.
[7] Ibid., 11 May 1967, 8.

At the fifth class on 16 May, Ralph McDade discussed the evaluations of the county's communities from the previous meeting. All five of the communities represented listed job training, nursing homes, and recreation as "poor." Four of the five communities considered local industry, garbage and trash disposal, flood control, roads, transportation, and parks and playgrounds as "poor."[8]

The sixth and final session was held on 23 May and consisted of a covered dish banquet provided by the members of the class and a graduation ceremony. Although Bill Grohse had expressed disappointment in his *Post* articles that more people had not attended the classes, his disappointment was likely inspired by the conspicuous absence of those Grohse thought *should* have attended: the "County Decision Makers," as he called the elected officials who did not participate. In any event, a core group of county leaders emerged from these meetings. They would operate independently of the "Decision Makers" and would be making big decisions in the coming months.[9]

Once the leadership classes were over, its graduates decided to continue meeting once a month, and they named themselves the Hancock County Resource Development Association (HCRDA). They immediately got involved in a new idea, a new direction for development of the county.

The previous year, two professors and their students conducted a study for the CPRVA. Carson-Newman College (now University) is a Baptist-affiliated institution in Jefferson City, about fifty miles from Sneedville. Gary Farley, from the department of sociology, and Joe Mack High, from the department of business administration, authored "Social Systems and Economic Development in a Rural Environment: Hancock County, Tennessee," and made summaries of the study available to the members of the HCRDA.

At the time of the study, Hancock County was the eighth-poorest county in the United States, with a per capita income of just $752 annually. They noted that "limitations of the physical environment have blocked adjustment by the county's economy to the newer economic reality." The county's 147,000 acres consisted largely of steep ridges and narrow valleys, and little of the land was suitable for agriculture. The only natural resources in the county were timber, which was second growth and of poor quality, and zinc, which was being mined and provided employment for between 75 and 150 people.

---

[8] Ibid., 18 May 1967, 5.
[9] Ibid., 1 June 1967, 1.

Another problem facing the county was politics. Farley and High wrote,

The people of the county have been traditionally Republican. *The basic problem is factionalism within this party.* This has been a reality for as long as anyone remembers. It is reported that each faction has been afraid that the other
one might get the credit for something good happening in the county.

Actually, the county is too small and too poor to be an economically feasible unit of government. Many officials lack the training to deal with the
political problems of the county.

*Essentially, then, factionalism and lack of trained leadership have com-
pounded the problem of poverty in the county.* With Federal assistance available,
the local government could meet the problems of the people if these political
problems could be overcome.

(Farley and High did note, however, that this conclusion did not apply to the
government of the town of Sneedville, led by Mayor Charles Turner.)

Farley and High also described the ways politics harmed education in Hancock County, particularly how the "patronage system" controlled the selection
and hiring of teachers. Education was not highly valued among county residents,
and the study "notes a tradition of anti-intellectualism and a fear of too much
education." Hancock County students also suffered due to a lack of vocational
education.

Farley and High saw little chance that industry would come into the county.

Factors which attract industry, such as infrastructure, raw or semi-processed
materials, and trained personnel, are lacking in Hancock County. Unless a
company is pressured into expanding into the area, or is looking for cheap
labor, it is unlikely that Hancock will be chosen. Realistically, primary attention should be given to other types of possible economic input.

As the Appalachian Regional Commission and other federal agencies had
already decided, Hancock County didn't have much going for it. There were few
natural resources to be exploited; the timber was of poor quality, there was no
coal or iron to be mined, and the zinc deposit at Flat Gap would someday be
depleted. The terrain was rough, and the county was isolated, lacking the population and resources to be an effective unit of government. The factions of the
political infrastructure were unconcerned with improving the county, only with
preserving their own positions. Conventional avenues for improvement were
closed to Hancock County.

What Hancock County had in its favor was natural beauty. It didn't have
the spectacular high peaks of the Smoky Mountains to the south, but its ridge-

and-valley terrain was largely unspoiled. The pace of life was slow and relaxed, the nights were quiet, and the people were friendly. It was the kind of place tourists would enjoy—if they had some reason to visit the county. So the professors described an unconventional idea.

> A natural possibility for such input is the idea of a drama featuring the mystery of the Melungeon settlement in the county. Interest in these people has been recently heightened by Jesse Stuart's novel, *Daughter of a Legend*. Similar projects have been successful nearby—Big Stone Gap, Berea, and Abingdon. This proximity to other successful dramas should enhance the chances of success in Hancock. In addition, the natural spin-off from the drama would be an outlet for handicraft items. It would also provide the basis for the development of food and lodging services for tourists and other economic impetus.[10]

The members of the HCRDA couldn't believe what they were reading. The county was going to hell in a handbasket, and these college professors thought the answer was *to put on a play*? Not only that, but a play about the *Melungeons*? No one in the county wanted to even acknowledge the existence of those people. Had these college eggheads lost their minds?

It wasn't a new idea, though. In September 1963, Louise Davis, journalist with the *Nashville Tennessean Sunday Magazine*, wrote:

> So far, no enterprising playwright has written a drama around the dark people of Hancock County. Roanoke Island, N.C., attracts tourists with its summertime spectacle, "The Lost Colony;" the Cherokee reservation draws its crowds with the Indian saga, "Unto These Hills." But the last Melungeon may vanish from Hancock County before the area capitalizes on its unique chapter in Tennessee history.[11]

As Farley and High talked with the HCRDA, the idea began to make a little bit more sense. Ever since 1937, when Pulitzer Prize–winning playwright Paul Green created *The Lost Colony*, an outdoor production about Sir Walter Raleigh's ill-fated settlement on North Carolina's Roanoke Island, similar productions had been growing in popularity. Green called his creation a "symphonic drama of American history"; other descriptions of the form included "musical drama," "historic drama," "musical romance," and, most commonly, "outdoor drama." Several outdoor dramas were being produced in high-traffic tourist destinations. Others were being staged in areas that hoped to *become* high-traffic tourist destinations. With very few exceptions, outdoor dramas were a Southern art form.

---

[10] Farley and High, "Social Systems and Economic Development in a Rural Environment."
[11] Davis, "Why Are They Vanishing?," 16.

Tom McElfresh, the drama critic for the *Cincinnati Enquirer,* noted other simi-larities.

> The word "drama" figures prominently in the descriptions of almost all of them. It's more sonorous than the word "play" or even "theatre." Has a ring of purpose to it. There's little frivolity to most of the presentation.
>
> Titles: They, too, run to sonority and a mighty ring. "Horn in the West." "The Common Glory"…"Honey in the Rock." And they're usually spoken with a deep and drawn-out reverence that just might be a little pretentious.
>
> Purpose is shared, too. All but one of them presents itself as somewhat historical. Are quasi-educational. More or less animated versions of those brass historical plaques you see along highways, they share [an] "on-this-hal-lowed-ground" quality. Though the scripts ring of history, I wouldn't trust the number of them I've seen to be factual. And, it's more than simple dra-matic license.
>
> They are endemic to their area. They were written specifically for the the-atres in which they now appear, and—linked to the soil as they are—aren't likely ever to appear elsewhere.…
>
> Physically the outdoor dramas resemble each other, too. Obviously they're outdoors. A few have indoor facilities to which they move in case of rain—and in one case for matinees. The amphitheaters seat anything from 400 to 2500 people. They all feature large and essentially unprofessional casts.… Most are "musical" in the sense that the performance is accompanied by a bombastic musical score—recorded or from an organ—and have woven into their patterns some elements of folk music and dance performed live. Most depend on actors who can fill the amphitheaters with their voices with-out amplification. Some have elaborate lighting designs on a variety of acting areas. Others are more simple in production…
>
> Some have gone through major revisions after their first couple of seasons. Logical. Broadway plays used to tune up out of town, but you can't move an outdoor drama. It belongs to the land.
>
> All share the same daylight saving time problem. With 8:30 and 8:45 cur-tains they are forced to begin in broad daylight when it is difficult to control audience attention on a specific action.[12]

By the mid-1960s, outdoor dramas were quite common. Within easy driv-ing distance from Sneedville, *Trail of the Lonesome Pine,* based on the novel by John Fox, Jr. was staged in Big Stone Gap, Virginia. Another Fox story, *The Little Shepherd of Kingdom Come*, was performed in nearby Whitesburg, Ken-tucky. *Davy Crockett* was performed across Clinch Mountain in Rogersville, and

---

[12] McElfresh, "Theatre for Vacationers," 1-G.

Daniel Boone was the subject of two outdoor dramas: *Horn in the West* in Boone, North Carolina, and *The Legend of Daniel Boone* in Harrodsburg, Kentucky. *The Book of Job*, in Pineville, Kentucky, was an anomaly among outdoor dramas, based not on local history, but on the Biblical story; it was also, according to some, the best of the lot. Cherokee, North Carolina, on the Qualla Boundary Reservation on eastern edge of the Great Smoky Mountains National Park, hosted *Unto These Hills*. On the western side of the park, outside Gatlinburg, Tennessee, the Hunter Hills Theatre was built to stage *Chuckey Jack*, the story of Tennessee's first governor, John Sevier. After the popularity of that three-hour drama waned, the owners of Hunter Hills gave the facility to the University of Tennessee's drama department, which by 1967 was staging three rotating dramas every summer.

The participants in the HCRDA meetings knew that lots of people attended outdoor dramas; many of them had themselves attended one or more of these productions and were familiar with the outdoor drama genre. The idea of developing Hancock County as a tourist destination was certainly alien to most members. But as Bob Dylan sang, "When you ain't got nothin' you got nothin' to lose." One HCRDA participant later recalled to Saundra Keys Ivey, "I think we decided that we didn't have the potential of a smokestack area, industrialized. We were in here between hills with a minimum of level land for industrial sites… So we decided our greatest potential was tourism."[13]

A drama committee was formed as a subcommittee of the recreation and tourism committee, which was chaired by Kyle Lawson. This committee began looking into the possibility of staging an outdoor drama.[14]

Though they were from outside the county, Farley and High were aware of potential problems with staging an outdoor drama about the Melungeons: "There is a history of tension between the Melungeons and the Scotch-Irish settlers, as was stressed in Stuart's book. Parenthetically, some of the town's people reacted negatively to this book."[15]

The book in question was Jesse Stuart's *Daughter of the Legend*. It tells the story of Dave Stoneking, a timber cutter who works in Cantwell County (a fictionalized Hancock County) in 1940. Stoneking meets and falls in love with Deutsia Huntoon, a beautiful Melungeon girl who lives on Sanctuary Mountain (Newman's Ridge). Stoneking knows nothing about the Melungeons and is puzzled as to why Deutsia seems unwelcome in the town of Oak Hill (Sneedville).

---

[13] Ivey, "Oral, Printed, and Popular Culture Traditions," 323.

[14] "Outdoor Drama Conference Concludes."

[15] Farley and High, "Social Systems and Economic Development in a Rural Environment."

Other people, including Stoneking's friend and partner Ben Dewberry, try to warn Stoneking away from Deutsia.

Stoneking finally learns about the Melungeons, and Dewberry—who has been dating a nurse in the county and has become something of an authority on the Melungeons—explains some of the exotic theories about their origins. Dewberry concludes by saying most of the people of the county believe the Melungeons to be "just a mixture of escaped slaves and trashy whites." Dewberry tries to console Stoneking by telling him other men had been taken in by the beauty of Melungeon women but rejected them once they learned of the Melungeons' uncertain racial origins.

But Stoneking rejects his friend's advice, alienating Dewberry and the rest of the town when he marries Deutsia. The couple can't get a marriage license in town but are married by a snake-handling preacher on Sanctuary Mountain. Stoneking wholeheartedly becomes part of the Melungeon community. The book takes a condescending tone as Stoneking works to "improve" the Melungeons, introducing his new in-laws to conveniences such as bathtubs and store-bought items the Melungeons can't afford. He seems content to settle into an idyllic existence on the mountain, but when Deutsia dies in childbirth, a heartbroken Stoneking abandons his daughter to the care of Deutsia's family and leaves Sanctuary Mountain, never to return.[16]

The story is reportedly drawn in part from Stuart's own experience. As a student at Lincoln Memorial University in Harrogate, Tennessee, just south of Cumberland Gap, Stuart met and fell in love with a Melungeon girl from Hancock County. Family pressure forced Stuart to end the romance. He tried to publish the book in 1945, while serving in the Navy, but *Daughter of the Legend* didn't see print until 1965.[17]

Reviews of the book are mixed. Katherine Vande Brake, author of *How They Shine: Melungeon Characters in the Fiction of Appalachia*, said, "I felt [Stuart] was a little bit condescending in his treatment of Melungeon characters. I didn't feel like he had the kind of respect some of the [later] writers had. He had kind of a 'we-they' attitude."[18]

However, a reader's review on Amazon.com from 2013 heaped praise on the book: "*Daughter of the Legend* is the best book I have ever read. There is love, suspense, and great sadness. It's a book I will read over and over again. The child

---

[16] Stuart, *Daughter of the Legend*.

[17] Overbay, presentation to tour group. Stuart was the college roommate of Overbay's father, Drew B. Williams.

[18] Vande Brake interview.

that was left behind I wonder where his ancestors are today. I worry about this baby. How could anyone just walk away[?]"[19]

An online reviewer from Kirkusreviews.com was intrigued by the subject matter but not the story itself:

> Stuart's story, which might even be true, seems to have been born from the hip of Gene Stratton Porter... Like Off-Off-Off-Broadway, this is back-back-backwoods Virginia, where the hill folk don't mix none with the valley folk. The hill folk have lived on their mountain tops for over a century and they apparently have tainted blood of sorts, Spanish or Moorish or Portuguese or maybe just plain Negro; nobody knows for sure. Well, Dave Stoneking, a 26-year-old lumberjack, falls axe over bootstraps for young Deutsia Huntoon, a hill girl whose blonde hair falls to her ankles. When the valley folk find out that he's going to marry her, their prejudice becomes overt and he is treated like a Negro. Meanwhile, up on the mountain, Dave is taken in by the Huntoons and made much of. Dave loses his best friend but is idyllically happy building a home and awaiting a child. When his wife dies in labor, Dave leaves the hills forever. The background is better than the foreground, which is appallingly banal.[20]

A review of the book in the *Daytona Beach Sunday News-Journal* on 9 January 1966 took a dim view Stuart's novel.

> Some years ago a poet who had celebrated the Kentucky hillbilly in a collection of better than passable verse brought out a mild shocker called "Taps for Private Tussy." The shock, it may be explained, was chiefly to Kentuckians who had some direct knowledge of mountain dwellers in the coal-bearing hills of the Bluegrass State. The book was part lampoon, part melodrama but all of it was readable. Since that time Jesse Stuart has written more poems (some very fine indeed), taught, lectured and, recently, produced a new parcel of hillbilly fiction. This one, "Daughter of the Legend" (McGraw Hill) is about a weird tribe of Tennessee mountain folk, the Melungeons. This quaint outfit, presumably an admixture of early Anglo-Saxon settlers with both Indian and Negro blood, lives on Sanctuary Mountain. (Symbolism, get it?) The Melungeons are snake worshippers, or perhaps it would be more accurate to say they use snakes in their divine worship. They also have a few more unhygienic habits, but in spite of these a flatlander white youth falls in love with a Melungeon maiden. Presumably Stuart expects readers to take this

---

[19] Code, customer review.
[20] Kirkus review, *Daughter of the Legend*.

mountain corn seriously, but it isn't even good moonshine. We still think his poems are great, however.[21]

As Farley and High noted, some Hancock County residents reacted negatively to the book and its unflattering portrayal of the county's white population; there was also residual wariness, engendered by the 1947 *Saturday Evening Post* article, of any publicity drawing attention to the Melungeons. But a good number of Hancock Countians, or at least that portion who read the book, seemed to have a favorable response to *Daughter of the Legend*. Racial attitudes had softened across America by 1965; the civil rights movement had created empathy for minorities. Stuart's portrayal of the Melungeons, while somewhat patronizing by twenty-first-century standards, was nonetheless positive, and the book remains popular in Hancock County to this day.

Still, Melungeons were a touchy subject in Hancock County. One man told Saundra Keyes Ivey in 1973 how Melungeons were viewed by many in the county: "They don't want nothing to do with these Melungeons. Some of them's prejudiced and always will be. They wouldn't want their girl to go with one of them, they wouldn't let me go with one of them…they're kind of a mixed race, and they'd just as soon they'd marry niggers as marry a Melungeon."[22]

Another told her that most Hancock Countians did not regard Melungeons as their equals: "As long as a dark-skinned race of people exists, they won't never accept them. You know, some whites, now, they never will. They never will. They want the Melungeons back on the ridge."[23]

Other county residents, still smarting from the 1947 *Saturday Evening Post* article, resented "outsiders" coming into Hancock County to ask questions and write about the Melungeons. One person told Ivey that the vast majority of people in the county had no interest in the ethnic heritage of the Melungeons but expressed bitterness over the *Post* article.

> I'd say 95% of the people in Hancock County are not interested at all in the Melungeons' origin, where they came from. We've decided it doesn't make too much difference. We wanted them to be accepted, of course, as citizens of society. And that's what made the people, along with the Melungeons, boil, a lot of them, to read things that weren't true, and say that Hancock County didn't have indoor toilets and so on…the Melungeons not only got angry, but it was sickening to us.[24]

---

[21] "Taps for Jesse Stuart," *Daytona Beach Sunday News-Journal*, 9 January 1966.
[22] Ivey, "Oral, Printed, and Popular Culture Traditions," 309.
[23] Ibid., 310.
[24] Ibid., 198.

Farley and High acknowledged these attitudes and suggested a separate committee be formed to study further the feasibility of staging and outdoor drama about the Melungeons, a committee representing "the factions and special interest groups of the community." In other words, they suggested a committee that included Melungeons. This idea was going to be hard to sell to the community; if the Melungeons felt exploited, the whole thing could backfire. They wanted to make sure the Melungeons were on board with the idea and recommended soliciting Melungeon support for the project before beginning. Due to the very subjective socioeconomic definition of "Melungeon," it didn't occur to anyone that Melungeons—including Claude Collins and several others—already were on the committee.[25]

But most Americans had never heard of the Melungeons, and it seemed likely that they never would. The Melungeons were disappearing—that's what all the newspaper and magazine writers said. The headlines of their articles shared that idea: "Melungeon Line Almost Extinct," "Mysterious Hill Folk Vanishing," "Melungeon Ways Are Passing," "Why Are They Vanishing?" The Melungeons were marrying outside the group, or moving away, or rising to a higher socioeconomic status. And most of them had never considered themselves "Melungeons," anyway; that was a name someone else called them. Hardly anyone would think an outdoor drama about the Melungeons was about them, or their families.

The Melungeons *were* disappearing, but they were a part of what made Hancock County unique. And because of more than a century's worth of newspaper and magazine articles, they were far and away the best known of the mixed-ethnic groups William Gilbert had catalogued for the Library of Congress two decades earlier. If the county put on a play about the Melungeons, the newspapers and magazines would likely write about it, and that would attract tourists. The more the members of the drama committee thought about it and discussed it, the more the whole idea made sense.

The *Hancock County Post* of 7 December 1967 devoted its front page to the news that Electric Motors and Specialties, Inc. of Garrett, Indiana, planned to build a factory in Hancock County that was expected to provide 135 jobs. Mayor Charles Turner's regular column, "This Is Your Town," expressed appreciation to the state agencies involved in securing the plant, and another story urged voters to approve a $150,000 bond issue to develop an industrial park, a prerequisite for the building of the plant. Inside the paper was a report that a committee

---

[25] Farley and High, "Social Systems and Economic Development in a Rural Environment."

formed from the leadership training classes was looking into the feasibility of staging an outdoor drama in the county.[26]

For some time after the initial proposal of the drama, many had assumed the play would be an adaptation of Jesse Stuart's novel. That idea posed several potential problems, not the least of which was money; Stuart would likely want to be paid for the use of his story. And it would somehow have to be adapted for the stage; a book can and does have its story take place in any number of places—homes, businesses, vehicles, a variety of outdoor locations, etc. A play can only have a limited number of settings, and an outdoor drama is even more limited. Clearly, some sort of adaptation would have to be made by someone who understood the limitations of the genre.

There was a man whom many thought equal to the task: Earl Hobson Smith, professor of English, speech, and drama at Lincoln Memorial University and a playwright whose works included the outdoor dramas *Trail of the Lonesome Pine* and *Davy Crockett*. Smith was born in western Kentucky and earned a degree at LMU in 1919. After graduate studies at Columbia University in New York, Smith returned to LMU as a professor of speech in 1926. Smith not only taught drama, he wrote plays as well, including outdoor dramas. His most successful works were *Stephen Foster: Or, Weep No More My Lady*, which was staged for many years in Bardstown, Kentucky, home of Stephen Foster State Park, and *Trail of the Lonesome Pine*, adapted from the John Fox novel by Smith and Clara Lou Kelly and staged since 1964 in Big Stone Gap, Virginia.

Smith wrote thirty or more plays over the course of his lifetime. Not all of them were staged. His 1940 work, *President Lincoln: A Two Hour Play in Three Acts with Three Scenes Each*, had problems that went beyond its unwieldy title. Writer Earl J. Hess describes it as "typical of Earl Hobson Smith's work—earnest, wordy, turgid, and playing very loose with the facts. It...fails in Smith's stated purpose to portray Lincoln with historical authenticity, verve, and understanding." A New York agent rejected it as unsuitable even for amateur productions, and the play was only performed at LMU. Smith went on to write several more plays about Lincoln, all of which Hess describes as "similar to the first."[27]

However, some of Smith's other works, like *Trail of the Lonesome Pine*, were successful. He was very familiar with the genre of outdoor drama and had been supportive of the proposed Hancock County drama since he first learned of it. After meeting with the Hancock County committee, he told a reporter, "It's a wonderful idea and I'd like to see it under production, even on a limited scale,

[26] "Ellington Announces Industry for Hancock," 1.
[27] Hess, *Lincoln Memorial University*, 189.

this coming summer."[28] And, perhaps most importantly to those who advocated adapting *Daughter of the Legend* for the outdoor stage, Smith had taught Jesse Stuart at Lincoln Memorial University and the two remained close friends. Stuart once said of Smith, "If I speak within a hundred mile radius of Lincoln Memorial, my teacher and friend Earl Hobson Smith will be there with a pad and pencil and grade me on my speech."[29] Smith's involvement might be the key to securing Stuart's permission to use the novel, and possibly even his cooperation in adapting it for the stage.

But *Daughter of the Legend* contained a serious, perhaps fatal flaw as an outdoor drama: there was no happy ending. The main female character dies, and the main male character abandons both his daughter and the Melungeons. *That* sure wasn't going to make audiences leave the amphitheater smiling. And when they went home and told their friends it was the saddest damn play they'd ever seen—well, that just wouldn't do at all. Outdoor dramas weren't supposed to be tragedies, after all; they were supposed to be uplifting, to make audiences happy.

The members of the drama committee were well aware of their own inexperience with staging any kind of a show. But many of them were at least familiar with outdoor dramas. "My wife and I had been attending outdoor dramas— *Unto These Hills, Trail of the Lonesome Pine*," recalled Claude Collins. "So we decided to invite the area colleges to send in the heads [of their drama departments] to talk about outdoor dramas."[30] With money from a grant provided under Title 1 of the Higher Education Act of 1965, the committee organized a conference and sent out invitations.

On Monday and Tuesday, 8 and 9 January 1968, the drama committee met at Sneedville Baptist Church. In addition to the local committee members and professors High and Farley, the attendees included Earl Hobson Smith; John Lee Welton, the director of the drama department at Carson-Newman College; Mrs. R. C. Lewis, who had helped stage Smith's *Davy Crockett* in Rogersville, and Mark Sumner, director of the Institute of Outdoor Drama at the University of North Carolina.

Also attending was Kermit Hunter, the dean of the Meadows School of Arts at Southern Methodist University in Dallas, Texas, and the author of dozens of commercially successful outdoor dramas, including *Unto These Hills, Horn in the West, Honey in the Rock, Chuckey Jack, Trail of Tears*, and many others.[31]

---

[28] "Hancock County Drama Is Hoped," 1.
[29] Hess, *Lincoln Memorial University*, 190.
[30] Claude Collins interview (2002).
[31] C. Bowlin, "Drama Committee Meets," 1 January 1968, 1.

Born in McDowell County, West Virginia, Hunter attended Emory and Henry College in Emory, Virginia, and Ohio State University, where he graduated in 1931. Joining the U.S. Army in 1940, he rose to the rank of lieutenant colonel and served as the assistant chief of staff of the Caribbean Defense Command. After the war, he began graduate studies in dramatic arts at the University of North Carolina. While studying in Chapel Hill, he won a commission from the Cherokee Historical Society to write an outdoor drama. The result was his best-known work, *Unto These Hills*, which opened in 1950 and is still staged at the Mountainside Theatre in Cherokee, North Carolina, on the Qualla Boundary reservation on the eastern edge of the Great Smoky Mountains National Park.

Hunter earned an M.A. and a Ph.D. at UNC, became director of drama at Hollins College in Roanoke, Virginia, and in 1964, took the job at Southern Methodist University.[32] When he came to Sneedville, Hunter was likely still a bit rattled from an incident that had occurred just a few weeks before. Dr. Hunter had been questioned by the Federal Bureau of Investigation in regard to a bizarre tale concerning the assassination of President John F. Kennedy.

A man named Terry Christie had sent a letter to U.S. Attorney General Ramsey Clark stating that Christie had heard from a friend that Dr. Kermit Hunter of Southern Methodist University had been visiting friends in Dallas on the night before the president was assassinated. Dr. Hunter reportedly told Christie's friend that Lee Harvey Oswald had come to the house Hunter was visiting and said he was looking for the home of Jack Ruby. Oswald was, of course, the presumed assassin of Kennedy, and Ruby had shot and killed Oswald on live television two days after the assassination, so this information certainly piqued the interest of the FBI.

The source of the story Christie related was one Helen McIntosh. FBI agents questioned Hunter on 27 November 1967, and Hunter said he did not know Ms. McIntosh although it was possible they had met at some point in connection with his work. Hunter told the FBI that he had not been in Dallas on the night of 21 November 1963, but that his brother-in-law, Floyd Chambers, had told Hunter that a man who had an office next to Chambers's office, a man named Jamison, had told Chambers that the night before the assassination, Jamison and some friends were playing poker at Jamison's house when a large man with red hair knocked on the door and said he was looking for the superintendent of the Texas School Book Depository. Since the Depository was where Lee Harvey Oswald worked and, reportedly, fired the fatal shots from a sixth-

---

[32] West Virginia Wesleyan College, *Guide to Resources.*

floor window, the incident was remembered and passed on to Hunter's brother-in-law and, eventually, to Hunter himself.[33]

The only possible connection this story had to the assassination was the coincidence of the Depository being mentioned the night before the shooting, and Hunter's involvement in the story was extremely remote. But even though the Warren Commission had investigated the assassination and concluded that there was no conspiracy and that Oswald had acted alone, the FBI was still following up on vague rumors connected to that event. Their questioning of Hunter had to have been at least slightly disconcerting to the playwright. It is likely Dr. Hunter had already been invited to Sneedville at the time he was questioned by the FBI.

A report compiled after the conference stated that the panel felt that an outdoor drama was entirely possible, providing the people of the county are willing to engage in a lot of hard, concentrated labor, working cooperatively toward their goal. Mayor Turner stated, "I feel the outdoor drama is completely worthy of our consideration. I am proud of the enthusiastic interest of our people and extremely grateful and highly honored to have the distinguished visitors to our town to assist us in this matter."

Kyle Lawson gave his reasons for his interest in the drama. "One, it has tremendous potential for increasing the income of our people. Two, it will give the youth of our area something to become actively involved in. And three, it will help us build an image of Hancock County that everyone will be proud of."

The vice-mayor of Sneedville, E. O. Parkey, echoed these sentiments, and added, "If there is ever the need in the drama for a tall, pioneer, mountaineer carrying an old brown jug and a hog rifle, I would be glad to try out for the part."[34]

The *Knoxville News-Sentinel* ran a front-page story titled "Maligned Mountain Folk May Be Topic of Drama." The previous night at the Methodist church, the Reverend Connor told a group of interested citizens that the drama would help eliminate the stigma attached to the word "Melungeon." Busting rhymes like a rapper decades before his time, Connor said the drama would "lift their name from shame to the hall of fame." He also shared his vision of Hancock County's potential economic revival, with tourist amenities including motels and restaurants, a golf course, a heated swimming pool, a chair lift on Newman's

[33] "Miscellaneous information regarding assassination of President John Fitzgerald Kennedy."

[34] "Outdoor Drama Conference Concludes," 1.

Ridge, living quarters for drama employees, and a landing strip for small airplanes. Connor even claimed to know of a financial backer who was willing to put up $50,000 in seed money.

The article went on to state, "One theme under discussion is author Jesse Stuart's new [sic] book, *Daughter of the Legend*."[35] That may have been the consensus among those who met at the church on Sunday night, but by the time the meetings had ended on Wednesday, Kermit Hunter was the playwright of choice for many members of the drama committee. Claude Collins and Dora Bowlin drove Hunter and Sumner to the airport in Knoxville, and along the way, asked Dr. Hunter if he would be willing to write an original play and how much he would charge. Hunter told them he would do it for 15 percent of the first year's gate receipts, and 10 percent of the receipts from subsequent years. Collins and Bowlin took the offer back to the group for consideration.[36]

In the *News-Sentinel* article, Willard Yarbrough wrote, "Key to an outdoor drama's success could well be the cooperation of the Melungeons themselves, who over the decades have come to mistrust those outsiders who distort their character and damage their image."[37] Of course, some of the people involved with the drama committee were Melungeon, at least in terms of ancestry.

It became clear to the committee that putting on this drama would mean dealing with the press, something with which only Mayor Charles Turner had any experience. And reporters were going to want to talk to a Melungeon. Very early in the process, Claude Collins found himself in a position that might be called the "designated Melungeon." He was certainly qualified; he grew up on Newman's Ridge, attended the Vardy Community School, and had the "Melungeon look," with dark skin and hair combined with bright blue eyes.[38] But he was also educated, a gainfully employed professional, well-spoken, and willing to acknowledge his Melungeon background. So, toward the end of January 1968,

---

[35] Yarbrough, "Maligned Mountain Folk," 1.

[36] Claude Collins interview (2002).

[37] Yarbrough, "Maligned Mountain Folk," 1.

[38] People often refer to "the distinctive Melungeon look." There actually isn't a "Melungeon look"—or at least, not just one look. If we assume (and not everyone does) that the Melungeons are a triracial mix—European, African, and Native American—that leaves a lot of variations that can, and do, occur, even within a single family. Claude Collins looked like he might have been Spanish or Portuguese. Many other Melungeons looked more Native American. One family well remembered by the author had children with what would have been called "Negroid" hair and facial features, but their hair was blonde and skin was a sort of yellow-ivory. Others lacked any distinctive features at all but looked like Appalachian whites or like African-Americans. When people spoke of a "distinctive" Melungeon look, what they usually meant was someone who didn't look "white," but whose ethnic background was difficult to ascertain based on appearance.

Claude Collins was quoted in the *Times-News* from nearby Kingsport, speaking a phrase he would repeat many times in the coming years: "Sure, I'm a Melungeon and proud of it."

> Probably for the first time in history, this statement came from one of a group of East Tennessee mountain-folk whose history and origin is steeped in legend and mystery. Heretofore, Melungeon was a fighting word in Hancock County and even in adjoining Hawkins County. You just don't ask a fellow if he's a Melungeon. North of Sneedville, high on a mountain known as Newman's Ridge, this group of people have lived and survived in what some would call primitive conditions.
>
> Their poverty and their lack of education have been a product of their isolation—from the world outside Hancock County, and more or less from their neighbors in the county itself. Now plans are underway for an out-door drama at Sneedville, based on the Melungeon story and on the frontier way of life as depicted by the Melungeons. Carson-Newman College received a Federal grant to survey the possibilities of such a drama "as a means to improve the socio-economic climate" of Hancock County.
>
> And when W. C. Collins, a supervisor in the Hancock County School system and co-chairman of a committee promoting the drama, made the above statement regarding his Melungeon heritage, he opened a door in overcoming the stigma which has been attached for centuries to a people maligned by the society surrounding them.[39]

Claude Collins would, from that point on, be the primary representative of the Melungeons when members of the press came to town. Before long, Corrine Bowlin also served as a Melungeon spokesperson. Of course, there were many in the county who disapproved of their role. "It wasn't easy for Corinne or myself," Collins recalled years later. "But we had to do these things to keep the play going and to keep people coming in."[40] Neither Claude nor Corrine fit the stereotype many people had of Melungeons, but their involvement with the play and willingness to acknowledge their Melungeon-ness to reporters established the approval and involvement of at least some Melungeons regarding the proposed play.

Equally important was the willingness of the community at large to support a play about the Melungeons, a topic Hancock Countians had long been reluctant to discuss. And there were skeptics and cynics, of course; there always are, especially in an area divided by political factions. Anthropologist Anthony

---

[39] Price, "The Melungeons Are Coming out in the Open," 4.
[40] Claude Collins interview (2002).

Cavender would write of the attitude held by some in the county that since the Melungeons had become a "hot topic," the "elites" of the county—merchants, educators, and prosperous farmers—had decided to exploit the widespread interest in the topic that had "put the county on the map."[41]

Despite the widespread interest in Melungeons, the drama committee faced a daunting challenge in putting on an outdoor drama. Mark Sumner, the director of the Institute of Outdoor Drama, had listed six prerequisites for a successful outdoor drama:

1. Access to a major highway
2. Proximity to another tourist attraction
3. Sufficient hotel and motel capacity
4. Adequate options for dining
5. An enthusiastic, energetic local board of directors and an interesting story
6. An attractive theater site

As John Lee Welton would later recall, the Hancock County Drama Association had only one out of those six prerequisites.[42] Would an enthusiastic and energetic board with a fascinating story be enough to make a drama successful?

In December 1967 and January 1968, the *Hancock County Post* ran several stories under the headline "Drama News," detailing the work of the Drama Committee in studying the proposal. Yet these stories were conspicuous in avoiding any mention of what this drama would be *about*, and they made no mention of Melungeons until 8 February 1968.

DRAMA NEWS

By Rev. R. B. Connor, Member of the Hancock Drama Committee and Pastor of the Sneedville Methodist Church.

WHY HAVE A DRAMA ABOUT THE MELUNGEONS IN HANCOCK COUNTY

1. This is the county's greatest asset at this time.
2. If we do not stage such a drama, some near-by county will.
3. The local drama committee can and will see that nothing goes into the drama to hurt any of our citizens.
4. Newman's Ridge, formerly known as "New Man's Ridge," because of the discovery of these new people living there, has been recognized as the main seat of the Melungeon colony.

---

[41] Cavender, "The Melungeons of Upper East Tennessee," 33.
[42] Welton presentation.

5. Such a drama will benefit every citizen of Hancock County and neighboring counties,

6. The struggle of the Melungeon people is in many ways closely similar to the struggle of all people.

WHO SHOULD BE INTERESTED IN A DRAMA IN HANCOCK COUNTY[43]

1. The Melungeons, those with some Indian heritage, the Negroes and the so-called pure Anglo-Saxon.

2. The poorest citizens as they will profit most.

3. The land-owners, for the end result will be better roads.

4. The uneducated because the inflow of tourists will broaden their vision.

5. The educated who are interested in seeing the reputation of our county raised to a higher level.

6. All business men, merchants, service station operators, motel owners, and those interested in operating eating establishments.

HOW WILL PROFITS COME FROM THE DRAMA

1. The drama itself will give part time employment to at least 125 people.

2. The drama will create a home market for many items, such as molasses, jellies, preserves, bedspreads, quilts, rugs, souvenirs, and here the field is wide open for those with a little imagination.

3. Many would be interested in guided tours to such places as the cave on Snake Hollow where moonshine liquors used to be "biled off."

4. More people coming into our county will put a demand on those responsible for better roads.

5. Accommodations for the tourists will create a demand for motels and restaurants. Since Ghost Town on top of a rugged mountain in North Carolina was opened there has been erected within three miles of the entrance, 32 motels in Maggie Valley, where just a few years ago there was not one.

6. Compare and contrast our possibilities with the drama "Unto These Hills" in Cherokee, N.C. I have been told that the drama itself in 1966 netted from 57 showings $300,000. In addition to the drama there are many other attractions. One is the Indian Village which is put on by the Indians themselves showing how the Indians lived many years ago. I suppose no one who has visited Cherokee has come away without purchasing a few of the many souvenirs offered for sale. I have visited many of the Indian homes far back up those steep hollows and have seen the pride the Indians take in making the souvenirs to be sold to the tourists. Several times I have visited in the

---

[43] The *Hancock County Post* was essentially a one-person operation. I have not attempted to correct the original punctuation and spelling, which often veer from convention, unless they interfere with comprehension.

home of the late Mary Coe and have seen her baking pottery in oven and grate of her wood cooking stove. I have seen the men making the blow guns, tomahawks, bows and arrows and other articles in their log cabins. Every Indian in the reservation has profited from the Drama about their struggle in life.

7. I would like to see this undertaking lifted above all party politics and group prejudices. This is not a project for and by a few; it must be an undertaking for and by all the people of Hancock County and the adjoining counties, then it can be an effort that will unite us all like nothing else has. I would offer a word of advice to everyone. Do not sell any of your old relics or antiques, these include the following and many more: old guns, iron cooking pots, skillets, wash tubs, rope beds, flat irons, water pitchers, bells, fire dogs, harness, cradles, spinning wheels, froes, homemade plows, hoes, etc.,-- in fact, just do not sell anything old.

There have been six committees appointed to inform you about what you can do to help and profit from the proposed drama. No one has been authorized to buy any of these antiques for the Drama Museum. You hold on to them and they will be placed in the Museum with your name on them and there they will become more valuable with every passing year. Remember this is a great undertaking for and by everyone of us.[44]

Although Claude Collins knew it was coming, he still cringed as he read the *Post* that Thursday morning. He worried about how the people of the county would react to the news that the Melungeon story would be staged for outsiders to watch. He noticed that the mayor's column, under the sub-headline "Our Interesting People," told the story of Vardy Collins and Buck Gibson that had been related by Will Allen Dromgoole. But he also noticed that the mayor had avoided using the word "Melungeon."[45]

The Rev. Connor clearly had other concerns besides the county's reaction to having the Melungeons as the subject of the drama. Political factionalism could wreck all of their efforts. So could the perception that the drama would only benefit a few people. By addressing these concerns directly at this time, Connor hoped to avoid problems as the project moved forward.

The Drama Committee met on 22 February 1968 and voted to have their outdoor drama written by Dr. Kermit Hunter. Earl Hobson Smith of Lincoln Memorial University had been seriously considered but lost out to Hunter. Pro-

[44] Connor, "Why Have a Drama about the Melungeons in Hancock County?," 1, 6.
[45] Turner, "This Is YOUR Town: Our Interesting People," 1.

fessor Joe Mack High wrote a letter to Smith, informing Smith of the committee's decision, acknowledging Smith's early support of the idea of an outdoor
drama and thanking him for his contributions to the project.[46]

Things were looking up for Hancock County. The prospect of creating a
tourist attraction to stimulate growth was encouraging. Even more encouraging
was the telegram Mayor Turner received in March from Senator Albert Gore,
informing Turner that the Economic Development Administration had awarded
a $98,000 grant to help develop Sneedville's new industrial park on the east side
of town. The industrial park project had gotten off to a good start the previous
December when almost 99 percent of the voters in the county approved a
$150,000 bond issue. Work needed on the site included the extension of water
and sewer lines. Electric Motors and Specialties, Inc. was preparing to build a
plant on the site. Mayor Turner said the new plant would employ 135 people.[47]

However, in the same issue of the *Hancock County Post* that announced the
EDA grant, Wayne Morrill of Electric Motors and Specialties said it was hard to
say how many jobs would be created, or how soon they would be available. In a
front-page column, Morrill wrote,

> If we were moving an established plant to Sneedville in which we were pro-
> ducing 200,000 electric motors per year, the answer to both of the above
> questions would be relatively easy because by experience we could expect to
> produce the same number, or more, electric motors and we would know by
> experience exactly how many people would be needed to produce that num-
> ber of motors. But we are not moving a plant to Sneedville because that would
> mean we would have to discharge people working in some other plant, and
> because most of these people are old friends, some of them friends for 20 years
> or more, we would not think of doing that. Even if they were not friends, we
> would not feel it would be fair to take away the jobs of people we already have
> and give these jobs to new people in another community.
>
> Since we are not moving an existing plant to Sneedville, we must build
> our business in Sneedville as we go and the jobs we provide in Sneedville will
> come as a result of our doing for ourselves in Sneedville work that we now
> hire done for us by outside companies, work that amounts to an overload on
> our existing plants or entirely new business we have never had before…. What
> I am saying is that to try and tell you how soon and how many jobs we will
> create with new products is about the same as your trying to tell me how
> many fish you will catch when you go fishing.[48]

---

[46] Joe Mack High to Earl Hobson Smith.
[47] "EDA Approves $98,000 Grant," 1.
[48] Morrill, "To the people of Hancock County," 1.

More federal money was coming into the county as the result of Title 1 funding for an expansion of Hancock County High School. This project would create a Commercial and Mechanical Arts room, along with four classrooms and two restrooms. Altogether, the school would be expanded by 7,000 square feet. School Superintendent T.J. Harrison also hoped to use some of the grant money to pave the school's parking lot and said the project should be completed by the beginning of the 1968–1969 school year. He said proudly, "Not one dime of Hancock County land tax will be used on this project."[49]

Mayor Turner was pleased to see this federal money coming into his town for improvements. But there still wasn't any money available to fix the highway over Clinch Mountain to Morristown.

There was, however, some reason for optimism. The state was talking about improving a few miles of Highway 31, from Mooresburg at the highway's junction with U.S. 11-W on the south side of Clinch Mountain to the Hawkins-Hancock County line at the foot of the mountain. It didn't solve the problems with the road on the mountain itself—but it was a start. Bids were taken and contracts expected by September.[50]

In June, Hancock County had a new corporation. The Hancock County Drama Association, Inc., filed with the Tennessee Department of State on 21 June 1968.[51] They registered as a Tennessee corporation for-profit. The Drama Association was now officially in business.

The *Hancock County Post* published a special edition of the newspaper dated 4 July 1968. Under the nameplate ("Hancock County Post—Striving for Development and Progress"), a headline stretched the entire width of the tabloid-sized paper, reading "Hancock County 'The Land of Enchantment.'" The rest of the front page was a photograph taken on Highway 31 on Clinch Mountain. This issue was clearly meant to serve as a sort of tourist guide to the county. Of course, no tourists were yet visiting Hancock County, but the *Post* was preparing in advance; this same issue would be reprinted, with minor variations, in 1969 and 1970.

Most of the second page was taken up with an article titled "Melungeons," which was reprinted from the *Tennessee Conservationist*. The article blends the scant known history of the Melungeons with many of the numerous theories

---

[49] "Title 1 Funds Approved for Hancock High School," 1.
[50] Turner, "This Is YOUR Town: Roads," 7 March 1968, 1.
[51] Tennessee Secretary of State.

regarding their origins. Other articles in the first section of the paper covered items of interest to tourists, including "Fishing and Hunting," "Elrod Falls," and "Floating the Clinch." Dora Bowlin contributed a piece titled "A Tour through Hancock County" while Elmer Turner described everyday life of an earlier generation in an article titled "Memories." Two of the VISTA workers assigned to Hancock County that year, Peter Dodge and Roger Markovics, contributed their impressions of the county. A pair of articles (each spread over three pages), "The County That Time Forgot," by historian and genealogist Alton Green, and "Hancock County: The Land of Mystery," by William P. Grohse, delved into county history, with the Melungeons figuring prominently in both stories.

The second section of the paper was primarily advertising but contained another article from Dora Bowlin, "Four Seasons on Clinch." The lead article of this section, "County Outdoor Historical Drama," begins "There is no richer segment of American history than those pages written by and about Hancock County's sons and daughters." There is a description of the planned 600-seat amphitheater at the foot of "Famous Newman's Ridge," and sets the target date of production for summer 1969. Strangely, although Melungeons are prominently featured in some of the other articles in this issue, no mention of Melungeons is found in this story. In fact, there is no indication at all of what this outdoor drama will be about.

Advertisements in this issue include several Sneedville businesses, including Turner's Department Store; Citizens Bank of Sneedville; Harrison Hardware Company; and McNeil Mortuary. But there were few of the type of ads that would be of the most interest to tourists: ads for restaurants and motels. Hancock County was woefully lacking in both of these amenities. The Green Top Inn, a rustic restaurant on Main Street in Sneedville, which served very good home-cooked food, has an ad, as does the Town Motel (also on Main Street), consisting of five small rooms above Fodell's Beauty Salon. There are ads for Kingsport's Peggy Ann Restaurant and The Little Tunnel Inn in Cumberland Gap, as well as the Big Chief Motel in Bean Station—none of which were located in Hancock County. Clearly the members and supporters of the Drama Association were counting on the reaction that had occurred in Maggie Valley, North Carolina, where restaurants and motels had sprung up once a tourist attraction had opened.[52]

---

[52] *Hancock County Post*, 4 July 1968.

The county's "elites," as Cavender called them, had long waited for the federal government or some other agency to help them arrest the decline and depopulation of Hancock County. Some help *had* been forthcoming, but it wasn't enough. So a group of people with no experience in show business at any level were going to put on a play. They had a playwright. Now all they needed was—well, everything else.

CHAPTER 6

THE VISTAS

You have come from every part of this country, from every age group, from every background. You have come to serve the poor and the unfortunate of American society, and to open the door of American opportunity to all of our American people. Your pay will be low; the conditions of your labor will often be difficult. But you will have the satisfaction of leading a great national effort, and you will have the ultimate reward which comes to those who serve their Nation and who serve their fellow man.

—President Lyndon B. Johnson
Remarks to members of VISTA, 12 December 1964

In 1963, President John F. Kennedy had the idea for a domestic version of the Peace Corps. Instead of going overseas to work with people in undeveloped or developing nations, volunteers would go to poverty-stricken areas of the United States. President Kennedy was assassinated before he could put this idea into effect, but his successor, President Lyndon B. Johnson, incorporated the concept into his broader War on Poverty. The Economic Opportunity Act of 1964 was the legislation that created Volunteers in Service to America.

As originally conceived, VISTA would send volunteers to specified locations, where they would work with existing community organizations to address local challenges such as literacy, employment, housing, and health. Volunteers would commit to a year of service, during which they would receive a poverty-level stipend to cover their expenses. Volunteers could be of any age, but the vast majority were college students or recent graduates.

"Seventy-five percent of our volunteers are collegians," according to Claire Palmour, VISTA's branch recruitment chief for the southeastern region (Mississippi, Alabama, Florida, Georgia, South Carolina, and Tennessee). Ms. Palmour was in Daytona Beach, Florida, in April 1968, along with six other VISTA recruiters, to connect with college students on spring break. "We're thinking of setting up office in a beach buggy, thinking that may get more attention," she said.[1]

---

[1] "VISTA to Seek Recruits Among Collegians Here," 5-A.

In those idealistic times, many young middle- and upper-class Americans didn't want to settle into a comfortable, suburban lifestyle after college. They felt a call to activism, and an opportunity to help alleviate the grinding poverty they had read about and seen on television was attractive to them. America was prosperous in those days; upper-middle-class kids did not feel the need to go straight to work right after college, to build their resumes and begin climbing the career ladder. Work and careers would be there for them when they were ready; they could take time off to do whatever they wanted—hitchhike across Europe, go to Haight-Ashbury or Greenwich Village, and "drop out" for a while—or join the Peace Corps or VISTA and try to make the world a better place.

Mary Bowler of Newark, New Jersey, was one such person. After college, she was a special education teacher. But she was looking for more.

> I traveled, like in the sixties scene; I went to San Francisco, the Summer of Love, and I traveled to Europe, and I came back to Newark and I decided I needed to—I wasn't satisfied with my life and I wanted to do some volunteer work and I always was drawn to working with the underprivileged, because that's what I did in Newark, where I taught. So I thought about, where could I go and have adventure and do something good at the same time, and I read about VISTA, and so I joined and went to Atlanta for training and from there to Hancock County.[2]

Young men had an additional incentive to join VISTA. Steve Nichandros of Orinda, California, was a nineteen-year-old junior college student when he was motivated to join VISTA. "Well, partly, [it was] the Vietnam War and the draft, and partly that there was somebody on campus talking about it, and it sounded like something I wanted to do."[3]

The war in Vietnam, in which America had been involved to some degree since the Eisenhower administration, had been heating up since 1965, and young men had been conscripted into military service in increasing numbers. Student deferments were becoming more difficult to get, and at the end of 1969 the Selective Service would adopt a lottery system in which nineteen-year-old men would be drafted according to their birth dates; student deferments would become available only to a select few, mostly graduate students in specified fields. It was widely believed that serving one year in VISTA would guarantee a deferment. A deferment wasn't automatic, as it turned out; deferments for VISTA workers were decided on an individual basis. But VISTA workers *were* serving their country and were often granted deferments on that basis. One year in

---

[2] Van Nest interview.
[3] Nichandros interview.

VISTA sure beat two years in the Army, especially since one of those Army years was likely to be spent in Vietnam.

Among the first VISTAs in Hancock County were two young women: Jeanette Bowman of Wooster, Ohio, and Fran Nenzel of San Francisco, California. They were assigned to Hancock County's Community Action Council in May 1967. The CAC director told them their primary job would be to "tell the people about the VISTA program so volunteers who follow this group will have an easy time." This was typical; the first VISTAs in any area were almost invariably viewed with suspicion by the people they came to help.

Bowman and Nenzel quickly found that a serious problem for many in Hancock County was transportation. Tennessee law did not permit welfare recipients to own a car, nor could a group of people pool their money to buy a car. Since public transportation didn't exist in the county, poor people had no way to get into Sneedville or Morristown for medical care or to find employment that might have taken them off the welfare rolls. Bowman and Nenzel saw this need as an opportunity for service and asked their supervisor to provide a car they could use to take people into town for necessary visits. A government-owned vehicle was promised but never arrived. The VISTAs borrowed cars when they could, but that was not often.

Jeanette wrote a letter to a newspaper back home, the *Cleveland Plain Dealer*, explained the problem they faced, and asked readers who had an extra car to contribute it to their project. A reader came up with a much-used 1956 Plymouth station wagon. Although the Plymouth was rusted and in poor condition, it ran, and the VISTAs were able to use it to provide much-needed transportation.

The old car also opened another door for service. Many of the local boys, most of them high school dropouts, hung around the only service station in the area. They lacked formal education but knew rudimentary auto mechanics, and—possibly motivated by the chance to be around two attractive young women—they volunteered to work on the Plymouth. They soon had the car in better condition, building their knowledge of automobile repair in the process. As Jeanette later told her college newspaper, "After we were able to get to see the people more often, they became more friendly and offered ways we could help the community."

Being accepted by the poor people of the county was relatively easy; more serious resistance came from those who should have welcomed the VISTAs but who instead saw them as a threat to their own power. As Jeanette Bowman recalled, "One of the big problems was the political hang-ups of the area. The superintendent of schools ran the local political machine. All the teachers were political appointees with little formal education of their own. The schools were serving no purpose except to teach kids to pledge the flag and wear shoes. No one went to college and few ever finished high school."

Bowman and Nenzel began an after-school tutoring program in one of the school buildings, helping children in all grades with their lessons. But after two weeks, the superintendent closed the program with no explanation. The VISTAs then started an after-school recreation program at their rented home. Once summer vacation began, they expanded it to an all-day program.

Then, according to Bowman's account, the superintendent began a rumor campaign against the VISTAs. Aided by one of his teachers, who was also the county sheriff, the superintendent spread stories about the "shady moral character" of the young women. The campaign of slander backfired; the program grew, attracting fifteen or more children to what locals called "the VISTA house" for games, hikes, and trips into town. The superintendent was voted out of office in the next election and replaced with a more progressive and open-minded educator, one who advocated tutorial and recreational programs.

Meanwhile, Bowman and Nenzel conducted a survey and determined that a lack of clean water was one of the biggest problems facing county residents. Most of the people outside Sneedville got their water from wells, which were often stagnant or contaminated with minerals from the soil. The VISTAs applied for a federal grant to build a water plant. The grant was approved, and a water system soon began serving some of the county's residents.[4]

Jeanette Bowman, Fran Nenzel, and the others in that first group helped get VISTA off to a good start in Hancock County, paving the way for the next crop of volunteers who arrived in summer 1968. Mary Bowler—now Mary Van Nest—doesn't recall being told a lot about Hancock County during her three weeks of VISTA training in Atlanta.

> Well, we had some—I don't know if you'd call them lectures, talks about general poverty in the South, and…we were told that it was the seventh poorest county in the country, I believe, something like that. I really don't remember being told too much specifically….[5]

Steve Nichandros recalls vague descriptions of what he would be doing in Hancock County: "Well, our general overall description was community development, as far as what to accomplish, to get the local people interested in getting

---

[4] Nichols, "VISTA Puts Community on Its Own Feet," 6.
[5] Van Nest interview.

together, to find out what they might want or need, what they considered something that they would want, and to facilitate them in accomplishing that, let's say. That's kind of a general description."[6]

The *Hancock County Post* printed a press release on 8 August 1968 from VISTA trainer David Mathieson, introducing the county's newest VISTAs.

Ten new VISTA trainees have come to Hancock County recently to replace the present volunteers who are now leaving. The new trainees arrived on July 15 and will officially become VISTAs on August 8.

Located in the Seal-Mathis Community are Mary Bowler, Susan Klein, and Julia McDevitt. Mary Bowler, 23, is from Newark, N.J. She received a B.A. from Newark State College in Education and has two years' experience in Newark teaching mentally retarded children and Adult Basic Education for the hard-core unemployed.

Susan Klein, 19, is from upstate New York. She has two years' schooling at Cornell University. She was raised on a farm and was editor of her high school newspaper.

Julia McDevitt comes from Cayuga [Cuyahoga] Falls, Ohio. She received a B.S. in Nursing and an R.N. from Ohio State University. During the last two years she has worked as a nurse in a large urban hospital in Ohio.

Situated in Mulberry Gap are Mr. and Mrs. Michael Hughes. Both Ann and Mike have a B.A. in Education from Chico State College in California. Both have two years' experience teaching school in Willows, California.

Ann Haralson and Dian Stallins are the VISTA trainees located in Kyles Ford Community. Ann comes from British Columbia, Canada and received a B.A. in Communications from Washington State University. She served as a VISTA Associate in Letcher County, Ky., during the summer of 1967.

Dian is a native of Henderson, Ky. She attended the University of Kentucky and has had a year of experience teaching in Henderson.

Stephen Nichandros, 19, living in New Hope Community, comes from Orinda, Calif., and attended Diable Valley College for two years. He is interested in electronics and auto mechanics.

Situated in Independence (third district) are Bob Van Nest and Ken Hatfield. Bob, 25, is from Summit, N.J., and has a B.A. in History from Saint Lawrence University and an M.A. in History from Columbia University. He was active in Scouting, rising to the rank of Eagle Scout. He has seven years' experience in camping and has received the Honorary Award for Distinguished Service in Conservation. Ken Hatfield, 22, is from Swansea, Mass., and attended the University of Massachusetts.

---

[6] Nichandros interview.

All of the trainees are impressed by the scenic beauty of Hancock County and the friendliness of its residents. They like the area very much and are looking forward to their year here.[7]

Mary Bowler, who later married fellow VISTA Bob Van Nest, the Eagle Scout, after their year in Hancock County, knew nothing about the Melungeons until arriving in the county. "No, I do not remember being told about Melungeons, at all. I don't even remember talking much about them until the play. (*to Bob*) How did we know about them? My husband remembers more about that than I do. He says we *were* told about Melungeons by some of the former VISTA volunteers that were leaving that year, that were there the year ahead of us."[8]

Speaking about his experiences more than four decades after his stay in Hancock County, Steve Nichandros recalled an admonition the new VISTAs received from their predecessors: "...we were advised not to say 'Melungeon,' or to talk about Melungeons, by the VISTAs that were there when we arrived."[9]

Those original VISTAs were justifiably proud of what they had accomplished. They had set the bar high for the VISTAs who arrived in summer 1968. When asked what she did during her year in Hancock County, Mary Van Nest recalls, "A little bit of everything."

When people ask us what we did, I say, sort of like, more like social work, I guess, than anything else. We did a lot of visiting. (chuckles) In fact, the locals referred to me and my roommates as "the visiting sisters."(laughs) And they loved it, because they were lonely, a lot of them, and we were really of great interest to them, coming from outside like we did. They were so isolated there, I think they really were intrigued with us and really got a kick out of us. We worked with a couple of nuns that were there, that were both nurses, and they were both health care workers in the district, and we did a lot with them with health fairs and trying to educate people about what was available, and trying to get women to come to the clinic to possibly discuss birth control, which did not go over very well. [We] did a lot of transporting of people to the doctors in Knoxville and Kingsport and various places because they had no way to get there. Did some tutoring; as a teacher I was interested in that.... But it was a very positive experience. We felt like we got so much more than we gave the people; we just loved them so much. We became really close to a lot of them, a lot of the local tobacco farmers. [They were] very, very welcoming. And very kind and generous. You know, they're the kind of people that,

---

[7] Matheison, "New VISTA Workers Ready," 3.

[8] Van Nest interview.

[9] Nichandros interview.

if they slaughtered a pig, would bring a loin of pork up to us rather than save it for themselves. They were wonderful.[10]

Steve Nichandros had fewer clear memories of the work he did as a VISTA.

The VISTAs as a group accomplished a couple of things, and the VISTA that was there before me had something to do with telephones coming into the community I was in. I worked with the—what was it called? OEO?

Yes, Office of Economic Opportunity.

Yes, I think there was an office in Sneedville, and I worked with them, however I could help out. Looking back on it, I don't really know what I did. I came away going, "Boy, I sure was young." (laughs)

The ten VISTAs there at that time lived in different parts of the county. Were each of you responsible for projects and tasks in the particular community in which you lived?

Yeah. Well, that second part of your statement is—well, in some ways it's true. Let's say on paper it's true. I guess that's a fair way of putting it. In other words, if there was something going on in a certain place, it would be the person living there that would be involved in it.[11]

Over the course of the next year, Scott Collins would come to know several of the VISTAs who served in Hancock County. Having just graduated from Hancock County High School, Collins was not much younger than the average VISTA. On one hand, they were young people of his own generation. On the other hand, they came from many different parts of the United States (and one was from Canada), with backgrounds and experiences vastly different from his own. A half-century after his experiences with the VISTAs, he still had somewhat mixed feelings about them:

They came here and they were supposed to help people learn how to do things, and of course the people here already knew more about what they were here for. [The VISTAs] were supposed to come in here and, I guess, nurture us back to how reality is. We were living in a county that was very poor, and we knew how to live off the land, and these folks tried to come in and do things—and I guess they did some things, maybe helped build some handicapped ramps for some folks, different things like that. But to teach [the locals] things, I don't know that they did a whole lot. And I'm not criticizing, I promise I'm not. I remember some of them. I got acquainted with several of the young men, and they were nice—young girls, too. Very good-looking young girls. (laughs)…But it was tough, it was really tough times for them.

---

[10] Van Nest interview.
[11] Nichandros interview.

They had to come in and find them a place to live, whatever it was. Some of them weren't very comfortable at all, I'm sure. But I'll tell you, for the most part, they got along really great with the people…I think they were taught more than they taught. They watched people plant gardens, things like that—they weren't used to anything like that; it was survival, planting and growing your own food, going out and milking cows. I mean, that was an experience for them, you know.[12]

In September 1968, the drama committee met to formally organize as the Hancock County Drama Association (HCDA) and to elect officers. Corrine Bowlin, a Carson-Newman student barely old enough to vote, was chosen to be president of the organization, with Kyle Greene, president of the Hancock County Resource Development Association, serving as vice-president of the HCDA. Claude Collins was elected secretary, and Martha Collins—Miss Martha of the Sneedville Bank—was treasurer. Three of the four officers of the Drama Association had surnames associated with the Melungeons.

The organization made plans for the weeks ahead. They discussed the amphitheater, which was to be built behind the former high school, now Hancock Central Elementary School, on Court Street at the foot of Newman's Ridge. They had received permission from the school board to use the property for the amphitheater. Claude Collins wrote a successful grant application for money to build a stage; according to the application, the stage was to be used as a teaching tool for his English classes. The school board also acquired a small adjoining piece of land in order to make broader use of the property.[13] Claude Collins handled the negotiations for that parcel of land. He knew the owner was not supportive of the idea of an outdoor drama about the Melungeons.

I went to talk to this man about it. I didn't tell him what we were going to do with the property. I just told him we wanted the addition to the school [property] 'cause it was right back of where I was teaching. And I said, "It's a possibility that I might carry on some classes down there in a theatre we might build." The man was not particularly pleased when the property was incorporated into the amphitheater for the outdoor drama.[14]

The Drama Association asked Mark Sumner of the Institute for Outdoor Drama to return to Sneedville at his earliest convenience to finish sketches and plans for the amphitheater. The HCDA and Sumner would work closely with the new school superintendent, Glenn Livesay, to make the best use of the site.

---

[12] Scott Collins interview.
[13] "Drama Group Makes Plans," 1.
[14] Claude Collins interview (2002).

The officers of the HCDA encouraged all members who were also members of other agencies and organizations to share information about what the Drama Association was doing. Many of those entities were in a position to offer help, and the HCDA hoped they would when it was needed.

The organization also authorized Carson-Newman College to submit a proposal under Title 1 of the Higher Education Act of 1965—which so far had been the sugar daddy of the drama committee—to organize and carry out a program of developing local handicrafts that could help draw tourists to the county. The sale of handicrafts by local artisans was always closely associated with the drama itself. The sale of hand-crafted items not only would draw tourists but also would provide income for the artisans.

Money was naturally of great concern to the group. They decided to immediately sell memberships in the HCDA to raise capital. They also began work on a brochure they would use to solicit members. Most of the members believed that some working capital could also be raised through interest-free loans from local residents.[15]

John Lee Welton was the drama instructor at Carson-Newman College. He was a native of Pampa, Texas, received his B.A. and M.A. at West Texas State University, and began teaching at Carson-Newman in 1960. He was involved in planning the outdoor drama from the beginning.

> We were brought into it because…[they] had nobody who knew how to put a drama together. I'd had some experience working with outdoor dramas; I'd worked with *The Lost Colony* and some of the other outdoor dramas. So I had a little background on that, and of course my experience in drama [at Carson-Newman]. Since it started at Carson-Newman with the [Farley/High] study I guess I just sort of fell into the position of it and was with it from the very beginning on through the end of it.[16]

Hancock Countians were disappointed by the news that contracts for the proposed improvement of a short stretch of Highway 31 would not be issued in September. In his regular column "This Is Your Town," Mayor Turner wrote,

> According to the Highway Department's Office of Research and Planning the deleay [*sic*] was caused by difficulties in rights of way appraisals, which should be worked out to some degree by the October letting of contracts. It might be well for us to familiarize ourselves with the fact that most of the better thing[s] are long range projects and usually come slow such as our road improvements.

---

[15] "Drama Group Makes Plans," 1.
[16] Welton interview (2002).

The low bid for the project was $468,608, submitted by Summers-Taylor Paving Company of Elizabethton, Tennessee, and preliminary grading began in late November. By the end of 1969, if a motorist from Sneedville survived the trip over the mountain, he or she would enjoy an improved road all the way to 11-W at Mooresburg.[17]

During most of 1968, the people of Sneedville were getting their town ready for an influx of tourists by making the town more attractive. Mayor Turner's "Clean Up-Fix Up-Paint Up Campaign" set out monthly projects for citizens in an effort to beautify Sneedville. May was devoted to picking up trash, scrap wood, and other rubbish, and setting it beside the streets where trucks would pick it up. June was devoted to improving the appearance of stores and other businesses in town, while July was spent cleaning streets and alleys and concentrating on weed and insect control. The focus in August was cleaning up vacant lots, particularly those located at the entrances to the town. "Residential beautification" was the project for September, and citizens were encouraged to plant trees and shrubs. The city gave a cash award for the most improved residential property. October was Fire Prevention Month, with emphasis on fire drills, demonstrations, and inspections, and November saw an extensive anti-litter campaign that included the addition of waste containers downtown. December was a month for holiday clean ups, Christmas decorations, and an extension of the fire prevention program. In an article in the *Post*, Mayor Turner's brother Sonny, who owned the department store in town, wrote, "Take an objective look at your store or business front to determine what can make your place look better. Painting buildings in harmonious colors, removing projecting or unsightly signs have proved to be successful projects in other towns. Why not let us give it a try?"[18]

Of course, not everyone in town was willing to give it a try, and Sneedville continued to be plagued by unkempt yards, unsightly buildings, and roadside trash piles—particularly at the entrance to town from the Clinch River bridge. What is remarkable is that a great number of people *did* follow the mayor's directives. Rural and small-town Appalachians have a well-deserved reputation for stubbornness and a disinclination to follow orders that are not accompanied by force. What is remarkable is the extent of cooperation displayed by the people of Sneedville. Mayor Turner prodded, cajoled, and sometimes shamed the people of his town into following his directives, and as a result the appearance of Sneedville was noticeably improved as 1968 came to a close.

---

[17] Turner, "This Is YOUR Town: Roads," 19 September 1968, 2.
[18] A. Y. Turner, "Clean Up—Fix Up—Paint Up," 1.

At the end of November, playwright Kermit Hunter returned to Sneedville to meet with the Drama Association. He explained that the outdoor drama must deal with the universal problems of mankind within the framework of the specific history of Hancock County and the Melungeons. "Dramas which successfully draw audiences year after year," he said, "are of a serious nature. Somehow, when the stars come out and the people sit in darkness, they are ready to think about greater things than a comedy provides." He added, "Such a play must end in hope."

Hunter told the Drama Association he would write a rough draft of the play to be read critically by members of the Association before completing the final script. He explained that he intended to set the play in the eighteenth and nineteenth centuries, which would allow for added dramatic effects in costuming. He also described the stage he wanted built, a large center stage with slightly raised stages on either side.

Hunter also told the Association that Hancock County could take pride in being the only county in the nation that could claim the Melungeons as residents. This was clearly not true; Melungeons lived in the surrounding counties in Tennessee, as well as in southwestern Virginia and southeastern Kentucky. Hunter's inaccuracy could be forgiven, however, since nearly all the historical articles available focused exclusively on Hancock County as the home of the Melungeons, and the county was unquestionably the only place in America willing to acknowledge their presence.

At the November meeting, the Drama Association selected a technical director to aid John Lee Welton, David Behan of Tusculum College in Greeneville. They also discussed drainage of the amphitheater site, which had to be accomplished before construction began. And, of course, fundraising was one everyone's mind. The Drama Association members were, of course, unpaid, and most of the labor for the construction of the amphitheater would be provided by volunteers and by workers and by workers with Operation Mainstream, called "Happy Pappies" for some long-forgotten reason, who were paid by the Federal government. Most of the lumber required for building the amphitheater, the box office, concession stand, and craft shop would come from various free sources. Still, many things would have to be purchased, from nails and screws to wiring to light fixtures. Jones Coal Yard provided drainage tiles at a reduced price, and bulldozer operator Junior Beckler agreed to a reduced fee for preparing the amphitheater site.[19]

---

[19] Haralson, "Drama Group on the Move," 1; Haralson, "Dr. Hunter Discusses Drama," 1; Haralson, "Construction Underway at County Drama Site," 1.

The progress of the Drama Association was reported in the *Hancock County Post* by VISTA Ann Haralson. Born in Oregon and raised in Quesnel, British Columbia, Canada, Ann had been a "stringer," or freelance reporter, for the *Prince George Citizen* while attending high school at the Auburn Academy. During her four years at Washington State University, she wrote for her college newspaper, the *WSU Daily Evergreen*, and served as a VISTA Associate in Letcher County, Kentucky, during summer 1967. When she graduated in 1968 with a degree in communications, she signed up for a full year's duty in VISTA and was assigned to Hancock County. *Post* editor and publisher John Montgomery would take advantage of her writing skills often during that year.[20]

John Lee Welton, who would direct the outdoor drama, recalls the fundraising efforts of the HCDA.

> There was a committee that went out and actually solicited funds—the Hancock County *Walk Toward the Sunset* drama group—to get the thing off the ground. Dora Bowlin…and [Corinne] Bowlin were very active in trying to raise money. They would go out and ask people for donations for the drama, and a lot of people said "Sure, be glad to donate to it. What is it?" They had no idea what it was. But with the idea that we were going to try to bring something in to help the community, help the county, and people were very generous—especially generous because this was a poor county. There was some funding from various historical and governmental organizations to help it along. So we got the thing going.[21]

Ross Hopkins chaired the fundraising committee. By early December, sales of the special Fourth of July souvenir issue of the *Hancock County Post* had netted $77.88. The Hancock County Farm Bureau contributed $100; the Chamber of Commerce, the Sneedville Women's Club, Howard Rhea, Burley Satterfield, and an anonymous donor had contributed $50 apiece, and Turner's Drug Store kicked in $25. In all, the HCDA had collected $350 by early December. Claude Collins headed a subcommittee that would sell individual memberships for five dollars each, entitling donors to a membership card and one free admission to the drama once production began.

No groundbreaking ceremony marked the beginning of construction of the amphitheater. The occasion was marked by a photograph in the *Post* on 12 December, showing HCDA member Kyle Lawson, soil conservationist Gordon Gibson, bulldozer operator Junior Beckler, and Operation Mainstream coordinator Kyle Greene gathered around Beckler's Caterpillar bulldozer. Ralph Green

---

[20] Smith, "Ann Piper 1946–2015."
[21] Welton interview (2002).

dug the drainage ditches at a reduced cost of two dollars per hour, and Happy Pappies laid and covered the tiles. Drainage water collected in a small creek at the bottom of the hill and wound its way into the nearby Clinch River. By mid-December, Junior Beckler and his "Cat" had cleared and leveled the seating area.

The New Jersey Zinc Company offered to donate gravel needed to raise the stage area to the desired height. The HCDA put out a call for posts and timbers to be used as bleachers. For a backdrop, playwright Kermit Hunter suggested old barn wood, so HCDA members were on the lookout for an old barn whose owner might volunteer it for dismantling and re-purposing.[22]

As 1968 closed, Drama Association members could look back with a sense of pride and wonder at all they had accomplished that year. There was still a lot to do, however, and they had just over six months in which to do it.

---

[22] Haralson, "Construction Underway," 1.

7

GETTING READY

The day after New Year's Day, 1969, the Hancock County Drama Association held a meeting at the Vardy School in Blackwater Valley—also known as Vardy Valley—across Newman's Ridge north of Sneedville. The HCDA planned to hold meetings in various communities around the county to give more people the chance to learn about the plans for the drama and to become involved. The meeting in Vardy was significant because the valley and adjoining Newman's Ridge were considered the epicenter of the Melungeon population, the place where writers had been going to observe the Melungeons since the mid-nineteenth century. The Vardy School had been established by Presbyterian missionaries to provide educational opportunities for the people of that isolated valley, including Melungeons, who had not been permitted in the county schools until relatively recently. The school had been taken over by the county but would soon be closing. So many people had left the valley—moving to places like Maryland, Michigan, Ohio, and Indiana to get factory jobs—that there weren't enough school-aged children left in the valley to justify keeping the school open.

Though many had moved away, there were still a lot of Melungeons living in the Vardy community, and the Drama Association wanted to make certain the play would not offend the Melungeons. It wasn't an easy task. "Melungeon" was still considered an epithet, and the mere mention of the existence of Melungeons was offensive to some, whether they shared that heritage or not. Many who did share that heritage wanted nothing more than to assimilate into the community and not be seen as different from their neighbors in any way. That desire for assimilation, as much as the desire for better economic opportunities, was the impetus for the outmigration of many Melungeon families to places where the word "Melungeon" was unknown. Many who remained in the valley saw the outdoor drama as unwelcome attention.

More than forty people came out on an unseasonably warm January evening to attend the meeting. After the officers of the HCDA were introduced, their duties were explained in order to provide an overview of the organization. Professor Joe M. High of Carson-Newman College explained that the purpose of the drama was to attract tourism to the county. The drama would also provide a

venue for the sale of local crafts, and High encouraged his audience to write letters to Congressman Jimmy Quillen encouraging him to support funding for
classes under the Manpower Development Training Act. The two proposed classes would train local residents to produce high-quality wood and fiber crafts. If
approved, the classes would have openings for twenty people in each nine-month
class, and class participants would be paid for their participation.

Once the classes were approved in Washington, Don Ward, a craftsman
from Gatlinburg, Tennessee, would help screen prospective participants. High
reported that one local girl had already been accepted in a ceramics class in Mon-
terey, Tennessee, and that a few craftspeople from Hancock County would have
the opportunity to exhibit their skills at Knoxville's Dogwood Arts Fair in April.

In other drama-related news, the attendees at the Vardy School meeting
learned that playwright Kermit Hunter had submitted a draft of the play to
members of the HCDA. Association members, as well as others in the community, were reading the script and considering possible suggestions. The costs associated with the drama were also discussed. The original estimated cost of the
project was $60,000, a sum that included the cost of the site, construction, and
the services of the playwright. As of January 1969, about $10,000 was still
needed, including $3,500 for lighting.

Fundraising chairman Ross Hopkins reported on the efforts of his committee. Elmer Turner, who had been principal of the Vardy School for a couple of
years in the 1940s, would create a newsletter that would go to individuals in the
school system; these newsletters would explain the importance of the drama to
the county. They would also solicit ideas for use of the amphitheater in the off-
season; some suggestions included local talent shows, singing conventions, and
public speeches. Claude Collins—an alumnus of the Vardy School—reported
that membership cards had been printed by the Reverend Carl Greene of
Sneedville and would be sold to individuals by members of the Drama Association, as well as by VISTA workers.[1]

Most people in Hancock County weren't yet convinced of the potential
value of the outdoor drama, but merchants in Sneedville were coming around.
In February, hardware store owner Kyle Lawson boasted that he would collect
$300 for the Drama Association over the course of a weekend. He more than
made good on his boast, collecting $320.[2]

A couple of other Sneedville merchants took an economic hit in February.
Shortly after midnight on Wednesday, 12 February, fire broke out in the Cash

---

[1] Haralson, "Drama Plans Announced," 1.
[2] Grohse, "H.R.D.A. Meets," 1.

n' Tote, a variety store owned by Morris Anderson and Sonny Turner. The Sneedville Volunteer Fire Department was augmented by units from Morristown, Surgoinsville, and Tazewell, as well as the rescue squads from Hancock and Hawkins counties. The blaze completely destroyed the building and threatened the Sneedville Motor Company, an auto dealership next door. Fire units were able to prevent the conflagration from spreading to the car dealership. Both buildings were owned by Lena Jarvis, and neither building was insured. Turner and Anderson, who had recently purchased stock for the coming spring and summer, lost their entire inventory, only a small portion of which was insured. Turner was undaunted and announced plans to re-open the Cash N' Tote in the building that housed another of his businesses, Turner's Fabric Shop. "We don't want to look back now," Turner said. "We appreciate the business the people of this county have given us in the past and we hope that soon we can be of service to them once again. Now we are looking ahead and planning for the opening of the new Cash N' Tote."[3]

The loss of a single merchant had a seriously negative impact on the tiny town of Sneedville. By the same token, however, the opening of a single small factory in Sneedville was cause for celebration, and in mid-March, Electric Motors and Specialties, Inc., announced they would be opening soon. "We have to have motors coming out of here next month," said William White, project engineer for the plant. County residents would be invited to submit applications as soon as equipment and furniture was in place at the factory. Ninety percent of the workforce would be hired locally, according to White, and more than two-thirds of those to be hired would be women. Resident manager Stephen Walko explained that women were more capable and adept at the type of production required to make electric motors for refrigeration units.[4] No one questioned what today would be seen as gender bias in hiring, nor did anyone ask if the women to be hired would be paid the same as the men, or if the workers in Sneedville would be paid the same as their counterparts up north. The prospect of jobs coming into the county would have overshadowed such questions, had anyone thought to ask them.

Another good thing coming into Hancock County that March came through the efforts of VISTA Mary Bowler, who organized a meeting to begin a group dealing with developmental disabilities, or mental retardation, as that group of conditions was known then. Bowler had been a special education teacher at home in Newark and saw that there was a need for such services in

---

[3] "Fire Destroys Cash N' Tote," 1.
[4] "Factory Opening Due Soon, Production to Begin in April," 1.

Hancock County. "I worked pretty hard with the superintendent to get some special ed classes started, because there were none," she recalled. "There were no special education services at the time. It was because there were no special ed teachers, for one reason; they weren't trained."[5]

Bowler brought eighteen county residents together with Eugene Nalir, the executive director of the Tennessee Association for Retarded Children and Adults. Nalir urged them to form an organization, which would make it easier to establish programs and offer serices. Officers were elected that evening; Lena Jarvis was the president, Sonny Turner the vice-president, and Mary Bowler was the secretary-treasurer. Bowler even wrote the story about the meeting that appeared in the *Hancock County Post*. The group would meet again in May at the Neighborhood Service Center.[6]

In the *Post* for 27 March, Dora Bowlin—the mother of HCDA president Corinne Bowlin—offered the first of several updates on the progress of the drama project under the headline "Drama News."

Our budget for the drama is based on the estimate that 5,000 to 6,000 people will come to see our play this summer.

These people will not be here for business or for visiting friends, but for the purpose of seeing an interesting drama, having an enjoyable time—and spending money.

Rev. R. B. Connor has figures that show that each tourist spends $11.41 per day. A small part of this will go for meals and tickets to the play. If we have quality products and quality service almost any business in Hancock County will get a large part of the rest.

Service stations, of course, are prime targets for the tourist dollar. Small groceries along tourist routes would profit. Any businesses handling items of a souvenir nature would benefit.

Then there are the organizations aimed primarily for the tourist such as the crafts organization. This beneficial project came into being solely as a result of the drama. The organization has been accepted into the Cumberland Mountains Crafts Guild and is presently hard at work in order to have their crafts ready for the tourists.

Five craftsmen in the county have been invited to display their art at Miller's Crafts Fair in Knoxville on April 17, 18, and 19. These five are Geraldine Southern, Leona Southern, Alex Stewart, and Mr. and Mrs. Jay Gillian.

They will show their crafts and demonstrate some of their handiwork. In addition to this fair there will be a Crafts Fair at Hancock High School on

[5] Van Nest interview.
[6] Bowler, "Retardation Group Formed," 8; "Meeting Set," 12.

April 12th. Something like 100 people have entered and many will be demonstrating their art on the premises....

Another idea that some of the VISTA are working on is compiling a cookbook to be sold at the drama site. Plans are to have pioneer recipes for such items as pickled beans, shuck beans, dried apples, kraut, pickled corn, stack cake, and even soap making. Ordinary recipes can be found anywhere, but this would be a gem that the tourist could find nowhere else...

Then, too, are the side benefits from the drama. The Mooresburg to Sneedville road improvement was approved after the officials called Mayor Turner to confirm the facts about the production of the drama. We hope to have more road improvements in the future.

Lastly, let us not forget the intangibles—Pride In Our County; In Our Way Of Life; In The Story We Have To Tell; In Our History. These can benefit all of us.

In closing, let me add one more statistic. The State of Tennessee takes in two and a half times as much money from tourism as it does from agriculture. We need to get our share of this.[7]

In the next issue of the *Post*, Dora Bowlin took the opportunity to thank many of the people of Hancock County who had contributed to the drama project. These included Joe High of Carson-Newman College, who had been instrumental in getting the project started and had also worked with the craft organization to insure outlets for the work of its members. Thanks also went to the teachers of the county, the PTAs, and the community clubs, all of whom had helped in various ways. Bulldozer operator Junior Beckler also received acknowledgment for his work in preparing the amphitheater site and for contributing about $100 worth of free work.

Recognition was also given to VISTA, Project Mainstream, the Tennessee Valley Authority, the University of Tennessee, the Hancock County Board of Education, the Neighborhood Service Center, and the County Agent's office, all of which had provided some degree of assistance to the HCDA.[8]

While members of the Drama Association and others were collecting contributions for the project, Sneedville mayor Charlie Turner was seeking funding from the state of Tennessee. Until about the end of the twentieth century, Tennessee was politically dominated by Democrats. The eastern third of the state, however, had been Republican territory since the mid-nineteenth century, reflecting that region's loyalty to the Union during the Civil War. Hancock County was almost solidly Republican, but the voters of Sneedville had chosen

---

[7] D. Bowlin, "Drama News," 27 March 1969, 1.

[8] Ibid., 3 April 1969, 6.

Turner, a Democrat, to be their mayor. As a result, Turner had some degree of influence with Democrats in Nashville, the state capital. That spring, he used that influence for the benefit of the outdoor drama.

Bruce Shine is an attorney in Kingsport, just over thirty-six miles east of Sneedville as the crow flies, but because of the mountains, more than fifty miles by car. In 1969, Shine was vice-chairman of the Tennessee Arts Commission.

> I had a phone call from Dick Barry, who was deputy—I think his official title was "executive assistant," what we now call "deputy governor" of Tennessee. He had been a former Speaker of the House of Representatives and he was the top assistant to Governor Buford Ellington. Governor Ellington, in one form or another, had been approached by Charlie Turner, who was the mayor of Sneedville and a member of the Democratic State Executive Committee, and a close friend of Senator Herbert S. Walters. Charlie Turner wanted to get some state money for the outdoor drama, and he had called either Hub Walters—Herbert Walters—or directly to Dick Barry. But Dick Barry was responsible for my being on the commission, because I was the youngest member; when I was appointed, I was like 26 or 27. Dick Barry called me up and said, "Charlie Turner up in Sneedville—do you know him?" And I answered, "I know him as a member of the Democratic State Executive Committee." He said, "Well, he needs help on this drama that they're doing up there." With that, I then talked with Norman Worrell [executive director of the Tennessee Arts Commission], and Dick Barry maybe also called Norman Worrell. But anyway, that's how I got involved, because Charlie Turner was good friends with the governor and the governor, by God, wanted something done for the drama in Sneedville.

Shine and Worrell journeyed to Sneedville to meet with Mayor Turner and Martha Collins, president of the local bank and a Drama Association member, and to take a look at the amphitheater, which was still under construction.

> I remember going up to Sneedville with Norman…I can't remember if the logs were in, if the seats were there or if they weren't. But I remember it was at night, and we had been at the drugstore, and we had gone over to the bank to visit with Martha Collins and both Charlie and Martha Collins gave us a general idea of what they were trying to do, and Norman and I said we wanted to see where it was, where it was going to be. Well, it was getting on, and it was probably March—February or March—and we went up there, and we walked up and down the bank. Charlie Turner showed us, and I know we never left Sneedville until about 10:30 at night because we had come back downtown after seeing the spot. But that was my first actual involvement.

But even when "the governor, by God, wanted something done for the drama in Sneedville," there were steps that had to be taken. Shine and Worrell encouraged the Drama Association to apply for a grant from the Tennessee Arts Commission. The application forms would have to obtained, filled out, and sent back to Nashville. There, they would be looked over by a committee that decided how grant money would be spent, and, if approved, the grant would be awarded to the Drama Association. Even with the governor's backing, this process would take time, and opening night was coming up quickly. *Walk Toward the Sunset* might get some financial aid from the state during its second season—if there *was* a second season.[9]

At the end of March, the *Louisville Courier-Journal Magazine* featured Hancock County and the Melungeons. Writer and photographer John Fetterman had visited the county and began his article with a descriptive passage:

> Soon, gaunt empty houses and overgrown graveyards will be all to mark lovely, lonely Newman Ridge in East Tennessee where they lived. For decades, these enigmatic, dark skin complexioned people confounded sociologist, anthropologist and historians alike. The riddle of their origin appears destined to remain forever unsolved.
>
> Newman Ridge, less than 50 miles beyond Cumberland Gap near Middlesboro, stretches some 25 miles from its northeast tip in northeastern tip of Virginia to its southwestern ending in Hancock County, Tennessee. On the other side it is flanked by lush valleys which drain the Powell River basin on the North and the Clinch River basin on the south. To this height came the dark ridge people to become the strangest legend of the Appalachians.

Fetterman's article continues with news of the outdoor drama, along with quotes from some Hancock Countians.

> The Melungeon legend gained new interest this year with the discovery of evidence that Phoenicians, indeed, may have found the western world at least 2000 years before Columbus.
>
> And this summer, the people of Hancock County hope to stage an outdoor drama to bring needed tourist money into the county of 8,000 people and to keep alive the Melungeon Legend. A script is being prepared by Kermit Hunter, successful writer of many such dramas, including "Unto These Hills" staged at Cherokee N.C. and the "Horn of the West" production at Boone N.C.
>
> Twenty-two year old Corinne Bowlin, a teacher in the county school system, is one of the drama organizers. "I have been fascinated by the Melungeon legend all my life," she said. "Bowlin, you know, is a Melungeon

---

[9] Shine interview.

name." Many of the other workers who helped to prepare a site for the drama and are seeking financing also bear "Melungeon" names.

Out along the unmapped ridge, away from paved roads, only two people live now, Mr. and Mrs. Ellis Stewart. He is 71 and she is 68 and they have spent their lives on Newman Ridge, "They'll all come back to this ridge someday" Stewart says. "Where they came from first I'll never know. But someday they'll come back up here like squirrels."

But they won't. As in all of Appalachia, the cities have drawn away the young people, and the older people have moved down by the paved roads and nearer the towns. Poverty has entangled some and success has found others. The days of moonshining and dirt farming up on the ridge will no more return to Newman's Ridge than they will to thousands of ridges like it.

Fetterman describes some of the theories surrounding the Melungeons, cites recent research that seems to bolster some of the legends of Phoenician, Carthaginian, and/or Portuguese ancestry. However, he concludes, the mystery remains.

Visitors—some curious, some scientific—still come intermittently to Hancock County. They search through the graveyards and prowl the abandoned houses. Outsiders have taken skull measurements and blood samples and made skin pigmentations studies. No answers have resulted. Meanwhile, time and change have sent the Melungeon to mix more and more with other segments of society. Their names appear all across the mountains, including East Kentucky, and in many places far from Newman's Ridge. It will probably be as Claude Collins says as he walks along the traces of the ancient roads up on Newman's Ridge: "I have heard all the stories, but we'll probably never know the truth."

In an East Kentucky county seat recently, a man patted a small, beautiful raven-haired girl on the head and asked the ageless question, "Where did you get your pretty hair?"

If the child had known, perhaps she could have told the most fascinating story ever to come from the mountains.[10]

In April, with opening night less than three months away, fundraising was of paramount importance to the Drama Association. Bill Grohse took a fairly stern tone in the *Post*:

---

[10] Fetterman, "The Melungeons." A version of Fetterman's story appeared in selected regional editions of *Life* on 26 June 1970.

I look through the list of donors to the Hancock Drama Association. I didn't see your name. Perhaps I overlooked it or it will appear in a later edition of the Post. Are "you" really interested in your county and community? Are "you" one of the persons who don't care?

I pity you if you don't care. No person is an island unto himself. How he lives, what he does affects us all. If he isn't interested in himself or his community—who can be expected to be interested in him? If we aren't interested in "our" county—who can be expected to be interested in us?

We ask the Federal Government for more free food stamps, more roads, more welfare, more tobacco allotments, more money for this or higher salaries. We ask the State of Tennessee for more of the same.

The politicians ask us for more votes. Yet we refuse to help ourselves. There is an old saying that the Good Lord helps those who help themselves. We Hancock Countians want to help ourselves. We don't want just a few people to carry the burden. We don't want just a few people to claim the credit for what has been done for the county or what is being done.

We want "all" Hancock Countians to claim the credit. We want "all" men and women of business, All [sic] Federal and State employees, "all" farmers, "all" retired people, "all" recipients of Federal and State Welfare to do their part.

We realize that some people cannot give much. Surely "you" can give something in the interest of your county and your community.

"Therefore all things whatsoever ye would that men should do to you, do ye even so to them; for this is the law and the prophets." Matt. 7:10…

We "are" asking, we "are" seeking, we "are" expecting to receive donations for the Hancock County Drama Association. As of July 1, 1967, Hancock County had a population of 7,775. If we just receive and [sic] average of two dollars per person we would be well over our goal.[11]

Grohse's approach to soliciting contributions might seem overly strident and accusatory, and certainly some in Hancock County took it in that way. But Grohse and the other members of the HCDA weren't professional fundraisers; most had never asked anyone for a contribution for anything. They were working for the benefit of the entire county, and many couldn't understand why others did not share their enthusiasm. And, since it was a small community where everyone pretty much knew everyone else, it was hard for them not to take rejection or indifference personally.

Publicly acknowledging the individuals who make contributions to a particular endeavor is common fundraising practice. Printing the names of contributors with the amount of their contribution is not. Individual contributors to

---

[11] Grohse, "Support the Drama," 6.

the HCDA were listed weekly in the *Post*, along with the amount of their contributions. This might have caused some concern among potential contributors; many likely wanted their names on the public list of contributors but didn't want their neighbors to see how much—or how little—they had contributed. To put the size of these gifts into perspective, it is good to remember that, according to the Social Security Administration, the average weekly salary in the United States in 1969 was $113.34. The average in Hancock County, Tennessee—one of the poorest counties in America—was considerably less. Five or ten dollars was a generous gift for a man trying to feed, clothe, and house his family on less than $100 per week.[12]

One gift that was not publicly acknowledged for several years came from three Sneedville businessmen, one of whom was Mayor Charlie Turner. These three signed a note for $6,000 to help finance the outdoor drama. If the drama made money, the $6,000 would be paid back from the profits. If not, the three individuals would be responsible for paying the money back to the bank. They were betting on their town and their county.[13]

Nonmonetary gifts were acknowledged in the *Hancock County Post*. Johnny Crippen contributed 20 tons of gravel. The Reverend Carl Green printed the membership cards. Boss Bowlin gave 6,000 sheets of paper.

Dora Bowlin's weekly "Drama News" column listed other non-monetary help that was needed: actors for the drama, extras to take nonspeaking roles to fill out crowd scenes, costumers, stage hands, make-up people, lighting and sound technicians, concession workers, ticket sellers—as many as 200 people in all. Bowlin reported that director John Lee Welton had addressed a meeting of the Drama Association and explained to the group what would be needed to make the production a success. "The days are swiftly passing," Bowlin wrote, "and before we know it July 3rd will be here. I cannot stress too strongly how important it is that those first people coming into the county find everything in readiness, there [sic] visit well organized and the people of Hancock County well prepared to show them a good time." Those first visitors, Bowlin wrote, could do more than any advertising to spread good word-of-mouth about the drama.[14]

Up to mid-April, the working title of the play had been *The Melungeon Story*. At the April meeting of the HCDA, John Lee Welton suggested changing the title to *Walk Toward the Sunset*. Playwright Kermit Hunter agreed to the change, and an HCDA member—likely someone connected to a school

---

[12] Social Security Administration, National Average Wage Index.
[13] Glenn, "Melungeon Drama to Reopen," 10.
[14] Bowlin, "Drama News," 10 April 1969, 1, 7.

equipped with a mimeograph—began cutting a stencil to run off copies of the script.

In her newspaper column for 17 April, Dora Bowlin wrote that the bleacher seats in the amphitheater were almost completed. Gravel had been hauled in to build up the stage area, and white pines had been planted along the perimeter of the amphitheater. Bowlin reported that the acoustics of the amphitheater were good; speaking in a relatively low voice from the stage area, Bowlin could be heard clearly from the top seats.[15] In fact, there *were* no seats at the top of the amphitheater, or anywhere else. The hillside had been terraced, and the logs that would serve as bleacher seats were almost ready to be installed, but much work remained to be done.

The Drama Association suffered a serious loss on Friday, 19 April, when Finance Committee chairman Ross Hopkins suffered a fatal heart attack. He was only forty-six years old. A rural mail carrier and former postmaster in Sneedville, Hopkins was involved in many community organizations besides the Drama Association. He was a past president of the Sneedville Chamber of Commerce and the Sneedville Lions Club. He was secretary of the Hancock County Citizens Participation Committee, a member of the Sneedville Industrial Committee, and a member of the Citizens Advisory Board to the Board of Mayor and Aldermen. A World War II veteran, Hopkins was a past director of the local American Legion Post, and a member and lay leader of the Sneedville United Methodist Church. He was survived by his wife, two sons, his mother, sister, and two brothers. The loss of an energetic, involved young man like Hopkins was a blow not only to the Drama Association, but to the community as a whole.[16]

On Saturday, 26 April, director John Lee Welton and technical director David Behan met with some HCDA members to finalize plans for the construction of the stage and to discuss costumes. They discussed changes to the stage, lighting, and costumes. The costumes would have to reflect two different time periods to correspond with the two acts of the play; Act 1 was set in the late 1700s; Act 2 took place in the 1890s. The costumes could not actually be made until casting was complete.[17]

While the main characters would be played by Carson-Newman drama students, dozens of nonspeaking extras would be cast from the local population. Local try-outs for the play were scheduled for Saturday, 17 May, at the Sneedville Elementary School, just above the amphitheater. Welton made an appeal to potential actors in the *Post* two days before the try-outs.

---

[15] Bowlin, "Drama News," 17 April 1969, 5.
[16] "Local Civic Leader Ross Hopkins Dies," 1.
[17] Bowlin, "Drama News," 1 May 1969, 8.

Should I try out for the play "Walk Toward the Sunset" that is to be given in Sneedville this summer?

What is a try-out like? Am I too old or too young to be in the play?

I have never been in a play in my life and know nothing about acting so should I go to the try-out?

These are just a few of the questions that arise when a community decides to produce a play such as the one which the Hancock County Drama Association has undertaken. Everyone is just a little unsure of what it is all about and nobody wants to make a fool of himself.

As director of the play, perhaps I can answer a few of these questions and let the people of the area know a little more about this great adventure which your people are about to embark upon.

First, let me say that I have seen communities in which these outdoor dramas have been staged suddenly come alive and change, in many cases, from run-of-the-mill places to exciting, alive and vibrant communities in which a common goal has pulled the people together, has made families engage in unified activity, has made new businesses move in and made the established businesses more prosperous.

But these things didn't happen without a great deal of effort on the part of the community itself....

Who is needed? Everybody. And especially men. There are a large number of male parts to be filled from this county. That does not mean there are no parts for women and girls. It's just that sometimes it's a little more difficult to convince "the old man" that he could ever do anything like act....

You don't know anything about acting? Fine! Neither will most of your neighbors who will be trying out. Your director doesn't expect you to. That's part of his job, to show you what to do.... Along with the director there will be several college trained people working in the play to act as guides for those who have never been on a stage before....

I think I can say, without any reservations, that those who work in Walk Toward the Sunset will find this summer to be one of the most exciting and rewarding times they have ever spent.

Welton needed a minimum of twenty or thirty extras to fill out the crowd scenes, but he made clear in the article that he could use as many as two hundred—the more the better. Significant public involvement in the play would certainly translate into increased local interest and better ticket sales. Welton wasn't likely to turn down anyone who wanted to be in the cast.[18]

---

[18] Welton, "Drama Try-Outs Saturday at Elementary School," 5.

The response to the try-outs was less than satisfactory. Getting people in a tiny rural community to voluntarily go onto a stage and perform in a play was a difficult challenge. Virtually none of the locals had ever acted; few had ever *thought* of acting. Men were particularly resistant to the idea; in their experience, acting was not something a man did. It would have been just about as easy to persuade them to put on pink tutus and attempt ballet dancing in public. The poor turnout was blamed on an alumni banquet held the same night as the try-out, so another try-out was scheduled for the following Saturday. While a few people showed interest, it was clear that more people would be needed for the production. No further auditions were scheduled, however.

Dave Behan chose Scott Collins to fill an important technical position. Collins, then a student at Lincoln Memorial University at Harrogate, Tennessee, had done audio-visual work as a student at Hancock County High School. "Because of my training in school," Collins recalled, "I was brought in to be the person who did all the lighting and audio, and I was kind of an understudy for one of the cast members."[19]

Meanwhile, the HCDA arranged for housing for the summer for Welton, Behan, and the Carson-Newman students who would be in the play. Some of them would be staying with Mrs. Edna Jones on weekends once the play got started. Others would have cots in the basement of Elmer and Hazel Turner, who lived less than fifty yards from the entrance to the amphitheater. Elmer Turner, a former Farm Agent and now an administrator with the Hancock County school system, was one of the founding members of the HCDA. His wife, Hazel, of Melungeon ancestry, taught fifth grade in the elementary school, behind which the amphitheater was sited.

Kyle Greene and the Project Mainstream workers brought in wood and rails from some old farm buildings for use at the amphitheater. The wood was donated to the drama project and was used to build the ticket booth, concession stand, and crafts building. Some of the locals were embarrassed by the rustic look of the recycled lumber, but the authenticity of the buildings would turn out to be well-received by playgoers. The old rails were used to build a rail fence around the site.

Meanwhile, the HCDA hired a publicity agent. Herbert J. "Jack" Love of Jefferson City, where Carson-Newman College was located, was brought in to get publicity for the drama and build public interest. One of his first acts was to get John Lee Welton and Mollie Bowlin on Knoxville television. Mollie Bowlin

---

[19] Scott Collins interview.

played the mountain dulcimer and had responded to Welton's invitation for musicians to try out for places in the cast. The pair appeared on *The Sunday Show* on WATE-TV, Channel 6, at 12:30 p.m. on Sunday, 8 June. They discussed the upcoming outdoor drama and Mollie played her dulcimer.[20]

On 12 June, the *Post* carried an engagement announcement for two of Hancock County's VISTA workers. Julie McDevitt worked in the Seal-Mathis community. She was a registered nurse from Cuyahoga Falls, Ohio, and a graduate of Ohio State University. Her fiancé was Peter Dodge of Ann Arbor, Michigan, who had served with VISTA in Hancock County from August 1967 to August 1968. He was now Specialist Fourth Class Dodge, a preventive medicine specialist with the United States Army, and would be spending the next year in Thailand. The wedding was tentatively scheduled for summer 1970.[21]

VISTA workers were in the news again the following week, but it wasn't a feel-good wedding announcement. *Post* editor John Montgomery, in what amounted to a multi-page editorial, wrote,

> The VISTA now serving in Hancock County[,] in appreciation of their efforts over the past year[,] failed to get a well deserved pat on the back last Friday night at the Citizens Participation Committee meeting held in Sneedville.
>
> What they did get in place of the pat on the back, was an undeserved kick—a little lower down.
>
> The Hancock County Citizens Representation Committee headed by Chairman Arnold Johnson, whose position in this authority is somewhat in question, voted not to replace the VISTA in the various Target Areas of Hancock County this summer. They did vote to have the VISTA Health Team operate in the county.
>
> However, by voting not to retain the valuable services offered by the VISTA, this small group of men who did the voting and which is really not entirely representative of the county as a whole, especially the poverty areas and the people most directly affected by the services of the VISTA, they may have placed this much needed Health Team service in jeopardy.
>
> In other words, the feeling in many quarters is that we just might not get it. After all, how can you have VISTA and not have VISTA?
>
> Chairman Arnold Johnson ??? voted in favor of the resolution not to replace the VISTA. Question: Does the chairman have a vote[?] Answer: As far as can be determined not unless the vote of the main body ends in a tie.

---

[20] Bowlin, "Drama News," 5 June 1969, 4.
[21] "VISTAs Announce Wedding Plans," 5.

In which area does Arnold Johnson live and which area does he represent? The answer of course must be Vardy. But it seems that on July 5, 1968 that the Vardy Community Club elected Willis P. Gibson to represent them at the Office of Economic Opportunity (O.E.O.) functions, of which the Hancock County Citizens Participation Committee is formed under.

Does Vardy have two representatives?

To say that something needs explaining here would be putting it mildly.

According to a notarized letter received by the Office of Economic Opportunity in Kingsport, Willis P. Gibson, duly elected by the Vardy Community Club, when he attended the C.P.C. meetings was given little or no voice, nor vote and if he wanted to attend, only did so as an interested spectator.

Some of those who may object to this, may say he didn't attend very often. Would you, if you were the person supposed to be representing this area and had no [voice] and no vote?

Others who voted in favor of the resolution not to retain the VISTA were Don Trent, Elmer Turner, Claude Collins and Warren Hurrell.

Trent said as a magistrate he had received complaints about the VISTA. He only named one of the youths in the complaint.

Because of a possible indiscretion of one person working with a program should the whole program be dropped[?] No is what the answer should be, especially if this supposed indiscretion cannot be proved.

To Magistrate Trent who is somewhat familiar with a little law in his capacity as magistrate, we could say if someone has done something legally wrong then take it to court.

"Don't gossip about it," as many of our good local citizens are now doing...[22]

It's easy to imagine the kind of rumors about the VISTAs that circulated around the county. Young men and women from other parts of the country, with strange accents; the men with hair a bit longer than the norm for Hancock County, the women with skirts a bit shorter—of course there was gossip about them, if for no other reason than the locals were bored with gossiping about each other.

It should be remembered that two of the previous year's female VISTAs were allegedly the targets of a rumor campaign started by the school superintendent. Magistrate Trent apparently did not elaborate on the nature of the complaint he had received, nor did he say there was any validity to the complaint. Since he was presumably aware of the laws concerning slander, it's not surprising that he didn't elaborate. Anyway, he didn't have to; the local rumor mill would

---

[22] Montgomery, "C.P.C. Votes to Discontinue Future Hancock VISTA Programs," 1, 3.

provide details, whether true or not. Were the VISTAs having sex, smoking marijuana, or traveling to Virginia to buy alcohol? Maybe. Certainly the rumor mill had them doing that and even more. But, as Montgomery pointed out in his article, if a VISTA had violated the law, he or she should be charged. If not, then the gossips should just shut up.

Rumored indiscretions, however, were not the reason Elmer Turner gave for voting not to have the VISTAs return. He told Montgomery he felt the individual VISTAs could do little in one year, that two years would be better. Turner had a point; it would take a year for many of the county residents served by VISTA to begin to feel comfortable with these young outsiders, and it would take at least a year for the VISTAs to become familiar enough with the power structure of Hancock County to become effective. However, VISTA was set up for one-year "tours of duty," and that was unlikely to change.

Claude Collins's reason for voting for the resolution was not apparent in the newspaper article. "Claude Collins justified his vote with a single shake of his head and a few words of which the meaning was taken to be that he wouldn't comment so there would be nothing about his feelings or reasons put in the paper."[23]

When asked about his vote forty-seven years later, Collins explained that he felt the VISTAs were given little or no direction from local authorities, that their effectiveness was thus hindered, and that if Hancock County wasn't going to use them effectively, they would do more good serving somewhere else.[24]

Elmer Turner and Claude Collins were not stereotypical small-town men, provincial in their attitudes and unfamiliar with the outside world. Both were educated men who had attended college and graduate school and had lived in other places. Collins had lived in Ellicott City Maryland, just west of Baltimore, where many Hancock County expatriates had moved in the 1940s and 1950s. Turner and Collins had both worked tirelessly to improve Hancock County, and neither was likely to reject help from outsiders due to suspicion or provincialism.

But Turner and Collins were not representative of the county as a whole. Steve Nichandros recalled difficulty in connecting with the people whom he was trying to help. When asked if the locals were welcoming to the VISTAs, he replied,

No, I would say not. Obviously, there were a select few that were. There were some people that were, and they really stand out as being special people,

[23] Ibid.
[24] Claude Collins interview (2016).

just because they were—let's use the words "forward thinking." Another way of saying it is "unusual for Hancock County." They were not outsiders but they had a surprisingly worldly view, compared to most Hancock Countians.

Did you encounter any hostility from the locals as a VISTA?

I remember accidentally winding up on someone's property, and being told later, "Well, that's a moonshine person." (laughs) That was a pretty big deal! That's probably not a good example, because that's the only example of someone being outwardly hostile, as opposed to someone quietly not wanting to have you around.

I was just wondering what kind of reception you got.

Cold. Cold is a good word. And we were told by the other two VISTAs that were there that really what our job was, was to get to know people, because you couldn't—nothing was going to happen until then. And what I would have called taking a few weeks to get to know somebody, it was probably, the honest truth, might have been a few years. I'd just say there were cultural differences between Hancock County and other places that are more urban, more modern. I remember at some point, after about three months, we were all bragging about how we had really gotten to know people in our community and we were accepted. And maybe three months after that we started to find out we had overstated it. (laughs)

How did you come to that realization?

I think it was Mary, or one of the VISTAs that lived where Mary lived—that told me they had really gotten into good communication and was accepted as a friend. But that was with just one person. I think I got to that point with my landlord.[25]

Mary Van Nest, *nee* Bowler, recalled her experience in Hancock County as a mixture of successes and resistance from the local power structure.

Actually we were supposed to be community organizers; that's what we were told, that's how we were described, but we met with some resistance from some of the local men in power. They were kind of suspicious of us and didn't share their power very easily. I know we had some disagreements with a couple of them. We tried to get water into our district; most of the people there had no running water. We tried to get a water system in. That was one of the projects. I think we tried to do too much, you know, too many different things rather than focus on any one, and we didn't really have a whole lot of guidance or direction once we got there, quite honestly—kind of on our own,

---

[25] Nichandros interview.

I think. But it was a very positive experience. We felt like we got so much more than we gave the people; we just loved them so much. We became really close to a lot of them, a lot of the local tobacco farmers.

Van Nest recalled Arnold Johnson with a lack of fondness.

Arnold Johnson—there were two Arnold Johnsons. One was a farmer in our district; he was married to Margaret and he was a good friend of ours. And the other Arnold Johnson was the head of the Community Action group that was supposed to be supervising us. And he had a sort of condescending attitude toward us and kind of a—I don't know; there was a lot of friction. He did not accept us, and he and a couple of his cronies, maybe, would have been the only people that would be critical of us or the college kids.

How do you mean "condescending"? Looking at you like "do-gooders"?
Yeah, exactly. "Coming here to tell us how to run our town, our county." There were some not very pleasant scenes between us and them. I remember I walked out on one meeting. I could get very indignant at that time, and I just didn't like it and walked out. But he was the only one who had that— he's the only one that's stands out in my mind, having that kind of attitude. He didn't want us there; he felt we were "activists," coming from the North, blah blah blah.

In his *Post* article, Montgomery cited the projects VISTAs either initiated or contributed to, including the outdoor drama, the crafts organization, the special education program started by VISTA Mary Bowler, the Big Springs bridge project, the Community Water Project, and others. He also pointed out that several of the VISTAs were planning to extend their service in Hancock County for another year, and that others intended to stay in the county after their year of service was completed—without pay and at their own expense—in order to help with the outdoor drama and the craft organization.

Montgomery concluded his article by pointing out that an election would be held in July to select members of the Citizens Participation Committee. "We can change some of the things wrong with this group there. Be sure to attend when the meeting is announced."[26]

The next issue of the *Post*, on 26 June, took a much more conciliatory tone on the issue of the CPC vote.

After hearing the pros and cons of the VISTA story for the past week there remains little or no doubt in the minds of most people that the five men who

---

[26] Montgomery, "C.P.C. Votes," 3.

voted not to have VISTA in Hancock County in the coming year took this action not out of malice, but because they sincerely belived [*sic*] this was the only course of action available to them at the time.... Most of the gossip angle has died away and from what can be learned the real reason seemes [*sic*] to be in the understanding of the over-all VISTA program and in matters of supervision.

However, it is still felt by this newspaper and many people throughout the county that VISTA should stay.

The problems regarding supervision, over-all aims of the VISTA program, conduct and appearance of the VISTA can and should be resolved.

Montgomery acknowledged that cultural and generational differences were a factor in the local acceptance—or lack thereof—of the VISTAs.

They have been criticized for their appearance, everything from haircuts, hairdos, clothing, etc. There is no doubt that they should be setting at the very least a good example in these areas of personal appearance.... What most people are saying is that they could be a lot neater and cleaner.

Each year it seems when a new group of VISTA head here from their training that a good part of them look more poverty stricken than anybody in this or any other county...But remember their reasons for joining this program is to help and this year and in past years in Hancock County they have helped.[27]

While some Hancock Countians may have been critical of the VISTAs, the cast of *Walk Toward the Sunset,* coming to Hancock County for the last two weeks of rehearsals before opening night, had some criticisms of Hancock Countians. When director John Lee Welton and the cast arrived in Sneedville, they discovered that the amphitheater was far from completed.

We had sent plans up for the theatre site to be constructed, which was a gully behind the school. We had sent those up, oh, several months in advance. And we started rehearsals here on campus, with the core of students who were going to be playing the leads. And then we were going to go up there and bring in the townspeople for the smaller roles and the crowd scenes and things of that sort. We had two weeks to rehearse up there. So we rehearsed here, on the Carson-Newman campus, and then two weeks before the show opened we went up there expecting to walk in and find a theatre. We found a gully behind the school and that was it, with a pile of dirt at the bottom of it. The Hancock County people, bless their hearts, just wanted to make sure they did

[27] "VISTA Question," 1, 2, 6.

it right, so they waited until we got up there and made sure we could oversee it and see how it was done.

In 2011, Welton spoke as part of a panel discussion on the play at Walters State Community College in Morristown.

> David Behan…designed the theatre sets and the theatre, and sent the plans to the county workers, to build seating on the hillside and a natural stage at the bottom…. We planned two weeks of rehearsals on campus [at Carson-Newman], then we were going to go to Sneedville for the last two weeks…. Well, after our two weeks at Carson-Newman College, we went to Sneedville for the last two weeks of rehearsal. We walked up to the theatre site eagerly— and our hearts fell. There was a hillside and a pile of dirt at the bottom. The county workers who were supposed to be working on it, in sometimes typical mountain fashion, said, "Well, we weren't exactly sure what you wanted, so we thought we'd wait until you got up here and do like you wanted to." (laughter from audience)[28]

In 1970, Welton would describe his dismay in an article for *The Student*.

> Although two years of planning had gone into the drama, the local work force simply had not moved on the construction of the theater. The people of Hancock County have a fierce pride, and, rather than make a mistake in following the theater plans, they simply waited until the production force arrived to make sure it was done right. Besides, the fund-raising campaign had brought in only about a third of the money needed, even though hundreds of Hancock residents had donated the little cash they could. There were no stage walls, no dressing rooms, no seats, no ticket booth; the recently-ordered lighting equipment was tied up in a rail strike—and with only three weeks until opening night.[29]

The county's VISTA workers turned out to be essential in getting the play ready for opening, taking vacant roles in the cast and helping to complete the amphitheater. Steve Nichandros recalled that the VISTAs' participation in *Walk Toward the Sunset*, to some extent, compensated for the lack of participation on the part of some locals.

---

[28] Welton interview (2002); Welton panel discussion.

[29] Welton, "Drama in Sneedville? You're Kidding," 46. In this article, Welton says he and the cast of Carson-Newman students arrived in Sneedville three weeks before opening night. In subsequent interviews and presentations, he would recall their arrival as two weeks before opening.

It was shortly after (the cast from Carson-Newman) got there, it was determined that we weren't going to have anybody volunteering from the community [to be in the play]. I remember it being kind of a last minute—well, whatever we have to do, we're gonna do, because we didn't want them to not have it. If that's what it takes to make it happen, we'll take the parts that are needed.

It's not surprising that [the locals] weren't keen on it. I think there was a tendency for—anything that was new or suggested by—well, there were different levels of outsiders. The people in my community would say, "Well, that was suggested by people with money who live in town." And even though that's not an outsider…We were not surprised when we would talk to people and ask them, "Do you want to have something to do with it," we got a pretty flat response on that.

Was it that they didn't think it would work, or was it the subject matter?

It was not the subject matter; that was my impression. It was just a fancy idea, and why would you want to do that? And who's going to cross Clinch Mountain to come see a play? That was the big hurdle—why would the county spend a dime on that? It would be money down the drain because no one would drive to see it. I remember there was some opposition in my community because it was considered entertainment, and that wasn't something you would do. Why do you need to put on entertainment? It was frivolous.

We probably were not planning to be so involved in general; we weren't trying to do things ourselves. But I do remember we were involved in the construction, along with some local people. I remember one of the VISTAs, Mike [Hughes], and I remember the two of us worked on it. That would explain why we did…I remember it was a gravel stage. I don't think that's what was originally intended; I think it had to do with the amount of money that was raised. I think that required some adjustments for the director. I remember working on the seating; it was pretty bare.[30]

Welton recalled two very busy weeks, getting ready for opening night,

Well, they, and the cast, crew, and anybody else who they could twist their arm, wheelbarrowed dirt…transplanted trees, built a fence, built seating along the hillside, built the two stages—and this during the two weeks we were supposed to be up there rehearsing. [We] worked all day long; we'd take a supper break, clean up a little bit, and come back and rehearsed from about 7:00 until about 10:00 each evening.[31]

---

[30] Nichandros interview.
[31] Welton interview (2002).

Raymond Buffington was a speech and theatre major at Carson-Newman College, and was a member of the cast of *Walk Toward the Sunset*.

> Well, at that point in my life I wasn't sure what an outdoor theatre should have looked like, but when we got there it was (pause) surprisingly rustic. (laughs)
>
> *So I suppose some of the first work you had to do was to get the theatre in some sort of shape for the production.*
> That sounds about right. I don't honestly remember any particular details because there *were* crew people who had been doing work. It was, again, very, very primitive, and essentially the amphitheater was just a big...ditch.[32]

Welton and the cast from Carson-Newman worked hard to make a good impression on the people of Sneedville. "[T]here was a great deal of suspicion as we came in there. As a matter of fact, to overcome that, we came into the community, we went around to all the stores, I asked the cast to go around to buy their supplies at each of the stores, maybe buy just one thing at each of the stores, to get acquainted with the community... and let them get acquainted with us."[33]

Doing business in local stores introduced the cast members to the merchants. On Sunday, they met even more locals in church.

> On the first Sunday morning all of the cast showed up for the morning worship service at least ten minutes early. Two of the musically talented members were asked to lead the singing and play the piano for the service—a job they were invited to keep for the rest of the summer.
>
> The students felt the walls of distrust were starting to crumble. However, their early missionary work apparently had not spread far enough. A preacher in an outlying area found his sermon topic for several Sundays in "the sin and shame brought to our fair county by this 'drammar' and them hippies runnin' it."[34]

The concept of the "drammar" itself was alien to many of the county residents who had never seen a play of any kind. And the subject of this particular "drammar" made many of the locals uneasy. Welton tried to dispel their fears.

> We opened up the rehearsals; we never had a closed rehearsal. People could walk in, sit down, watch us work, and realize that we were not there to make

---

[32] Buffington interview.
[33] Welton interview (2002).
[34] Welton, "Drama in Sneedville?" 47.

fun of the Melungeons but rather to try and promote an interest in their heritage and a pride in their heritage.... [O]nce we got the show open, people were able to sit at rehearsals, as I said, and watch and see that we weren't doing that, and then once we got the show open there tended to be a great deal more enthusiasm.[35]

While the director and cast worked to make a good impression on Sneedville, the leaders of the town were working to make a good impression on the visitors that would be coming into town. Most of those visitors would be coming from Morristown over Clinch Mountain on Highway 31. They would come into town across the Clinch River bridge and be treated to a view that impressed Raymond Buffington both positively and negatively.

I can remember vividly to this day arriving into Sneedville, across the river, and the first view of the town in that little tiny valley there was just totally charming, you know, it was a very pretty sight, a pretty setting. It was almost a storybook, just that entrance right there into the town. Of course it changed as soon as you drove 500 yards, but it was a very, very pretty entrance to the town.... Coming in it was a very pretty sight, but if you got a little bit further in there were old rusted out cars and farm equipment and refrigerators and all kinds of things like that on the sides of the road. What could have been a real pretty entrance into the town proper was a mess because of that stuff. So that was one of the projects for these guys, the Happy Pappies, to clear out, to move all that stuff so that as tourists came into town, they wouldn't see it. And what they did was, they removed it all, but they took it through Sneedville to the other side of town and dumped it off over there. (laughs) Our little college-educated liberal-minded do-gooding play-actors' point of view was not always in touch with reality there on the ground in Sneedville. But I remember those things pretty clearly and they stuck with me over the years.

Working with the people in Hancock County also exposed Buffington to something else he'd never experienced, something that remained in his memory more than four decades later.

The men who built the amphitheater...the site was constructed by OEO, the Office of Economic Opportunity, which was a federally-funded thing, and they were called Mainstream workers, and a man named Kyle Greene was, I guess, the head guy. I remember locally they were referred to as the "Happy Pappies," because I think they were all middle-aged men who couldn't work or didn't work or had no jobs. And I remember—this is going to be hard for

---

[35] Welton interview (2002).

you to picture, maybe, if I don't explain it clearly—I was a pretty well educated kid, I guess. Again, I was a kid, and I hadn't traveled all that much. Carson-Newman opened a lot of doors for me. Some of the men we met there were the first functionally illiterate people I'd ever met in my life, which was kind of a strange thing, which is probably why I remember it. And one of these men—I don't remember if it was Kyle Greene or not; I do remember his name was Kyle; I think that summer I met more people named Kyle than I ever heard of in my life. And I remember one of the jobs that this guy had to do was to paint parking signs for the traffic that would be coming into Sneedville. And the way he went about it—because I don't think he knew how to read or write—but it was his task to do these parking signs and I remember seeing these things and I just marvel at it because now I'm in education and I teach kids how to read and to write. These signs were just simple little hand-painted wooden things, and all they had was the word "parking" and an arrow pointing. And if the arrow pointed toward the right and the word "parking" was written above it, that's what you would expect to see. But if the sign was directing you to go to the left, and the arrow was pointing to the left, they wrote the letters "parking" *backwards*, starting at the right side of the sign and writing them backwards toward the left; it was like a mirror image of the proper way to do it. And that has stuck with me all these years. It's not like a dyslexic kind of expression; it was literally a mirror image. And, you know, to someone who doesn't read or write, it makes perfect sense. It's very logical to just turn the arrow around and turn the letters around, too. It was a very interesting thing; I'd never seen anything like it before or since.

The amphitheater remained, as Buffington described it, "rustic," but as opening night approached, it came together well enough.

It seems to me the seating area was boards or logs; it was a tiered amphitheater, or that's how it ended up being constructed. The stage area was, uh, let's see—I remember there was a central playing area, then there was a small stage left area, and there was probably a small stage right area, too, I believe. The stage left area—that's where my scene in Act 1 was, okay; I think that was an interior, and so it was constructed—probably board walls or flats or something, I don't recall precisely. And then on the stage right, that was probably—I recall foliage, bushes around there, so it was probably an exterior, but a small, confined area. And then the main stage was all exterior; I seem to recall board fencing was the backdrop of the whole thing. And then Newman's Ridge was right beyond that, so it was ideal, it was really perfect for the show. It was really rough, unfinished—you know, a lot of outdoor theatre can be that way. There was no sidewalk or finished backstage; it was all dirt. But I remember all those kind of sounds and smells you get in the evening in the mountains; there were cattle on the hill behind us at different times. So it was just ideal. I remember liking it a lot.[36]

Workers completed construction of the concession building, the box office, and the Sunrise Craft House building at the drama site. The buildings were made of re-purposed barn wood. The craft organization chose Geraldine Southern of Mulberry Gap to be president, with Dolly Gilliam elected vice-president, Hattie Parkey as secretary, and Margaret Johnson as treasurer.[37]

The Drama Association received a donation from a group of soldiers serving in Vietnam. Staff Sergeant Rector Bowlin, the nephew of Mr. and Mrs. Bill Tyler of Sneedville, along with four of his buddies, identified only as Sp/4s Kiebach, Boos, Young, and Jordan, sent a contribution of $50 to the organization.[38]

Reporter Willard Yarbrough and the *Knoxville News-Sentinel* gave the drama a pre-opening boost by designating opening weekend in Sneedville as the paper's "Trip of the Month."

> You've heard about and read about the mysterious Melungeons of New-man's Ridge whose origin is lost in romantic antiquity. Now you can see them and talk with them.
>
> Better still, you can see them perform in the new outdoor drama, "Walk Toward the Sunset: The Melungeon Story," written by noted playwright Kermit Hunter and based on Jesse Stuart's novel "Daughter of the Legend."[39]
>
> The July Trip of the Month coincides with the opening of the drama about the maligned Melungeons. But the three-day weekend trip also includes a July 4 horse show and fireworks, a giant parade by East Tennessee Rescue Squads on Saturday, three days of barbeque, three days of mountain crafts exhibits, and even tours into Melungeon Country such as Newman's Ridge, Mulberry, Little Sycamore and Vardy—all communities near Sneedville.
>
> "We have planned hospitality and a welcome for News-Sentinel Trippers that will long be remembered," said Miss Martha Collins.
>
> And who is Miss Collins? She's N-S Trip Host Committee chairman and president of Citizens Bank, where she has served for 50 years. More than that, she herself is of Melungeon extraction. Her own theory of the Melungeon origin will be told in a later article.[40]

---

[36] Buffington interview.

[37] Haralson, "Craft News," 1.

[38] Bowlin, "Drama News," 26 June 1969, 1.

[39] Yarbrough had covered this story from the beginning when the idea was to dramatize Stuart's book. The play written by Kermit Hunter had no relation to Stuart's novel.

[40] Yarbrough, "Come Enjoy a Piece of History with Melungeons," 1.

Although the Green Top Inn on Main Street in Sneedville served excellent food, its rough exterior was likely to scare away out-of-towners. A new eatery, the Sunset Restaurant, had opened in anticipation of serving the tourists. Barbeque chicken or beef would be available for $1.59, and for *News-Sentinel* Trippers, full dinners would be available at the special rate of 75 cents and 60 cents—bargain prices even for 1969.

The only motel in Sneedville was the five-room Town Motel, located above a beauty shop. However, free primitive campsites were available on Newman's Ridge and along the Clinch River. "As long as rooms last," wrote Yarbrough, "Sneedville townspeople will host overnight guests in their homes." Most of the Trippers, however, would be staying at motels in Tazewell, Bean Station, and Morristown, and taking chartered buses into Sneedville.

While Yarbrough's earlier articles on the outdoor drama indicated that no Melungeons were involved with the project, a photograph of Kyle Greene, Kyle Turner, Frank Louthron, Clyde (Susie) Roberts, and Obie Collins working on the amphitheater was captioned "Melungeons All," and stated that the men were proud of their Melungeon ancestry.[41] John Lee Welton recalled how a sense of pride among local Melungeons had developed as work on the play progressed. "We had people coming and saying—toward the end of the season, especially—who had never said they were Melungeons, to come up and kind of nudge me on the shoulder and say, 'I'm a Melungeon—did you know that?' So we were quite proud that at least that change had come about."[42]

Despite Yarbrough's claim that Trippers would be able to see and talk to Melungeons, he qualified that with a warning:

> Now a sincere word of caution to Trippers: Don't come rushing into Sneedville, jump out of your car, and ask the first person you see, "Where's a Melungeon?" The name was once a fighting word, a bad word, and a Melungeon didn't want to be called a Melungeon. While this is rapidly changing, and folk now are seeking to prove they are of Melungeon ancestry, there are still some sensitive men and women among this maligned people.
>
> Listen to Kyle Greene, a Melungeon himself who as coordinator of Operation Mainstream has directed construction of Sunset Hills Amphitheater: "If your Trippers come in here and yell out, 'Where's a Melungeon? Where's one? I want to see a Melungeon!', he might wind up with a face full of

---

[41] Yarbrough, "Trippers Take Melungeon Tour," 21.
[42] Welton interview (2002).

clinched fingers. But if the visitor asks how he can see or meet a Melungeon, my people will be glad to cooperate. After a century of ridicule some of us are still sensitive."[43]

However, the day before opening night of *Walk Toward the Sunset*, Yarbrough informed prospective *News-Sentinel* Trippers that Claude Collins would lead tours into Melungeon country.

> A Melungeon has agreed to conduct tours for News-Sentinel Trippers beginning tomorrow deep into Hancock County where descendants of these mysterious settlers live today.
> He is William C. Collins, who will drive a lead car when Trippers can go in groups of three or more vehicles in a caravan.... Newman's Ridge, Mulberry, Vardy and Little Sycamore are the community names where the caravans will move. Collins will explain Melungeon territory and, as your guide, you should heed his advice on your deportment.[44]

Mayor Charles Turner wasn't in town that weekend before the play opened. He was being honored at the thirtieth annual convention of the Tennessee Municipal League in Gatlinburg. The TML named Turner "Typical Mayor of the Year," an honor Turner had missed by a single vote the previous year. Turner received this honor out of a field of more than three hundred Tennessee mayors and received a certificate citing his "outstanding public service and devotion to duty." The citation went on to commend Turner for "his leadership which has helped bring an infusion of governmental and private funds into the county to provide public facilities and new jobs for his isolated municipality." The citation mentioned, among Turner's accomplishments, the development of an industrial park and recruitment of Sneedville's first industry, Tennessee Electric Motors; completion of a $300,000 sanitary sewer project; a city street paving program carried out with a combination of federal and local funds; the repaving of Highway 31 between Sneedville and Mooresburg; and the beginning of an $800,000 project to build twenty-two units of low-rent housing in Sneedville.[45]

On the eve of the opening of *Walk Toward the Sunset*, the tiny, impoverished town of Sneedville was riding the crest of a wave of accomplishment and

---

[43] Yarbrough, "Come Enjoy a Piece of History with Melungeons," 1.
[44] Yarbrough, "Trippers Take Melungeon Tour," 21.
[45] "Sneedville Mayor Named 'Mayor of the Year," 1.

good publicity. There was just the little matter of a bomb threat that could ruin the play's opening night.

8

SHOWTIME

Afterward, no one could say how the rumor got started, but by lunchtime on Wednesday, 2 July, nearly everyone in Sneedville was talking about a bomb that would explode at the amphitheater before opening night on Thursday. In a way, it was like a manifestation of the collective skepticism with which so many Hancock County residents had viewed the entire outdoor drama project. If "nothing we do ever works," then something would have to happen before opening night to keep the show from going on. At that point, it would have taken a bomb to stop the momentum of *Walk Toward the Sunset*.

Of course, there was no bomb, but Claude Collins and some others spent the night in the amphitheater to make certain nothing happened. "We were really worried," he recalls. "We sat up the entire night at the theatre, afraid somebody would bother it."[1]

The cast members weren't told about the bomb threat. Years later, Raymond Buffington thought that not telling the cast was a good idea: "Sometimes you're better off not knowing."[2] VISTA and cast member Mary Bowler was certainly better off not knowing about it; when told about it four decades later, she was shocked.

> No! (rising inflection—obviously this is the first she's heard about it.) A bomb threat?
>
> *Maybe you weren't told about it.*
> You're kidding! Opening night—the very first night?
>
> *It was the night before opening night.*
> No! (incredulous) They never found out who did it?
>
> *I think Claude Collins had a suspicion about who might have started the rumor. The person who owned the property the amphitheater was on wasn't told exactly how the property would be used because of the stigma about Melungeons.*

---

[1] Claude Collins interview (2002).
[2] Buffington interview.

Oh…interesting. You know, now that you say that, it does sound familiar, what you said about the landowner. Hmm—well.[3]

Director John Lee Welton had a different take on the source of the bomb
rumor. "As I understand, [it was] one of the more fiery Melungeons who thought
we were coming in to make fun of them and deride them in different ways."

Costumes were, of course, a crucial part of the play. Given the last-minute
effort it took to build the stage, it wouldn't have been surprising for Welton to
learn that the costumes weren't ready in time for opening night. But he had some
help in that department. "Fortunately a fellow named [Dave] Behan, who was
with Tusculum College, had just finished doing their, I think it was their cen-
tennial celebration," Welton recalled, "and had done a pageant over there, so we
borrowed their costumes, borrowed some of their set pieces, and were able to get
by on those for that rush issue of getting the thing put together."[4]

As audience members approached the ticket booth, manned by Elmer
Turner, they were treated to the dulcimer playing of Mollie Bowlin. The dulcimer is a member of the zither family of instruments, and the fretted dulcimer
Mollie Bowlin played had its origin in Europe but was primarily associated with
the Appalachian Mountains. Mollie was accompanied by cast member Reba
Ramsey, who sang the Appalachian ballads and Carter Family songs Mollie
played on the dulcimer.

Some of the locals were embarrassed by the re-purposed wood used for the
construction of the ticket booth, the concession stand, and the Sunrise Craft
House. They felt that the buildings, constructed of boards salvaged by Kyle
Greene's Happy Pappies from an old unused church, looked like shacks. But the
rustic structures added to the overall atmosphere and were much admired by the
out-of-town visitors.

Tickets for the play were $2.50 for adults, $1.00 for children. Shortly after
8:00 p.m., with the summer sun low in the sky, the audience started filing into
the 750-seat amphitheater. At the bottom of the hill was the stage—an elevated
surface made of dirt and gravel. The back wall of the stage was a high fence of
weather-beaten boards, such as might be found on an old barn. The side stages
were slightly raised, and on the right-side stage was the front of a church, made
of the same weather-beaten wood as the back wall. There was a low steeple, and
two steps lead up to the front door. The other side stage had bushes and small
trees and would be used to represent outdoor settings. The program—a single

[3] Van Nest interview.
[4] Welton interview (2002).

sheet mimeographed on both sides—listed the cast members. Most of the cast had roles in both acts, and some had multiple roles within a single act.

The setting for the first act is a village along the Holston River in August 1782. There was still daylight as Mike Atherton walked out to center stage and spoke to the audience.

> Good evening. Welcome to Hancock County. My name in the drama is Pat Gibson. I play the part of a Melungeon. If you don't know what that is, perhaps our play will tell you. We are going back a long way, to the year 1782. The Revolutionary War had just ended, and I was living with friends in the wilderness country down west of what is now Knoxville.[5] At that time it was still part of North Carolina.[6]

Atherton starts off, then stops and smiles at the audience. "Oh, I forgot: my sweetheart and I talked so long one Sunday morning that we were late for church." He then hurries offstage.[7]

A choir is heard singing "Holy Manna." A man tiptoes out of the front door of the church. He's wearing knee-breeches, a loose shirt, an open vest, and shoes with large buckles. His escape from the church is thwarted by a woman in a homespun dress and bonnet; presumably his wife, she takes him by the ear and leads him back inside. Two boys furtively escape the church and begin tossing a rag ball back and forth. A grim-looking woman emerges and commands them back into the building, delivering a swat across the rear to each of them as they pass.

A young man and a young woman approach the church, holding hands. The character of Pat Gibson has already been introduced to the audience, who will soon learn that the young woman is Alisee Collins. The two young people are obviously sweethearts and have lost track of time, arriving at church too late to go inside. The singing ends and the minister pronounces the benediction. Pat and Alisee brush their clothes and fix their hair, then back away from the church a few steps to wait for the congregation to emerge. They notice that they are holding hands; they let go and step apart as the congregation fills the stage. A

---

[5] Although the script has Atherton saying his character lived "in the wilderness country west of what is now Knoxville," the printed program sets the Melungeon village along the Holston River. There are references to the Holston River area elsewhere in the play. The Holston does not extend to the west of present-day Knoxville. It joins the French Broad River on the east side of Knoxville to form the Tennessee River.

[6] Script quotations in this chapter are from the 1969 version of *Walk Toward the Sunset*, the unpublished script by Kermit Hunter. The 1969 script is in the possession of John Lee Welton, who loaned it to the author.

[7] This spoken preamble to the play was dropped after the first season.

woman scolds Alisee for missing church; a man is likewise upbraiding Pat, but the Preacher calms the older folks with a few words and pats on the shoulders.

By now, the audience is aware that there are different types of people represented on stage. There are a few African Americans in the crowd. Other people smile and talk to them, but they stand slightly apart from the others. An Indian man and three Indian women are also in the group; the man wears a feather in his glossy braided black hair and wears buckskin, while the women wear narrow beaded headbands and skirts with horizontal stripes around the bottom. They also seem a part of the community and yet somehow separate. Most of the other people look like typical frontier men and women of the time, but with dark skin. Only the minister, Preacher Givens, is white.

Much care was taken by the director to select the appropriate makeup for each group. The black characters—played by white actors—have rich, dark-brown makeup, while the Indians—also played by whites—have a reddish tint and glossy black hair. The others have dark skin as well, but of a different tone, and several of them have blonde or light-colored hair. These people, the audience will learn, are the Melungeons.

Preacher Givens moves down to the center of the stage and looks at the sky.

> PREACHER: Looks like a right good day for the trip to Jonesboro. Who-all's a-goin'? Who's gonna do your talkin'?
>
> SYLVESTER: Preacher, we-all kinda hopin' you'd go along.
>
> PREACHER: I'll go with you, help argufy if you want me to. Trouble is, I don't read none too well. What if they fetch out a lotta papers or sumpin'?
>
> SYLVESTER (indicating the boy upstage) Pat Gibson's ma taught him to read. He reads better'n anybody, 'ceptin maybe his sweetheart Alisee. They both read, both talk real good.
>
> PREACHER: Well, they both got a heap o' good sense. You can tell that by the way they stayed away from my sermonizin'.

The Preacher summons Pat and Alisee. As they come down to the group, they both seem to be braced for further scolding. They both apologize for being late to church, but the Preacher cuts them off.

> PREACHER: Never mind. I can tell when the Devil gets into somebody, and you'uns got no Devil in you. You two figgerin' to get married?
>
> PAT: We are, Preacher. We've been talkin' a long time, I reckon since we were little 'uns.
>
> PREACHER: Well, that's the way it oughta be. One o' these days we'll have a real church weddin'.
>
> ALISEE: I always wanted a church weddin'.

> PREACHER: Meantime, we got work to do. Talkin' now about you two goin' to Jonesboro with these men to see John Sevier.
> ALISEE (in awe) Jonesboro?
> PAT: Why you want us along?
> PREACHER: 'Cause you read an' write, son, you and Alisee both. You got sumpin' not many of us have. That makes you important in this country, and don't you forget it. One o' these days you'll be a leader.

Putting his arm around Alisee, Pat acknowledges he'd been wanting to take Alisee to Jonesboro to buy material for a wedding dress. To pay for it, he had two sacks of ginseng, the roots of which were valued as a folk medicine. As the preacher and the others make their way home for the evening, Pat and Alisee move to the left side stage; Alisee sits on a rock while Pat paces back and forth.

> PAT: You know why they're goin' to Jonesboro?
> ALISEE: Somethin' about this bottom land here along the Holston River.
> PAT: Before my Ma died, she used to tell me about how they once lived way east o' here, along the ocean, in a big town. And then one day they all up and moved, wagons and baggage and all, out across the country till they hit the mountains, kinda the jumpin' off place to nowhere. Winter time…they lit out across the mountains in snow and sleet…finally got down into the valleys…Indians ever'where. Ma was just a little girl, maybe five or six years old…she watched 'em cut down trees and build houses…Indians sittin' around watchin'…she played with little Indian children, taught 'em to play a game called Chickamy Chickamy Craney Crow.

Pat dances a sort of hop-scotch step as Alisee laughs and asks about the game. Pat explains that it's "some kinda jumpin' around and singin'."

> ALISEE: You can jump around but you sure can't sing.
> PAT: All right Mistress Smart, you sing a little.
> ALISEE: Not unless you ask me right.
> PAT: (smiling and lifting her to her feet) Dear Miss Alisee Collins, will you be so kind as to sing Ca' the Yewes?
> ALISEE: (with a formal curtsey) Only because you insist.
> PAT: What do the words mean? Ca' the Yewes?
> ALISEE: Call the ewes—call the little sheep from the heather. That song came over from Scotland many years ago.
> PAT: Where did you learn it?
> ALISEE: From my mother—like you. Funny, us both being orphans.

Pat looks at Alisee, tenderly brushes her hair, then holds her as he gazes off into the distance with a worried expression. "Orphans," he says, "but that's not all."

Scene 1 ends as the waning summer sun dips below the western ridges and Pat and Alisee walk offstage. On a side stage, lights come up revealing John Sevier's office, signaling the beginning of scene 2. On opening night, the lighting equipment that had been ordered was still on a train somewhere, held up by the railroad strike. The lighting crew had hobbled together a system using lights borrowed from hither and yon, and the audience saw John Sevier, sitting at a rough table. He's dressed as we might imagine George Washington to be dressed, with riding trousers and boots. Daniel Boone enters the room; dressed in buckskin, he puts one foot on a chair and rests his chin on his hand.

SEVIER: You've been all over this country, from the coast into Kentucky. People say Daniel Boone knows every man, woman, and child in North Carolina and Virginia. Yet when I ask you about *these* people, you say you don't know.

BOONE: Well, I don't, and that's that. I don't know what they are, don't have the least idea where they come from. Melungeon...just what does that mean, colonel?

SEVIER: It must be French...my father is French...he says it sounds like "mélange," meaning mixture.

BOONE: Mixture of what?

SEVIER: If I knew that, I would have the answer. Are they part Indian?

BOONE: Whoever saw an Indian with yellow hair? Whoever saw a Neegro slave with yellow hair? With blue eyes?

SEVIER: Couldn't it be a mixture?

BOONE: I don't think so.

SEVIER: Why not?

BOONE: Somewhere along the line you'd see that straight black hair, or high cheekbones, or wide faces. If they were mixed with slaves, you'd see some kinky hair, or flat noses, or thick lips. You put a yellow cat and a black cat together, you get yellow and black cats.

SEVIER: Not always.

BOONE: Mr. Sevier, you can't tell me that a little mixture of Indian or Negro blood is gonna produce this kinda people. They're different. They look just exactly like you an' me, only their skin is a little darker. They don't look a bit like any Indians I ever saw or any slaves either, Course, they got Indians livin' among 'em, and they never turned their back on a runaway slave or anybody else needin' help, so they may have some mixture develop later. Anyway, they're a good kind of people. What's the problem?

SEVIER: No Indian or black man can own land. You know that. It's been on the statute books ever since these colonies existed.

BOONE: Ain't it about time to make some new statute books? We defeated the British—we got our own country here now—you yourself are talking about a new state out here—why can't they own land?

SEVIER: (rising grimly) You know why, Mr. Boone...white people won't
allow it.

BOONE: How do you know they ain't white people?

SEVIER: I don't. All I know is they got dark skin.

BOONE: And they claim some of the richest bottom land in this whole
country.

SEVIER: (bristling) What do you mean by that, Mr. Boone?

BOONE: You'd be glad to see 'em forced out, wouldn't you?

Sevier slams his hand on the table in anger and demands that Boone retract his
statement. Boone won't back down; the Melungeons live on land that future white
settlers will covet. Sevier insists that even if the Melungeons move out, he won't
benefit personally. "A fine help you are," he tells Boone. "I asked you to stop by on
your way back to Kentucky, and you end up by accusing me of stealing land."

Boone denies that he intended to make such an accusation and suggests that
perhaps Sevier feels guilty about what he knows is in store for the Melungeons.
"Maybe so, Mr. Boone," Sevier replies. "Perhaps I'm ashamed to admit that a man
with colored skin cannot own land in this territory."

Boone replies, "It's been my experience that a man can be good or bad, whether
he's black, or red, or white, or anything else." Boone has just stated the premise of
the play, the idea of tolerance and equality Kermit Hunter hopes the audience will
take from *Walk Toward the Sunset*.

But tolerance is not what Sevier has in mind today. White settlers want the
Melungeons' land, and Sevier wants Boone to talk to the Melungeons, to persuade
them to move away. Boone argues that whoever got there first and claimed the land
owned it. Sevier, however, knows the whites want the land and are putting pressure
on him to remove the dark-skinned people who already occupy it.

Pat, Alisee, Preacher Givens, and Mr. Sylvester arrive and are introduced to
Sevier and Boone.

SEVIER: I know why you're here, and I wish I could be more encouraging.

PREACHER: Col. Sevier, these people come into this country twenty,
thirty years ago, maybe longer. Who's got any better right to this land?

SEVIER: Preacher, I don't make laws. I don't judge human action. I too
left my home in Virginia to make a new place out here in the wilderness. I'm
just like everybody else

PAT: Col. Sevier, we are told that you intend to set up a new state.

SEVIER: If the people ask me, I will do whatever I can to help.

BOONE: Ain't you awful independent about human rights all of a sudden?

SEVIER: What does that mean?

BOONE: You took a company of men to King's Mountain, your brother died there, to make this country free. You've been a *leader* in persuadin' settlers to open up this land across the mountains. Now all of a sudden you do "whatever the people ask you." Just what do you mean by freedom, Colonel? What was you fightin' for at King's Mountain?

SEVIER: To protect my home! The British threatened to come and burn it down!

ALISEE: Shall we fight to protect *our* homes, Colonel?

Mr. Sylvester points out that he served during the Revolution. "I was at King's Mountain, Colonel Sevier, General Cleveland. This boy's pappy, Rafe Gibson, died from his wounds a few days later. I buried him myself."

SEVIER: I think I remember that man...dark skin...I thought he was a runaway slave. What did you do after King's Mountain?

SYLVESTER: I joined Daniel Morgan, went into South Carolina, finally went toward Yorktown. I saw Cornwallis surrender his sword to General Washington.

SEVIER: I'm proud to know you, Mr. Sylvester.

SYLVESTER: Corporal Sylvester, sir.

Sylvester snaps a salute to Sevier. Sevier hesitates, then returns the salute. Clearly, the Melungeons had fought for the new nation, just as Sevier had. The audience can clearly see the injustice of the situation. They can also see that John Sevier, a hero of early Tennessee history, is not quite so heroic in this situation. Alisee asks, "Why can't *we* buy our land?" Boone replies, "There's a law saying nobody but a white man can own land." There is an embarrassed silence, and the preacher turns away. He knows the Melungeons' argument is lost.

PAT: Col. Sevier, if you should set up a new state, would you have a law like that?

SEVIER: The people would make the laws, young man. The legislature.

BOONE: You mean, people with *white skin* make the laws.

SEVIER: The *majority*, Mr. Boone, whatever color they happen to be. In this country, the majority is *white*.

BOONE: No, the majority is red, Colonel. This is Indian country.

SEVIER: (irritated) Well...they fought on the side of the *British*.

BOONE: The British are white, Colonel. (Sevier turns away in confusion.) So it is color, after all. Somehow being white is supposed to make a man better. He can rob and cheat and murder, but as long as he's white, he can own land. These people live godly lives and walk straight in the eyes of the Lord, but they *can't own land.* Look at me, dark as any Melungeon in this country!

Sevier cannot win the argument, but it doesn't matter. The whites will take what they want—Sevier knows it, Boone knows it, and the Melungeons know it. John Sevier recognizes the injustice of the situation but will do nothing to correct it. Pat, Alisee, Preacher Givens, and Mr. Sylvester leave. Boone delivers some harsh parting words to Sevier, then Sevier is left alone, slumped in a chair as the lights go down. Drums are heard as the lights come up on the other side stage, revealing a circle of Indians gathered in a woodland clearing. Atalullakula, the Cherokee chief, addresses the Indians briefly; he knows the Melungeons will lose their land. The chief motions to an Indian offstage, who leads in Pat, Preacher Givens, and Mr. Sylvester. Pat steps up on a stump in the center of the clearing to address the Indians.

PAT: Some of our people say take guns and fight to keep our lands. Once upon a time the Cherokee had to decide. What do you say?

ATAKULLAKULLA: Like grains of sand along these mountain rivers, like yellow leaves blowing on the north wind, settlers cross the mountains and come down the valleys. The Red Man had two paths to go: fight, or scatter in the forest like animals. Either way, the Cherokee walk toward the sunset.

PAT: The law is against us. We cannot own property. If we stay here, we will be like slaves working in the fields.

ATAKULLAKULLA: You must move toward the west.

The chief describes a land, a hidden valley, seven days' journey from where they stand. The land is between that of the Cherokee and the Shawnee, "cut off from the rest of the world, so far that not even the Red Man travels there."

PAT: How soon can we go?

ATAKULLAKULLA: Let the Dark People make their harvest and load their wagons. One month from today we will come and show you the way.

PAT: (raising his right hand) May God turn his face with joy toward the Cherokee people.

ATAKULLAKULLA: Many times you have taken care of the Red Man, nursed our wounded, given us food for the winter. On your farms along the Holston you give us grain and livestock from your barns and granaries. In your churches we stand side by side and learn of your God. You have done good for us. Now the Cherokee give back to you. We will come to your village with the full moon.

Pat, Preacher Givens, and Mr. Sylvester leave as the chief mounts the stump and intones a prayer. Drums are heard, along with rattles, gourds, and knee bells. Lights rise on the center stage as a group of women dance as men bring gifts to an altar: pumpkins, gourds, blankets, hatchets, and various other items. The men then join the dance, which builds in energy as an Indian woman runs down the aisle where the audience is seated, jumps onto the stage, and joins the dance.

Dance scenes are standard fare in outdoor drama, and the Indian dance in *Walk Toward the Sunset* is particularly exciting, with torches and wildly whirling actors portraying Indians. Mary Bowler—now Mary Van Nest—recalls the scene fondly.

My most starring role was as "The Seed." I was an Indian in a ceremonial dance. Steve [Nichandros] didn't tell you about this?

Steve didn't remember a lot about it.
Oh, he knows *this*, come on! He was the "The Sun God."

He remembered that, yes.
He *should* remember—he danced with me and jumped over me and fertilized me in this dance. And then I'd get up and dance around after he jumps over me, and I think—oh, yeah, I'd go running down the aisle to get into the dance. It was center stage—a big deal. I was really quite funny.

That was one of the highlights of the play, as I remember it.
Absolutely, absolutely. (laughs)[8]

As the dance concludes, lights come up on a side stage where Pat Gibson, Preacher Givens, and Mr. Sylvester stand; they have been summoned by Atakullakulla. Only two weeks have passed since the Melungeons met with the Cherokees, but the chief now tells Pat they must leave in three days.

PAT: But we need another week to finish our harvest!
ATAKULLAKULLA: You have plenty of grain. Cherokee will finish your harvest and keep the grain for the winter. You leave in three days.
PAT: (looks at the Preacher and Mr. Sylvester, then turns to the chief) Why does the principal chief want us to hurry?
ATAKULLAKULLA: Word comes to us of a wagon train moving down the valley from Virginia, thirty families, more than two hundred people. At

---

[8] Van Nest interview.

Jonesboro they buy lands along the Holston River…lands where you now live.

PAT: (hotly) They can't even wait 'til we move out! I'll go to Jonesboro and see Governor Sevier!

ATAKULLAKULLA: (stops Pat with his hand) The settlers come with guns, perhaps with militia. Let the Dark People be gone when they arrive. We will come to your village in three days.

As the lights dim on one side stage, they come up on the other, as scene 5 opens with Alisee churning butter and singing "Chickamy, chickamy, craney crow." Mrs. Bolton—played by Annette Turner—enters the scene. The two women talk of Alisee's upcoming wedding, but the talk soon turns to the move the Melungeons will soon have to make. Alisee begins to cry, and Mrs. Bolton takes over the churning.

ALISEE: Mrs. Bolton, what's wrong with us Melungeons?

MRS. BOLTON: Ain't nothin' wrong, Alisee. You're so pretty you got ever' boy in this country after you. They tell me in Jonesboro the men followed you around like flies.

ALISEE: That's not it. They look down on us, as if we were slaves or Indians. They didn't think I was pretty; they thought they had a right to follow me because I was dark. They don't follow white girls around.

MRS. BOLTON: No white girls in Jonesboro look as good as you do.

ALISEE: Mrs. Bolton, how do we know we won't have to move again? What if settlers come into that new country? Then what do we do?

MRS. BOLTON: (gazing off sadly) Jist keep a-movin', child, jist keep a-movin'. Like the Children o' Israel in the Wilderness—jist keep a-movin'. Some people destined for one thing, some another.

ALISEE: But why?

MRS. BOLTON: I quit askin' myself a long time ago. I know I'm different, so I don't ask questions any more. It don't do any good.

ALISEE: Jist give up? Surrender? Well, I won't surrender! I'll fight!

MRS. BOLTON: When I was your age, I felt the same way. I wanted to grab people by the throat an' tell 'em I was as good as they was. I used to rub my skin feel how smooth it was, look at myself in the glass an' I was clean and smooth. I said what makes anybody better'n anybody else? (A shrug) Then I give up. We can run away, or we can join 'em. If we join 'em, we have to be slaves, so they's nothin' to do but keep a-movin'.

Pat arrives and tells them they have to move the next day. He and Alisee will have to get married right away. Preacher Givens begins giving orders; Mrs. Bolton is to get Alisee's dress ready as Mr. Sylvester rounds up the choir. After making sure Pat has the ring, the preacher goes to get the wagons ready for the journey. Pat and Alisee talk for a moment, then Alisee goes to put on her wedding dress. Pat sits on a stump and gazes at the ground. A bearded white man cradling a long rifle enters the scene, and Pat leaps to his feet.

> PAT: Who're you? Whaddya want?
>
> SCOUT: Never mind, black boy. Wagon train sent me on up ahead to spot their new land. Near as I can figger, this is it, all this bottom land for the next twenty miles. Looks like they won't have to build any barns or houses a'tall.
>
> PAT: Our people plan to move tomorrow mornin'.
>
> SCOUT: That'll be about right. The wagon train'll get here 'bout noon tomorrow. You wanta be outa here when they pull up.
>
> PAT: (grimly) What if we decided to stay 'til the next day.
>
> SCOUT: (fingering the rifle) That wouldn't be a bit healthy for any o' you'ns.
>
> PAT: Why don't you ride back there an' tell 'em we jist might stay here another week or ten days.

The scout casually lowers his rifle, but Pat wrenches it out of his hands and tosses it aside. The scout pulls out a large hunting knife and moves toward Pat, threatening to cut Pat into pieces, to scalp him. He lunges at Pat a couple of times, but Pat easily sidesteps him. Pat then gets the scout's arm in a lock hold, forcing him to drop the knife. Applying more pressure, Pat has the scout crying out in agony. "You git back to that wagon train," Pat snarls, "an' tell 'em if they come nigh this place 'fore tomorrow evenin' they all end up floatin' down the river 'ith their heads cut off."

The scout runs away and Pat sits on the stump, gazing at the audience. The choir begins softly humming "Ca' the Yewes" as the lights rise on center stage, showing the churchyard. Pat stands and straightens his clothes, brushes his hair, and moves to center stage as the lights dim behind him. Alisee enters, wearing her wedding dress. Preacher Givens invites anyone who wants to stay for the wedding to get inside the church. "Rest o' you'ns git them wagons and haul out! Leave one Indian here to lead the rest of us!"

The stage empties and the lights dim—once the rest of the lighting equipment arrives, the stage will be bathed in a soft blue light, but on opening night, they make do with what they have. A guitar is heard, then Alisee's voice singing a folk song. Boys and girls appear onstage to do a dance representing the wedding. As their dance ends and they leave the stage, the lights come up and Pat and Alisee hurry out of the church, followed by the others. The newlyweds move to center stage and Alisee turns to look at the church.

> ALISEE: You reckon we'll ever see our old church again?
> PAT: I'll build another one. That's the first thing we'll do.
> ALISEE: I don't want to go! It's wrong! Maybe we could stay here and work our way into this new state…
> PAT: I told you what Col. Sevier said.
> ALISEE: (sadly) I wonder if the time will ever come…
> PAT: It'll take a long time. Maybe our grandchildren…

Alisee looks at the church, then runs offstage. Pat takes one last look at the church, then follows his bride. Preacher Givens and the others move to center stage, and the preacher asks, "Did you get the word out?" Mr. Sylvester replies, "'Fore sundown this evenin' ever' house, barn, granary, shed, ever' pigsty for twenty miles'll be set on fire."

Preacher Givens leads the group in prayer, and the people begin singing "Holy Manna." They all walk away, leaving the stage empty. Then two Indians carrying rifles appear. They quickly glance around, then another Indian runs in with a lighted torch, runs to the back of the church, and sets it on fire. The choir bursts forth in a dissonant chord as the lights go down quickly, ending Act 1.

As Katie Vande Brake points out in her book *How They Shine: Melungeon Characters in the Fiction of Appalachia*:

> Hunter's use of Daniel Boone and John Sevier is worth noting. Daniel Boone's name is familiar to most Americans who would see him in their mind's eye wearing a coonskin cap and carrying a long rifle, as he opened up Kentucky by creating the Wilderness Road through the Cumberland Gap. Many could recall the story of Boone killing a bear at the foot of a huge oak tree. Boone is a part of American folklore. By putting him in the story at the center of the land controversy involving the Melungeons right after the Revolutionary War, Hunter ties his story to something with which the audience would be familiar. If people are expected to remember new information, it helps to have a "peg" to hang the new information on. Daniel Boone—the westward pioneer movement that Boone represents—is just such a peg for most Americans.[9]

Of course, there is no record that Daniel Boone was involved in a controversy about Melungeon lands—or that any such controversy ever occurred. The work of researchers including Jack Goins indicates that the Melungeons did not

---

[9] Vande Brake, *How They Shine*, 173.

move west from the Carolinas and Virginia in unison as part of any cohesive group, but rather as individual family units. There may well have been disputes over the right of Melungeons to own land stemming from their uncertain racial status, but these disputes would have affected individuals and families, not the Melungeon population as a whole. Indeed, before their arrival in east Tennessee, there is no indication that anyone recognized a cohesive Melungeon population at all. Hunter sets Act 1 in a framework of historical events, but his portrayal of the Melungeons' role in those events is based entirely on his own imagination and is at odds with more recent research.

John Sevier, who led the short-lived movement to create the State of Franklin and became the first governor of Tennessee, is less well-known to most Americans. His connection to the Melungeons, however, is of interest. In her articles on the Melungeons published in the *Arena* magazine in 1891, Will Allen Dromgoole refers to a letter from Sevier in which he recounts meeting a colony of people in 1784, people he believed to be of Moorish descent who claimed to be Portuguese. Dromgoole got this information from a letter to the *Nashville American* newspaper following the publication of her two articles about the Melungeons in summer 1890.[10] The information, provided by Dan Baird, publisher of the *Southern Lumberman* magazine, appears to be apocryphal; no such letter from Sevier has ever been found. However, this claim regarding Sevier's meeting the Melungeons in Tennessee has been central to the Melungeon legend ever since Dromgoole wrote about it in 1891. Hunter makes no reference to this supposed meeting in *Walk Toward the Sunset*, but Sevier has been a permanent part of the Melungeon legend ever since Dromgoole's articles were published, and the elusive "letter from Sevier" has been cited by many writers since then.

Although most outdoor dramas are based on historical events, rarely do they let history get in the way of the story. And Hunter had less documented history with which to work than he usually did when writing historical dramas. In the first act, Hunter wrote about Melungeon history as it *might* have happened. The second act is purely drama, with no reference to any historical events at all, real or supposed.

A fifteen-minute intermission after Act 1 concluded with fireworks, and not just because the opening weekend of the drama coincided with Independence Day. The fireworks segued into the second act, which opens in Sneedville on the Fourth of July, 1870. The façade of the church from Act 1 is now a courthouse, a transformation accomplished by removing the steeple, adding an American

---

[10] Baird, "A Backward Glance," 2.

flag, and mounting a wooden sign beside the door reading "Court House." Otherwise, the stage is the same as before. Upstage is a sort of market, with carts containing items such as cloth, shoes, and other wares. A peddler is showing some carpet to a group of women, who are dressed in calico and sunbonnets. Downstage, a crowd has gathered near a stump. Most of the people are white, but there are a few Melungeons who stand close to each other, slightly separate from the whites. They're listening to one of the Knoxville lumbermen.

> LUMBERMAN: Folks, I hate to interrupt this Independence Day celebration, but business is business. Now as I said before—you all know me...been knowin' me for twenty years...right over there next to Kingsport...an' you know I ain't one to come in here tryin' to hoodwink nobody. After all, I ain't runnin' for no political office. (The people laugh with him) I say use your heads: sell off a little timber an' make some *money*.

The people murmur in agreement. Pat Gibson, the grandson of Pat Gibson from the first act, is at center stage as the lumber buyer addresses him. "Pat Gibson, yore granddaddy come into this country near on a hundred years ago. Watta you say?"

> PAT: I say this country been timbered plumb to death already. Where you aimin' to find any more good trees?
> LUMBERMAN: You got good timber back in the mountains.
> PAT: That's jist what I figgered. Us Melungeons been pushed outa here back into the high ridges. You timbered out all the valleys for fifty years. Now you wanta come up thar, take our land again. Why don't you go sommers else an' cut railroad ties?
> LUMBERMAN: We ain't talkin' about railroad ties. We're lookin' for chestnut, poplar, oak, and walnut...furniture factory goin' up in Knoxville sometime this year...pay good money.
> PAT: Our people ain't interested.
> LUMBERMAN: Times is changin'. What're you gonna do to make a livin'?
> PAT: Work our farms back on Newman's Ridge an' Powell Mountain, all up an' down this country.
> MAN IN CROWD: Work? You mean moonshine!

The laughter from the crowd onstage blends with laughter from the audience. Pat takes no offense at the remark; he grins knowingly.

PAT: Nobody's gonna work less'n he has to. Man don't have to be a plumb fool about it. I'm standin' in the way of my people gettin' robbed, that's all.

LUMBERMAN: Now looky here, don't be accusin' me o' robbin' nobody.

PAT: What else you call it? The price you offer ain't half enough. Nobody on the Ridge gonna sell timber for a price like that.

Sneedville businessman Ezra Johnson, who has been standing near the timber buyer, steps up to address Pat.

JOHNSON: How does anybody on Newman's Ridge know what an acre o' timber's worth?

PAT: I *tell* 'em how much it's worth. That way they don't git robbed.

LUMBERMAN: You're a big help to jist about ever'body, ain'tcha?

JOHNSON: Pat Gibson, you're doin' your duty towards your people, an' that's fine. But you also got a larger duty, to *all* the people.

PAT: (skeptical) Is that a fact?

JOHNSON: Yessiree, to the people of Hancock County. You wanta see this region grow an' prosper, an' that means bringin' in new capital. You're standin' in the way o' progress. We need a new furniture factory in East Tennessee.

VOICE IN THE CROWD: Why don't you build a furniture factory right here in Sneedville?

LUMBERMAN: No way to transport furniture out of here, dang it! Knoxville's got railroads.

SECOND VOICE: I say let 'em bring a railroad through Hancock County. (The crowd agrees loudly.)

LUMBERMAN: Takes money to build a railroad. Besides, it's gotta go where people live, not out here in this wilderness.

JOHNSON: Pat Gibson, if you got one ounce o' pride in your own country where you was born, you'll tell those people to sell their timber. It'll make jobs around here for two years or more!

PAT: (cooly) Mr. Johnson, you'ns talk about me and *my people*, like we was some kinda freaks...curious...tell us to work for the good o' Hancock County, have pride in it, sell our timber for half what it's worth, then in the next breath you settin' us apart like slaves or Indians or sumpin', makin' us different!

VOICE IN CROWD: Well, you *are* different!

Uh-oh! There it is; it's out there now. The audience sees that, for the Melungeons, 1870 isn't much better than 1782. They're still "different," still not fully accepted by the whites. Onstage, the white characters in the crowd murmur

their agreement. The Melungeon characters edge away from the center, antici-
pating trouble. Ezra Johnson also sees trouble coming and tries to stop it.

JOHNSON: Now wait a minute! No use to start this kinda stuff all over.
In 1867, just three years ago, the State o' Tennessee declared that every man
had a right to vote. That includes you, too.

PAT: That's plumb nice o' the State o' Tennessee seein' as how our ancestors fought at King's Mountain an' a few more places…that's awful nice.

LUMBERMAN: No call to be a smart aleck. You know the way things
are. It'll take more'n us to change 'em.

PAT: I ain't tryin' to change anything. You're the one; offerin' us half of
what our timber's worth an' then gittin' riled up 'cause we got sense enough
not to sell it!

MAN IN CROWD: You're keepin' us from gittin' jobs! (The crowd
shouts approval.)

PAT: You know who's keepin' you from gittin' timberin' jobs? Ask Mr.
Ezra Johnson, standin' right there. (The crowd mutters angrily.) Ask him
about his stock in Southern Railroad…goes to Knoxville but not through
Hancock County.

LUMBERMAN: How you gonna run a railroad up and down these
mountainsides? You crazy?

PAT: Ask him about the stock he owns in the new furniture factory in
Knoxville. If he can git us to sell timber for half of what it's worth, that means
twice as much profit for him an' the rest of the rich men in Knoxville.

JOHNSON: Folks, don't you believe that! We've heard these kind of
yarns before. Pat Gibson, looks like you an' your crowd don't cause nothin'
but trouble.

The crowd murmurs angrily again; the white townspeople seem to have all
taken Ezra Johnson's side in this dispute. Johnson, emboldened by the support
of the crowd, suggests that someone who refuses to cooperate with his neighbors
should move somewhere else. The townspeople cheer, and Johnson takes it a step
further. "An' if he don't move sommers else, we oughta *make* him move!" The
darker people in the crowd are wielding clubs and knives, and move into position
to defend Pat, who waves them back, sends them offstage. There are shouts to
"ride 'im out on a rail" and "string him up."

Johnson sees that it's gotten out of hand and tries to stop the crowd, which
ignores him. They grab Pat's arms and take him across the stage as a voice calls
out about getting a rope. When they get halfway across the stage, Pat's daughter
Alisee appears, holding a long rifle, and says "Take your hands off'n 'im." Johnson tries to calm her down, but she repeats her threat to shoot anyone who lays

a hand on her daddy. Knowing that Alisee's muzzle-loader can fire only one round at a time, Johnson tells her, "Don't be foolish. You'd get one shot, then they'd crush you." From the darkness, a voice calls out, 'No, they wouldn't."

The lights come up on the side stage to reveal Vance Johnson, standing in the doorway of the courthouse. He's holding a rifle. "In fact, this is a Springfield repeater. You touch Pat Gibson, an' I'll lay out six of you. Now git back ever'body."

Vance's parents are shocked that their son has taken the side of "them dang Ridge people." His mother declares that the boy has gone crazy, and Vance orders his father to take his mother home. He tells the Melungeons to go on about their business and asks Pat and Alisee to come to him. Pat takes a furtive drink from a bottle in his pocket, then he and Alisee cross the stage to Vance.

> PAT: You sure got nerve, boy. But you got no business foolin' around 'ith us Melungeons. Won't bring nothin' but trouble.
> VANCE: Tell 'em to get back toward Newman's Ridge 'fore any more trouble starts.
> PAT: Yeah. He's right, folks. Git a-goin'. We'll catch up.

The Melungeons move offstage. One Melungeon, however, comes across to Alisee. He's Tom Robertson, and he's clearly sweet on Alisee.

> TOM: Come on, Alisee. I'll take you home.
> VANCE: Who're you?
> TOM: A Melungeon, jis' like she is.
> VANCE: I'll take care of her.
> TOM: Alisee's figgerin' on bein' my wife 'fore long.
> ALISEE: He's…Tom Robertson…lives on the Ridge.
> VANCE: Please to meet you, Mr. Robertson. Now move along.
> TOM: You give orders right good, seein' you got a rifle in yer hands.
> VANCE: Same rifle I was carryin' at Appomattox. Now you go catch up with the others.

Tom looks at Pat, who looks away. He looks at Alisee, who looks downward, unwilling to meet his eyes. He looks at Vance, who is becoming impatient and cradles the rifle in his arms. Tom starts to leave, looks back, then runs offstage. Pat is uneasy about the situation. "I don't like seein' Tom Robertson git mad," he says. "He's like his daddy…take on a wild bull…"

Vance pays no attention. He has other things on his mind. He turns Alisee toward him and says, "Nothing's changed, is it?"

ALISEE: No.

VANCE: You still willin' to marry me?

ALISEE: Yes.

VANCE: Mr. Gibson, we're gonna make a trip to Nashville.

PAT: Ain't no use, son. We'ns can't legally own land. They can take the timber if they want to, and they know it.

VANCE: That letter from Mr. Netherland was very friendly. If they get that bill through the legislature...

PAT: All right. You been to school, boy, even college, you're readin' law, an' you know some of them politician fellers over at Nashville. Whatever you say, we'll do.

VANCE: You go home and pack. Meet me here tomorrow mornin', early.

ALISEE: Pack what? This is the only dress I got.

VANCE: Shoes?

ALISEE: I never owned a pair in my life.

VANCE: (holds Alisee closely) I guess that's why I love you so much. One old dress, no shoes, and still you're the prettiest, sweetest girl in Tennessee. Maybe in Knoxville we can find you a new dress an' a pair o' shoes.

ALISEE: I don't care about a new dress.

VANCE: You think I want my wife to have just one dress and no shoes?

PAT: Son, you got trouble. Your old man ain't gonna 'low this. An' he's got powerful influence. You got Tom Robertson fightin' mad...

Vance doesn't pay any attention to Pat's worries. Instead, he suggests the three of them leave right away, just walk across the mountain until they get to the railroad, then catch a train to Knoxville and then to Nashville. Pat and Alisee look at each other, then give in. Vance places his rifle inside the door of the courthouse, and the three walk offstage and out of sight. A string band plays a mountain ballad for a few moments, then the lights come up on the opposite side stage to show the interior of John Netherland's office in Nashville.

In 1870, John Netherland held no public office. He had been one of the leaders of Tennessee's Whig Party, and had served in both the Tennessee House of Representatives and the Tennessee Senate. He ran unsuccessfully for governor in 1859 and supported the Union during the Civil War. Netherland maintained a law practice in Rogersville, and in 1870 he was a delegate to the Tennessee Constitutional Convention.

Dewitt Clinton Senter had also supported the Union during the war. He was elected to the State Senate after the war and became speaker of the senate in 1867. As the speaker, he automatically assumed the office of governor when Governor William Brownlow resigned to take a seat in the United States Senate in 1869. Senter was elected in his own right a few weeks later. As scene 7 opens, he is talking with Netherland in Netherland's office.

> SENTER: What got you so worked up about Melungeons? What in the world *are* Melungeons, anyway?
>
> NETHERLAND: Dark-skinned people living on the high ridges in Hancock County...scattered all through the Clinch and Powell country.
>
> SENTER: Dark-skinned? You mean...?
>
> NETHERLAND: No, I don't...not Indian, not black. But I reckon there's been a lot of intermarriage by now, even with whites. The pure Melungeon of fifty years ago was exactly like you and me, except with a dark skin.
>
> SENTER: Dark-skinned...why? Where'd they come from?
>
> NETHERLAND: Nobody knows for sure, not even the Melungeons...perhaps around the Mediterranean...they don't look like Indian or black. During the Revolution they fought on our side, used to claim fine lands along the Holston River. Then they got shoved out because dark people couldn't own land. They moved north and settled in the upper Clinch and Powell valleys. Little by little they got pushed back onto the high ridges. Now they sorta keep to themselves.
>
> SENTER: Why are they coming here?
>
> NETHERLAND: People want to cut the timber off of those high ridges and pay them little or nothing. They're afraid they still can't own the land.
>
> SENTER: Well, the new Tennessee Constitution takes care of that.
>
> NETHERLAND: I doubt if they know it yet. It was ratified in May...this is July. They probably haven't heard.
>
> SENTER: (looks at his pocket watch) I was supposed to attend a committee meeting, but I think I'll stay a minute. I want to see what they look like.
>
> NETHERLAND: Only two are Melungeons...man named Gibson and his daughter. The third is a white man, a young lawyer by the name of Vance Johnson. He helped make you governor last fall.

A clerk steps in to signal the arrival of visitors. Netherland nods, and Vance, Pat, and Alisee enter the office. Introductions are made, and, after some small talk, the governor gets to the heart of the matter. "I am happy to tell you, Mr. Gibson, that you can now legally own land in Tennessee." Netherland concurs. "The land you now claim on the ridges is yours. They can't cut any timber without making a deal with you."

Governor Senter then looks at Alisee and admires her beauty. He then tells Vance to let him know if he'd be interested in taking a job with the state. As he prepares to leave, the governor shakes hands with the visitors.

SENTER: Mr. Gibson, I guess Tennessee owes a lot to you and your people. If these two ever move to Nashville, you come and see 'em.

PAT: Thank you, Governor. You want a little taste of Hancock County corn likker?

As the audience laughs, Pat offers the bottle in his pocket to the governor. The governor demurs, and leaves for his committee meeting. Netherland paces slowly in the office; he has some questions for Pat.

NETHERLAND: Mr. Gibson, what church do you claim?

PAT: I reckon you call it the Holiness Church, Mr. Netherland. We git a preacher 'bout once a month in the spring and summer, then maybe once or twice in the winter.

NETHERLAND: What religion was your grandfather?

PAT: Baptist…there was a Baptist preacher, a white man name o' Givens, come on the march with 'em outa the Holston Valley.

NETHERLAND: And before that…didn't your people live along the coast somewhere?

PAT: The old folks used to tell about livin' close to the ocean. I always figgered it 'us Charleston, or Wilmington, or sommers like that.

NETHERLAND: What church before the Baptist and Holiness?

PAT: A lot of families still have Church of England prayer-books, Mr. Netherland, published in 1745. What are you getting at?

NETHERLAND: How many can read and write?

PAT: I was taught by my granddaddy, fine old man. I was named after him. Then my daddy taught me some. Alisee can read and write…

NETHERLAND: How many more?

PAT: I reckon that's about all.

VANCE: Sir, what are you getting' at?

NETHERLAND: (gently) The whole history of the Melungeons has been sort of…downhill, hasn't it?

VANCE: It hasn't been their fault!

NETHERLAND: Of course not. It is the fault of unscrupulous, greedy people for a hundred years. What I'm saying is that you cannot afford to go back to the primitive.

PAT: I reckon I don't understand.

NETHERLAND: This is an age of railroads, and cities, and big development. If you try to stay in the past, pretty soon you lose contact with the world, then you lose dignity and self-respect. It's not just a matter of color. The law is on your side, so you can keep your timber; but you have to build schools and churches. You have to learn new ways, mingle with the white society around you, make yourselves a part of the life of Hancock County and east Tennessee.

VANCE: Suppose they choose to live in the quiet beauty of those mountain ridges and not get mixed up with the white people?

NETHERLAND: Then they will become just like the Indians. They will die out. They will sink farther and farther into the primitive, and after a while they will be forgotten. It's all right to keep their culture and their beliefs and their homes, but they have to be a part of this world, too.

PAT: I never thought of it quite that way.

NETHERLAND: I don't blame your ancestors for retreating to the mountain-tops, Mr. Gibson. They had to. But you must come down and mingle with the world, be part of the world. You have to have pride. You have to meet the world on even terms. You got nothing to be ashamed of. Any man whose great-grandfather gave his life at Kings Mountain got nothin' to be ashamed of.

Netherland invites Pat, Alisee, and Vance to stay at his house for a few days and look around Nashville. The lights dim on the side stage, and a string orchestra is heard. The lights come up on center stage to show a garden party at the home of Ezra and Millie Johnson. Several couples perform a lively country dance while others watch and clap their hands.

As the music ends, Ezra Johnson thanks everyone for attending and apologizes for the absence of his wife, who isn't feeling well. He comments that several people up and down the valley are ill. As Johnson invites the partygoers to partake of refreshments, Vance and Alisee enter. Alisee is dressed in a new gown and is wearing shoes. There is an uncomfortable silence, which Vance tries to dispel by introducing Alisee to various people, all of whom nod politely and turn away. It is obvious that Alisee is not welcome in this group, and she protests to Vance that she should leave. Vance stubbornly insists that she stay, but Alisee turns to hurry away. She stops abruptly as a group of Melungeons enters the scene, led by Tom Robertson. All the Melungeons are carrying rifles. Pat Gibson tries to speak to Tom, but Tom pushes Pat away.

TOM: Alisee, you comin' back to the Ridge. Resta you people stand right still. We don't want no trouble.

VANCE: Alisee's gonna do what she wants to do.

TOM: She's doin' what I say.

VANCE: Which is it, Alisee? ...Me or him?

ALISEE: Tom, I done promised Vance to marry him.

At that, Ezra Johnson protests, "*Marry?* Your mother wouldn't 'low *her* in the *house!*" That seems to settle the matter for Tom, and he repeats that he is taking Alisee back to the Ridge. Alisee concedes that she might be taken back to the Ridge at gunpoint, and that Tom might force her to marry him, but sooner or later she'd run away; no one can make her do what she doesn't want to do. Tom insists, "You don't belong here!" Alisee looks at Ezra Johnson and his guests, and replies, "I reckon you're right, Tom."

> TOM: You think they're gonna take you in like you 'us one of 'em?"
> ALISEE: No, I don't think so.
> TOM: Then whatta you hangin' around 'em fer?
> ALISEE: I done told you.
> TOM: You don't belong here! In sight o' six months you'll be back on Newman's Ridge.
> ALISEE: Maybe. But I keep rememberin' what a man in Nashville told us…this is a new day, an' we can't go on backin' farther an' farther, hidin' off up there in the mountains. We got to be part o' this country. We run away long enough!
> TOM: Alisee, you know things ain't never gonna change!
> ALISEE: We got to try!
> TOM: We tried before! My daddy tried to be part o' this country around here, this valley, an' what happened? They shot 'im down one night from behind! Nobody would stand up to my daddy face to face an' fight! No siree! They had to shoot 'im in the back! I don't recollect anybody even bein' tried in court for his murder!
> VANCE: You think this town's *proud* o' that? You can't blame decent people for what a few scum did!
> TOM: (coldly) I ain't blamin' nobody. I'm jist tellin' ye they ain't no place for a Melungeon 'cept back on the ridges. And I'm tellin' ye *you* better stay *off* the Ridge!
> VANCE: Long as you keep livin' by yourselves the world's gonna pass you by. You'll get more and more ignorant and illiterate, an' after a while you'll all die of poverty and starvation.
> TOM: (fingering the rifle) You callin' my people ignorant?
> VANCE: Can you read and write?
> TOM: No, but I can raise cattle an' sheep an' I can take an ax an' bring down a twelve-inch oak in five minutes!
> VANCE: How many sheep you got? How many cattle?

There is an ominous pause as Tom glares at Vance. Clearly, Vance is pushing Tom too far. Tom grimly answers, "None."

VANCE: An' you talk about marryin' Alisee an' keepin' 'er back there on that ridge, when you don't even have one cow or one sheep! What kinda love you call that? Why don't you start getttin' some book learnin', make sumpin' outa yourselves? ...all of you? Alisee took the time to learn...why don't the rest of you?

TOM: We done argified enough. Alisee, you comin'?

ALISEE: No. I'm stayin' here.

TOM: You done this, Vance Johnson...all this sweet talk an' big promises about "the new day." You'ns know better, all of ye...lyin', connivin', greedy, uppity! (He hands his rifle to one of the other Melungeons.) All right, Mr. Vance Johnson, last time I 'us here you kept your rifle in yer hands. I'm puttin' my rifle away! You want Alisee? Le's see you take 'er.

Vance takes off his coat as his father protests. "Vance, we ain't gonna have any fightin' with the Ridge people! Leave 'em alone! Let the girl go!" Alisee begs Vance not to fight. But Vance know things have gone too far for him to back down.

Tom lunges at Vance, who sidesteps him. Tom sprawls on the ground but quickly regains his feet. The women scream, and Ezra Johnson calls for somebody to go and get some guns. The Melungeons level their rifles and no one moves. Tom swings again, and again Vance sidesteps the blow. Tom takes another swing and Vance hits him. Tom goes down but comes up holding a knife. Tom tries to stab Vance, who grabs Tom's wrist. Tom is obviously more powerful than Vance, and little by little forces the knife closer to Vance. Suddenly, Vance kicks Tom's legs out from under him and they both fall to the stage, Tom falling on his knife. Alisee runs to Tom and Vance kneels beside them, but Tom dies without a word.

Pat quickly tells the Melungeons, "I reckon ever'body saw how it happened. Wasn't Vance's fault." The Melungeons pick up Tom's body and carry him offstage in silence. Pat looks at Vance, pats his arm, then follows the Melungeons offstage. A white man tells Vance, "Don't let it bother you, boy, nobody blamin' you. Anyhow, he's jist a Melungeon..." Vance grabs the man by his lapels and almost hits him, but then relaxes and lets the man scurry off. Everyone is now offstage except for Vance, his father, and Alisee. Mr. Johnson says, "Reckon you didn't mean what you said."

VANCE: I meant all of it. I'm leavin'. I'm movin' out.

JOHNSON: What're you talkin' about? Where you aimin' to go?

VANCE: Nashville. I been offered a job on the staff of Governor Senter.

JOHNSON: I'm right proud to hear it, son. What about that other...?

VANCE: Alisee and I are going to be married tomorrow in that little church up on the Ridge. Twelve o'clock noon, if you wanta come.

JOHNSON: Vance, you don't mean that! You can't do it! Your mother'd never git over it!

VANCE: She'll get over it. Anyway, we'll be livin' in Nashville.

JOHNSON: We'll talk about it in the mornin'. Come to bed.

VANCE: I'm not stayin' here tonight. I'm goin' with Alisee up on Newman's Ridge.

JOHNSON: Vance, they'll kill you.

VANCE: No, they won't. (Takes Alisee's hand) I sorta want to, on account o' Tom Robertson. Looks like all the Melungeons ever get from us is trouble. We should be doin' what we can to draw 'em out, make friends, get 'em educated…goodnight, Paw. Tell Momma I hope she feels better tomorrow.

Vance goes offstage with Alisee. Ezra Johnson kicks the ground in frustration. Mrs. Farley enters the scene to tell Johnson he should try to get a doctor; his wife appears to have the fever that's going around. Johnson tells Mrs. Farley to stay with her and goes off to find someone to ride to Kingsport for a doctor.

The lights fade out, then come up on a side stage. Vance and Alisee are sitting in a clearing on top of Newman's Ridge. They discuss their future life in Nashville; Alisee is concerned that she won't fit in. "I can't talk good," she says. "I can't cook fancy like what we had in Nashville. I have a hard time wearin' shoes…"

Vance reassures her that he doesn't care about any of that. Alisee asks if he is sad that none of his folks came to their wedding; Vance replies that he's sorry for his folks, not for himself or Alisee. Pat comes onstage with a worried look on his face. "They sent word up from Sneedville," he tells Vance. "Your ma's got the fever…real bad off. I reckon she got it several days ago. Said she was feelin' sick the night o' that party. Doctor from Rogersville still ain't got there…sick people all over the country…he can't get loose."

VANCE: Looks like I'll have to ride over there an' bring 'im.

ALISEE: They's no time. She's got to have treatment right now.

VANCE: Yeah, but what kind of treatment?

ALISEE: Vance, we been takin' care of ourselves up here for a hundred years, an' I know all the old remedies. I can cure that fever.

VANCE: (restraining her) Fever's contagious. Remember they told us in Knoxville there was smallpox in the Clinch Valley…it could be smallpox…

ALISEE: (calmly) She's sick…don't nothin' else matter. Pa, run on ahead an' git Miz Goins to start mixin' roots an' stuff…she knows which'uns to use…git 'em b'ilin' in a pot o' ginger. I'll be there in a minute.

VANCE: You're not gonna expose yourself to smallpox! You fix the stuff an' I'll take it to 'er.

ALISEE: We don't know it's smallpox yet. Anyway, it's better for me to go.

VANCE: You crazy?

ALISEE: This is the first time in my life I had a chance to do sumpin' for the very ones that hate us the most. I got to, Vance. Maybe the Lord's suddenly decided to test me. I got to go.

Vance continues to protest, but Alisee's mind is clearly made up. She makes Vance promise not to come down from the Ridge until she sends for him. The lights go down as Vance watches Alisee leave. The lights rise on the opposite side stage, showing the parlor of the Johnson house, now a sickroom.

Mrs. Johnson is propped up on a sofa that has been turned into a bed. She is pale and weak, her eyes closed. Mrs. Farley enters with a pan and a towel; she wets the towel and dabs Mrs. Johnson's forehead. Alisee enters with a cup; she stirs the contents of the cup, pours out a spoonful, then gently opens Mrs. Johnson mouth and pours in the liquid. Mrs. Johnson coughs and gasps. Alisee repeats the process twice more.

Ezra Johnson watches Alisee tend to his wife. Alisee tells him to go to bed and rest; she'll call him if anything happens. The lights fade out and rise again on the opposite side stage, the same woodland clearing as before. Pat is reading the Bible, commenting on a passage. Vance is not interested in the Bible passage; he wants to go into town to see about Alisee and his mother. Pat tells him to wait until tomorrow, that the treatment takes seven days and tomorrow will be the seventh day. Vance turns away, tired and exasperated, as the lights dim on the clearing and come up again on the Johnson parlor.

Alisee is watching Mrs. Johnson, who suddenly gives a little cry and begins to gasp. Alisee quickly wets the towel and begins wiping Mrs. Johnson's forehead and calls for Mrs. Farley. "Bring another pan o' water, some more towels! I believe the fever's broke! Look at that sweat on 'er forehead!" The two women work on Mrs. Johnson, restraining her when she tries to sit up. Mrs. Farley dabs at tears in her eyes and says "She's goin' right to sleep. Praise the Lord! Alisee, child, you're gonna have stars in your crown!"

Mr. Johnson appears, and Mrs. Farley tells him that his wife's fever has broken. Johnson gazes upward, closes his eyes, and says, "Lord, I thank you." Then he looks for Alisee.

JOHNSON: That girl saved her life, Miz Farley...Alisee...where is she?

MRS. FARLEY: Went out towards the kitchen. I 'spect she's wore out...a whole week a-settin' here day and night. Mr. Johnson, if they ever was a fine 'un, she's it. You shore oughta be proud Vance gotta holt-a her.

JOHNSON: Yes, I know. I've been a plumb fool, Miz Farley. There's somethin' I got to do. (He goes out, then comes back in.) She's gone. That girl saved Millie's life. An' I didn't even git a chance to say anything.

Johnson sinks to his knees by his wife's bed, then slowly covers his face with his hands. The lights fade. A string band is heard, and the lights come up on the center stage to show a crowd on the street, with several couples dancing. The song ends and the people applaud. Vance and Alisee appear on one side, followed by Pat. Alisee seems more confident, more serene. Her hair is brushed and she's wearing shoes. As they enter, the crowd falls silent. As the crowd stares at Vance and Alisee, the silence becomes uncomfortable. Then a woman walks up to Alisee and offers her hand. Alisee takes it, and the woman smiles and envelops Alisee in a hug. Then other women come to thank her, shake hands, and hug her. Pat dabs at his eyes and turns away, but Vance makes him face the crowd. Several people come to shake Pat's hand, and soon Pat is smiling. Then Mr. and Mrs. Johnson enter.

JOHNSON: Howdy, Vance.

VANCE: Hello, Pa. You all right? Hello, Ma. How you feelin'?

MRS. JOHNSON: Feel fine now, Vance. I been up more'n two weeks.

JOHNSON: Ain't seen neither one o' you in all that time. I 'us beginning to think we'd have to climb up onto Newman's Ridge to get a look at you. Howdy, Alisee.

ALISEE: Howdy, Mr. Johnson, Mrs. Johnson.

MRS. JOHNSON: Alisee, I...I had a speech all figured out...I knew what I was going to say...wakin' up all those nights and having you sitting there smiling, like an angel of the Lord...I...

Mrs. Johnson breaks into sobs and hugs Alisee. The crowd applauds. "What's everybody clappin' their hands for?" Vance asks. "Didn't you ever see two women cryin'?" The people laugh and applaud some more.

JOHNSON: They say you're headin' for Nashville.

VANCE: We'll be comin' back here for a visit 'long about next spring.

JOHNSON: Your job supposed to run out then?

VANCE: No, the job'll wait all right. But we want our baby to be born in Hancock County.

Johnson shakes his son's hand and the people cheer again. Mrs. Johnson hugs Vance and Mr. Johnson hugs Alisee.

>JOHNSON: Pat Gibson, while we're straightenin' out things, they's sumpin' else I want to git cleared up. You had the right idea about what's good for Hancock County and its people. The company wants to double the askin' price for that timber.
>
>PAT: By dang, Mr. Johnson, we'll sell 'er! (More cheers and applause from the people.)
>
>JOHNSON: Seein' you know the ridges an' coves as well as anybody, I wanta hire you to boss the whole shootin' match. Will you do it?
>
>PAT: Well, Mr. Johnson, that means I'd have to work, an' I ain't hankerin' to git too involved.
>
>JOHNSON: Will you do it, Pat?
>
>ALISEE: 'Course he will, Mr. Johnson, an' he'll do you a good job. If he don't, I'll come back here and knock 'is brains out. (She hugs Pat.)
>
>VANCE: Got to make it across the mountain today to catch that train. We better be leavin'. We'll be expectin' all of you to visit us in Nashville.
>
>MAN IN CROWD: Me an' my wife an' fourteen young'uns? Boy, you better watch out what you're sayin'!
>
>MRS. FARLEY: Wish we had a goin' away present for you two.
>
>VANCE: That's mighty nice of you. Why don't you sing a hymn for us? Sing it so we can hear it down the road.

The choir sings softly as Vance and Alisee cross to a side stage. The lights on the center stage dim out.

>VANCE: Alisee, we're lucky to be livin' in a free land. I see a great future out there for America…a place where our baby can grow up with neighbor livin' next door to neighbor no matter who or what he is. We've had our troubles, but they don't matter much if that can happen.

Alisee and Vance walk off and the stage goes completely dark. There is silence for a moment as the audience realizes the play has ended, then the silence is broken by hearty applause. The lights come back up as the entire cast comes onstage to take their bows, and the audience gives them a standing ovation. Many in the audience have never seen a live play before and are amazed at how they have been transported into another time. And a large portion of the audience had been involved with the play in one way or another for the past year or more. They'd done it! Their applause was as much for their community as it was for the actors onstage.

Playwright Kermit Hunter attended the second night's performance on the Fourth of July. Prior to the first act, Hunter addressed the audience.

> There are many routes this play could take. It would be impossible to tell the whole story because it would take a dozen plays and would be twenty hours long. We simply selected those parts which seemed to be more dramatic. We told the story from the viewpoint of the Melungeons, just as "Unto These Hills" is told from the viewpoint of the Cherokee, and for this reason both plays show the white man in his worst and his best light. He is a land grabber, and a selfish, materialistic, thoughtless creature, but he is also kind and progressive and courageous. In fact, the play says that nearly anybody is good or bad by his nature and not by the color of his skin.[11]

Four years later, Hunter wrote in a letter to author Jean Patterson Bible:

> The story of the Melungeons is typical of some of the darker impulses in the American dream: those moments when the American dream gets crowded by white supremacy, the arrogance of wealth and position and power. The Melungeons happened to have dark skin, and for this reason they were buffeted and shunted by the white society moving across the mountains toward the west. It is significant that they were cared for and aided by the Red Man, who himself had felt the injustices of white supremacy.[12]

Writing about the play in her book *How They Shine: Melungeon Characters in the Fiction of Appalachia*, Katherine Vande Brake says *Walk Toward the Sunset* seems shallow.

> The characters are like one-dimensional icons instead of real people. One could argue that the form, that of outdoor theatre, is a constraint; however, the ancient Greeks worked in the same sort of physical setting and added masks to the characters' costumes so that even the tool of facial expressions was lost. No one can accuse Antigone or Oedipus of being a one-dimensional character.
>
> Furthermore, someone writing such a drama today might focus on the same issues—racial prejudice and local history—but in different ways. Racial equality was a 1960s crusade, and while still a problem in our society, the focus is different. The laws of the land now mandate equal opportunities for all; the problems are the more subtle ones of attitude. Certainly the Indians would also be treated differently as well. In his play, Hunter buys into the

---

[11] "Drama Off to a Good Start," 1.
[12] Bible, *Melungeons Yesterday and Today*, 115.

stereotype of Native Americans as violent warriors. The fact that the Cherokees invite the Melungeons to settle in their hunting ground seems unrealistic
as well.[13]

Vande Brake recognizes that Hunter was writing about themes of racial
equality in the 1960s, and that the topic would have been handled somewhat
differently, possibly with more nuance, had Hunter been writing in the late
twentieth or early twenty-first century. But Hunter, an experienced writer of
outdoor drama, knew his audience—or, more properly, his audiences. *Walk Toward the Sunset* was written, as many—if not most—outdoor dramas are written:
for two distinct audiences.

The first audience the writer of an outdoor drama must satisfy is the sponsoring group. In the case of *Walk Toward the Sunset*, that sponsoring group was
the Hancock County Drama Association, made up of both Melungeons and
non-Melungeons. Since non-Melungeons are decidedly the bad guys in the play,
the non-Melungeons in the Drama Association, as well as in Sneedville and Hancock County, were pretty good sports about having their ancestors portrayed as,
in Hunter's words, "selfish, materialistic, thoughtless creature[s]." However, the
play also portrayed the whites as—again in Hunter's words—"kind and progressive and courageous." The play could have portrayed the discrimination against
Melungeons in even more harsh terms and been more historically accurate. Instead, the play has a "happily ever after" ending, with the white people of
Sneedville grateful and accepting of the Melungeons, and the Melungeons gaining a favorable deal on their timber. The play implies that the discrimination and
prejudice the Melungeons faced had ended by the last quarter of the nineteenth
century, when in fact Melungeon children were not permitted in Hancock
County schools until the mid-twentieth century, and Melungeons faced legal
discrimination, such as Virginia's Racial Integrity Act, until the 1970s. Portraying whites in a more villainous manner might have been more accurate, but such
a portrayal would have likely offended some of the members of the Drama Association and the white citizens of Hancock County. A more historically accurate
version of history would likely have never gotten past the first reading of the
script by the Drama Association.

The second audience Hunter had to satisfy were the potential playgoers, the
people of northeast Tennessee, southwest Virginia, and southeastern Kentucky—the people most likely to travel to Sneedville to attend the play. With
several exceptions, these were not people we would generally think of as "theater

---

[13] Vande Brake, *How They Shine*, 178.

people;" they were, for the most part, unfamiliar with the works of Ibsen, Tennessee Williams, or Edward Albee. They didn't want complex characters. They wanted a straightforward story: "A" is followed by "B," leading to a conclusion, "C." This is not to imply that the people who enjoy outdoor theater are in any way unintelligent; rather, they are generally unfamiliar with more sophisticated forms of theater and aren't seeking nuance or complexity in an outdoor production. They simply want a good story about local history, with a few dance scenes and a happy ending. *Walk Toward the Sunset* fit the bill.

Kermit Hunter's play presented issues of race to an audience of people living in the upper South in the late 1960s. The area surrounding Sneedville, like much of southern Appalachia, was made up primarily of people of northern European descent; there were few African Americans living in that region, and many potential playgoers could not claim to know even one black person well enough to talk to him or her. That doesn't mean they didn't have strong opinions on racial questions. The racial turmoil of the 1960s—the marches led by Dr. Martin Luther King; the rise of militant blacks such as Malcolm X, H. Rap Brown, Stokely Carmichael, and the Black Panthers; riots in Watts, Detroit, Newark, and other cities—might be happening somewhere else, but it was still disturbing to the vast majority of whites in the region. More than a few of the cars that came over Clinch Mountain bearing playgoers still had "George Wallace for President" stickers adorning their bumpers. The people who would attend *Walk Toward the Sunset* were not, for the most part, racially enlightened people.

Many of these same people had seen and been moved by Hunter's *Unto These Hills*, which dealt with the mistreatment by whites of the Cherokees. A large percentage of Appalachian people were beginning to boast of Indian ancestry, whether genuine or of the "Cherokee princess" variety. By downplaying the African component of the Melungeons' ancestry and focusing more on the "mystery" of their origins, Hunter was able to move his audiences a step toward racial enlightenment. A baby step, to be sure, but a step nonetheless.

The play was generally well-received by both locals and out-of-towners. "Great," "Wonderful," "The best ever," were comments noted in the *Hancock County Post* after the play's opening weekend. Near-capacity crowds filled the amphitheater during that Fourth of July weekend. The following weekend saw the official dedication of the play, an event attended by such dignitaries as Jimmy Quillen, U.S. Representative from the First Congressional District; Knoxville mayor Leonard Rogers; and the president of Carson-Newman College, Dr. John

Fincher. The drama was dedicated "To the preservation of the Melungeon heritage. May it always succeed in this purpose and may the history of the Melungeon people be a continuous thread that reaches out to a bright future."[14]

---

[14] "Drama Off to a Good Start," 1.

9

LOOKING FOR MELUNGEONS

On the second weekend of *Walk Toward the Sunset*, Calvin Beale came to Sneedville.

Beale had written about the Melungeons and other mixed-ethnic communities in 1957 in the unfortunately named journal *Eugenics Quarterly*. Eugenics—from the Greek *eugenes*, meaning "well-born," is a social philosophy that aspires to improvement of the human population by promoting the reproduction of individuals with "good" genetic traits, while conversely discouraging the reproduction of those with "bad" traits. Very popular during the early twentieth century, the belief in eugenics led to measures such as Virginia's Racial Integrity Act of 1924, as well as the involuntary sterilization of individuals in many states who were believed to have "bad traits." The ultimate expression of the eugenic philosophy occurred in Nazi Germany, where millions of people with "bad traits"—including Judaism or other ethnic backgrounds considered undesirable by the Nazis—were put to death. As Beale later said of his article, "Today, I wish that I didn't have to say it was in *Eugenics Quarterly*—not because *Eugenics Quarterly* was a bad journal. It was a very reputable journal....But 'eugenics' had become a bad word, particularly after World War II, and it wasn't more than a couple more years before the journal took a different name."[1]

Calvin Lunsford Beale was a lifelong resident of the District of Columbia. Born in 1923, he studied geography at Wilson Teachers College in Washington D.C., which later merged with the all-black Miner Teachers College to form District of Columbia Teachers College. Beale also studied history at the University of Maryland and received a master's degree from the University of Wisconsin, where he studied demography. His interest in demographics led him to the Bureau of the Census, where he worked from 1946 to 1953.[2]

When Beale began working at the Census Bureau, the agency was preparing for the 1950 census. "There was at least one person there in authority," Beale

---

[1] Beale interview.

[2] Calvin L. Beale, *A Taste of the Country: A Collection of Calvin Beale's Writings*, Peter Morrison, editor, University Park, PA: The Pennsylvania State University Press, 1990, 2.

recalled in 2002, "who knew of William Gilbert's work [on mixed-ethnic communities] and who knew that…many of these groups [Gilbert] had looked at had been counted in the census inconsistently, say, from one census to another as to their race, or that different enumerators would treat them differently within the same census." Officials in the Census Bureau decided to pay close attention to the counties listed by Gilbert in his survey of "racial islands," and any person listed as "Indian" would be placed in a separate category designated "other." This would separate these presumed tri-racial people from federally recognized Indians, an idea Beale conceded was "a little bit misbegotten."

When the 1950 Census was complete, Beale, who was working on a different project, did some independent research. He had access to every portfolio of census returns, including those from counties that Gilbert had identified as containing mixed-ethnic communities. Portfolios from those counties bore a stamp indicating "Mixed Stock." Using the surnames identified by Gilbert, Beale began studying the census forms to see how the race of individuals had been identified.[3]

In 1953, Beale joined the Department of Agriculture, but his interest in mixed-ethnic communities continued. He was particularly interested in groups that Gilbert had missed or about which Gilbert had little information. Rather that study them from afar—"You can't know what's going on in the country from behind a desk in Washington," he later asserted—Beale traveled on his own time and at his own expense to visit mixed-ethnic groups such as the Gointown community in Rockingham County, North Carolina; the Alabama Creeks; the Carmel, Ohio, Melungeons; and the Smilings of Robeson County, North Carolina.[4]

Beale coined the term "triracial isolates," borrowed in part from a term common among anthropologists, "racial isolates." "I wondered what to call these people collectively. Because I wasn't interested in an individual group, but in providing, as [Gilbert] had done, a synoptic of all of these groups. And I limited myself only to those who had, either by self-identity or local ascription, three races—whether or not any individuals in [those groups] were necessarily of *triracial* descent."[5]

His article, "American Triracial Isolates: Their Status and Pertinence to Genetic Research," appeared in *Eugenics Quarterly* in December 1957. In the article, Beale estimated the triracial population as at least 77,000, distributed over 100 counties in 17 states, in groups ranging from 50 individuals to more than 20,000.

---

[3] Beale interview.
[4] Beale, *A Taste of the Country*, 38–39; Beale interview.
[5] Beale interview.

While many of these groups were associated with origin theories similar to the Melungeons, involving ancient seafaring people or other romantic legends, Beale took a more pragmatic view.

> [T]hey seem to have formed through miscegenation between Indians, whites, and Negroes—slave or free—in the Colonial and early Federal periods. In places the offspring of such unions—many of which were illegitimate under the law—tended to marry among themselves. Within a generation or so this practice created a distinctly new racial element in society, living apart from other races. The forces tending to perpetuate such groups, and the strength of these forces, differed from place to place. Some groups subsequently dispersed or were assimilated during the nineteenth century. Some waxed in numbers; others waned. Most have persisted to the present day.

Indian groups that had, in Beale's words, "absorbed both white and Negro blood," such as the Pamunkey, Narragansett, and Shinnecock were excluded from this study because they had "retained their tribal identity and historical continuity." Other Indian groups, including the Lumbee, Mattaponi, Monacans, Potomac, Nanticokes, and Rappahannocks, were deemed triracial isolates.

Like beauty, however, racial identity can be in the eye of the beholder. In those days, people did not fill out their own census forms, nor did they self-identify their racial or ethnic category. Beale, working with raw census data, acknowledged that his designation of groups as triracial was often based on the conclusion of the individual census takers rather than the generally accepted opinion of those who lived in the area where the supposed triracial people were found. He accepted those conclusions at face value. However, his travels to visit several of these groups had given him an insight not available through the census data.

> In general, all local informants will agree that the mixed population is partly white. (Blue eyes are commonly in evidence to validate this.) The white informant will insist that the mixed-blood people are partly Negro. Perhaps he will agree that they are partly Indian, perhaps not. The mixed-blood individual will usually insist—with vehemence, if necessary—that there is no Negro ancestry in his family (although he may not make this claim for all other families in the settlement) but that he is partly Indian. In a minority of communities unmistakable elements of Indian culture have been found. Presence of Negro ancestry may or may not be evident in some families from the occurrence of Negro hair forms or facial features. If evident, it tends to jeopardize the claims of the group to non-Negro status. In sum, the groups described are with few exceptions considered only of white and Indian descent by their members but are regarded to be partly Negro by neighboring whites or Negroes.

Beale noted that the Melungeons had commonly been listed as "mulatto" prior to the Civil War, but, by 1950, nearly all were listed by census takers as "white." It was a pattern he saw repeated in other groups; when a change in social status was experienced, it was generally to a "lighter classification."[6]

It is fortunate that Beale and other scientists, including William Gilbert and Edward Price, studied these triracial groups when they did, in the 1940s and 1950s. Social and legal segregation were already beginning to abate. It was much easier to identify members of a triracial group if they attended separate churches or their children attended separate schools. Outmigration and marriage outside the group further blurred the lines that identified the members of triracial groups. Within a few years, some of these groups would simply cease to exist as a distinct community, while identifying members of other groups would become more difficult.

However, at the time Beale and others published their articles, segregation and discrimination were still in force, and the members of the groups they studied were doing all they could to avoid being categorized as "Negro." Beale acknowledged that visible evidence of African ancestry tended to "jeopardize the claims of the group to non-Negro status." Publishing articles that suggested the members of the groups were even "partly Negro" also jeopardized those claims. Members of the tri-racial groups might never read *Eugenics Quarterly*, but it was highly possible that state legislators, county officials, and school board members might be aware of the information contained in articles about these groups and use that information to maintain segregation against them. After hearing that point made in a lecture in 2002, Beale said, "I have to admit that I never thought of that before."[7] The positive value of the work of Beale, Gilbert, and Price certainly outweighs the temporary problems their articles might have caused, but those problems did exist and may have been exacerbated by the publication of scientific articles.

In 1961, Beale became head of the Population Section of the Department of Agriculture's Economic Research Service. He eventually became the Senior Demographer for that service. Beale spent a great deal of time studying rural areas, combining statistical data with firsthand observations. As Peter Morrison noted in the introduction to a collection of Beale's writings, "Beale was the first to detect in some regions that more people were leaving metropolitan areas than were moving in—this in the late 1960s, when the government was contemplating the construction of new cities to handle urban spillover. Small wonder that

---

[6] Beale, "American Triracial Isolates," 187–96.
[7] Beale interview.

his discovery met with widespread skepticism until massive new evidence bore him out."[8]

In July 1969, Beale participated in a conference on Urban Decentralization at the Oak Ridge National Laboratory. Newspaper articles on the outdoor drama caught his attention, and he realized the play was a significant event for one of the triracial communities about which he had written. So, on Saturday, 12 July, Beale drove from Oak Ridge to Sneedville to see *Walk Toward the Sunset*.

> Along the way, I went through Grainger and Claiborne counties, which also have part of the Melungeon population. The countryside is a mixture of mountains and valleys. I went into Hancock County from Claiborne County following a road up the Clinch River Valley. [Beale came into Sneedville on the bucolic and level Highway 33 from U.S. 25-E, rather than the hair-raising ride over Clinch Mountain on Highway 31.] This valley I found very beautiful, with a bottomland of perhaps one-sixth to one quarter mile wide that is cultivated in corn and tobacco. Sneedville is a small town of just 800 population covering a fairly level area but surrounded by hills. The courthouse occupies a small square, which was filled with many men lounging around on the wall and the steps in the old-time southern Saturday afternoon courthouse manner. There were a good many men in bib overalls, a style of work clothes not much seen anymore.[9]

Sneedville's five-room Town Motel was full, but a young woman working at the amphitheater's box office agreed to find a place for Beale to spend the night. Then Beale asked if anyone was available to ride along with him as he drove through the county, pointing out areas of interest, particularly areas with Melungeons.

> She took me up to one of the school administration buildings and we found Mr. Claude Collins there, who is one of the men whose picture was shown in a recent article on the Melungeons published in the *Louisville Courier-Journal*. Collins is thirty-three years old, according to the article, and is the librarian of the school and also does certain administrative work for the school system. He agreed right away to act as my guide. This was a very fortunate circumstance for me because he is not only a Melungeon but one of the comparatively small number who are well-educated, being a college graduate and having a very objective view about the group and its history.
>
> Collins is white, yet there is something different about his appearance. He has very black hair, very dark eyes, and a somewhat sallow or slightly tan

[8] Beale, *A Taste of the Country*, 2.
[9] Beale, "Notes on a Visit to Hancock County, Tennessee," 42.

complexion, which is his natural color and not the result of sun. He was easy to talk with and we got along well together right away.

Collins told Beale he would show him Snake Hollow—Snake Holler to the locals—and Vardy Valley. Since the amphitheater and school administrative offices were at the very foot of Newman's Ridge, Beale's car began the climb right away. At the bottom of the other side of the Ridge, Collins directed Beale to turn left on a one-lane gravel road into Snake Hollow. Much of the land had been abandoned and was overgrown with brush. That land still under cultivation was occupied primarily by "poor people of lower socio-economic status," as Beale described in a chapter of his writings titled "Notes on a Visit to Hancock County, Tennessee."

> Snake Hollow contains one of the four remaining one-room schools in Hancock County. There are only eight left in the entire state. We stopped at the school, which is known as the Ramsey School. It is simply an old one-room wooden building with old-fashioned desk-and-chair units, in which one-person's chair is attached to the desk of the person behind him. There was an old coal stove and a pile of coal outside of the building. The building had electricity but no running water. The kids have to use a privy about seventy-five feet away. All or nearly all of the children are from Melungeon families. The county once had fifty schools. As a result of consolidation this is now down to fourteen and there is only one high school. However, Collins said the Ramsey School could not yet be discontinued because of lack of sufficient space in the school in Sneedville to take more elementary pupils. He said that he had been asked whether he would teach the school and told the person who asked him that the first thing he would do if assigned to teach that school was to set a match to it and burn it down. He felt that strongly about the inadequacy of education that the Melungeon children could get in this little school.

Leaving the Ramsey School, Beale and Collins continued up the Hollow on the narrow gravel road. Soon they met a car coming in the opposite direction. Beale stopped immediately but the other driver apparently didn't see Beale's car until the last moment and slammed on his brakes. Collins didn't recognize the glaring driver and told Beale, "Well, I guess he is going to cuss us out." The other driver held his tongue but wouldn't back up, even though he could have backed up to a wide place in the road easier than Beale. Wishing to avoid a confrontation, Beale backed up carefully and the other driver inched past and drove on, without raising his index finger from the wheel, a traditional Hancock County greeting to friends and strangers alike.

As they drove further up Snake Hollow, Collins told Beale they were going to meet a man named Bell. Along the way, they passed the homes of two other families named Bell. Beale noted that most of the people he saw had very dark complexions.

> By that I mean that they were people who were distinctly brown in color and who would under no circumstance be taken as being of unmixed white ancestry. However, these people did not have negroid features. Eventually we came to where the family lived that Collins wanted to see and we found them all out in the road near the house. There was a husband about fortyish who was the darkest person and who did have rather tightly curled hair, but without negroid facial features; his wife who was lighter and who was barefoot; his son who was probably about ten years old and fairly dark; and a somewhat lighter man who may have been his father. The husband had once taken an adult education class that Collins had taught, and Collins had become friendly with him in this connection.
>
> When we pulled up and stopped, Collins became very animated in his manner, in a way that rather surprised me, for he had been somewhat mild mannered and even a little feminine in his personality. Apparently one way of dealing with these families was on a jocular basis. Collins had a freshly lit cigarette in his hand and after he had greeted Bell, he said to him, "Gimmie a couple of cigarettes." Bell started to say, "I don't have none." But then he noticed Collins with his cigarette and said in a very rapid manner of speech, with a thick mountain accent, something like, "Goddamn, here this man just lit up a cigarette and he's trying to bum one off of me." But this successfully set a tone of banter between the two of them. Bell then took over and started joking [with] Collins. Collins was wearing a pair of shorts, checked shorts at that, and Bell said something like, "Look at this man with a pair of girls' shorts on. Come on, get out of this car here and let me see what those things look like." He tried to open the door to the car on Collins's side. Collins started fending him off saying, "Get away from me now, get away from me." Collins then sort of pointed to me, I guess after Bell had asked what we were doing up there, and said, "I brought the law along. We want to know who's making liquor up here." I thought this was an outrageous way to introduce me and would queer the conversation for sure. But apparently it would have been such an unthinkable thing for Collins to have brought the law in that Bell didn't for a moment believe that I was the law, and he joked right back. Collins said, "We want to know if you're making any whiskey up here." Bell said no, that he wasn't making any, but he could get us some. Collins said, "Who's making it?" Bell said, "Ain't nobody making it up here." Collins said, "Where you getting it from?" "Bringing it in from Claiborne County."

Beale had trouble understanding Bell's rapid and staccato speech. But he was impressed with Bell's display of Hancock County humor. Bell told a story of an incident that occurred when Collins was teaching the adult education class Bell had attended. Bell and several other men had jacked up Collins's car and put cinder blocks under the rear axle, lifting the wheels off the ground by only a couple of inches. When Collins was ready to go home, he started the car and put it into gear, but the car wouldn't move. While Collins tried to figure out why his car wouldn't move, the Melungeon men couldn't contain their laughter. When Collins realized what was wrong, he joined in the laughter. The Melungeons then charged him a quarter apiece to jack the car up again and remove the blocks.

Despite the joking, Beale quickly realized there was violence very close to the surface in Snake Hollow. Seated in his car, Beale first had thought Bell was holding a stick or shovel in his arms. But then he saw that the object Bell was cradling was a rifle. Beale also noticed that Bell's wife was carrying a rifle or shotgun.

> Bell asked, "Did you meet (so-and-so) on the road back there?"—meaning, as it turned out, the man with whom we almost had the head-on accident. We said yes. Then Bell said, "He shot at my feet up here a few minutes ago." He proceeded to tell us how the man in question, whose last name we did not catch, but which was not a Melungeon name, was angry about something Bell's son had done, and came there with a gun, apparently wanting the boy to be corrected in some way and threatening to shoot Bell if he didn't do so. Bell had told him that he might just as well shoot and kill him because he wasn't going to do anything. The man then fired his gun near Bell's foot. Bell rushed at him before he could do anything else and wrestled the gun away from him. I suppose in the meantime Mrs. Bell had run into the house and gotten their own gun. They had then forced the man to leave his gun and go away. It wasn't until this part of the story that Bell said rather casually, "He's married to my sister." So it was a family fuss with guns, and I think nothing typifies better the traditional, mountaineer nature of this rather isolated community of Melungeons.

Beale and Collins drove back the way they had come, leaving Snake Hollow and crossing Highway 63 into Vardy Valley. Beale noticed that the people in Vardy seemed to be of a higher socio-economic status, and not all the residents of the valley were Melungeon. The road was well paved, and the valley was wider, with more open area. Collins showed Beale the Vardy School, founded by Presbyterian missionaries and now operated by the county, despite steadily declining enrollment. They drove up on Newman's Ridge on a rough and poorly maintained road to visit the cabin of legendary Melungeon moonshiner Mahala Mullins.

Beale learned that in the previous twenty years, *all* the Melungeon families had left Newman's Ridge; only one family, non-Melungeon, lived on the Ridge by the summer 1969.

> I asked Collins whether the Melungeon people who moved away from Hancock County went to any particular locality. He immediately said yes, and named Ellicott City, Maryland, and Kokomo, Indiana. He went on to say, "If I walked down the streets of Ellicott City, I would recognize more people than I do here in Sneedville." Two of his brothers live there, his mother lived there for a period, and he himself taught school in Edmonston, Maryland, near Ellicott City, for a short period of time after losing his teaching position in Hancock County two or three years earlier when the school board administration changed.

Beale discovered that Collins had never heard the word "Melungeon" until Collins was a college student. The word was never used by his family or other Melungeons, nor was it used by local whites, at least not in his presence.

> Collins knew about Melungeons in neighboring Grainger County and also up into Virginia (certainly Lee County, which Hancock borders). I do not know whether he knew how extensive they are in Virginia. However, he knew nothing about Melungeons and similar types of people in either Campbell or Claiborne County, and when I told him about the existence of such people and some of the names, this was news to him.
>
> Collins had never heard of the Lumbee Indians of North Carolina. Nor did he know of the Rockingham, North Carolina, people who are named Goins and Harris and who used to include Gibsons (all relevant Melungeon names), nor any of the other Goins communities along the Virginia-North Carolina border, although he knew that the Melungeons had originally come to Tennessee from the Carolinas and Virginia. My point is, he did not know of the existence of present-day communities in those states where some Melungeon names are found. Nor did Collins know of the English ancestry of the Mullins family that I found in the 1880 census. He was quite interested to learn of this.

Beale took Collins back to his home, a modern brick house on Main Street east of downtown Sneedville, where they had a cold drink. Beale then went into town to have a bite to eat at Turner's Drug Store before the play.

> That evening at about 7:30 I went to the open-air amphitheater where the play was to be held. When I entered the amphitheater to take my seat, the young man taking tickets looked at me and asked, "Are you Mr. Beale?" I said yes. Then he said, "Well, we have a seat for you in our dignitary section." So

I guess Collins had tipped them off to watch for a stranger with a mustache and a slightly receding hairline. At any rate, my dignitary status got me a seat in the middle of the center section.[10]

Several years later, Beale recalled his evening in Sneedville for a gathering of the Melungeon Heritage Association. He recalled looking at the crafts available for purchase in the craft shop. He spent a few moments contemplating some homemade soaps when he heard Claude Collins's voice behind him: "Mr. Beale, are you planning on taking a bath?"[11] After a description of the plot of *Walk Toward the Sunset*, Beale wrote,

> What the playwright has done is to demonstrate to the whites the rather mindless racial prejudice that they have had against the Melungeons, and the injustice that the Melungeons have suffered as a result. But, in the second half of the play, he very distinctly and deliberately portrays the Melungeons as having gone downhill socially and culturally in the previous hundred years. They are pictured as being for the most part barefooted hillbillies given to moonshining and quite disinclined to work for a living. His message to the Melungeons is that "the world was passing them by" and that despite the injustices of the past, they could not simply continue to retreat to the mountain ridges. Their youth would get nowhere anymore without an education and it was necessary for them to change their attitudes if they were not to completely degenerate.
>
> Today, another century after the setting of the play's final act, some of the older isolation and mode of living remains. But an enormous amount of material and social progress has been made in the last generation. The play has been well received by most of the Melungeon element of the population. Bell of Snake Hollow said that he had seen it, enjoyed it, and planned to go again. The act of sponsoring the play and thus confronting publicly the mystery of their origin and their inferior status in the past seems to have been liberating in itself.[12]

Congressman Jimmy Quillen, who attended the play for its official dedication on the second weekend, called *Walk Toward the Sunset* one of the best outdoor dramas he had ever seen. Knoxville Mayor Leonard Rogers went further, calling it the best drama he had ever seen.[13] Of course, politicians have been known to engage in hyperbole. Still, audiences did seem well pleased with the

---

[10] Ibid., 42–50.
[11] Beale, "Researching Triracial Communities," presentation.
[12] Beale, "Notes on a Visit to Hancock County, Tennessee," 50–52.
[13] "Drama off to a Good Start," 1.

drama. Perhaps even more significantly, most Hancock Countians were impressed with the play and the number of people who made the journey over Clinch Mountain to see it. VISTA and cast member Steve Nichandros, recalls his landlord's shift in attitude about the play.

> Yeah, I did hear from my landlord and his family, because they were so—I don't want to say, *against* it—more like, not in favor of it. But they did come and see it—that was in the first season—and they didn't have anything bad to say about it. Rather, they had something good to say about it. There was just a general feeling I had; I don't have a specific—because this is what Hancock County was famous for, not speaking openly about something that needed to be discussed, which keeps it, uh, call it a "dirty rumor." So I think in that respect it was tremendously positive.[14]

Country singer Brenda Carter attended the drama on Friday, 18 July. The year before, she had released what would be her biggest hit, a duet with George Jones titled "Milwaukee, Here I Come." Jones recorded for the Musicor label at that time, and his usual duet partner, Melba Montgomery, had left Musicor and gone to Capitol Records. Jones's future duet partner (and future wife), Tammy Wynette, recorded on the Epic label, and Musicor wanted to pair Jones with someone who was on their roster of performers. So the producers of the record tapped another Musicor artist, Brenda Carter, to sing the song with Jones. As one reviewer put it years later, "To put it charitably, she was no Melba or Tammy." Still, the record was popular, and Carter would record another duet with Jones, "Great Big Spirit of Love." Brenda Carter was booked to perform at the Tazewell Speedway in neighboring Claiborne County on Saturday night. So on Friday, she came to Sneedville, toured the county, had dinner at the Sunset Restaurant, and attended the play.[15]

For the first two weekends of *Walk Toward the Sunset*, the cast performed under minimal lighting; the equipment they had ordered was still delayed by the rail strike. The new equipment arrived in time for the third weekend. But on that third weekend, even with the additional lighting on the stage, many audience members couldn't help taking their eyes away from the stage from time to time to look up toward the thin sliver of crescent moon that was visible. On the morning of Wednesday, 16 July, a Saturn rocket had lifted off from Cape Kennedy to fulfill the late president John F. Kennedy's 1961 promise to put a man

---

[14] Nichandros interview.
[15] "Brenda Carter at Tazewell This Saturday," 1; Razor X, "Classic Rewind: George Jones & Tammy Wynette—'Milwaukee, Here I Come,'"; "Album Review: Porter Wagoner & Dolly Parton—'Always, Always.'"

on the moon before the decade was out. As cast members delivered their lines on Saturday night, the command module and lunar lander of Apollo 11 were orbiting the moon. On Sunday, the lunar lander, with astronauts Neil Armstrong and Edwin "Buzz" Aldrin aboard, separated from the command module, piloted by Michael Collins. Although the astronaut Collins was of Irish descent, some people in Hancock County noted that he shared a surname with a good many Melungeons.

The lunar lander, named Eagle, touched down on the moon on Sunday afternoon. Just before 11:00 p.m. in Tennessee, Neil Armstrong exited Eagle and became the first person to step on the moon. Mary Bowler was watching on television.

> I remember the power went out for some reason—it was really weird. The men landed on the moon and all of a sudden our power went out. And people said "That was because we were up there doing something we shouldn't have been doing. Shouldn't have been up there on the moon." They did—they said that. I don't know what caused the power to go out; I guess maybe it was a storm.[16]

On 22 July, director John Lee Welton appeared on *The Betty Adler Show*, a morning program on WBIR-TV, Channel 10 in Knoxville. Welton and Adler discussed the drama, and cast members Annette Turner, Nancy Pierce, Roger Hopkins, and Nancy Johnston performed one of the musical numbers from the drama, "Chickmey, Chickmey," accompanied by the dulcimer playing of Mollie Bowlin.[17]

Some of the people attending *Walk Toward the Sunset* came into town on a bus operated by Knoxville Tours, operated by Larry Phillips and bus driver Vaughn Wilson. Other tour bus operators began regular weekend runs from Knoxville and Morristown. At least one bus driver found the narrow, twisting Highway 31 across Clinch Mountain more than he could handle alone; he had some of the passengers get off the bus to guide him through some of the hairpin turns.[18] Once a tour bus got to Sneedville, the visitors were invited to ride over Newman's Ridge in school buses. Claude Collins or Elmer Turner would serve as tour guides as the bus crossed Newman's Ridge into Vardy Valley, pointing out sites such as the Presbyterian mission school and the cabin of fabled moonshiner Mahala Mullins. The passengers would see the rustic county museum created by Lena Jarvis and have a meal at the Sunset Restaurant. Once the play was

---

[16] Van Nest interview.
[17] "Drama Off to a Good Start."
[18] Welton interview.

over, the tour buses would take their passengers back to Knoxville or Morristown.

"There were buses that came into Sneedville on Friday or Saturday nights, sometimes 10 or 12 buses in an afternoon," recalled Claude Collins. "Well, I'd do a bus tour over into Vardy Valley and show them the Presbyterian National Board of Missions, and this and that."[19]

A lot of the tourists weren't particularly interested in seeing an old schoolhouse or a museum. They wanted to see Melungeons. Of course, they'd been seeing Melungeons since they first arrived in Hancock County, but usually didn't recognize them as such. Claude Collins had the black hair, swarthy skin, and blue eyes the tourists expected to see, but Claude was—well, too *normal* looking. He was college-educated and articulate, and dressed more or less the same as the tourists. Many of the visitors expected to see the Melungeons they'd read or heard about: wild, feral people with olive skin, and perhaps six fingers on each hand. The Melungeons they'd seen didn't fit the bill.

These tourists weren't the first to come into the county hoping to see some exotic-looking Melungeons. Sociologist John Shelton Reed, a native of Kingsport, wrote about visiting Sneedville as a youth. He and a friend hoped to catch of glimpse of the Melungeons of legend.

> I wish this story had some drama to it, some fateful encounter or embarrassing discovery, but as a writer of non-fiction, I'm stuck with the facts. What happened was that we cruised Sneedville's down-at-the-heels main street, circumspectly eyeing the locals (we knew better than to stare). We were checking for extra fingers, but we didn't see any. Nor did we see any "olive" skin, which we imagined to be green. We stopped in a general store to buy some junk food—I was partial to Dolly Madison cream-filled cupcakes—and we made idle conversation with the man behind the counter. We talked about this and that, but not about Melungeons. Oddly, for a couple of bumptious teenage city boys, we were reluctant even to say the word: it didn't seem *polite*. So we left Sneedville no wiser than we'd come.[20]

Reed's sister, novelist Lisa Alther, made a similar journey to Sneedville, hoping to see exotic-looking Melungeons. She was fortunate enough to meet a woman who had one of the surnames identified with Melungeons, but when she asked the woman if she was a Melungeon, the frosty look Alther received told her that she had offended the woman by asking. That just wasn't done.[21]

---

[19] Claude Collins interview (2002).
[20] Reed, "Mixing in the Mountains," 25.
[21] Alther, *Kinfolks*, 57–58.

Despite the willingness of Claude Collins and a few others to acknowledge their heritage, most folks in Hancock County still considered it rude to ask an individual if he or she were Melungeon—especially if the individual in question was *not* a Melungeon. Some tourists drove their own cars over Newman's Ridge and set out to find Melungeons in Vardy Valley. Sometimes they would pull into someone's driveway and ask the startled residents where Melungeons might be found.

Though Collins was careful to point out places of significance rather than individuals, the buses came to be resented by several Valley residents who were concerned that they were being pointed out and stared at. Such incidents particularly rankled those residents who *weren't* Melungeons. One Valley resident was visibly upset when, years later, he told anthropologist Anthony Cavender about one such incident. One of the buses had stopped in front of his house while he was sitting on his front porch. He learned that he was being pointed out to the tourists as a Melungeon.

"Why, I couldn't believe it," the man recalled. "I walked over to [the tour guide] standing by the bus and said, pointing to that bus full of people, 'Why, that's the biggest bunch of Melungeons *I* ever did see! They ought to put all of *you* in a zoo!'" Cavender wrote that when he asked the tour guide (likely Claude Collins) for his version of the story, he was told that "the whole affair was but another example of the conservative, unprogressive outlook of the people in Hancock County."[22]

"Well, I was all but drug off that mountain," Collins recalled years later. "People in the valley didn't appreciate me doing it. So I soon had to quit doing that, because people resented it.... I stopped over there in Vardy Valley once and there were some men who were going to drag me off there." After receiving several complaints, a local magistrate advised Collins to quit taking tour buses into the valley.[23]

Still, tourists continued to cross Clinch Mountain to see the play. Mayor Charles Turner wrote in his *Post* column, "It is very true that we are somewhat handicapped by lack of accommodations compared to other areas, especially in housing. These things are understandable and can be excused for the present at least...."[24] Clearly, Sneedville was experiencing an unprecedented influx of visitors. But there were no other attractions in the county to keep visitors (and their money) in the county once they'd seen the play. And there was still practically nowhere in town for those visitors to stay.

---

[22] Cavender, "The Melungeons of Upper East Tennessee," 33–34.
[23] Claude Collins interview (2002).
[24] Turner, "This is YOUR Town," 31 July 1969, 1.

Sneedville, Tennessee, ca. 1973.

Mayor Charles Turner.

W. C. "Claude" Collins.

Dora Bowlin.

Concession stand, box office, and craft shop.

John Lee Welton.

Kermit Hunter.

Amphitheater.

Scott Collins.

A. Y. "Sonny" Turner.

From left to right: Charles Turner, John Lee Welton, Nancy Johnston, and Mike Atherton, prior to opening night, July 1969.

Molly Bowlin performs
before the show.

Kyle Green.

Charles Turner (left) and Congressman Jimmy Quillen (third from left)
attend a performance, Saturday, 12 July 1969.

Scene from *Walk Toward the Sunset.*

Scene from *Walk Toward the Sunset.*

Miss Martha Collins.   Mike Hughes.

Congressman Quillen visits the cast after the show.

Annette Turner.

Roy Garland.

Turner's Drug Store.

Ben Harville.

Dr. Truett Pierce.

Carol Ann McGuire and Patrick Crouch onstage, Summer 1973.

Tennessee Ernie Ford.

Larry Clifton.

A dance scene from *Walk Toward the Sunset*.

Souvenir program from the 1973 season.

Mike Murphy (top), Rose Williams (bottom),
and Reba Ramsey wearing an antique dress.

Pamphlet (cover) for the 1976 season,
distributed to highway rest stops and visitor centers.

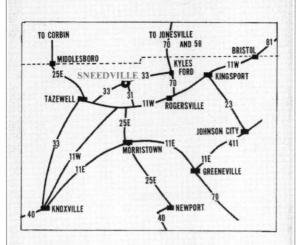

Sneedville is easily accessible amid some of the area's most spectacular scenery. The amphitheater is located near the center of town north of the courthouse about one-half mile. The Sunrise Craft House, located on the drama site, sells Tennessee handicrafts.

Another area attraction is Elrod Falls Park located off State Highway 31 near the Treadway community, with camp sites and stocked trout streams.

THEATRE TICKETS
Adults $3.50—Children (under 12) $1.50
(Group Rates Available)
WALK TOWARD THE SUNSET IS PRESENTED EVERY
THURSDAY, FRIDAY AND SATURDAY
DURING JULY AND AUGUST
PERFORMANCE TIME 8:30 P.M. (EDT)
For Tickets Write "Walk Toward the Sunset"
Sneedville, Tenn. 37869 or Telephone (615) 733-8810
Name _____
Address _____
City_____ State _____ Zip_____
(No. Tickets) Adults_____Children_____
_____ performance
          day   date

Enclosed is my check or money order for $ _____
Please allow ample time to mail tickets or confirmation. If time does not permit this, you may pick up your tickets at the box office.

TICKETS ARE ALSO ON SALE
AT THE BOX OFFICE.

Pamphlet (back).

Walk Toward the Sunset

THE MYSTERY...

The theory that the Melungeons discovered America is only one of the dozen unproven legends about the origins of this dark-skinned people, who for years have lived quietly on Newman's Ridge high in the East Tennessee mountains near Sneedville, Tennessee.

Some say the Melungeons are descendants of Sir Walter Raleigh's colony of Englishmen at Roanoke Island, which mysteriously disappeared around 1560. Another bit of folklore declares that the Melungeons originated with the deserters from DeSoto's Spanish expedition of 1540. One of the most popular theories among the Melungeons themselves is that they are of Portuguese descent, related somehow to a long-ago band of shipwrecked sailors. There are also those who claim to trace the Melungeon ancestry back to one of the lost tribes of Israel. Some romanticists believe that Shakespeare's Othello was an ancient Melungeon. Others subscribe to the belief that the Melungeons are descended from a group of dissident Welshmen led by Prince Madoc. But the theory that excites the most interest and has gained much scholarly support recently is one claiming that the Phoenicians, highly skilled sea-going people who ruled the oceans before Rome was built, may have found the Western World some 2,000 years before the time of Columbus.

The Melungeons were never adherents to the Indian religions and rites, but adhered to the Christian religion. The cross was ever held by them as a sacred symbol.

Where did they come from and who were they? No one knows. Many guesses have been made. Historians have studied it and scholars have contemplated it, but no answer is available. See the passionate story of the courageous Melungeon people in their fight for the freedom to be left alone with their mysterious background and unknown heritage.

The Author
Kermit Hunter

Kermit Hunter has emerged as one of America's foremost exponents of the outdoor drama. He has been instrumental in restoring the outdoor theatre to a level of dramatic art transcending typical local or historical pageantry. In the nationally famous **UNTO THESE HILLS**, Dr. Hunter inaugurated his successful authorship of this new form. He has written numerous dramas for localities all over the United States. A native of West Virginia and the mountain country of the Alleghenies, Dr. Hunter's concept of American History is that of one who loves the land and its people.

In 1964 Dr. Hunter was appointed Dean of the School of Arts at Southern Methodist University, Dallas, Texas.

WALK TOWARD THE SUNSET deals with the universal problems of mankind within the history of Appalachia and its people.

Pamphlet (inside).

10

THE FIRST SEASON

The cast and crew of *Walk Toward the Sunset* was a mix of drama students from Carson-Newman College in Jefferson City, about forty-five miles southwest of Sneedville, VISTA workers from various parts of the United States, and local people from Hancock County.

As noted earlier, the director, John Lee Welton, had been instrumental in the drama project from the very beginning. A native of Pampa, Texas, Welton received his B.A. and M.A. from West Texas State University and had been with the drama department at Carson-Newman College for nine years. He had directed more than fifty plays, including outdoor dramas, and had received a Danforth Grant to study drama across the South. He lived in Jefferson City with his wife and two children, but during the drama season, resided in Sneedville four days each week.[1]

David Behan was the Designer and Technical Director. Born in Evanston, Illinois, Behan received a B.A. in Speech and Drama from Lake Forest College in Lake Forest, Illinois, and his B.A. in Drama from Indiana University. He had taught high school drama and had also worked in commercial film production in Chicago. When he became involved with *Walk Toward the Sunset*, he had been teaching drama for three years at Tusculum College in Greeneville, Tennessee, where he lived with his wife and two children. Behan had arranged the loan of Revolutionary-era costumes from Tusculum College.

Husband and wife Joe and Patsy Craver served as stage manager and music director, respectively. Joe was a native of Davidson County, North Carolina, and following his graduation from Carson-Newman College with a B.A. in speech and theater, he attended Southwestern Baptist Theological Seminary in Fort Worth, Texas. In summer 1969, while playing the role of Cherokee Chief Atakullakulla in Act 1 of the play, and John Netherland in the second act, he was also working on his master's degree in drama from the University of North Carolina at Greensboro. Patsy Craver, originally from Greensboro, North Carolina, had graduated from the University of North Carolina and studied music at

---

[1] *Walk Toward the Sunset* souvenir program, 1970, 5.

the University of Salzburg, Austria. Patsy played one of the Sneedville villagers in Act 2.

Gene Mathis served as production manager and played two roles: the farmer Mr. Sylvester in the first act, and Sneedville businessman Ezra Johnson, the father of lead character Vance Johnson, in the second act. A native of Winters, Texas, Mathis received his B.A. at McMurray College in Abilene, Texas, and his M.A. from Baylor University in Waco. In 1969 he was an assistant professor of speech at Carson-Newman.

Liz Highers of Chattanooga, Tennessee, was the assistant to the director and appeared in all the dance scenes. She was also an understudy for the roles of Alisee Collins in the first act and Alisee Gibson in the second act. Alisee Gibson was the granddaughter of Pat Gibson and Alisee Collins. The similarity of names, plus the fact that the two characters were played by the same actress, sometimes caused confusion. Highers, a junior at Carson-Newman was studying speech and theatre.

Nancy Johnston played the lead female roles of Alisee Collins and Alisee Gibson. A native of Decatur, Georgia, she was a junior at Carson-Newman, majoring in English. The lead male roles of Pat Gibson and Vance Johnson were played by Washington, D.C., native Mike Atherton, who had just graduated Carson-Newman College but stayed in Tennessee to perform in *Walk Toward the Sunset*.

Jacksonville, Florida, native Ron Brannan played Preacher Givens in the first act, and was one of the villagers in the second act. He was a senior at Carson-Newman, studying philosophy.

Gayle Clevinger played Mrs. Farley, a Sneedville woman, in the second act. She was also one of the Indian dancers in the first act, and one of the wedding dancers in the second act. A Jefferson City native and senior History major at Carson-Newman, Clevinger received the "Best Student Director" award at Carson-Newman for her work with the 1968–1969 production of *Finian's Rainbow*.[2]

Raymond Buffington of Gainesville, Georgia, was a senior at Carson-Newman, majoring in speech. He played John Sevier in the first act, and Pat Gibson in the second. Years later, he recalled,

> I probably would not have done it at all if I had completed my degree on time, so it was really a kind of situation where I kind of messed up my senior year and didn't finish one of my major requirements, so I had to stay on at Carson-Newman during that summer to meet that requirement and graduate

---

[2] "A History of the Drama," 7 August 1969, 2; "Well Done…Thank You," 1.

in August. So since I was there and this project was in the works, I had the time available, and Dr. Welton made the situation, uh…I honestly don't recall if there was an audition process, or the typical kinds of things that you do when you're casting a play. But nevertheless, I was happy to do the part, or the two parts.[3]

Mike and Ann Hughes were VISTAs from California. They had both received B.A. degrees in education from Chico State College before joining VISTA. They lived in the Mulberry Gap Community in Hancock County. Mike played the scout in Act 1, and a lumberman in Act 2. Ann played a villager and was also involved in the Sunrise Craft Guild, which sold crafts local crafts from a log structure outside the amphitheater.

VISTA Susan Klein was from upstate New York, a student at Cornell University, and played a villager. Bob Van Nest was a VISTA from Summit, New Jersey. A history major, with a B.A. from St. Lawrence University and an M.A. from Columbia University, he played Governor Senter in the second act. VISTA Julie McDevitt worked with the costumes and played both a Melungeon villager and an Indian in Act 1 and was a dancer in the second act.[4]

Steve Nichandros, a VISTA from Orinda, California, played Tom Robertson in the second act. In the first act, he was the Sun King in the dramatic Indian dance, symbolically fertilizing Mary Bowler, a VISTA from Newark, New Jersey, who also played a Melungeon from Newman's Ridge in the second act. Mary recalled learning of the drama in its planning stages:

> There were meetings to discuss it, and the people from Carson-Newman College came to talk to us, and I think we knew right from the beginning that we were going to be involved in it. I don't know if they assumed we would be involved in it; I just remember thinking, "Oh, the drama is going to happen and we're going to be in it." …I remember thinking it would be fun.…[5]

Ann Haralson, who played a Sneedville villager in the second act, was a VISTA from British Columbia, Canada, and lived in the Kyles Ford community. An experienced newspaper reporter with a degree in communications, Ann also contributed several articles about the drama and other topics to the *Hancock County Post*.[6]

Annette Turner, an English teacher at Hancock County High School, played Mrs. Bolton in Act 1, as well as Melungeon from Newman's Ridge in Act

---

[3] Buffington interview.
[4] Matheison, "New VISTA Workers Ready," 3.
[5] Van Nest interview.
[6] Matheison, "New VISTA Workers Ready," 3.

2. Her husband, Sonny, played a villager in the second act. John Montgomery, publisher of the *Hancock County Post* and an important booster of *Walk Toward the Sunset*, played one of the Knoxville lumbermen in the second act. Dora Bowlin, one of the founding members of the Hancock County Drama Association, played Vance Johnson's mother Millie in the second act. Sneedville hardware merchant Kyle Lawson played Daniel Boone in the first act and served on the lighting and sound crew with Junior Collins, Paul Mullins, and Scott Collins.

Other locals who filled out crowd scenes and took part in dance scenes included Keith Greene, Roger Hopkins, Janice Kinsler, Patricia Pierce, Lucille Trent, Zella Mills, Betty Lawson, Reba Ramsey, Norma Campbell, Lonnie Bowlin, Rosemary Mills, John Gillis, Lucille Mabe, E. G. Parkey, Linda Mullins, Linda Mabe, Mike Clonce, and Carol Campbell. Kyle Greene supervised the construction crew of Operation Mainstream workers—the "Happy Pappies"— under the auspices of the federally-funded Office of Economic Development.[7]

Housing for the Carson-Newman students was a concern from the very beginning of the drama. Jefferson City was more than an hour away via the treacherous Highway 31 over Clinch Mountain. There had been improvements made on both the northern and southern approaches to the mountain, but on the mountain itself the highway was a nightmare of hairpin turns without guardrails. No one wanted the student actors driving that road at night after the Thursday, Friday, and Saturday performances, so places were found for the actors in town.

Ray Buffington and several male members of the cast stayed in the spacious basement of Elmer and Hazel Turner, just a hundred yards or so from the amphitheater. The Turners were both educators—Elmer was a school administrator, and Hazel taught fifth grade at the Sneedville Elementary School. Others stayed at rental houses in the area, with rent paid by the Drama Association. There were few options for eating out. Buffington recalled often taking lunch at Turner's Drugstore, and he quickly learned that the food at the rustic Green Top Inn was much better than the dilapidated exterior led him to expect.

> There was a restaurant called the Green Top Inn, and that's where we had supper every day. And that was one of the finest places I've ever been in my life. Absolutely. It was extremely humble, and the dining room had picnic tables inside. But the food was great, you know? It was great Southern-style cooking, and that's what I grew up on, so I enjoyed it. It was dirt cheap, and it was always crowded, every day, because it was such a great bargain and the food was so good. And I can remember—I think there was a grocery store

---

[7] *Walk Toward the Sunset* souvenir program, 1969.

right next door to it, and I can remember on more than one occasion if they ran out of something in the kitchen of the restaurant, one of the girls would come through the dining room real fast, go out the screen door to the grocery store, and come right back in with a couple of things in her hand, and after a couple more minutes they would be serving it to us on the table. It was a great place. I doubt if that exists any more.[8]

Mary Bowler also had fond memories of the Green Top Inn.

That was one of our favorite places. We used to get such a kick out of that because the fellow that owned it—I can picture him so clearly now, a big tall, lanky guy with a crew cut. He would carry out one plate at a time and bring it to you and would never use a tray—it would take him forever to bring everybody's food out. Yeah, that was a great place. That, and...Charles Turner's place was the best place to get cheeseburgers. And then there was another place that had great milkshakes and cheeseburgers. It was on the right hand side; I think it was a drive-up, too.[9]

The students and VISTA workers probably didn't realize that the owner of the Green Top Inn, who also served as the waiter, didn't read or write—or at least, not well enough to write down orders. That's why he took the orders one at a time. He also served "country-style," that is, men were served first. If two couples were seated at a table, the owner would ask one of the men what he wanted. Then he'd go to the kitchen, where his wife did the cooking, and put the food on a plate and carry it back to the dining area and serve his customer. Then he'd ask the second man what he wanted and repeat the process. Only after the men were served did he ask the women what they wanted. The food was apparently so good that none of the student or VISTA actors recalled the "men first" policy at the Green Top Inn.[10]

Hancock County had few opportunities for entertainment, but Raymond Buffington recalls a few opportunities for fun.

I remember there was a movie theater or some public space in some building where movies were shown, and I remember one day all of us from school went to see *Gone with the Wind*, and I don't remember if it was a legitimate movie theater or if it was some other space. Sometimes we would just drive around, out in the country, just to see where we were, to scope out the area outside the town proper....I think that summer, too—because we weren't that far from Kentucky—some of us went to Kentucky once to see another outdoor

[8] Buffington interview.
[9] Van Nest interview.
[10] Welton interview (2002); author's recollection.

drama there—oh, boy, it was Pineville, or Pikeville, Kentucky—it was a great
show called, I think it was called *The Book of Job.*[11]

It was natural that the actors from Carson-Newman College and the VIS-
TAs in the cast would socialize. As Buffington says, "We were all young and
educated and from somewhere else. And, you know, that has its hazards, too. I'm
sure we didn't think about it at the time, but you know, do-gooders from out of
town, coming in and stirring things up…(chuckles)."

VISTA Mary Bowler got to know some of the student actors after hours.

> Oh, yeah, definitely. Because as much as we [the VISTA workers] liked
> each other—and we did; we were a tight-knit group—our social contacts were
> rather limited, other than visiting with our neighbors. We spent a lot of time
> with our neighbors, but as far as socializing with anybody our own age or
> with our interests—yeah, we were ready for some new faces. Yeah, we got
> quite friendly with them, especially with a couple of them….
>
> What did we do? Sometimes we'd go to Morristown, but not much. We
> might go to see a movie, but not very often. We just hung out together, you
> know—hung around each other's houses, listening to music, whatever….
> During the day we were always busy, and we often had meetings at night; we
> were always going to meetings. So we really didn't have a whole lot of time
> to socialize. And we didn't have television, most of us, so at night we just
> read.

The VISTAs were a little older, on average, than the students, and were
living in rented houses rather than boarding with locals. As a result, Bowler recalls entertainments of a more adult nature. "Well, we'd go to each other's houses
and drink the beer that we had to travel quite a way to get." Hancock County
was "dry," and although there were bootleggers scattered across the county, purchasing alcohol legally required a drive to Gate City, Virginia, forty-five miles
away.

Years later, Mary Bowler Van Nest recalled several of the locals with fondness but admits not having much in common with most of the people in Hancock County.

> No, we didn't. No, not at all. The Bowlins—their kids are the only ones
> I can think of right off hand that had been to college. It was interesting—
> some of [the locals] were very bright; they just didn't have the opportunities
> to go to school. So, no, we did not have that much in common with them….

---

[11] Buffington interview.

[But] the poor folks, the ones we worked with? ...[F]or some reason, we all felt an instant connection with them, I think. We really—I mean, we knew we were different, but we really built up some close relationships very quickly. And I don't know if it was our idealism at the time, or—I don't know. I had been working with poor people for a long time in Newark, so it wasn't that alien to me. And I also had relatives in New York State, and some of them were quite poor. But as far as the other VISTAs—I don't know. We all—I don't think we ever looked down on them, by any means. We just really respected them, and really got very close to them in a very short time. To this day, I think about them a lot, with such fond, fond memories. I just feel really fortunate that we had that opportunity...

I know we had a place [at the drama site] where we sold locally made trinkets, or trips as they would call them down there—you know, crafts. They sold quilts, I believe, and nicely done creations that women sewed and dolls. I remember one of the things we tried to do was to get locals to make crafts for this shop as a way of earning a little extra money. And I had my dear, dear neighbor Wilf Drinnon, who was a wonderful man who died the year we were there—I'm looking at a picture of him right now that I took of him on his porch; he was just the greatest guy. He lived just down the road from us, and he would do just everything we asked him to do, you know; he was just so sweet. He came up with this plow that he had made out of wood and painted it blue. I still have it.... I don't remember him making more than that one, and I kept it.

Van Nest recalled that some of the VISTAs put together a souvenir booklet for sale at the craft shop. The project was an outgrowth of the VISTAs' efforts to understand the unique dialect spoken in Hancock County.

I'm looking at this book here, this little booklet that we VISTAs put together called *Hancockiana*. We were selling it at the drama. It says *Hancockiana, or a casual collection of words and sayings common to Hancock County, Tennessee and other folksy places, summer of 1969. Our price is 35 cents.* We had a little introduction about language...and then we have a glossary of terms common to Hancock County, terms that Bob and I still use. Like today when we heard it was going to snow, we said, "Hit's a-gonna snow. Yep, a big-un's a-comin'. But it's not gonna lay on very long, this time of year." We had a lot of fun putting this together. Mostly it was Bob and I—and Mike Hughes. I'm sure Steve had something to do with it, too. He acquired quite an accent; he loved using these expressions, too. I'm sure he had something to do with it.

Well, nobody comes to Hancock County without taking a bit of it with them.

No, gosh no—that's for sure.[12]

VISTAs and students alike recall being cautioned about referring to Melungeons or asking if someone had Melungeon ancestry. Steve Nichandros remembered,

> We had an informal introduction from the two VISTAs that were there before the nine of us arrived. And those two VISTAs were leaving; I think there was a week of overlap—might have been two weeks. We were advised not to say "Melungeon" or to talk about Melungeons by the two VISTAs that were there when we arrived.

> *What do you remember being told?*
> That they were either a real or a mythical race; that it was not known. And that they were—I don't want to say persecuted—put down, or thought very poorly of by other people. I pretty much remember being told that it was without any justification, and that it was arbitrary—somebody would point a finger and say, "That's a Melungeon," but where does it say that person is a Melungeon? So I got the impression it was a bad thing.[13]

Raymond Buffington also recalled being advised to be careful about discussing Melungeons.

> I mean, it would have been very presumptuous of us to ask around town, as we were having lunch or whatever, to discuss those kinds of things, so, as young as we were, we still knew our manners.

> *Did anyone have the opportunity to tell you beforehand that this is not something you want to bring up, or was it something you just picked up when you were in Sneedville?*
> Yeah, I think when we had talked about the whole purpose for being there, and the fact that this was—why this project was put together, and that there were still Melungeon families in the area, and it was explicit in the play that there was great prejudice against them, I think that we did discuss that. I mean, I don't remember anything specific, but my sense is that we knew to be judicious in who we talked to and what we talked about. We were the outsiders coming in, so—there's always a degree of skepticism and suspicion over people like us.
> You know, I think, at the time—because we were very curious; we were playing Melungeons, the play was about the Melungeons—we were always

---

[12] Van Nest interview.
[13] Nichandros interview.

on the lookout for Melungeons and we never knew if we actually saw a Melungeon, so I'm not sure if we had any preconceived notions that were confirmed or disproved or what, you know? My general sense was that they were poor country people who had been there longer than I had and that it was their land, their territory, their turf, and I was an outsider, so my sense was that they were just poor country Tennessee people. That was it, end of story. I learned a lot from the script and from the information that was available at the time—I mean, people are people, Melungeons or not.[14]

Mary Bowler recalled meeting a family that acknowledged being Melungeon.

I got to know the Tuckers. They were black folks up on Newman's Ridge. I worked with them quite a bit, and they had—there were some members of that family that certainly looked Melungeon, and I'm quite sure claimed to be. And then there was—I don't remember her name; she was a very nice young woman who was quite friendly with some of the VISTAs before us. I remember she claimed to be [Melungeon]—and they seemed to be proud of it, from what I remember. I really don't remember hearing [negative comments about Melungeons]. And I don't remember hearing any negative talk about the blacks, the few blacks that we had, either. I really don't. I'm sure there probably *was* prejudice; maybe they kept it hidden from us.... And also there had to be a lot of intermarriage.... They may have been talking about a relative.

As a VISTA, Bowler had occasion to meet—and sometimes get to know—most of the prominent people in Sneedville and Hancock County.

Yeah, we knew Charles Turner, but we were much more friendly with Sonny, his brother. Sonny Turner ran a women's clothing shop in town, and he was very, very friendly with us. He was always giving us presents, taking us places, treating us royally. But his brother was OK. He was rather—I don't know, Sonny was very outgoing, but his brother was more, I don't know, more serious, I guess, less approachable. He seemed to be a fair person.[15]

More than four decades after his summer in Sneedville, Ray Buffington recalled several of the local people as he looked through a mimeographed program from the play's initial season. Buffington also had a more elaborate program from a later season, which featured a photograph of Reba Ramsey wearing an unusual dress.

---

[14] Buffington interview.
[15] Van Nest interview.

There was a woman named Reba Ramsey; she was a young woman who was in that area, and I remember her because of that dress that she had that was featured on the program for the show. I remembered that pretty vividly before I went through the program again; that was a pretty amazing story, I thought. Are you familiar with that story?

That was a dress that had been handed down through her family, hadn't it?
Right, right. If I recall, it was silk, and it had been stamped with Andrew Jackson's face on it. Just a remarkable thing, and she actually wore the dress in the show, which I remember thinking once—probably not the best thing…. Dora Bowlin was in the show, too. And there were a bunch of names here in the [list of] Sneedville villagers. I honestly don't remember too many of them. The one guy I did remember, oddly enough, was one of the tech guys, and his name was Scotty Collins. And I don't know why I remembered him, but I do…. I think that there was a lighting booth at the top of the amphitheater, and I remember he was there; I remember meeting him. He had real dark hair, and that's about all I remember. (chuckles) For some odd reason I remember his name.

Scott Collins was in a unique position among those involved with the outdoor drama. He was a local, born and raised in Hancock County, a graduate of the county's high school. He was of Melungeon ancestry, with dark skin and hair, bearing one of the traditional surnames of the group. He was young—nineteen years old that first season—and a college student, as were the actors from Carson-Newman and as the VISTAs were or had recently been. While the Carson-Newman students were in the county only for the weekends, the VISTAs lived there full-time for their year of service. Scott knew that living in Hancock County was not easy for them.

They were living all over the county, up in Seal-Mathis, in the Big Springs area, it was an all-over-the-county thing. There was one young lady that invited me to her home one night—seems to me this was over in the Mulberry area—and I mean she lived out in the boonies! Of course, about anywhere you go in the county, you're in the boonies, but she lived—it was a little bit unusual to find her where she told me she lived. I mean it was just a little old shack of a place, but she loved it—and I did, too; I mean, it was OK. She had done a lot of work on it, just manual labor, and getting it kind of in shape to live. She rigged up a little thing there from the spring so she could take a shower, various things to make it just a little more homey. But it was tough, it was really tough times for them. They had to come in and find them a place to live, whatever it was. Some of them weren't very comfortable at all, I'm sure. But I'll tell you, for the most part, they got along really great with the people.[16]

The Carson-Newman students usually came to Sneedville on Wednesday night or Thursday morning. "I can remember—we played on Thursday, Friday, and Saturday evenings, I think, and on Saturday evenings we'd go back to Carson-Newman late at night, after things were over."[17] The drive over Clinch Mountain could be scary, especially at night. VISTA Mary Bowler sometimes drove across the mountain to Morristown where she had a cousin.

We would go and visit when we needed a shower or a good meal. Oh, that road was incredible. Coming back at night—whoa, that was scary. I remember one night I was driving back and I had a flat tire, and I was so naïve I didn't even know what it was; I just knew something was wrong. I just kept driving; I didn't want to stop on that road. The next morning I went out to look at our van and saw the tire, and I couldn't believe I had driven that far. Yeah, it was scary at night. There were no guardrails, and it was just a twisting, turning....[18]

Director John Lee Welton felt that the road over Clinch Mountain hindered attendance at the play.

The problem with the first year was the roads going up there were just awful. They were very narrow; they were very crooked. As a matter of fact, the first year, one of our senior citizens groups from one of the churches brought a bus up there, and at one point they had to all get out and direct the driver, move him around, to get that bus around one of those curves and then get back on because it was so curvy. It's about forty-five miles from my house to where the theater site was, and it took an hour and a half, any way you went, because it was up and down and around, very slow travel.[19]

Despite the difficulty in getting to Hancock County, people were coming from near and far. On Thursday, 31 July, Mr. and Mrs. Albert Goldsmith came all the way from Pittsburgh, Pennsylvania, specifically to see the play. Mayor Turner talked with the Goldsmiths after the play and invited them to visit his drugstore the following morning so he could take their photograph. They arrived at the store first thing the next morning, and Turner took their picture. The mayor didn't have much time to talk with them, but asked Mr. Goldsmith to write something in his notebook. Goldsmith wrote,

[16] Scott Collins interview.
[17] Buffington interview.
[18] Van Nest interview.
[19] Welton interview (2002).

8:00 a.m.—August 1, 1969—I don't know why all the fuss to take my picture just because I came from Pittsburgh especially to see "Walk Toward the Sunset." There should be lots of people from Pennsylvania and further who ought to come and see this excellent historical play. I enjoyed meeting many of the local folks. Their enthusiasm for the play and for their very beautiful part of the country is catching. I shall hope to come again and tell my friends.[20]

As the play entered its final weeks, the audiences grew. On Saturday, 9 August, the cast performed to its largest audience yet; with 674 people in attendance, the amphitheater was filled almost to capacity. To keep the momentum going, and to urge locals to attend, the Drama Association announced a second "Hancock County Night." County residents would be able to see the play on Thursday, 14 August, at special reduced rates: one dollar for adults and 50 cents for children.[21]

Weather can be a problem for any outdoor production, and the southern Appalachian Mountains usually have an abundance of rain in the summer. Ray Buffington, who would perform in other outdoor productions, learned how rain is often handled by outdoor dramas.

I don't know when I learned this—I may have learned it in Sneedville, but a few years later I was in another big show in the Smokies, *The Smoky Mountain Passion Play*, and I honestly don't know where I learned this, but I know I learned it in one of those two shows. There's something in outdoor theater called a "rain pace," and like in any business, once you collect the ticket money you never want to give it back. So the goal is, if there is a threat of rain, you speed up the pace of the show, you possibly eliminate a scene or two to make it through all the key information of the show. And if it *does* rain, you keep doing the show as long as possible until it becomes impossible to do the show, and if you can make it through—I'm not sure what the official policy typically is, but if it's a two hour show, if you can make it through Act 1, you don't have to refund the price of admission. So—outdoor theater, it's almost a given that you take your chances.[22]

On the final Thursday of the drama, Mark Sumner, the director of the Institute for Outdoor Drama, was in the audience. He experienced this production's method for handling rain. With the elementary school at the top of the hill behind the seating area, the cast could carry vital props up the hill and perform in the school's auditorium. On this particular evening, the first act was

---

[20] Turner, "This Is YOUR Town: Enjoyed the Drama," 1.
[21] "Hancock County Night Thursday," 1.
[22] Buffington interview.

performed indoors, but the cast and audience returned to the amphitheater for the second act after the rain stopped.

Despite the rain, the isolation of Sneedville, and the frightening road over Clinch Mountain, attendance for the first season of *Walk Toward the Sunset* was over 10,000. On the final Saturday of the production, the cast and crew held an afternoon picnic. Hancock County's Farm Agent, Hubert Lambert, prepared chicken barbeque. The picnic didn't last long because everyone had to be at the amphitheater to prepare for the final performance.[23] Raymond Buffington recalls an after-show party at the Green Top Inn, where community members gathered with Carson-Newman students and VISTAs from the cast.

> There was a lot of gratitude and a lot of warmth. I can remember—I guess it was the closing night, and we had a party or something at the Green Top Inn, and everybody was there. The Turners were there, Dora Bowlin was there, and everybody sang "Should old acquaintance be forgot...." It was one of those emotional closing night things; everybody had worked really hard on it, and for a long time; weeks of performance, and ups and downs and all that stuff, and then—clearly, we were leaving and they were staying, and they had a lot of hope that this was going to continue and meet their expectations. I remember that it was overall just a very positive, warm experience between us who were from out of town and all those people who were part of the project who were there.

Prior to each performance, the cast had gathered in a circle in the backstage area, holding hands, creating what they called "The Magic Circle." This pre-show ceremony always ended with a prayer. On the Sunday following the final performance, Mayor Turner stood at the top of the Sunset Theatre, empty now except for a few of the cast members who had not yet left Hancock County. He described the scene in his regular newspaper column.

> There from the hill above the theater I saw Nancy Johnston who had done her part to delight over ten thousand people since July 3 sitting alone among all those empty seats, just looking around. And Ray Buffington who had won the hearts of all with his superb performance as Pat Gibson was just walking around on the stage alone. Then as they quietly began to appear on the stage and join hands to form the "Magic Circle" for the last time.... I thanked God for such an example of genuine American youth.[24]

Two of the cast members weren't there. The VISTAs term of service had ended in mid-summer, but most of the VISTAs in the cast stayed on until the

---

[23] Bowlin, "Drama Season Highly Successful," 4.
[24] Turner, "This Is YOUR Town: The Magic Circle," 1.

end of the season. Mary Bowler and Bob Van Nest, however, had fallen in love and decided to get married. Five decades later, they are still together, and Mary Bowler Van Nest recalled leaving Hancock County.

> We both left a little early. I remember it caused a scene between me and my roommates—one of them in particular, because she was very critical of my leaving before the play was over; I remember she gave me a really hard time about that. So yeah, I left a little early.... Was it romantic? Oh, yes. (*laughs*) Oh, yeah. And it's like—we were both from New Jersey. Actually we were on the same plane out of Newark but we didn't know it until the next day. I saw him in the airport, and then I saw him again in Atlanta. I said "Oh—hmm. I remember him." So, yeah, that was definitely a plus for joining (VISTA).... We got married that fall when we got home, in '69.[25]

Summer 1969 was a special time for all who were involved with *Walk Toward the Sunset*. For the members of the Hancock County Drama Association and all who had worked with them, there was a great feeling of accomplishment. An idea that had seemed rather far-fetched in 1967 had become a reality. Because of their efforts, a noted author had written a play, an amphitheater had been built, and people from all over the country had journeyed to Hancock County to see a bit of local history—or at least a playwright's version of that history. For the people of Hancock County, many of whom believed "nothing we do ever works," the play was a positive affirmation—something they did *had* worked. And for the student actors and VISTAs, it was an adventure in an unfamiliar place, one which left them feeling that they had done something worthwhile with their summer. As Raymond Buffington recalled,

> From my point of view—let's face it, it was kind of a romantic adventure. We were doing what we liked to do; we considered ourselves performers and artists and we had an opportunity to do this, but at the same time it was a big social project. We were doing something that should have good results. We met all these people, these VISTA workers from all over the country who were there for similar reasons, so it was like being a part of something much bigger than just who we were. Everybody had good intentions... All in all, it was one of the best summers of my life. It was really a great experience.[26]

---

[25] Van Nest interview.
[26] Buffington interview.

11

THE SECOND SEASON

On Sunday, 17 August 1969, the Hancock County Drama Association met to assess the previous year's work, and to plan for the coming year. As Dora Bowlin wrote in the *Hancock County Post*, "We found, from this year's experience, that there is much to do before we are once again ready to open our drama next year. The stage area needs improvement, rest rooms need to be installed, more lighting needs to be added, greenery needs to be planted, and so on down the long list of items that need taking care of."[1]

Some of those suggestions came from Mark Sumner of the Institute for Outdoor Drama at the University of North Carolina at Chapel Hill, who saw the show during its final weekend. However, Sumner saw very little he would change about the script or production. Overall, Sumner said, director John Lee Welton had done "a tremendous job."[2]

Welton expressed his gratitude to the people of Hancock County in a "Letter to the Editor" of the *Hancock County Post*.

> I came to Hancock County with the feeling of an "outsider"—I left at the end of the summer with the feeling of leaving loved ones and life-long friends.
>
> I had long heard of the reluctance of the people of Hancock County to accept outsiders, but this summer has changed that image of the County as indicated by many of the persons coming to see [the] play who stated that this was one of the friendliest outdoor theatre areas they had ever visited...
>
> I have had the opportunity to see seven of the other outdoor dramas now playing, some of them in splendid and magnificently constructed theatres, but I think I can say without reservation that "Walk Toward the Sunset" equals, if not surpasses, [any] one of them. I see no reason why, with the continued support and enthusiasm of the people of Hancock County, this play cannot continue for many years to come, bringing new economy to the area as has been done in other areas such as...Boone and Cherokee, North Carolina.[3]

---

[1] Bowlin, "Hancock County Can Be Proud," 1.
[2] Bowlin, "Drama Season Highly Successful," 4.
[3] Welton, "A Promise of Greater Things to Come," 1.

Sneedville and Hancock County were praised by the Tennessee State Planning Commission. An article in the summer edition of the Commission's newsletter *Local Planning News* was reprinted in several state newspapers, including the *Hancock County Post*.

> [W]ith a rugged harsh topography which limited many economic activities, coupled with inadequate highway access to surrounding employment and service centers, the future of Sneedville definitely did not look bright. Since there were no manufacturing concerns located in Hancock County, the citizens of Sneedville were forced to commute to other employment centers in Upper East Tennessee over inadequate highways, or migrate to other places across the state or nation to earn a living. From 1910 until the present time, with the exception of the decade between 1930 and 1940, the population of the county declined. The people who stayed and tried to earn their living in Sneedville were confronted with an economically depressed area and chronic unemployment.
>
> The future of Hancock County and Sneedville, from the study of past and present conditions, indicated a continued decline of the economy and population. This would be enough to force all but the most dynamic and rugged to give up and let Sneedville pass into oblivion. To effect a change in the prevailing economic conditions, isolation from urbanizing areas of the region must be overcome.
>
> In 1961, however, the situation started to change and what has been accomplished in an eight-year period is almost unbelievable. It all started in July 1961 when Charles Turner was elected mayor of Sneedville.

The article went on to list some of the accomplishments and improvements made under the leadership of Mayor Turner, including the paving of downtown streets; the development of a sewage system, including a sewage treatment plant; the inauguration of the "Fix-up Clean-up" campaign; the creation of an industrial park and the recruitment of a factory; receiving a grant for a community center and swimming pool; the building of a new city hall and library; the improvement of highway access to Sneedville; the beginning of a low-rent housing project; the creation of the Sneedville Planning Commission; and the successful acquisition of federal funding for many of these projects. The article noted that Sneedville won first place in a statewide community progress contest sponsored by the Division for Industrial Development in 1963 and was listed by the Tennessee Municipal League as an all-municipal city in 1964. Charles Turner's recognition as Tennessee mayor of the year was also noted. "No town in Tennessee has made such progress as Sneedville when you consider how little it had to begin with," the article concluded. "Now the future of Sneedville and Hancock County does indeed look bright."[4] The article made no mention of the outdoor drama; it had originally appeared in the July/August issue of *Local Planning News*, so the first performance hadn't been staged when the article was written.

While the first season of *Walk Toward the Sunset* had resulted in very little material improvement for Sneedville or Hancock County, the supporters of the play were confident those improvements would come in time. In that first season, the total income for *Walk Toward the Sunset* was $27,539.57, which included $18,688.65 in ticket sales and $8,850.92 from non-ticket sources—primarily contributions from supporters in the community.[5]

Fifteen percent of the gate receipts—$2,753.57—had gone to the playwright, Kermit Hunter. The director, John Lee Welton, received $1,000 for his summer's work. Technical director, designer, and all-around go-to guy David Behan was paid $900. The salaries for the stage manager, music director, and actors went beyond the originally budgeted amount because the performing season was extended from 18 performances to 25. The drama also went over budget on housing for the out-of-town performers and crew: only $55 had been budgeted, but actual rental expenses were $370. The Drama Association had originally planned to spend $1,000 on publicity and advertising; the actual cost for the season was $2,642.16. The HCDA's decision to hire a publicity and promotion man from nearby Rogersville added an additional $1,509.03 to their expenditures. And $2,500 had to be spent to repay various loans from local people that had been necessary to get the play started.

However, several budgeted items were donated, ranging from materials for scenery, costumes, and sound equipment rental to duplication of scripts, office supplies, and the cost of printing tickets. The expenditures for the first season of the play totaled $21,986.87. The Drama Association had a small nest egg of $5,552.70 to carry over into the next season.[6]

The major impact of the play was psychological. Sneedville and Hancock County had attracted national attention and had drawn visitors from many places, including a few from outside the United States. They had accomplished something only a few people had believed could be done when the idea of the outdoor drama was first proposed.

---

[4] "Sneedville Sets an Example for Other Areas in the State," 1.

[5] Hancock County Drama Association, report, 21 October 1975.

[6] Hancock County Drama Association, budget worksheet for Tennessee Arts Commission proposal, 1970.

The impact on the Melungeons themselves was more complex and harder to measure. People like Claude Collins had publicly acknowledged being Melungeons, something that simply wasn't done before the drama began. Collins did it at first because reporters needed a Melungeon spokesman, but others in the county began acknowledging their Melungeon ancestry because it was now a source of pride, and that was a direct result of the play. In 1947, people in the county were upset that an article in the *Saturday Evening Post* even acknowledged the existence of such a people. Now they were proudly displaying Hancock County's Melungeon heritage for the world to see. Writing for the *Chattanooga Times*, Mouzon Peters noted, "Nowadays, a Hancock County resident who can claim to be a Melungeon or a kinsman to a Melungeon is quick to admit it." As people all over the county were saying, "It used to be no one ever said the word 'Melungeon,' now everybody wants to be one."[7]

Well, not everyone. While the play and the nationwide publicity about the Melungeons downplayed the Melungeons' presumed African ancestry, emphasizing instead their "mysterious" origins, some people in Hancock County maintained their traditional prejudices. A decade after the opening of the play, one country resident told researcher Anthony Cavender that a Melungeon was someone who "had nigger blood in 'em." Another resident told Cavender, "Twenty years ago if you called one of them a Melungeon, he would have beat the hell out of you. It's still that way with some of them." Relating a conversation among teachers in the lounge of an elementary school, one teacher commented that another teacher, "Jim" (a pseudonym) was a Melungeon because he had a Melungeon surname. Everyone laughed because no one actually considered Jim to be a "real" Melungeon, nor did Jim consider himself to be one. One teacher said, "Well, Jim, I didn't know you had nigger blood in you!" Jim, referring to the number of reporters and outsiders who had come into the county seeking Melungeons, laughingly replied, "Yeah, I'm going to have to start charging money for you all to talk to me!"[8]

Some locals resented outsiders coming into the county and resented the way the people of the county were portrayed in *Walk Toward the Sunset*. Sociologist Melissa Schrift, who interviewed several Hancock County residents about the play decades later, noted that those who expressed displeasure about the play did

---

[7] Peters, "Melungeons Steeped in Mystery."
[8] Cavender, "The Melungeons of Upper East Tennessee," 31.

so primarily on the basis of socioeconomic class and how the Melungeons—and the county—were represented. Schrift observed that "[t]he media portrayals of more exotic Melungeon origins seemed secondary and even irrelevant to many with whom I spoke." Schrift quoted one individual who recalled, "There were some folks in town that didn't particularly like the idea that we were having the play, because it was a put down, they felt like, on the county, to portray the poor Melungeon people and basically, to make them look like they were just...well, they were very poor." Another woman recalled that, as a child, she was not allowed to see the play because her mother felt that the people of the county would be depicted as stereotypical hillbillies, barefoot and dirty.

One person Schrift interviewed claimed that "the organizers solicited the poorest local people to hang around the amphitheater to create a more authentic environment."

> They had hired these same people to pass out the brochure and to walk around with their feet dirty. Everything they did was really just to embarrass.... Everybody was really upset. I thought the Sheriff was really going to do some damage to them.... And I didn't like it, either. I think I went a couple of times, and you'd go up to where the drama site was, they'd have every one of these kids out here, none of them cleaned up, their hair not combed.... And they'd get them to wear the kind of clothes they wanted them to. And they were payin' them, too. It just put a bad taste in everybody's mouth.

Schrift seems skeptical of that account and was unable to corroborate the claim that someone paid local people to look poor for the tourists.[9] The members of HCDA had no desire to show Hancock County or its people in a bad light and certainly didn't have the funds to pay anyone to do so.

One of Schrift's interviewees objected to the way Hancock Countians were portrayed by the Knoxville television stations. The play organizers "were doin' all the publicity they could with channel 6 and channel 10. Every night they would come on, they woulda went up some holler, woulda found somebody too sorry to scratch their head, on TV every night. Everybody got tired of that."

Only one person interviewed by Schrift hinted that ethnic considerations contributed to antipathy toward the play.

> We did have some people who were objecting to the play. Even the sheriff at the time was objecting, because he felt like...he just liked to run everybody out on a rail, because...he was harassing everybody come into the county and wanted to see the play. He felt like they were just running the Melungeon

---

[9] Schrift, *Becoming Melungeon*, 83–84.

folks down. And he certainly didn't like any locals who were involved with it, because they had the makeup on...yeah, some of them had to put makeup on and had to play the role...because, you know you had to do those things to be on stage, had to make sure you separated the Melungeons from the white folks, because that's what the play was about, how they were treated.[10]

Although Scott Collins felt that most of the people of the county supported the outdoor drama, he recalled hostility from the sheriff.

I remember the sheriff at that time...didn't like the idea of the outdoor drama at all; he felt like they were trying to make fun of our county, and more or less he felt like it was totally negative. I don't know whether he harassed any-one or not; I don't guess he did that, but he was open about it, that he didn't feel like it was a benefit to the county, it was more or less a smack in the face.[11]

For many in Hancock County, the word "Melungeon" still held a negative connotation. One local merchant commented that many Melungeons had moved from remote areas of the county to live "closer to the welfare office" in Sneedville.[12] Cavender observed that the definition of "Melungeon" in Hancock County depended largely on socio-economic status, and, to a lesser extent, the willingness of the individual to proclaim a Melungeon heritage.

The definitional rules...are not uniformly applied to all individuals. Members of the middle and upper socio-economic levels who could be referred to as Melungeons are not overtly referred to as such. Thus, it appears the term Melungeon is used to both identify and stigmatize the poor. This observation is supported by the fact that some people use the term Melungeon in reference to any person who is on welfare, regardless of their kinship relations or ances-try.[13]

Other county residents simply denied the very existence of Melungeons. When Cavender spoke with a sixty-seven-year-old man, a lifelong Hancock Countian, if he knew anything about Melungeons, the man replied that he had never heard of the word "Melungeon." Cavender concluded that the majority of whites he interviewed in the county believed the Melungeons no longer existed.[14]

Two professors at the University of North Carolina at Chapel Hill not only believed the Melungeons existed, they were trying to determine their origins by

---

[10] Ibid., 84.
[11] Scott Collins interview.
[12] Cavender, "The Melungeons of Upper East Tennessee," 28.
[13] Ibid., 34.
[14] Ibid., 31.

studying their blood, and in September 1969 they published their findings. William S. Pollitzer was an anatomist and would later serve as the president of the American Association of Physical Anthropologists and the Human Biology Council. William H. Brown was a serologist, one who studies blood and other bodily fluids, in the Lab Animal Medicine Division at UNC. Pollitzer and Brown contacted Dr. Truett Pierce, whose medical practice in Hancock County made him familiar with the Melungeon families who lived there. They wanted some Melungeon blood samples to study.

In 1965, Doc Pierce invited some of his Melungeon patients to participate in a health survey. In a 1974 interview, Pierce said of the subjects, "We worked on the basis that they would have free physicals and they would be asked questions about the Melungeons." He said that he and the researchers tried to make sure the testing was performed on "true" Melungeons, meaning the descendants of Melungeons who had married Melungeons.[15]

Pierce was able to provide 72 blood and urine samples to Pollitzer and Brown. In 1966, Pierce gave the professors an additional 105 samples. These 177 samples came from 50 adult males, 78 adult females, and 49 children, aged 6 through 15. In addition to taking blood and urine samples, the professors observed hair form and hair color, as well as height, weight, the length and width of the subjects' faces, and length and width of their noses. Skin color was measured on the second group of 105 subjects, using a photometer.[16]

Questions about the birthplace of the test subjects revealed both the past isolation of the Melungeons and the more recent mobility of members of the group.

> Of birthplace recorded for 125 adults, 118 were born within the area, i.e., Hancock County, Tennessee, or Lee County, Virginia, and the remaining seven were born in immediately adjacent counties of Tennessee, Virginia, or Kentucky. Of these 118 adults 52 knew the birthplace of both parents, and 48 had both parents born within the area and the remainder in the immediate adjacent counties. Of 85 children whose birthplace was known, 76 were born within the area, usually in the same small community as their parents and grandparents. One child was born in the adjacent area, and eight were born in cities as far away as New York and Baltimore. In some cases natives of the local area had moved out, married, and returned to the area, but many more have moved permanently away to northern cities. These findings suggest the

---

[15] Ivey, "Oral, Printed, and Popular Culture Traditions," 263.

[16] Pollitzer and Brown, "Survey of Demography, Anthropometry, and Genetics in the Melungeons of Tennessee," 389–90.

long isolation and probable inbreeding of the past and their present break-up so characteristic of the population isolates in the Southeast.[17]

In their conclusions regarding the origins of the Melungeons, Pollitzer and Brown accounted for the widespread belief that the Melungeons had Portuguese ancestry. They were unable to differentiate between English and Portuguese ancestry but stated that their data could be interpreted to mean that the Melungeons could be 90 percent Portuguese with a slight Indian and Negro admixture, or possibly 94 percent Portuguese and 6 percent Indian. However, if the European component were English only, that component made up 94 percent of the admixture, with the remaining 6 percent representing Negro ancestry. Factoring in all the data, they estimated the Melungeons could well be 84 percent English and 16 percent Negro. "In short, due to the similarity between English and Portuguese gene frequencies no clear resolution is possible as to the certain contribution of one or the other," Pollitzer and Brown noted. "But all methods do agree that a European element predominates, bearing out the supposition from morphology and appearance."[18]

In short, the Pollitzer and Brown study more or less verified the widely held local opinion that a Melungeon "was someone who has got nigger blood."

One season of an outdoor drama was not going to radically change the attitudes and prejudices of everyone in the county. But it *had* changed the attitudes of many, and it had begun the process of change in many others. Not long before, the word "Melungeon" had rarely been spoken, and when it *was* used, it was used as an insult. Now the word was on everyone's lips and was being used in a positive way. It was a process that would continue as the outdoor drama prepared for a second season.

On Saturday, 18 October 1969, Jimmy Quillen, who represented the First Congressional District in the northeastern corner of Tennessee, held an "Open Door" session in Sneedville. Participants asked if federal money might be available to support and improve the outdoor drama. Quillen replied that he had supported a measure in the U.S. House of Representatives to make federal money available through the states for such purposes. He said he would contact officials in Washington and in Nashville urging that funding be provided to the Hancock County Drama Association.[19]

---

[17] Ibid., 390.
[18] Ibid., 398.
[19] "Quillen Discusses Grant for Drama," 1.

Quillen wrote to Dora Bowlin, telling her, "I have written the appropriate letters recommending a grant for 'Walk Toward the Sunset,' pointing out the desperate need for restrooms, lighting, and so forth." He also sent a list of private charitable foundations from which the Drama Association might obtain funding.[20]

The congressman also wrote to Norman Worrell, the executive director of the Tennessee Arts Commission.

> "Walk Toward the Sunset," sponsored by the Hancock County Drama Association, is one of the most moving plays I have had the opportunity of seeing.
>
> When you were up for the luncheon on July 30, I talked with you about a grant for this production.
>
> As you know, Hancock County is either the seventh or tenth poorest county in the United States, but they have a lot of initiative and a story to tell.
>
> "Walk Toward the Sunset" is the story of the Melungeons who live on Newman's Ridge there in the county.
>
> There is a great need for restrooms, lighting, and you name it, and I would like very much for you to earmark funds for this production for next year.
>
> As to the amount, they are very much in need of funds up to $35,000, and I will appreciate your consideration and advice.[21]

Worrell's reply indicated that funding for the physical improvements the congressman had requested would not be available. However, there might be other ways the Tennessee Arts Commission could help.

> You are aware, of course, that the National Endowment for the Arts does not have funds available in its State grants for a program for building and facilities projects, nor does the Tennessee Arts Commission because of our severely limited funds.
>
> We will, however, give every consideration to supporting the Hancock County Drama Association for projects involving certain activities other than the building and facility projects.
>
> I will talk to the Hancock County group to explore ways in which we may be of assistance to them.[22]

In December, Arts Commission vice-chairman Bruce Shine contacted Joe High at Carson-Newman College to arrange a meeting with the Hancock

---

[20] James H. Quillen to Dora Bowlin, 20 October 1969, Quillen papers.
[21] James H. Quillen to Norman Worrell, 20 October 1969, Quillen papers.
[22] Norman Worrell to James H. Quillen, 30 October 1969, Quillen papers.

County Drama Association for Thursday evening, 15 January 1970. He and
Worrell would also visit Rogersville the evening before to discuss that community's Davy Crockett drama.[23]

The Clinch River flooded at the end of 1969. Four to six inches of snow
fell on Christmas Day, followed by warmer temperatures and a two-day rain that
swelled the river over its banks. Highway 33 between Sneedville and Tazewell
was under water in several locations, and the highway was also closed between
Sneedville and Kyles Ford in the other direction. Many county residents were
isolated for days, and Sneedville itself might have been isolated if not for the
recent repair and raising of the road between the city limits and the bridge at the
southern end of town.[24]

On 15 January, Norman Worrell and Bruce Shine from the Tennessee Arts
Commission visited Sneedville and praised the outdoor drama. In a statement
released to the press, Shine said, "The Hancock County Drama Association has
performed a valuable service to the people of Tennessee in presenting their production on the Melungeon people." The statement urged people from Tennessee
and other states to visit Sneedville and attend the drama during the coming summer and stated that the Tennessee Arts Commission would list the drama in their
summer catalogue of cultural events in the state. More than 100,000 people
would receive that catalogue.

Shine and Worrell met with Mayor Charles Turner and members of the
Hancock County Drama Association and praised the professional manner in
which the business side of the production was handled. They explained, as Worrell had explained to Rep. Quillen, that the Arts Commission could not provide
funding for building projects. They could, however, help fund the salaries for
the student actors and cover some of the other expenses involved with the play.
Shine also helped the HCDA prepare a proposal for funding to submit to the
Arts Commission and pledged to solicit support from his fellow Commission
members when grant awards were decided in the spring.[25]

Some of the HCDA members were pleasantly surprised by the cooperative
attitude of Worrell and Shine. Despite over a half-decade of the War on Poverty,
relatively little had been done to alleviate poverty in Hancock County. These
folks were used to hearing empty promises from Washington and from Nashville. When they learned that the Arts Commission would not—actually, could
not—fund the improvements they wanted for their amphitheater, restrooms,

---

[23] Bruce Shine to J. M. High and Dr. Thomas Slaughter, 18 December 1969, Quillen Papers.

[24] "Then the Floods Came," 1.

[25] "Arts Commission Commends Local Drama," 1.

and lighting, most of them expected to hear praise for their efforts and nothing more. And many felt that the Tennessee Arts Commission was interested only in "higher" forms of art: symphony orchestras, art galleries, and professional, "legitimate" theater. They doubted that the Commission was seriously interested in a rustic outdoor drama performed by student actors and local amateurs in a rough amphitheater in a tiny, isolated rural town, nor would they have any interest in a play about an obscure group of people of which most Americans had never heard.

The HCDA members left the meeting feeling encouraged, and Joe High expressed his gratitude in a letter to Worrell, with copies sent to Bruce Shine, Jimmy Quillen, and other members of the Drama Association.

> Until that meeting I was one of those who viewed the Tennessee Arts Commission as being interested in only the performing and fine arts. Your interest in our project and suggestions as to how we might improve our service to the project and, perhaps to the Commission and the State, is greatly appreciated. Let me say that you now have an advocate where before you had a critic.[26]

The Hancock County Drama Association wasted no time in submitting a proposal to the Tennessee Arts Commission. The "Uniform Proposal Form" submitted to the TAC for the project "*Walk Toward the Sunset* Outdoor Drama" requested $2,500, to be matched with $2,500 from the HCDA. The project would run from 2 July 1970 to 29 August 1970.[27] Accompanying the form was a description of the project. As advised by Worrell and Shine, the HCDA was no longer requesting restrooms, lighting, or other physical facilities.

> I. Aid is requested to assist in obtaining trained personnel to perform in and help produce the outdoor drama *Walk Toward the Sunset.*
> A. This drama is a professional production and as such it demands highly skilled actors who demonstrate the qualities of good acting to the audience and also to the drama cast, predominantly local citizens, who have no stage experience, save for the drama itself.
> B. Since this is the only cultural activity of any magnitude within the county, the drama possesses a high potential of cultural exchange. Young college actors can bring such an exchange. But, in order to do so they need a reasonable salary to live on during the summer, to help with their schooling, and to be attracted to the drama itself. The drama is a valuable opportunity for the serious student of acting to pursue his or her own craft.

---

[26] J. M. High to Norman Worrell, 17 January 1970, Quillen papers.

[27] Tennessee Arts Commission, Uniform Proposal Form for Hancock County Drama Association, Quillen Papers.

C. Thus, to guarantee a successful season, the Hancock County Drama Association must hire a certain number of college-trained personnel, primarily those in need of funds to continue their education, who would act as the main core of the production and assist the local people in making their production as artistic and esthetically perfect as possible.

D. The personnel would be selected by the director of the drama with the approval of the president of the Hancock County Drama Association. The personnel selected would be studying or residing within the State of Tennessee.

II. The amount of funds requested would be based on a $25 per week supplement for ten trained persons for a ten-week rehearsal and production schedule. The total amount requested would be $2,500.

A. The salary supplement for the selected persons would be matched by the Hancock County Drama Association so that each of these persons would receive a minimum of $50 a week for ten weeks. Facilities will be provided by the Hancock County Drama Association so that the selected persons will have adequate rooming accommodations.

B. No [funds] from the Tennessee Arts Commission would be used for administrative or directorial functions or for facilities.

III. The drama would serve as a keystone of a county tourism and cultural enrichment program being planned by local citizens and officials, as well as state and federal officials. The drama attempts to breakdown racial and other prejudices and to instill a sense of pride and worth in all people.

IV. A successful drama will provide a new base for county income, which is important, since Hancock County is not only the eighth poorest county in the United States but also the second poorest in Tennessee and is in a population decline.[28]

Jimmy Quillen, a Republican in the U.S. House of Representatives, had no direct influence on the Tennessee Arts Commission, which was a state agency in a state with a Democrat governor, Buford Ellington, and a legislature dominated by Democrats. However, he had considerable indirect influence in the state, and the Hancock County Drama Association greatly appreciated his support. Mike Hughes, who stayed in Hancock County with his wife, Ann, after their term of service with VISTA had ended, and served as the general manager of *Walk Toward the Sunset*, expressed his appreciation in a letter to Quillen.

---

[28] Hancock County Drama Association, Proposal for Aid from the Tennessee Arts Commission for the Outdoor Drama "Walk Toward the Sunset" 1970 season, Quillen papers.

Speaking on behalf of the Hancock County Drama Association I would like to thank you for agreeing to serve as an Honorary Board Member of our organization. We are indeed grateful for your support of this work and for your kind remarks concerning "Walk Toward the Sunset."…I am enclosing a copy of our proposal to the Tennessee Arts Commission for student-actor funding. This proposal has been submitted to the board members of the Tennessee Arts Commission and they will be acting upon it in several months. After talking with Mr. Norman Worrell, executive director of the TAC, and Mr. D. Bruce Shine, the Commission's vice-chairman, I am very optimistic that the proposal will be approved, since both men are actively supporting it.[29]

To no one's surprise, the Drama Association chose John Lee Welton to direct *Walk Toward the Sunset* in the summer. He had worked hard to make himself and his student actors fit into the insular community of Hancock County. He made sure that he and the cast members patronized local businesses and occasionally attended local churches. If he had criticisms of the county or some of the people who lived there, he kept them to himself. These efforts had paid off; Welton and the students were accepted by most county residents.

Welton told the *Post* that the playwright, Kermit Hunter, was expanding the script. The amphitheater was expanding also; Welton said the seating capacity of the facility would be increased from seven hundred to nine hundred. And he hoped to see an expansion of the cast as well.

"Last year the cast consisted of forty-two people, but I expect the number to be larger this year because more of the people in Sneedville have expressed an interest in the production," Welton said. "I hope we can have a larger cast. Last year several cast members had to play multiple parts."[30]

There would be a real need for more local people in 1970; there would be no VISTAs to fill out the cast. In March, the local VISTA supervisor, James Hornik, reported to the Office of Economic Opportunity that no new VISTAs would be trained to go into Hancock County. That decision, he said, had been made by the Tennessee program officer for VISTA, Ron Kalil, and VISTA's southeast region director, David Danon.

Kalil and Hornik both told the *Kingsport Times-News* that this decision had nothing to do with the previous year's dispute between the Hancock County Citizens Participation Committee and the VISTAs. The CPC had voted to have no more VISTAs in the county due to what they termed "lack of communication," but the CPC subsequently rescinded that decision. The current chair of the CPC, Broton Livesay, told the *Times-News* that the CPC had been satisfied

---

[29] Michael Hughes to James H. Quillen, 19 February 1970, Quillen Papers.
[30] "Welton Again Named to Head Local Drama," 1; Welton interview (2002).

with the volunteers and with their work, and that the VISTAs now reported to
the CPC. Livesay was unaware of the decision not to send new VISTAs to Hancock County until he learned of it from a *Times-News* reporter.

Kalil explained the decision by saying that Hancock County had had VIS-
TAs for six years, and that other areas of the state had had none and were requesting them. Still, it could easily be argued that Hancock County—the poorest
county in Tennessee and now ranked as the seventh-poorest county in the
United States—should take precedence over other areas in the state. And Kalil
told the newspaper that while VISTA's aim was to help the poor and then move
on before the poor became dependent on the volunteers, he did not feel the job
in Hancock County had been completed.[31]

There were those in the county who did not welcome the VISTAs, who saw
them as outsiders who threatened the existing power structure. The experiences
of earlier VISTAs who found themselves in conflict with the school superintendent and the county sheriff demonstrated the hostility that some in the county
felt toward the young outsiders. Despite denials by Hornik and Kalil, the previous year's vote by the CPC almost certainly made VISTA officials doubt that the
volunteers could have much impact in Hancock County.

Hornik said that VISTA was failing in one important aspect in Hancock
County: they were developing projects faster than they were developing local
people who were involved with those projects. He blamed "bad VISTA training"
for that failure, saying that VISTA would now be less "project-oriented" and
would now focus on "making the poor aware of each other's common experiences and positions in society…with the aim of working toward solutions."

The next group of fifty volunteers would be assigned to the Shelby County
Penal Farm in Memphis, to a community action agency in Memphis, and to
Nashville. However, Hornik said that some of the VISTAs currently in Hancock
County might stay on a second year.[32] Steve Nichandros, the Californian who
played the Cherokee Sun King, would be returning to the cast of *Walk Toward
the Sunset* for the 1970 season—not as a VISTA, but as a paid cast member.

Another former VISTA might have been planning to perform in the cast in
1970. Ann Haralson, who had written several articles in the *Hancock County Post*
about the drama in 1969, and had performed in the original cast, had stayed in
East Tennessee after completing her year of VISTA service. She took a job on
the staff of the Morristown *Citizen-Tribune* and could easily have returned to
participate in the drama again. However, on 4 May 1970, National Guardsmen

---

[31] Atkin, "Vista Won't Go Back to Hancock."
[32] Ibid.

opened fire on an antiwar protest at Kent State University in Ohio. When Ann found her newspaper colleagues celebrating the shooting death of four student protesters, she was horrified. She immediately typed her resignation from the newspaper, packed her dog and whatever possessions would fit into her old British MG sports car, and returned to her home in Canada.[33]

Meanwhile, the Tennessee Arts Commission had come through with funding for the outdoor drama. On the evening of Thursday, 16 April, Bruce Shine, the vice-chairman of the TAC, announced that the commission had awarded a $2,500 grant to the Hancock County Drama Association to assist in funding the student actors who performed in the play. Speaking at Hancock County High School, Shine discussed what the outdoor drama could mean to Hancock County and explained the various ways the Tennessee Arts Commission could help.[34]

While he was in town, Shine met with Mayor Charles Turner on political business unrelated to the outdoor drama. In June, Shine would announce his candidacy for the First Congressional District seat held by Republican Jimmy Quillen, who, like Shine, lived in Kingsport. Shine was certainly qualified for the job; he had served on the staff of the North Atlantic Treaty Organization in Paris, as well as on the staffs of two United States senators from Tennessee and as an aide to the vice-president of the United States. But his bid to unseat Quillen was quixotic at best. Tennessee's First District had not elected a Democrat to Congress since the Civil War. And Shine opposed the war in Vietnam, a stance that put him at odds with the majority of voters in the district. Despite the long odds against Shine's success, Charles Turner agreed to chair Shine's official campaign organization, "Citizens for Shine." Shine may have recognized that a Democrat like Turner, who was repeatedly elected mayor in one of the most decidedly Republican areas of the state, could possibly help a young, liberal attorney to win a seat in Congress. In November, however, voters would re-elect Quillen to his fifth term in Congress; he received 67.9 percent of the vote, compared to Shine's 32.1 percent.[35]

The Hancock County Drama Association was engaged in its own brand of politics during spring 1970. In June, they announced the formation of an honorary board of directors, which included several prominent Tennesseans including Congressman Jimmy Quillen, U.S. Senator Howard Baker, Governor

[33] *Walk Toward the Sunset* souvenir program, 1971, 34; Smith, "Ann Piper 1946–2015."

[34] Turner, "This Is YOUR Town," 30 April 1970, 1.

[35] "Bruce Shine Announces as First District Congressional Candidate," 5; "Sneedville Mayor Heads Citizens for Shrine [*sic*] Campaign," A-6. "United States House of Representatives elections, 1970."

Buford Ellington, Tennessee House speaker William Jenkins, and former U.S. Senator Herbert Walters. An important and relevant non-Tennessean was also chosen for the board: John B. Waters, the co-chairman of the Appalachian Regional Commission.[36]

As the HCDA geared up for opening night of the 1970 season, Sneedville was mentioned in an Associated Press story about outdoor dramas. "Outdoor Dramas Aid Economies" listed several communities (Beckley, West Virginia; Canyon, Texas; Tahlequah, Oklahoma; and Cherokee, North Carolina) that had attracted thousands of tourists by staging outdoor dramas. Beckley, West Virginia, had suffered economic doldrums with the downturn in coal production. But in 1961, local citizens, with assistance from the state, had raised more than $100,000, built a theater in the scenic New River Gorge outside the city, commissioned Kermit Hunter to write a play, hired a director and a production staff, and staged *Honey in the Rock*, a drama about the birth of the state of West Virginia. The play drew an average of 35,000 people each season, and now, in 1970, the 1,200-seat theater would present a new musical, *Hatfields and McCoys*.

The article also mentioned Columbia, South Carolina, which had to compete for tourist dollars with beaches on the coast and mountains to the west. A group of private citizens began working to develop an outdoor drama, commissioned Kermit Hunter to write yet another play, and premiered *The Liberty Tree*, a drama about South Carolina's role in the American Revolution, in 1968. In 1970, *The Liberty Tree* would be paired with a long-running musical favorite from Broadway, *Annie Get Your Gun*, and the entire production had been taken over by the University of South Carolina Theatre Department.

All in all, prospects looked good for communities staging outdoor dramas, but the article concluded with a note of warning: "For every outdoor drama that has been a success, however, dozens have failed for one reason or another. Many of the dramas closed because they were produced in large urban centers or were underfinanced at the beginning. Experts in the field say city dwellers will travel miles to see an outdoor drama back in the hills, or at seaside, but seldom ever support a production in their own backyard."[37]

Sneedville was about as far from being a large urban center as could be imagined, so that pitfall was never going to be a factor for *Walk Toward the Sunset*. But the project had lacked financial support from the very beginning. Only the determination of a few county residents—and the willingness of many more to

[36] "Hancock Drama Association Honorary Directors Named," 7.
[37] Associated Press, "Outdoor Dramas Aid Economies."

volunteer their time and effort—got the production onstage for the 1969 season. But attendance had been good, and the HCDA had high hopes for 1970.

Dora Bowlin had succeeded her daughter Corrine as president of HCDA. In the fall, Corrine would begin teaching at Tusculum College in Greeneville. The drama now had a general manager: Michael Hughes, the VISTA from California who was known around the county for his bushy mutton chop sideburns. In 1969, he had portrayed the scout in the first act, and a lumberman in the second. For the 1970 season, he would play the role of Governor Senter. His wife, Ann, was active in the craft guild and would be in the play as a square dancer and a villager. Steve Nichandros was back in Sneedville following his year as a VISTA. He was now a paid cast member and stage manager of the production and would reprise his role as Tom Robertson.

Nancy Johnston of Decatur, Georgia, returned to the cast, portraying Alisee Collins in the first act and Alisee Gibson in the second. The male lead for the 1970 production was Phillip Dorr, who would play Pat Gibson in the first act and Vance Johnson in the second. Dorr was born in Yemen, where his parents were missionaries, and he had just completed his freshman year at Carson-Newman College. Clifton "Kip" Marshall was a native of Dublin, Georgia. He had just graduated from Carson-Newman, where he studied drama and appeared in a number of productions including *Inherit the Wind, You Can't Take It with You, Our Town,* and several others. After spending the summer portraying Col. John Sevier and old Pat Gibson, Marshall would attend the University of Georgia as a graduate student of drama.

Eugene Mathis, like director John Lee Welton, was a transplanted Texan who served as an assistant professor of speech and director of forensics at Carson-Newman. He would reprise his role as Ezra Johnson, the father of Vance. Ron Brannan of Jacksonville, Florida, who had played Preacher Givens the previous year, had just graduated from Carson-Newman and would play the roles of Daniel Boone in the first act and a fast-talking lumberman in the second. Another Floridian, Ken Brunson of Venice, had just completed his sophomore year at Carson-Newman, where he appeared in a number of plays. He would portray Atakullakulla and John Netherland.

Dora Bowlin would again play Millie Johnson, mother of Vance, in the second act. Donald Lamb of Knoxville studied music at Carson-Newman and would appear as Preacher Givens in the first act. Roy Garland of Sneedville, a Marine veteran of World War II and director of purchasing for the Powell Valley Electric Cooperative, took the role of Mr. Sylvester in the first act. Annette Turner would again play Mrs. Bolton in the first act, while Sonny Turner would be onstage as a villager in the second act. Sharon Kaye Smith of Frederick, Maryland, was a drama major who had just completed her sophomore year at Carson-Newman; she would be Mrs. Farley in the second act.[38]

There were more local people participating in the play for the second season. Dozens of county residents, many with Melungeon ancestry, appeared in crowd scenes. Greg Marion, who would grow up to become the county mayor (in Tennessee, the chief county executive is called "mayor"), was still in elementary school in 1970. "Larry (Turner, the author's cousin) and I were the first people onstage every night. We'd come out and throw a ball back and forth while everyone else was in church, singing." Marion recalled one of the benefits of being in the cast. "They didn't have dressing rooms backstage. There were just these little shed-like things that were open on one side. We would stand around behind the stage and we could watch the college girls changing costumes. They didn't pay any attention to us, but we sure paid attention to them!" Marion recalled that some of the college girls in the cast who played Melungeons or Indians requested assistance putting makeup on the backs of their legs, requests with which Greg and Larry happily complied.[39]

From his perch in the lighting booth at the top of the amphitheater, Scott Collins watched the play every night and recalls that some of the local people had a knack for acting.

> One of the other characters I'll never forget, who played in crowd scenes, was Lonnie Hugh Bowlin. Lonnie Hugh was just a fine gentleman, just an old farmer, country fella. He came onstage with a hog rifle in his hands. He had something wrong with one of his eyes, kind of like Jack Elam, I guess—one eye went one way and one eye went the other. He'd get in character and he just played the part so well. He was on target. When his facial expressions changed, you could tell something was about to happen.[40]

Lonnie was the husband of Mollie Bowlin, who played the dulcimer beside the box office each evening before the play started. On many evenings, Lonnie sat beside his wife as she played, giving playgoers the opportunity to see a real Melungeon.

The mimeographed program of the 1969 season had been replaced by a program book printed by the East Tennessee Printing Company of Rogersville, which sold for a dollar at the box office. The program contained a page, spon-

---

[38] *Walk Toward the Sunset* souvenir program, 1970.
[39] Marion interview.
[40] Scott Collins interview.

sored by the Hamilton National Bank of Morristown, which provided some historical background for the play. Robinson Freight Lines of Knoxville sponsored a page containing biographies of playwright Kermit Hunter and director John Lee Welton. Dora Bowlin contributed a page titled "From Dream to Reality: The Creation of Walk Toward the Sunset." That page was sponsored by Dr. Truett Pierce and the staff of Hancock County Hospital. Five pages of the program book were taken up by John Fetterman's article, reprinted from the *Louisville Courier-Journal and Times Magazine*. Those pages were sponsored by Hugh S. Moles Lumber and Building Supplies of Rogersville; Dr. Roy Jarvis, Electric Motors of Tennessee; Oakes Motor Company of Morristown; and Prater Oil Company of Morristown. Powell Valley Electric Cooperative of Jonesville, Virginia, sponsored the cast page.

A page listing the scenes in each act was sponsored Harris Motor Court and Restaurant of Bean Station, and Camelot, a new resort development at Pressmen's Home outside Rogersville, the headquarters for the International Printing Pressmen and Assistants Union of North America from 1911 to 1967. The final six pages of the program book (sponsored by the Hancock and Claiborne Counties Co-Op, J.C. Penney of Morristown, the Bank of Morristown, and the Citizens Bank of Sneedville) contained a reprint of Alton Green's "The County That Time Forgot."[41]

Walk Toward the Sunset opened for its second season on Thursday, 2 July, with improved lighting and seating. Once again, the *Knoxville News-Sentinel* made opening weekend their "Trip of the Month." Tour buses again made the journey over Clinch Mountain, and over the course of the summer, visitors came from as far away as Pennsylvania, New York, and Illinois—and even further. "There were some foreign countries that were represented," Welton recalled; "...this became a place to stop on the circuit. A lot of people do the outdoor dramas, just sort of take a vacation and hit a lot of these things. We had a lot of out-of-state visitors, by all means."[42]

Outdoor drama aficionados knew of the play from newsletters and recommendations from other enthusiasts. Word-of-mouth advertising—the only kind HCDA could afford—drew others into Sneedville from significant distances.

The *Hancock County Post* ran its Independence Day weekend issue on Thursday, 2 July, opening night of the play. It was more or less the same issue the paper had put out the previous two Fourth of July weekends, with articles about Hancock County, Melungeons, and the outdoor drama. Two weeks later,

---

[41] *Walk Toward the Sunset* souvenir program, 1970.
[42] Turner, "This Is YOUR Town," 16 July 1970, 1; Welton interview (2002).

Sneedville mayor Charles Turner congratulated the play organizers and the residents of Hancock County in his "This Is YOUR Town" column.

> The success of the outdoor drama at this point can be attributed to the fact that there are a good number of people in our county who were willing to follow through—who were willing to disregard obstacles and press on. I am proud of these people, I congratulate them, and I hope that the citizens of our town will be more seriously considering their effort and assisting in sustaining this progressive endeavor. To all who had seen to it that their property was looking its best on July 2, 3, and 4th, and were out talking with visitors and driving them around, or helping in any way we are indeed grateful.[43]

The issue of 16 July 1970 was the last for the *Hancock County Post*. There was no announcement, no word of farewell. There was simply no newspaper on the following Thursday. Operating a small-town weekly newspaper is rarely a lucrative endeavor, and it would appear that publisher, John Montgomery, simply ran out of money and had to close.[44] Montgomery had been an enthusiastic booster of Hancock County, and of *Walk Toward the Sunset* in particular. The closing of the *Post* was a serious loss to the county and to the play.

Fewer people attended the drama in 1970; ticket sales totaled $12,380.40, which was $6,308.25 less than in 1969. Despite the sale of a souvenir program, and the sale of advertising within that program, total income for the drama in 1970 was $17,814.20, a $9,725.37 drop from the previous year. However, expenditures were slightly more in 1970 than in 1969—$22,519.52, which was $532.65 higher than 1969. *Walk Toward the Sunset* ended the 1970 season with a deficit of $4,705.[45]

Many local residents were discouraged that the play hadn't resulted in visible improvements for Hancock County. "Our biggest problem is our lack of motels and restaurants," Claude Collins told Juanita Glenn of the *Knoxville Journal*. "We can't keep people here when they come to see the play, and that keeps the drama from having as big an impact on the county's economy as it should have."[46]

Even the play's most ardent supporters were disappointed that the second season had ended with a deficit. But the Drama Association was undeterred. In fall 1970, Eugene Mathis a circulated a letter:

---

[43] Turner, "This Is YOUR Town," 16 July 1970.
[44] Dykes interview.
[45] HCDA, report, 21 October 1975.
[46] Glenn, "Hancock Countians Aiding Dream with Drama."

AN OPEN LETTER OF INTRODUCTION
Hello to the people of Hancock County,

To those of you who do not know me, my name is Eugene Mathis. Some of you may know me as Mr. Ezra Johnson or the Scout—the roles I have played in WALK TOWARD THE SUNSET. There are a few of you who may recall that I also played Mr. Sylvester in the show during its first season. By whatever name you call me, I will probably answer; but I prefer "Gene." For the past two years I have been an assistant professor of speech at Carson-Newman College in Jefferson City, but recently the Hancock County Drama Association hired me to be the general manager of WALK TOWARD THE SUNSET for the 1971 season. This "open" letter is to let you get to know me, and I hope that you will let me get to know you: so, if you see me on the streets of Sneedville or at the drama site, stop me and introduce yourself; I cannot promise I will remember your name the next time, but I will try.

Permit me now to get serious about the future of WALK TOWARD THE SUNSET, Sneedville, and Hancock County. In all three of these, you have something of which to be proud, and rightfully so. Many visitors to the drama have remarked about the excellence of the show (many say that it is better than UNTO THESE HILLS and THE LOST COLONY—and I believe them!), about the friendliness of the people, and about the beauty of the county. They are not just being nice; they are sincere. And you would believe it if you were to attend one of the other outdoor dramas where all you are is just another number or tourist about whom they care only because you spend money. But you have offered our visitors more: here is a place in which they can feel at home, be neighborly, and have someone concerned about their well-being. Do not ever let this change, and this county will grow because word-of-mouth is your best advertisement.

Ladies and gentlemen, you have the potential to become just exactly what you want to become. I hope that part of your dream is to help Hancock County become a center for tourists: a place where they can come for a day or two or a week or longer and get away from the noise and confusion and filth of an urban area. But I do not believe that any of you, and me included, want Hancock County to become a Gatlinburg. And we do not have to be a Gatlinburg to get people to come here, but we do have to offer more than we have now to get them here. We need more restaurants, and we need a motel or motels. We need campgrounds and hiking trails and horseback trails and fishing areas and picnic grounds—these are attractions that will bring people here and make their visit enjoyable. And most important, it will bring money for you and Hancock County. How much? Let me include this excerpt from the August 15th edition of Family Weekly to give you an example:

Suppose one touring couple spends one day and night in your town. This couple will spend at least $35 dollars for a room, meals, gasoline, shopping, and sightseeing. If you attracted just one couple a day, every day of the year, it would mean a tourist income of $12,775. Just 100 couples a day would mean a tourist income of $1,227,500. This in turn would cause employment of approximately 127 people—waitresses, bus boys, tour guides, life guards, bell hops, parking attendants, sales clerks—jobs that require little training and can absorb the normally hard-to-employ: the young and unskilled. This added payroll of about half a million dollars spent in the community would set in motion economic activity that could result in another million dollars in local business.

Now, the drama cannot do this alone. Many of you think that we are making lots of money. Well, you are wrong. We are a non-profit organization designed not to make money, but to break even, and, perhaps, make enough to run another season. We have been able to do this these past two years, but this may not always be true. Most of our success has resulted because many of you have contributed your time and effort, without payment, to make the drama a success. For this, I thank you. But, at the same time, I ask that more of you help us and, in turn, help yourself.

How can you help? If you will come by the drama office, I am sure that we can find something for you to do. This winter, we want to landscape the theatre site and will need men who know when and how certain trees and shrubs can be transplanted. We want to build new walls for the theatre, and this means we will need people to put them up and to donate any old, weathered timber that will be suitable. These are just a few of the improvements we need, and we need your help.

There is another way you can help and also make some money out of it. This is to erect and operate a county cooperative motel and restaurant. How? Well, you have the most necessary material—timber. And you have some of the best carpenters around—I know because I saw your men build a theatre from scratch, not knowing what a theatre should be. And you also have some of the best cooks in the world—I know this too because I have eaten with some of you. How do you go about building such an operation? First, get someone to donate or to rent you adequate and suitable land. Second, have an old-fashioned "house raising," only this time build a motel and restaurant. Make all the buildings out of logs. Let the men cut and trim the timber and raise the buildings. The women could fix meals on the days that work was done. And let this be a county project and enjoy it. After the structures are completed, donations of sheets, pillows, bed frames, mattresses, and whatever else is needed could be made. Now, how do you make money from such an operation? First of all, you will need cooks, waitresses, maids, dishwashers, clerks, and others to run the restaurant and motel; these can be paid out of the money taken in. Next, you will need produce to cook, and this can be supplied by the farmers in the county who could raise corn, tomatoes, beans, peas, et cetera, and sell to the restaurant. And many of you could take turns working and earning money, and no one would be tied down. From the profits, you could then buy better equipment, needed furniture, and other accessories—eventually having a first-class business. And what is more, such a venture would bring more people to the county to see your project and to avail themselves of your offerings. I hope someone will take this idea and make it a reality—by next summer, I hope!

Let me now return to the drama, and what we are doing for next year. Our biggest effort will be publicity. We are writing magazines across the nation asking them to let us tell our story, and some have already said we could. Also, plans are being made to have pictures and a story in the 50 major daily newspapers in January and February telling the people about Hancock County and the drama. From these efforts, we hope to have the biggest year ever. Secondly, we hope to have a large membership drive that will enable us to get needed revenue to finance the drama. Along the same lines, we will make applications to various foundations for grants. We also hope to get the State of Tennessee to support us more actively. And finally, we want more of you to help us as actors, technicians, and workers. We want this to truly be Hancock County's project.

Citizens of Hancock County, I have been using the pronouns "our" and "we" in referring to the county and the drama. I truly believe that both are a part of me. During the past two years, you have become my second home, and I thank you for letting me come into your homes and hearts. You are just as friendly and neighborly—maybe more so—as the people I left in a small West Texas farming community. There we had miles and miles of miles and miles; it is the same here, except some of your miles are straight up and have trees on them. I promise to work as best as I am able to make the drama an enormous success. Please help me.

Sincerely yours,
"GENE"
General Manager
WALK TOWARD THE SUNSET[47]

The Hancock County Drama Association had high hopes for the 1971 season. A few widely-scattered newspaper stories brought visitors from Illinois, New York, Indiana, Pennsylvania, and elsewhere. The HCDA was going to expand its fundraising efforts and hoped not only to wipe out the deficit but also to wind up with a bit of a surplus. After two seasons, all the bugs had been worked out and everyone knew their jobs. Surely 1971 was going to be the breakthrough year for *Walk Toward the Sunset*.

---

[47] Mathis, "An Open Letter of Introduction."

That optimism was shaken when they learned that their director wouldn't be available for the 1971 season. John Lee Welton had been working toward his doctoral degree and would be spending the next summer at the University of Southern Illinois at Carbondale. The play would be going into its third season with someone new at the helm.

12

STORM CLOUDS

A public relations representative/press agent hired by the Hancock County Drama Association contacted Tennessee Ernie Ford sometime in 1970, when Ford came back to his hometown of Bristol, Tennessee, after the death of his parents.[1] Ford agreed to serve as campaign chair of the "Friends of the Melungeons" fundraising group.

Ernest Jennings Ford was born in 1919 in Bristol, a town on the Virginia-Tennessee border about seventy miles east of Sneedville. He worked at local radio station WOPI but left in 1939 to study vocal music at the Cincinnati Conservatory of Music. During World War II, while Ford served as a bombardier trainer in the Army Air Corps in California, he married Betty Heminger. After the war, Ford was hired by KFXM radio in San Bernardino to host an early-morning country music program. There, he developed a comic persona, "Tennessee Ernie," and was popular enough to be hired away by KXLA in Pasadena. At KXLA, he hosted a program and sang on Cliffie Stone's live radio show, *Dinner Bell Roundup*. Soon, Ford was appearing on Stone's popular *Hometown Jamboree* television show. Stone, a part-time talent scout for Capitol Records, helped Ford get a recording contract.

Although Ford was originally considered a country singer, many of his recordings in the early 1950s helped lay the groundwork for rock and roll. "Shotgun Boogie" and "Blackberry Boogie" were driving, uptempo numbers, and his cover of Willie Mabon's "I Don't Know" was one of the earliest examples of a white singer making a pop hit out of a rhythm and blues song by a black performer. Ford had a hit duet with Kay Starr, "I'll Never Be Free," and another with Ella Mae Morse, "False Hearted Girl." He ended his morning radio show and replaced bandleader Kay Kaiser as the host of the NBC television show *Kollege of Musical Knowledge*. In 1954, Ford appeared on the popular CBS program *I Love Lucy* as Lucy's country bumpkin Cousin Ernie.

In October 1955, Ford released his biggest hit, a cover of Merle Travis's "Sixteen Tons." A year later, he was chosen to host the variety program *The Ford*

---

[1] Welton interview (2017).

Show, named for its sponsor, not its star. Ford ended each episode with a hymn, and his first gospel record album, *Hymns,* spent 277 weeks at the top of *Billboard* magazine's gospel album charts.[2]

By 1971, Ford was known primarily as a gospel singer and was a household name across the United States. When newspaper stories appeared in late January and early February about his involvement with the "Friends of the Melungeons" group, it was a powerful endorsement.

"Of course, I've known and heard about the Melungeons all my life up in Sneedville and Hancock County," Ford said from his office in San Francisco. "In fact, I've heard some pretty wild stories about the goin's-on up there in Sneedville! And further, I wouldn't be a bit surprised if there was some Melungeon in me."

"There isn't any 'might' about it," asserted Jeffrey Buckner "Buck" Ford, Tennessee Ernie's eldest son.[3]

> His mother, Maud Long, could trace her kin—and in fact, I did a moderate bit of backwards tracing on Maud Ford's line, tracing her back to most probable Melungeon stock in the beginning. My grandfather was Dutch, primarily; he was European, but Grandma Ford was—there was a lot of Melungeon in her somewhere. I mean, I have to tell you something right now. I have to tell you that it's a source of pride for me, and my late mother-in-law used to tell people on a regular basis, "Well, this is my daughter Murphy, and this is my son-in-law, our Melungeon boy." I was always tied to the tribe, if you will. And I make it a point, when people ask, 'Well your father was...and your mother was...," to tell them, "Well, on my father's side there was some Melungeon."[4]

The involvement of Tennessee Ernie Ford in the drama's fundraising efforts was a welcome boost, especially after the deficit of the 1970 season. Attendance had been down a little, compared to the drama's first season, and that was to be expected. Although *Walk Toward the Sunset* had been mentioned in several newspapers during the summer, the HCDA couldn't afford the type of advertising—billboards, brochures at interstate rest stops, radio and television—that would have brought in more tourists who were unfamiliar with the Melungeon story.

Claude Collins and the rest of the Drama Association wanted to see the production become profitable enough to pay the local actors and workers; only

---

[2] Olson, liner notes, *Tennessee Ernie Ford.*
[3] "Ford Heads 'Sunset' Drama Drive," 33.
[4] Ford interview.

the principal actors and the production staff had been paid for the first two seasons. "We have young people who are so interested in the play that they walk across Newman's [Ridge] each night to take part in it," Collins told a reporter. "It doesn't seem right that we can't afford to pay them something."[5]

The drama had been underfunded from the very beginning, but the HCDA hoped to go into the third season with a nest egg of contributions. Their goal was to generate $30,000 through donations and ticket sales, which would wipe out the 1970 deficit and leave the production with a profit. To raise money before the 1971 season began, the HCDA formed a fundraising committee, the Friends of the Melungeons. Fundraising campaigns often have a celebrity serving as the chair of the committee, and now the Friends of the Melungeons had Tennessee Ernie Ford.

"Friendship" levels were established. The *Friend* level was a $5 contribution, *Family* was $25, *Companion* was $50, and *Patron* was $100. A Lifetime Friendship was available for 20 times the amount for the friendship level desired; for instance, a Lifetime Friendship at the *Friend* level was $100, while at the *Patron* level it would be $2,000. The donor received tickets to the drama—the number of tickets depended on the Friendship level chosen—and a souvenir program in which the donor's name was listed.

Only a dozen names appeared in the 1971 souvenir program. Eight of those names were in the $5 *Friend* category, and four were in the $25 *Family* group. There were likely many more contributors by the time the season opened in July, but the lead time for getting the program to the printer was likely several weeks, at least, so some names could not be included. Other contributors probably didn't want recognition for their gifts, like Mayor Turner or Doc Pierce.

Still, the addition of Tennessee Ernie Ford to the "Friends of the Melungeons" did not have the impact the HCDA had hoped for. Decades later, one person familiar with the drama said of Ford, "I don't remember him doing anything... I don't know what he was going to do."[6]

In all fairness, when a celebrity is chosen to head a fundraising effort such as "Friends of the Melungeons," the celebrity is not usually expected to do any actual fundraising. Unfortunately, the members of the Hancock County Drama Association had no experience with any type of fundraising other than calling on friends and neighbors and asking for a contribution. When Tennessee Ernie Ford agreed to serve as chairman of the "Friends of the Melungeons," he was contributing the use of his name and notoriety.

---

[5] Glenn, "Hancock Countians Aiding Dream with Drama."
[6] Shine interview.

Unfortunately, no one in the HCDA had the expertise to imagine, create, and implement a fundraising strategy to capitalize on Ford's name recognition. A direct mail campaign, for example, might have been effective and required only small investment of labor and of funds to pay for materials and postage. To make matters worse, Ford expected to return to east Tennessee to settle his parents' affairs, but he couldn't commit to attending the play, and there is no record of either his attendance or any further participation with the Friends of the Melungeons.[7] Ford has been criticized by some people who thought he should have done more, but the HCDA missed the opportunity.

In March 1971, several HCDA members and members of the 1970 cast traveled to Nashville to talk about the drama to a joint session of the Tennessee state legislature. They outlined the progress of the play from its inception and performed a scene about the Melungeons' effort to secure the rights of citizenship. Mollie Bowlin performed a medley of mountain songs accompanying herself on the dulcimer.

With John Lee Welton working on his doctorate in Illinois, the Drama Association chose Ben Harville to direct *Walk Toward the Sunset* for the 1971 season. A native of Morristown, Harville had received a B.A. in political science from the University of Tennessee in Knoxville in 1967, but his first love was clearly theater. He studied dance and choreography at the Dancers' Studio in Knoxville, had been involved in theater productions while an undergraduate at U-T, and, when he moved to Florida to teach, worked with the Lakeland Little Theatre. In 1969, he moved back to Knoxville to work toward a master's degree in theater.

In November of that year, Harville played the title role and directed the choreography in Carlo Goldoni's *Arlecchino: Servant of Two Masters*, staged by the University of Tennessee Theatre. He performed in several productions at U-T's Carousel Theatre, and by 1971 had five summers' worth of experience in outdoor drama at the Hunter Hills Theatre in Gatlinburg. As an undergraduate in 1966, Harville was a dancer in *Annie Get Your Gun*, the first production at Hunter Hills after the facility was given to the U-T Theatre Department. The following year, he was the first student to play John the Witch Boy in Howard Richardson and William Berney's Appalachian-themed *Dark of the Moon*, a role he repeated for the next three summers to considerable acclaim. With multiple productions at Hunter Hills each summer, Harville learned all aspects of theater,

[7] "Ernie Ford is Drama Campaign Chairman," 4.

working as an actor, dancer, company manager, assistant choreographer, and assistant director.[8] "[In 1970] I was company manager [at Hunter Hills], and I directed a production of *Agamemnon*, which showed one night through the summer. A lot of people came to see it, and I think some of the people from *Walk Toward the Sunset* came to see it. That's one of the reasons they offered me the job."

Harville's work at Hunter Hills was theater, and it was outdoors, but it wasn't "outdoor theater," in the sense that term is usually used. The company at Hunter Hills performed established Broadway shows, usually musicals, but also works like Shakespeare's *A Midsummer Night's Dream*.

Harville was aware of *Walk Toward the Sunset* even though he didn't make the trip across Clinch Mountain to see it during its first two seasons. He had also met John Lee Welton, who came backstage after Harville had performed in *The Robe* during Harville's senior year at U-T.

> [The Hancock County Drama Association] sent notices to the [Drama] Department at UT to see if anyone might be interested [in directing]. My professors suggested that I go interview for it, and I did. I think I only interviewed the one time, as best I can remember. They were very thorough in the interview. I was very impressed with several members of the board. They explained the conditions and the situation with the budget and the conditions of the residency.

Harville visited the amphitheater, and thought it was "very primitive, but I thought it had possibilities." Still, "I was surprised when they asked me to do it, because I was so young. I readily accepted."[9]

Despite his youth, Harville seemed like a good fit for *Walk Toward the Sunset*. He was from nearby Morristown and had family connections in Hancock County. Later, he would discover that some of those connections were Melungeons. One of the members of the Drama Association, Dora Bowlin, was a distant relative—"a second cousin, I believe," Harville recalled.

Directing *Walk Toward the Sunset* in 1971 would take Harville away from Hunter Hills and the U-T Theatre Department for the summer, but it was an opportunity for him to be in charge of a production, one that had not yet realized its potential. Sure, it was an outdoor drama in a remote little flyspeck of a town, but the unique subject matter had attracted attention in various parts of the country; with a little effort and a little luck, even more publicity might be generated. It was a chance for an ambitious young man to make a name for himself.

---

[8] Buttrey, "A History of the Hunter Hills Theatre, 1956–1977."
[9] Harville interview.

Harville rented a small house just north of town and set out to direct the third season of *Walk Toward the Sunset*.

While the first two seasons of the drama had relied on students from Carson-Newman College, Harville wanted to draw young actors from all over east Tennessee. He scheduled tryouts on 26 April at the ballroom of the student center at U-T Knoxville, on 27 April at the Drama Den in the Henderson building at Carson-Newman in Jefferson City, on 28 April at the amphitheater at East Tennessee State University in Johnson City, and on 1 May at the elementary school in Sneedville. Harville could offer ten paid positions, at $50 per week plus lodging in Sneedville.[10]

Sharon Smith, a speech and drama major at Carson-Newman, won the female lead roles as Alisee Collins and Alisee Gibson. She had played Mrs. Farley in the 1970 cast. Rod Tallant, a West Virginia native and speech and drama major at Carson-Newman, would portray Pat Gibson and Vance Johnson. Kip Marshall returned once again to play the roles of Colonel John Sevier and old Pat Gibson. A graduate student of theater at the University of Georgia, Kip would also serve as technical director and stage manager.

Patrick Crouch, a senior at the University of Tennessee, would play three roles: Cherokee chief Attakullakulla, Ezra Johnson, and Governor Senter. Crouch had served as assistant technical director for the Panola Players in Sardis, Mississippi, and had acted in a number of productions. David Reynolds, who would graduate that spring from East Tennessee State with a degree in theater and English, would play Daniel Boone and Tom Robertson.

Larry Clifton, a Knoxville native, had worked with Harville at Hunter Hills Theatre on *Dark of the Moon*, as well as *Li'l Abner* and several other roles at U-T. He would graduate that spring and spend the summer playing Preacher Givens and John Netherland. Another spring graduate from U-T, Carol Ann McGuire of Alcoa, Tennessee, would portray Mrs. Farley. She had previously acted in productions of *Cindy* and *Bye Bye Birdie* and had directed an educational production of *The Trial of John Green*.

Bristol, Virginia, native Penny Hernandez, a junior at Carson-Newman, won the role of Mrs. Johnson. Her credits included roles in *Who Wields the Hammer*, *The Gift*, and *Into Thy Kingdom*, as well as experience directing high school dramas and doing makeup and costuming for several religious dramas. And Gail Moody of Jefferson City would understudy all the female roles in the play. She would graduate that spring from Jefferson High School, where she had acted in

---

[10] "Hancock Drama Set Again," 22.

Cheaper by the Dozen and *Professor, How Could You!* and planned to enroll at Carson-Newman in the fall.

Two local actors would be returning to the cast. Annette Turner would spend her third season in *WTTS* playing Aunt Marthie Bolton, and Roy Garland would reprise his role as Mr. Sylvester and would also play the fast-talking lumberman. Marvin McCarson, a senior at Hancock County High School who had served as assistant stage manager in 1970, would portray the Scout.

The supporting cast, portraying Melungeons, Indians, and townspeople, was made up of local volunteers. They included Lonnie Bowlin, Mollie Bowlin, Becky Clonce, Donald Collins, Darise Dendler, Michelle Dendler, Harry Hopkins, Lila Hopkins, Roger Hopkins, Herbert Horton, Gary Johnson, Ronnie Johnson, Gary LaForce, Joyce Maloney, Chris Provost, Mark Provost, Tom Provost, Donald Rhea, Terry Smith, Debbie Sword, and Larry Turner.

Harville brought in a colleague from the Dancers' Studio, Betty Orr, to serve as costume mistress and house manager. Orr lived in Seymour, Tennessee, and owned a shop in Knoxville, The Leather Carrot, where she designed leather clothing. She had designed costumes for *Fantasticks*, *Othello*, and the annual recital at the Dancers' Studio, and while she had no particular major in mind, had completed coursework at five different colleges and universities in three years.

Scott Collins, now a junior at Lincoln Memorial University at Harrogate, Tennessee, and a teacher in the Hancock County school system, would return for a third season as lighting director. Kyle Greene, the coordinator for Operation Mainstream and an HCDA board member, would again serve as plant manager. Elmer Turner, vice-president of the Drama Association, would be the ticket manager; his wife, Hazel, would serve as concessions manager, and their son Larry was in the supporting cast again. Again, some of the student actors would stay in the Turners' basement, just a short walk from the amphitheater.[11]

Claude Collins was now the president of the Hancock County Drama Association. He also continued to be the primary spokesman for the drama, and by extension, for the Melungeons. In that latter role, he was a natural; he wasn't shy about talking to reporters, and with his obvious Melungeon features, was often photographed. Some folks in the country resented him for representing the Melungeons—some of them still hadn't gotten used to anyone speaking openly about the Melungeons—but, as Claude later said, "We had to do these things to keep the play going and to keep people coming in. It was not easy."[12]

---

[11] *Walk Toward the Sunset* souvenir program, 1971, 18–23.
[12] Claude Collins interview (2002).

Walk Toward the Sunset opened a week earlier than usual, on Thursday, 24 June. From the beginning, attendance was lower than in the previous two seasons. "It wasn't very well attended," Harville recalled. Cast member Larry Clifton remembered, "One night we played for three people."[13]

One big problem that summer was frequent rain. Because Harville chose not to move the play into the nearby elementary school gymnasium when rain fell, many performances were cancelled and tickets refunded.[14] Though Harville had experienced several years of outdoor drama in the often-rainy summers of East Tennessee, he may not have fully appreciated how different this situation was. Hunter Hills Theatre was located in tourist-heavy Gatlinburg, where there were many more tourists to fill seats on clear nights, making up to some extent the loss of revenue on rainy evenings. In any event, the plays at Hunter Hills were subsidized by the Drama Department of the University of Tennessee, so the director didn't really have to worry about keeping the seats full. Outdoor theater in remote Sneedville was much more precarious, and a few missed performances could put the production in the red for the entire season.

Saundra Keyes Ivey, a Ph.D. candidate who did fieldwork in Sneedville in 1973 for her dissertation on Melungeons, identified another problem. She noted that in 1971, the primary cast was not made up entirely of students from nearby Carson-Newman College, but included students from other institutions, "and there were apparently students among them whose lifestyles did not agree with the prevailing Sneedville mores. Some community support was apparently alienated by the behavior of some cast members."[15]

The social upheaval of the 1960s had yet to reach Sneedville in 1971. Local men still wore their hair short although long sideburns were becoming more commonplace. In the record bin at Turner's Drugstore, one could purchase current country hits like "Running Bear" by Sonny James or Jack Greene's "Statue of a Fool"; current rock hits like the Rolling Stones's "Brown Sugar" or The Who's "Won't Get Fooled Again" were nowhere in sight.

Illicit drug use was practically unknown in Hancock County; if any locals were using marijuana, LSD, or other illegal substances, they were extremely discreet about it. Alcohol was the drug of choice for those citizens of Hancock County who indulged in any sort of intoxicants. While it was a dry county, alcohol was available to members of the Veterans of Foreign Wars Post 9654 on Highway 66, just outside town. Hancock County also had numerous bootleggers

---

[13] Harville interview; Clifton panel discussion.
[14] Ivey, "Oral, Printed, and Popular Culture Traditions," 335.
[15] Ibid.

who legally purchased alcohol elsewhere and re-sold it in Hancock County at inflated prices. Locally-distilled moonshine was also widely available. Alcohol could be purchased legally from a state-owned ABC store in Gate City, Virginia, an hour away from Sneedville.

The VISTA workers who had come to Sneedville were suspected by many of being closet hippies; some of the men had long hair, and rumors circulated about the behavior of both the men and the women. But the VISTAs had been trained to fit in as much as possible with the locals where they worked, and they weren't going to jeopardize the VISTA program or their own freedom by being indiscreet with alcohol or illegal drugs. The Carson-Newman College students who came to Sneedville in 1969 and 1970, for the most part, shared the mores and values of places like Sneedville. In 1971, however, the student actors who performed in *Walk Toward the Sunset* came from places like the University of Tennessee and East Tennessee State University. Neither of those institutions was considered a hotbed of radical thought or hedonistic student behavior—President Richard Nixon spoke at ETSU in October 1970 because it was a college at which he could be fairly certain he wouldn't be heckled and jeered—but these schools had a wider variety of student behavior than did Carson-Newman. The young men from U-T and ETSU may have had (slightly) longer hair than their Carson-Newman counterparts. And their idea of a good time might have involved more alcohol than Hancock Countians thought proper.

"We were near the Virginia border where there was no tax on liquor," Larry Clifton reminisced four decades later, "so our automobiles were very heavy when they would come back."[16] But that couldn't have been cause for much alarm among Hancock Countians; Tennessee had lowered the legal drinking age to 18 earlier in 1971, and all the out-of-town cast members were over that age. Besides, Hancock County, like most dry counties, had several serious drunks living there; a few college students imbibing after a show weren't going to upset too many people.

One heard rumors of marijuana use among cast members, but few people in Hancock County at that time would have known what marijuana smelled like. None of the cast members ran afoul of the law, at least not in any serious way. So why were the lifestyles and behaviors of these students more offensive to Hancock Countians than that of the Carson-Newman students?

In truth, the tensions between the student actors and the townspeople probably had little to do with the actual behavior of the student cast members. Rather,

---

[16] Clifton panel discussion.

it was simply that Hancock County was finally catching up with the social up-heavals of the 1960s. The isolation of the county was being breached by news-papers, by radio and television, and by movies, which were readily available in nearby Morristown. The people of Hancock County were finding it harder to feel separated and protected from the events of the world.

Five years earlier, it would have been difficult to find anyone in Hancock County who opposed the war in Vietnam. By 1971, several young men from the county had served in Vietnam; a few had been wounded or killed. Opposition to the war was seeping into the county; even one of Tennessee's United States senators, Albert Gore, Sr. (father of Vietnam veteran and future vice-president Al Gore, Jr.)—publicly opposed the war.

Rock and roll records might not have been available at Turner's Drug Store, but kids heard the songs on radio stations from Knoxville and Kingsport. The hair on the male students from U-T and ETSU might have been a little bit longer than that of the Carson-Newman students of 1969 and 1970, but even at Car-son-Newman, young men were letting their hair grow longer.

In other words, even if John Lee Welton had remained in charge of the production of *Walk Toward the Sunset*, and even if the cast members all came from Carson-Newman College, Hancock Countians might still have felt threat-ened by the generational and cultural divides that were affecting the rest of the country.

Harville acknowledged a bit of culture clash that summer—"a little bit, a little bit, yes," he recalled. "Nothing major. I remember none of my actors were especially outrageous-looking or acting. My 'Preacher [Givens]'…was an impos-ing 6-foot-2, dark skinned, Melungeon-looking man with a bass voice who drew attention everywhere he went, but other than that, I don't remember very much reaction at all."[17]

Larry Clifton, who played Preacher Givens, recalled, "We were all treated so well that [we] merged into the county…. We had a good time, a very good time, and everyone appreciated our being there, so my memories are very fond ones."[18]

Locals' negative feelings toward the 1971 season may have had less to do with the cast than with the director. While Ben Harville acknowledged that di-recting *Walk Toward the Sunset* was a good opportunity for him, he was not particularly fond of the outdoor theater genre—or of *Walk Toward the Sunset*.

---

[17] Harville interview.
[18] Clifton panel discussion.

It was formulaic. [Hunter's] plays were formulaic.... If you were to look at his plays in some detail, they all follow the same formula: the romantic lead, the suppressed group of people.... You know, his play *Unto These Hills* [the story of the Eastern Band of Cherokees, performed since 1950 in Cherokee, North Carolina] has been completely re-written by Cherokee writers, and a new production has been mounted for several years there, completely by the Cherokee nation.[19] I have no idea about the rest of his plays, but his play *Chuckey Jack*, which opened the Hunter Hills Theatre, died after a few years.... I just didn't see *Walk Toward the Sunset* as telling a real story about the persecution of the Melungeons at all, especially from the beginning of the Tennessee Constitution and all of that. [It] just wasn't explicit enough, in my mind.

Harville conceded that Hunter had very little to work with in writing the play; very little scholarly work had been done on the Melungeons at that time. Still, Harville couldn't resist making some changes in the script. John Lee Welton had asked for Hunter to make some changes himself, but Harville wasn't that diplomatic.

I have to say I made a few changes to the script.... I made some changes in the opening scene, and I think I added [the song] "We're Bound for the Promised Land." I don't think that was part of his [script]. And the others, I can't remember exactly what changes I made.... And when Kermit Hunter came to see the play that summer—which I had no idea he was going to be doing—he did pull me aside afterwards to say, "Well, I suppose it should read in the program 'Written by Kermit Hunter and Ben Harville.' (laughs) He was not pleased.... Dora Bowlin's son said it seemed a little more contemporary in interpretation than the ones before. That's about the only particular comment I remember.[20]

The regional press had generally been supportive of the outdoor drama, and usually—with some exceptions, as noted earlier—cast the Melungeons and Hancock County in a positive light. But the national press was less supportive. Researcher Saundra Keyes Ivey asked one woman from Hancock County who had frequently been quoted by reporters whether the stories written by outsiders had generally been accurate.

---

[19] According to Robert Jumper, writing for the *Cherokee One Feather* in January 2017, "[t]he Cherokee Historical Association decided to revert to the original script in hopes of a boost to sales and attendance, introducing a new generation to the drama of the Cherokee."

[20] Harville interview.

Fairly so. Fairly so. Um, I don't know if I can quote his writings, but there's a William Endicott, I believe from the *L.A. Times*. His article, it was a reflection on us, and too much so. We resented it a little, and some of the people let him hear about it, too.

Ivey: What type of thing did he write?

Informant: Oh, that we were almost animals.[21]

Dealing with reporters was often difficult when the reporter had little or no background information on the Melungeons, or worse, relied on some of the more outrageous and negative stereotypes of Melungeons and Appalachians. Reporters often came to Appalachia with preconceived notions and their stories mostly written before they arrived; they simply sought out individuals or groups who fit the narrative the reporters had concocted before arriving. One reporter found the college-educated and eloquent Claude Collins unsuitable for the story he intended to write.

They wanted to take my picture and interview me and so forth. I said, "Fine, when do you want to interview me?" So we decided on a time, and I said "Well, now, you'll have to meet me at my house and let me dress up in my best suit and sit on my front porch. Because I don't want to be depicted in a little mountain cabin where I never lived. I never experienced that." So they didn't interview me.[22]

Claude did grow up on Newman's Ridge; his home may not have been a mountain cabin, but it was rather primitive. He had been a poor, undernourished child, but that's not who he was in 1971. Claude Collins was rightfully proud of his accomplishments and wanted his photograph to reflect the person he had become.

Collins may have been referring to Jon Nordheimer of the *New York Times*. John Lee Welton was also apparently referring to Nordheimer when he told Saundra Keyes Ivey, "A man from a large newspaper came down here, spent maybe one day, possibly two days in town, became suddenly an expert on it. He took pictures of the worst places he could find in the county...."

On 10 August 1971, the *New York Times* published an article by Jon Nordheimer, titled "Mysterious Hill Folk Vanishing."[23] Nordheimer's article was rife

---

[21] Ivey, "Oral, Printed, and Popular Culture Traditions," 371. The Endicott reference is likely to "Mystery of the Melungeons" in the *San Francisco Examiner & Chronicle*, 15 November 1970.

[22] Claude Collins interview (2002).

[23] See www.nytimes.com/1971/08/10/archives/mysterious-hill-folk-vanishing-mysterious-mountain-folk-are.html.

with inaccuracies. His estimate of 3,000 slaves living in Hancock County prior to the Civil War was way off. The total population of the county was 5,660 in 1850 and 7,020 in 1860, according to the U.S. Census. With no large-scale agricultural operations in the county, the slave population was very small, one reason most of the county's residents remained loyal to the Union during the Civil War.[24]

Nordheimer also wrote that after the war, intermarriage between Melungeons and whites became more acceptable, but, while he opined that these intermarriages usually involved a white man "taking a hill girl for his bride," he cited (without attribution) "reports of Melungeon males abducting white girls from distant farms to take into the hills with them." Nordheimer combined racial/sexual tension with the television image of Ernest T. Bass swooping out of the mountains into Mayberry to make off with an unwilling bride.

The people quoted in Nordheimer's story—Taylor Collins and his wife, who were preparing to move north to Indiana, and Monroe Collins, who said, "All the Ridge people have gone up from here and left, or else they're sleeping in their graves, and the ones that leave don't ever find their way back home no more"—fit the point Nordheimer was making: that the Melungeons were disappearing, moving away to be assimilated into industrial Northern cities and towns. No one could dispute the truth of that view. But many felt that Nordheimer had failed to see the people as more than stereotypical impoverished Appalachians with an exotic twist.

One woman told Ivey that she had become ambivalent about introducing her Melungeon neighbor to outsiders.

> I feel like I'm taking advantage of him [a neighbor] and he doesn't know it. And it makes me really feel bad. Now, if people could see_____ the way I see him, because I like the man. If everybody was more like him, we probably wouldn't have as much material things, but we wouldn't be too bad off, I think. He's so gentle, and I just…. So if people could just see him that way, I don't mind a bit, but I can see where some people only see his poverty. Now this fellow from the *New York Times*, Jon Nordheimer, was here, and I swear, I tried harder with him than with anybody I guess. He's a very intelligent person, and I tried my best to picture—to him as I saw—and it just didn't work. Nordheimer could have stayed in Atlanta—he works out of Atlanta— and wrote his preconceived notions, because that's all he wrote anyway.[25]

However, Nordheimer's portrayal of the Melungeons fit the widespread stereotypes of Appalachian people, compounded by the Melungeons' uncertain ethnic status. More positive examples of Melungeons were not included. Claude Collins

---

[24] Nordheimer, "Mysterious Hill Folk Vanishing," 33, 38.
[25] Ivey, "Oral, Printed, and Popular Culture Traditions," 372–73.

was not quoted; in fact, aside from a brief reference to bank president Miss Martha Collins, there is no indication anywhere in the article that some Melungeons were college-educated, reasonably prosperous, and held prominent positions within the county. There was no photograph of Claude Collins in front of his attractive ranch house. Instead the article featured a photograph of a man and a child in the shadows of the front of a weathered mountain home. The photograph is similar to the hundreds of images portraying Appalachian poverty in those years of the War on Poverty, VISTA, and other programs meant to alleviate that poverty. These images are not false; rates of poverty in Appalachia were and still are above the national average, but such pictures do not tell the entire story of the Melungeons.

Nordheimer's article also completely ignored an important and relevant aspect of the story—the fact that the night before the article appeared, an audience of people from all over the southeastern United States and beyond had come to Sneedville to watch a drama about the Melungeons, as audiences had done on summer weekends for the past two years. It is inconceivable that Nordheimer was unaware of the outdoor drama. No one could have been in Hancock County that summer, or any of the previous three summers, without hearing about the "Melungeon drama," which was the talk of the county a year before the play opened.

In fairness to Nordheimer, he may well have written about the play and about some of the Melungeons who, instead of moving away, were staying to improve their community. But reporters are subject to the dictates of editors and page space, and it is possible that any such material was cut in the interest of space or because it didn't fit the central theme of the story. That theme, of course was that the Melungeons were impoverished and disappearing. The very existence of the outdoor drama at the very least provided a contrast to this theme; at most it contradicted the whole concept. One could say that instead of disappearing, Melungeons were coming out in droves. The common joke in Hancock County was "It used to be no one even said the word 'Melungeon'; now everyone wants to be one." At the same time some Melungeons were moving away from their homes and heritage, others were staying in the community and proudly celebrating that heritage.

On 24 August, Nordheimer appeared on ABC-TV's *The Dick Cavett Show*, along with actress Carol Channing, jazz pianist Mary Lou Williams, and baseball legend Willie Mays. In the brief time he was allotted, Nordheimer essentially gave a condensed version of the information in his article, which had been reprinted by several newspapers across America. He still didn't mention the outdoor drama, and by late August he couldn't have done much to improve the season anyway. Welton recalled that Nordheimer appeared on television with both film and still pictures taken in Hancock County: "[He] showed pictures of old ladies who were snaggle-toothed. He went in and showed the flimsiest shacks he could find, and these were the Melungeons.... It was really sad." A young local man expressed his resentment about Nordheimer's appearance on *Cavett*:

THE MELUNGEON OUTDOOR DRAMA, 1969–1976

He said the Melungeons talked about going "over yonder" [meaning across the ridge to Sneedville] like it was a big deal. They come "over yonder" every day to the hospital where I work. And he showed pictures of the poorest-looking houses and people he could find. He mostly said they were isolated and poor, and that their big treat was to go to town. He said most of the Melungeons had never been out of Hancock County.[26]

Whether the one-sided portrayal by the *New York Times* reporter was caused by poor observation or by poor editing, his failure to mention the outdoor drama was unfortunate. The Hancock County Drama Association struggled to keep the production going despite constant shortages of money. Had the play been discussed in the Sunday *New York Times*, attendance during the final few weeks of the play's 1971 season would almost certainly have been improved. The mere mention that there *was* a play might have made the season profitable, and *Walk Toward the Sunset* needed all the help it could get.

The play lost money during the 1971 season. Total income for the play was slightly more than the previous year—$18,641.19. That was $826.99 more than 1970, but $8,898.38 less than in 1969. Expenses had gone up to $25,422.04; that was $2,902.52 more than in 1970. Ticket sales totaled $8,780.95, a drop of $3,599.45.

Non-ticket income was greater in 1971 than income from ticket sales— $9,860.24 came from the sale of concessions, souvenir program, contributions, and other sources. The play ended the season with a deficit of $6,780.85.[27]

Director Ben Harville was not involved with the financial aspects of the production and was not aware of any concern or dissatisfaction on the part of the Hancock County Drama Association or anyone else in Hancock County. He expressed positive feelings about his summer in Hancock County and the people who lived there, and said, "I thought that there were forward-looking people in the county who felt like [the play] would help the county in many ways—tourism, a sense of community—and I appreciated them for doing that." He recalled Mayor Charles Turner as a very affable person, saying, "I liked him. Very helpful; he helped us with financial considerations: where we should cash checks, and things like that."

Remembering the 1971 season, Scott Collins felt that the loss of John Lee Welton as director was "the worst thing that could have happened that year."

It just couldn't gel that year. Seemed like no one was on the same page; the cast wasn't.... The glue that held [the] Carson-Newman [cast] together was

---

[26] Ibid., 372.
[27] HCDA, report, 21 October 1975.

John Lee Welton and the closeness the students had at Carson-Newman. But when you got U-T, LMU, East Tennessee State, and various other colleges and universities that came in…. Ben Harville was the director that year, and he just couldn't—I mean, Dr. Kermit Hunter, who wrote the play, told the Drama Association in no uncertain terms that if Carson-Newman wasn't in the play, and Dr. Welton is not directing it, the play will not be ongoing. What Ben Harville did was not what [Hunter] wanted that play to be. Overall, I think they did a pretty good job, it's just—I think Ben took a little different approach to it. At the time I thought it was different and I think it was—what that difference was at this point in time I don't remember. It seemed like they just didn't have those themes that showed the discrimination, I guess, between the white people downtown and the Melungeons. And I think Dr. Kermit Hunter was looking at it just exactly that way, that they were discriminated against, back in the day…. It was not a good season, and it was not going to run any more if someone other than Carson-Newman produced it. That was the bottom line.[28]

Harville was not invited to direct the play in 1972 and wouldn't have accepted the position had it been offered. "It was such a remote place," he recalled, "and I was much too social an animal at the time. And I was offered a chance to direct *A Midsummer Night's Dream* at Hunter Hills the next summer." But his experience with *Walk Toward the Sunset* had an immediate benefit to his career. "I think it helped me get a position teaching at Walters State [Community College in Morristown] the next year."

Though Ben Harville considered the 1971 season of *Walk Toward the Sunset* a success, the Hancock County Drama Association did not share that feeling. Attendance was poor, compared to 1969 and 1970. No one could tell whether the lack of audience was caused by the weather, or if everyone who cared to see the play had already seen it during the first two seasons. Whatever the reason, the Hancock County Drama Association ended the season close to $7,000 in debt, and the group voted not to stage the play in 1972 unless the debt was paid off.[29] What's more, John Lee Welton had not yet completed his doctoral work, so if the show went on, it would again have to be staged with another director.

[28] Scott Collins interview.
[29] "Melungeon Drama to Be Staged Again," 4.

13

GETTING BACK ON TRACK

On 20 April 1972, the *Kingsport News* reported:

> "Walk Toward the Sunset," a story of the Melungeons of Hancock County, will be presented again this summer, despite financial problems which almost closed the three-year old drama after last season.
>
> The finances still aren't fully cleared with $3,000 of a $7,000 debt still to be paid, but supporters of the Kermit Hunter drama are planning to open again July 4 weekend and run through Labor Day...
>
> Carson-Newman College at Jefferson City will provide a director, stage hands, and some actors for the drama. The school has supported the play since it opened in 1969.
>
> Many Melungeons will take part in the drama themselves, giving it an authenticity it would lack without their participation.[1]

This small news item reflected some significant activity on the part of the Hancock County Drama Association. In just over six months, they managed to pay more than half the $7,000 deficit incurred during the 1971 season. Some creditors forgave their debts, while others were repaid through the sale of memberships and contributions from supporters. While $3,000 in debt remained, and the HCDA had previously stated that they wouldn't continue producing the play until their debts were paid, the Drama Association realized that they'd have to continue the drama in 1972 in order to raise the money to pay the remainder of the deficit.

Carson-Newman College was also committing its resources to the play, pledging to provide salaries for a director, technical staff, and actors during the 1972 season. This would relieve HCDA of a major financial burden for the coming season.

---

[1] "Melungeon Drama Goes on Despite Money Problems," 27.

Willard Yarbrough, the *Knoxville News-Sentinel* reporter who had been supportive of the drama from the beginning, wrote another article about the Melungeons, this one echoing Jon Nordheimer's *New York Times* article and its theme of disappearing Melungeons.

> Spring air was nippy along Blackwater Creek in Vardy Valley.
>
> So chilly, in fact, that Howard Mullins lifted his hands with palms exposed to coal-fed flames of the open fire.
>
> Such delicate hands, calloused from field work and 110 winters spent in isolated hill country—where necessities of life long since have become luxuries to a mysterious people to whom Mullins belongs.
>
> He is one of the last of the Melungeons, oldest of them all in Hancock County. Which has been home to the Melungeons for 200 years.
>
> Those left—in Snake Hollow, Blackwater, Vardy, and Mulberry—are few in number. Most have left the hills for jobs in cities far and near. And time is catching up with those remaining.
>
> In 1931 there were 40 Melungeon families living on Newman's Ridge above their ancestral home. Today, only two families remain on the steep ridges. Genealogist William P. Grohse, Sr., who lives near Mullins, estimates there may be under 200 families left in the county.
>
> Melungeon youth, just as others, are leaving rural America for jobs in towns and cities, Hancock's population of 12,000 in 1900 dropped to 6719 by 1970, according to the U.S. Census....
>
> The Melungeons...like many American traditions, are passing, just as are some of their own traditions. Graveposts are disappearing from their cemeteries....

Yarbrough, unlike Nordheimer, departs from the "disappearing Melungeon" theme to acknowledge the existence of the outdoor drama.

> The Melungeons aren't so reticent anymore, or so skeptical of strangers, and this is largely because of Kermit Hunter's outdoor drama that's shown here each summer, beginning July 4. "The Melungeon Story: Walk Toward the Sunset" is staged at the base of Newman's Ridge in Sneedville. It depicts their travail and the discrimination against them, from the time John Sevier found them in 1784. It tells how racial bars were broken with the marriage of a Sneedville white to a beautiful Melungeon lass. These "people of free color" [*sic*] finally were permitted by the Legislature to vote! And famed author Jesse Stuart tells in his book "Daughter of a Legend" [*sic*] how he dated a Melungeon when he was a student at LMU.

Even today, however, Melungeons are lampooned. A recent magazine article said the drama was concocted to bilk money from tourists at a Melungeon trap that featured no Melungeons. How sad! Melungeons built the outdoor theatre, helped stage the play, and performed in it. And Hancock Countians gave money and labor, signed notes for operating capital, and lost money in efforts to preserve the Melungeon culture and tradition.[2]

Yarbrough's story contains a few errors. Jesse Stuart's book was not autobiographical and does not mention his own ill-fated romance with a Hancock County Melungeon. Yarbrough treats the plot of the play as though it were history, rather than fiction. And the primary purpose of the play was not to "preserve the Melungeon culture and tradition," but to create a tourist attraction that would create jobs and help alleviate the county's poverty.

On the other hand. Yarbrough acknowledged the involvement of Melungeons in the project and credited the people of the county with investing money and labor to make the play happen and to keep it going. Supporters of the play appreciated Yarbrough's positive coverage of *Walk Toward the Sunset*, which dated back to the planning stages of the outdoor drama.

But in early May, a director had for the play still had not been found.

> SNEEDVILLE, Tenn., May 9 (Special)—Help wanted: One director for "The Melungeon Story: Walk Toward the Sunset."
>
> Apply to Joe Mac High, Carson-Newman College, Jefferson City, Tenn. 37760.
>
> Employment immediately, compensation, competle [*sic*] satisfaction in the theater, with curtain time July 4 weekend here.
>
> The college, again in a supporting role for the outdoor drama that depicts the life and times of Hancock County's mysterious race of olive-skinned people, is attempting to find a director for this season.
>
> UT's Paul Soper and Dr. Herman Middleston [*sic*], University of North Carolina, are aiding the search for a director. But those who have a desire, along with qualifications, are urged to apply immediately.[3]

Dr. Paul Soper was the head of the University of Tennessee's Department of Speech and Theatre and had been instrumental in the university's acquisition of Hunter Hills Theatre in Gatlinburg. Dr. Herman Middleton was the head of the Department of Drama and Speech at the University of North Carolina at Greensboro. Their involvement in the search for a director was indicative of the

---

[2] Yarbrough, "Melungeon Ways Are Passing," 33.
[3] "Melungeon Play Director Sought," 5.

support *Walk Toward the Sunset* enjoyed in the academic theater community of the Southeast. But it wasn't enough.

NO CAST, NO CROWD—ANOTHER DRAMA FAILS

It was a bad year for outdoor dramas and the Hancock County production of "Walk Toward the Sunset," like some others throughout Appalachia, never got off the ground…

For the past three years the Hancock County Drama Association has been working with drama majors from Carson-Newman College.

The college students have been taking the lead parts but no one appeared this year for try-outs. The lack of interest, plus some financial trouble, kept the community drama from opening.

Charles Turner, former Sneedville mayor and a member of the drama association's board of directors, said Tuesday the group finished last year's production some $7,000 in debt.

"We got the money any way we could," Turner said, "and by opening time (July 4) this year, [we] had reduced the debt to $2,800."

The drama could have received some state money, had it been presented, but with no one applying for the lead parts and the bad past season the directors decided not to open at all.

"If we can get enough money and enthusiasm we will open again next year," Turner stated.

Dr. John Lee Welton, director of the play the first two years, but absent last year, will return next season and directors hope a lot of the following will also…

"We're trying desperately to hang on. We didn't have enough money our first year and if it weren't for the cooperation of area newspapers we would have never had a crowd," the former mayor said. Turner said that the local residents, and tourists, spread the word of the drama by word-of-mouth and the first two years were successful.

But last year the rains came and the audiences became smaller and smaller.

The Davy Crockett Drama, an annual event in Hawkins County, also failed to open this year for much the same reason.

The Trail of the Lonesome Pine drama, in Big Stone Gap, Va., reported its smallest crowds in the history of the production and it seems the smaller productions may be doomed unless more money can be obtained and local participation encouraged.[4]

Old ways were passing, and new ways were coming in. Charles Turner was no longer the mayor of Sneedville; after serving for ten years, he declined to run

---

[4] "No Cast, No Crowd—Another Drama Fails," 22.

for re-election in 1970 and his office was taken by the town's physician, Dr. Truett Pierce. Howard Mullins, 110 years old and the subject of Willard Yarbrough's newspaper piece in April 1972, died in August of that year. And Sheriff Kyle Seal, elected that same month, died in office the following spring. The quarterly court selected Seal's wife, Ora, to serve out the remainder of his term. And Sneedville would soon have its first female magistrate, Sara Trent.[5]

In December 1972, Claude Collins and Elmer Turner attended the Eastern Indian Conference in Washington, D.C. The conference was organized by Chief Curtis Custalow of the Mattaponi Reservation near West Point, Virginia, and sponsored by the Coalition of Eastern Native Americans. Turner and Collins registered as "Melungeon Indians." One conference attendee remarked, "First I ever heard of anyone *claiming* to be a Melungeon."[6]

For members of tribes in the eastern United States, ethnic identity could be a sore point. Under Virginia's Racial Integrity Act of 1924—which would not be fully repealed until 1975—Indians were classified as "colored." This reflected a long-standing prejudice against tribes whose members had intermarried with African Americans. (Tribes whose members intermarried primarily with whites had relatively little difficulty establishing an official "Indian" identity, which could be accompanied by federal and state benefits.) When Collins and Turner identified themselves as "Melungeon Indians," acknowledging a mixed ancestry, many of the attendees must have felt the men from Sneedville were undermining the "Indian" identity these tribes were trying to establish.

Decades later, Claude Collins recalled that their identification as "Melungeon Indians" allowed him and Turner to receive a grant enabling them to attend. "I think maybe what we were doing [at the conference] was trying to find money [for the outdoor drama]," Collins recalled. "And, probably too, we were trying to figure out if we were connected to them."[7] Melungeons were beginning to ask questions about their own heritage, trying to determine for themselves who they were, rather than simply accepting whatever outsiders said about them.

The failure to stage *Walk Toward the Sunset* in 1972 was a blow to the members of the Hancock County Drama Association. They could blame the young director from the 1971 season, the student actors, the rain, or anything else, but the bottom line was there hadn't been enough people in the seats to make the season successful. Hancock County was full of people who "knew all along" that the play would be a failure, that nobody wanted to come across

---

[5] "Man Dies, 110 Years Old"; Steely, "The Lady Wears a Star," B-1.

[6] Everett, "Melungeon History and Myth," 358–404.

[7] Claude Collins interview (2002).

Clinch Mountain to see a play about the Melungeons, and the members of the HCDA heard those sentiments expressed constantly. They must have had moments when they thought the naysayers were right; maybe they'd just been lucky the first season, maybe the novelty of the subject had worn off and everyone who might want to see the play had already seen it.

The high hopes of the play's original backers hadn't been borne out. No new jobs had been created by the play, at least not paying jobs for local people. No other tourist attractions had materialized, nor had an infrastructure been developed to support them. The Town Motel remained the only commercial lodging in the county. A new drive-in restaurant, the Rock Hut, had opened, but other than that, there was no solid evidence that the outdoor drama had brought any improvements.

Nonetheless, the past decade had brought improvements in the county and in Sneedville. Streets in Sneedville had been paved and curbed. The capacity of the county's hospital had been doubled. Schools had been consolidated. A new community center had been established with funding from the Appalachian Regional Commission. A low-cost apartment complex was being developed. Electric Motors of Tennessee had brought some jobs to the county and had won the Westinghouse Electric Corporation Quality Certificate of Excellence. Although the section of Highway 31 that crossed Clinch Mountain was still a narrow, twisting terror, both ends of the highway had been improved, and county and state officials were discussing improving the mountain portion of the road. The leadership classes sponsored by the University of Tennessee had increased citizen involvement in county affairs. A report by the Tennessee State Board for Vocational Education claimed that Hancock County was no longer one of the poorest counties in the United States.[8] The staging of *Walk Toward the Sunset* could be viewed as a part of an overall progressive trend in the county, one that had made impressive gains in a decade's time.

The most significant change caused by the drama was not economic, but psychological. Being a Melungeon was no longer a source of shame. As one county resident recalled, "Before the drama started, if you'd walked up to someone on the streets of Sneedville and asked if they were Melungeon, they'd probably have hit you." "The thing I like," Dora Bowlin remarked, "is that the drama has made the name Melungeon more respected now."[9]

A local minister told researcher Saundra Keyes Ivey,

[8] Barnett, "Hancock No Longer 'Poor' County?," 9.
[9] Ivey, "'Walk Toward the Sunset' Tells Melungeon Story," 6-E.

I think this drama has helped a lot to change attitudes toward the people. Several years ago if anybody had a Melungeon background, they didn't want to admit it. Now they boast about it. I print these programs for the drama, and I had some one time I didn't have time to fold, and I took them down and let some of those children help fold them, and two of the little Melungeon children who were there helping fold—they called it doubling—and one of them said to the other, "Hurry and double them, you little 'lungeon." So they were boasting, calling each other Melungeon. But a few years ago they wouldn't have wanted anyone to know it. So I think it's changed a lot in that respect. And I think it gives them something to be proud of, when they do talk about their ancestry...[10]

So, despite the discouragement caused by the missed 1972 season, the members of the HCDA looked forward to putting the show back onstage in 1973. Ivey, who was doing fieldwork in the county for her Ph.D. in Folklore from Indiana University, writes, "Although many persons were willing to discuss the factors which entered into [the decision not to stage the play in 1972], few wished to comment for publication—not because scandalous matters were involved, but rather because there is a feeling that the past should be left behind." One person she interviewed later in the 1973 season said, "It's not good for the drama for people to come and ask 'How's the drama doing?' and for someone to say, 'Oh, it's in bad shape.' Or 'We didn't play last year.' See, people coming now mostly don't know we didn't play last year, so we don't tell them. There's no use telling them that we've had difficulty in starting it back."[11]

"Starting it back" didn't depend on the county's naysayers, the ones who "knew all along it would fail." It depended on the people who had worked on the project from the beginning. Those people were understandably wary; the failure to recover from a bad season in 1971 left many of them doubting the wisdom of the project—or their own ability to carry it out. But in the end, they believed in the story they were telling, in its appeal to a large number of potential outdoor theater-goers. And they knew that the small group of people who made up the Hancock County Drama Association, along with several allies in the county, had created this drama against long odds. There was no reason to think they couldn't re-start it. They had learned a lot since the drama was first proposed seven years earlier. And there were three positive factors to consider.

First, John Lee Welton—soon to be *Dr.* Welton, as he was finishing work for his Ph.D.—would be at the helm again as director. Second, the past debts—or most of them, anyway—had been paid. And, third, Carson-Newman College

[10] Ivey, "Oral, Printed, and Popular Culture Traditions," 345.
[11] Ibid., 336.

would be responsible for the future salaries of the director, cast members, and stage hands. HCDA members had reason to feel confident about the future of the production.

In late May, the *Kingsport Times-News* reported that John Lee Welton, "whose absence from the production spelled death for the drama last year," was back in charge of *Walk Toward the Sunset*, bringing with him a troupe of student actors from Carson-Newman College. Since the amphitheater had been idle for almost two years, the actors were clearing brush, building and painting scenery, and restoring bench seats, on top of rehearsing their lines. "But Professor Welton," Mike Seely wrote, "dressed Monday in shorts and a T-shirt said that despite the grumblings that his crew is having a 'wonderful time' and expects to be ready by opening night."[12]

Mike Murphy had just graduated from Carson-Newman and took the role of Governor DeWitt Clinton Senter. He recalled hours of hard work getting the amphitheater ready.

> Well, we had a lot of work to do, physical work. We were outside a lot. I could barely hit a nail with a hammer, so I just did the best I could do. There was a lot of work involved in it—not as much as Dr. Welton was talking about the first time they went over there [in 1969], expecting an amphitheater to have been built, and there was just a pile of dirt (laughs). But I remember we worked pretty hard there, and also trying to do the rehearsals. We didn't mind doing that, but it was work; we were tired at the end of the day.[13]

Rose Williams (today Rose Grayson) was cast in the lead female roles of Alisee Collins and Alisee Gibson. She recalls that nearly all the preliminary work done on the play was done on-site in Sneedville.

> I really don't remember working on it at Carson-Newman. We may have, and Papa might remember better. That's what I always called Dr. Welton. But I remember the rehearsal up there in Sneedville, it seemed like a couple of weeks before [opening night]. We may have rough-blocked it or had a read-through at Carson-Newman, but I don't remember doing a lot of work on it. I do remember the newness of trying to do it from such a distance. Papa would sit way up there on the hillside, and we'd be down on the stage, and the projection, you know, to get the sound to carry, and the lines and the action for that big a space, getting adjusted to that.... It was at least two weeks, possibly three. We would have gotten out of school in May and not had that much time off before we started, because it was a paying job for the summer, so those of us who relied on that—you know, it wasn't enough time

[12] Seely, "They're 'Working Up' a Drama," 22.
[13] Murphy interview.

to get any other kind of job. So it seems like there wasn't much lag time between when school got out and we started working.[14]

Rose Williams, like most of the 1973 cast, was a student at Carson-Newman College. Dr. Welton was sticking with Carson-Newman students, young people who called him "Papa," rather than casting from other college drama departments in the region. It was a decision that reassured the locals in Hancock County; these were good kids, kids that "Papa" knew. They might be theater kids, but they were theater kids at a Baptist college in nearby Jefferson City. Williams was a junior drama major who had appeared in numerous college productions.

> I grew up in Dayton, Ohio, but my parents were from South Carolina. After I graduated I moved back to South Carolina, and I've been in South Carolina ever since. I don't really feel like Dayton was hometown, even though I was there for about 11 years. (laughs)
>
> *What were your impressions of Sneedville?*
> It was a culture shock, I would say. We were not used to a place where you didn't have a choice about where to go to eat. But then, coming from Dayton, Jeff City was a culture shock, because Jeff City was really small. But Sneedville was even smaller. It was a different experience, but I really—I don't know what the right word is—not admired, but appreciated, maybe—I loved being away from the city. It wasn't like I missed being in downtown Dayton. It was like, "Oh, let's get away and be in nature and out in the mountains and clean air." And I think part of that also was the times. It was the '70s, and we were all kind of anti-whatever was the establishment. It seemed like everything was "back to nature." I had a couple of friends who got married out in the middle of a field, or top of some mountain, rather than in a church. And so there was a whole kind of atmosphere of get away from cities and go rural. And we were as rural as you could get up there in Sneedville. It was different because there were no stores, but I think we looked at it as, "Wow! Isn't this unique, isn't this different?" And we felt at the same time that we were part of something, trying to do something, as far as bringing attention to the Melungeons and bringing people to the area.[15]

Mike Murphy found Sneedville not so different from his hometown.

> I'm from Galax, Virginia, which is right on top of the Blue Ridge Mountains and is very similar to Sneedville—you have to be driving *to* there to get there. You're not really passing through. Very small, population-wise—

---

[14] Grayson interview.

[15] Ibid.

maybe three to seven thousand. When I went to Sneedville I fit right in, but I could see someone coming from Atlanta—Sneedville would really be an adventure....

What was your major at Carson-Newman?
Political science. I think I was the only non-theatre major in the play. [*Walk Toward the Sunset*] might have been the first thing I did in Carson-Newman theater. I did some [theater] in high school. And I had graduated— I was a senior, and I graduated in May, so I was out. I just did it because I thought it would be interesting.[16]

Paul Kersey, a Carson-Newman freshman from Atlanta, played the lead male roles of young Pat Gibson and Vance Johnson. Rodney Clark, a native of Anniston, Alabama, had the roles of Daniel Boone and old Pat Gibson. He was a graduate of Presbyterian College in Clinton, South Carolina, where he majored in drama. Like Paul Kersey, he had shoulder-length hair that would have disturbed people in Hancock County as recently as 1971, but, to paraphrase Bob Dylan, the times they were a-changin', even in Sneedville.

Donald Lamb of Knoxville returned for his second season in the drama. In 1970 he had portrayed Preacher Givens; in 1973 he would play the Scout and Ezra Johnson. A senior speech and music education major at Carson-Newman, Lamb would also serve as the drama's music director. He had been an actor at Goldrush Junction, a theme park in Pigeon Forge, Tennessee, and had served as minister of music at churches in Knoxville and Dandridge.

Gene Ellis served as stage manager and played the roles of the Cherokee chief Atakullakulla and the attorney John Netherland. The Lawrenceville, Virginia, native was a Carson-Newman graduate with a degree in English who had performed in and directed several plays. Willa King Bagwell of Oak Ridge, Tennessee, portrayed Millie Johnson, served as a lighting technician, and managed the costumes for the play. She was a junior at Carson-Newman, where she had appeared in a number of productions.

Wayne Venable had just graduated from Carson-Newman, where he majored in religion and performed in a few plays. In *Walk Toward the Sunset*, he portrayed John Sevier and a Sneedville villager. David LaPrade, a Carson-Newman senior majoring in music, played Mr. Sylvester and one of the lumbermen. Jamie Callaway of Erwin, Tennessee, portrayed an Indian dancer and a

Sneedville villager and also made several of the costumes. A recent Carson-New-man graduate, she had appeared in some production and had served as assistant director for *The Silver Whistle*.

Local members of the cast included Annette Turner, the Hancock County High School English teacher who had performed in every season of the play so far and would portray Mrs. Bolton. Roy Garland returned for a third season to play Preacher Givens; his daughter, Virginia Garland, a secretary at Hancock County Hospital, would perform as Mrs. Farley, as well as understudy the role of Alisee. And Tim Wilder, a 1971 graduate of Hancock County High School and employee of Turner's Market in Sneedville, had the role of Tom Robertson.

Scott Collins returned as lighting director, a job he had performed since he was in high school. Now a college senior, he was also an alderman for the Town of Sneedville and a board member of the Hancock County Drama Association. Marvin James, a Sneedville resident and an Air Force veteran, was plant manager for the drama; his day job was with the Upper East Tennessee Office of Economic Development.

Dora Bowlin was the president of the Hancock County Drama Association for the 1973 season; Kyle Greene was vice-president, Claude Collins was secretary, and the treasurer was bank president Martha Collins. Former mayor Charles Turner headed the publicity committee, Michael Hughes was back in the job as general manager of the drama, and other board members included Steve Walko, Elmer Turner, Kyle Lawson, Bess Jaynes, Gordon Gibson, Lena Jarvis, John Lawson, Dr. Esco Mills, Howard Rhea, and Don Trent.[17]

While female cast members boarded in town, John Lee Welton recalls that he and some of the male cast members spent their summer weekends living on Newman's Ridge.

> Doctor Pierce had some cabins up there, some vacation cabins, and he donated them to us. One cabin that we had was just a beautiful cabin—carpeted, had a telephone, electricity—but no running water. So when we would start off in the morning, I would take a tobacco sprayer, one of these metal tobacco sprayers, fill it full of water and set it on the back porch. And then we would come home and the sun had warmed it that much, and that was my shower for the day. If we didn't do that, there was a creek that we had to go down to, probably half a mile away, to bathe. There was a spring right behind the house where we could get water. We had an outhouse. So some of these kids, city kids, learned some interesting things while they were there with us.[18]

---

[17] *Walk Toward the Sunset* souvenir program, 1973.
[18] Welton interview (2002).

Mike Murphy was one of the young men in the cast who stayed on the Ridge for at least part of the summer.

> That was such an experience. It was out in the middle of nowhere on top of that Ridge; I think the road was pretty bad to get up to it. I don't remember any neighbors. As Dr. Welton said at Walters State the other day, it had electricity but it didn't have any running water, so you had to take a bath in the creek behind the house. But that was wonderful; I mean, you'd pay big money to stay in a place like that now.[19]

Rose Grayson (then, Rose Williams) recalled a lot of traveling back and forth between Jefferson City and Sneedville, slightly more than an hour's drive, during that summer.

> I know some of us moved into apartments in Jeff City and were paying rent for two or three months for the summer there. Because when we were not playing, when we were dark—once the show opened we were only rolling on Thursdays, Fridays, and Saturdays. So a lot of times we'd come back down to Jeff City for Sunday night—Monday—Tuesday, maybe go back up on Wednesday, to make sure everything was ready to go on Thursday. But we were kind of back and forth, some of us. It seemed like at that time, all the girls in the cast would be in one apartment in Jeff City, even if we were staying in different places in Sneedville. I know in '73 there were three or four of us girls who stayed with a family, or in somebody's basement that they rented out. And then all the guys were up at Doc Pierce's place on the mountain.[20]

The drama was set to open on Thursday, 21 June. The Sunday prior to the opening, Ric Larue wrote in the *Morristown Citizen-Tribune,*

> An outdoor drama is a different animal. It is half theatre, half movie location shooting, and half professional baseball game. No exception to this is "Walk Toward the Sunset," set for its grand opening this Thursday in Sneedville.
>
> It has all the problems of an indoor play—acting, costumes, stage-setting and props. On top of this are the added problems of a movie company in a more or less remote location, where equipment must either be created or carried from other areas. As in location shooting many non-actors must also be recruited from the surrounding area and trained in their parts to complete the production.
>
> As in a baseball game, "Walk Toward the Sunset" is totally at the mercy of the elements. For a sudden shower not only dampens the enthusiasm of

---

[19] Murphy interview.
[20] Grayson interview.

the audience, but does wonders for the equipment. (Although provisions have been made to perform the play in the nearby elementary school in case of rain.) Like a pro baseball game it is most often played under lights with the audience enduring a two-hour session on unyielding bleachers.[21]

The new cast was enthusiastic about what they were doing with their summer. They felt they were a part of something more important than merely staging a play. Rose Grayson recalled,

> I think we looked at it as, "Wow! Isn't this unique, isn't this different?" And we felt at the same time that we were part of something, trying to do something, as far as bringing attention to the Melungeons and bringing people to the area. I think we were conscious of trying to present going to Sneedville in a positive light. There were several outdoor dramas in Tennessee, and there was a sort of outdoor theatre community, and we encouraged each other— "you really ought to come up to Sneedville and see *our* show." We tried to get other people to come up and see it who hadn't been exposed to the story, or to the people.

For the most part unaware of the tensions that involved the 1971 cast, Grayson felt welcomed by Hancock Countians, but she acknowledged a feeling of separation as well.

> I don't remember any open problems, or hostility, or judgment, but there was some feeling of difference—those are the drama people, and we're the townspeople. There was a dividing line. I think it's pretty safe to say that during those years, most of the college students used the down time to do a lot of partying. And I'm sure that didn't go over with a lot of the townspeople. Not everybody in the cast was that way; there were some that were still pretty strong Baptists, so within the cast there were some differences between who was partying and who wasn't. I remember joking about spending time up in the mountains, where we were considered "the drammer people." It was just a separation; we were the drama people. But I don't remember any uneasiness, I don't remember being scared to go around in Sneedville, or feeling uncomfortable. The people that were dealing with the show, the Drama Association people, they were *so* gracious and welcoming to the cast.[22]

Mike Murphy recalled feeling a sense of responsibility for the how the actors were perceived in the community.

> It had been drilled into our heads not to blow it, to do anything that would bring shame to Carson-Newman or to the town or the play. And I

---

[21] Larue, "Sneedville Drama Is Product of History and Hard Work," D-1.
[22] Grayson interview.

tried to think the other day, before I talked to you, who instilled that in us; it was like breathing air, it was just something that you knew. You were always conscious of that. You just didn't want to do anything that would harm the play. Carson-Newman had invested a lot in that play, and Dr. Welton had invested a lot of his time.... It's kind of amazing when you've got 21-year-olds, and most of those people are theater majors, and there's really no supervision and you're up in the wilderness of Hancock County, you could get in a lot of trouble. I mean, you might be bored and just be doing something to get out of the boredom, but I never heard of anything that was out-of-the-way—no messing around by the people in the play, no drinking, cussing, drugs; you just didn't see it. To this day I'm amazed, it just floors me to think that, voluntarily, someone would be able to restrain himself and act as perfect gentleman—and ladies—for that time period. It's pretty amazing for 21-year-olds.

In 1973 there was a fairly big cultural divide in America, with young people on one side and older people on the other, and I wouldn't have been surprised to hear that there had been some friction between the college students and the people in Sneedville.

No, it was really the opposite. I mean, I was there one week and I knew everybody in town on a first-name basis. They were just so friendly, and the actors were friendly, too; it was a big adventure for us. But there was no "them versus us." That might have been because the play had been running for a while; maybe in the first years it was like that. But when we got there it was just, "Come home to supper with us tonight."[23]

Once the play started, the cast members began to encounter the challenges of their particular roles. For Rose Grayson, in the lead roles of Alisee Collins and Alisee Gibson, singing was required.

There was a little bit where Allisee had to sing a refrain or something. I'm not a soloist, and I just remember that was the most difficult part for me, and I didn't ever think I could project it, and I never really did that well with it. And I half-talked my lines where I was supposed to sing. Oh, goodness.

When you performed it in Sneedville, did they have recorded music, or did you have actual musicians performing?
There was a woman—I want to say Martha—Bolton?

Mollie Bowlin.

---

[23] Murphy interview.

Mollie! She used to sit out there and play dulcimer. Now, for the show itself, I believe [the music] was recorded. I remember us singing "Bretheren, We Have Met to Worship," and we probably did it *a capella*. There was a scene where we came out of the church. The church was on a rolling thing, and they would roll it out for one scene and then roll it back. I remember us being in a small space singing, (sings) "Bretheren, we have met to worship…." (Laughs) But we had all the extras from the town also singing. I guess it was enough to carry for that song. But other music—I think there was some Indian music, drumming, but I don't remember using live drummers.[24]

For Mike Murphy, makeup was a challenge.

I had to be an Indian in one of the scenes, and they used to give me a hard time about not putting on enough red paint. You know, they would critique it, and they'd see this white kid running around trying to be an Indian…[M]y problem with the makeup was that my skin was allergic to it, and I didn't want to have permanent acne scars. I remember one of the girls in the play— I guess there was an Avon Lady that used to come by and she offered, at her own expense, to get me some non-allergic stuff to put on my face. I declined because I knew she couldn't afford that, but that's just how nice those people were.

Rose Grayson recalled the makeup in more detail.

We used pancake makeup, and there was a variety called "Texas Dirt" that was a little more red, for the ones playing Indians, and there was a darker shade for those playing Melungeons. We used wet sponges and put makeup everywhere we thought skin was going to show if we were playing the darker-colored. Some of the people in the cast were already tanned—we got tanned as we stood out there rehearsing—and they didn't have to go as dark. Some of us who were lighter-complexioned—and I've always sunburned, so I had to put a good bit of it on. We spent a lot of time washing it off (laughs)— making up and washing it off. Fortunately, playing [another Melungeon character] in the second act, I didn't have to wash off the makeup between acts. In later years, I was an Indian in the first act and then Miz Johnson in the second act, playing white in the second act, so I had to change makeup between acts. It pretty well washed off with soap; you had to do a little scrubbing.

We had a mirror in there, but the lighting was not great. I don't think that we sat down to put makeup on. There was like a little bar shelf and a light and a mirror, but a lot of times we did makeup outside just to have

---

[24] Grayson interview.

daylight to see better by. Girls were on one side, on stage left, and guys were stage right. It wasn't a lot of room when you get that many people in there trying to change and put makeup on. I think a lot of the townspeople came ready; they came in their costumes.

As noted earlier, Greg Marion recalled that one of the pleasures of being a child extra in the play was the proximity to college girls changing clothes and asking for help with their makeup. Grayson was amused to hear of his recollections.

> There were a couple of big sinks on the back of each dressing room; kind of deep, like washtubs, sort of. That's where we were out of our costumes and washing off the makeup, and we were thinking we had, like bathing suits on, but I guess the little guys thought differently. That kind of came with the territory when you're in theater, in tight spaces with not much room to change. You tried to keep modesty, but—That may have added to the difference with the townspeople (laughs) if we weren't as aware as we should have been.

Grayson also recalled one of the particular hazards of their dressing area.

> We made a habit out of shaking our shoes out to make sure there were no black widow spiders in our shoes that had been left in the dressing room. When you went from being barefoot Indians or Melungeons in the first act to being townspeople in the second act, you had these black patent leather button-up shoes, and we left those in the dressing rooms. I remember we all learned rather quickly that you needed to shake everything out.[25]

When told of Rose Grayson's memory about spiders, Mike Murphy exclaimed, "They never told me *that*; I would have never gone in there! That doesn't surprise me a bit."[26]

Saundra Keyes Ivey described the activity at the drama site on the evening of a performance:

> Tickets for the drama are purchased from the window of a log building. Refreshments—soft drinks, sandwiches, and candy bars—are served from two converted corncribs. A crafts building, also made of logs, contains items ranging from quilts to candles and oil paintings. In the grassy space which separates these structures, a number of log benches are available; some of these are occupied by tourists, while one row of them, against the back of the crafts building, is almost always occupied by a group of Hancock County men who

---

[25] Ibid.
[26] Murphy interview.

come to the drama site an hour or so before the performance begins. These men pass the time in talk, sometimes with tourists, but more often with each other; occasionally an older resident will whittle as he talks, and sometimes all will sit quietly, simply observing the activity in the area.

Another log bench, always placed in front of the ticket office, is occupied by Mollie Bowlin, who arrives about an hour before each performance of "Walk Toward the Sunset" to sing and play her dulcimer. A number of tourists usually stand or sit near Mrs. Bowlin's bench to listen to her singing; often, a group will approach her to request a specific title or simply to compliment her on her performance. Near Mrs. Bowlin's bench, tourists may purchase souvenir programs containing a variety of articles on the Melungeons and on selected aspects of local culture....

In the course of these activities, tourists converse among themselves or with local persons working at the drama site. Comments such as "I've always heard they were descended from the Lost Colony," or the question "Are there any Melungeons here tonight?" are often heard during this period of conversation outside the theatre, and depending on the tact of the visitor or the patience and goodwill of the county resident who has been addressed, traditional information about the Melungeons and the county's history may be given in response.[27]

Prior to a show, the actors would be backstage at the bottom of the hill, while the box office, concessions, craft shop, and lighting booth were at the top of the hill. Grayson recalls that there wasn't a lot of contact between the two groups before curtain time.

With any production like that, front of the house is not as close with back of the house. They were busy with what they were doing, and we were busy getting ready for the show, and so everybody's job happened at a different spot. We had walkie-talkies, so we would ask them, you know, how was the house, are we filling up, or do we need to hold? Sometimes, like if a bus pulled up right before we were getting ready to start, they'd let us know, "Don't start yet, we've got a bus full of people coming in." But I think we were so busy dealing with what we had to deal with to get ready down on the stage, and they were so busy up at the top—some of them may have had more contact with them, but my memory is down on the stage, and making sure everyone was doing what they were supposed to be doing....

Now, there were only a couple of times we had to do this, but if it rained, we dreaded that. We would have to move everything up to the school and do it... trying to translate that show and put it into the gym, with rain pouring

---

[27] Ivey, "Oral, Printed, and Popular Culture Traditions," 361–62.

down on the tin roof, and you weren't miked and you couldn't hear—it was just an awful experience to have to call a rain show. You didn't want to have to give people's money back, and they had driven all the way up there and you wanted to give them a show. We had a policy of waiting till a certain time to call it, depending on how much it was raining, or how wet the seats were. Sometimes it would clear off but maybe the stage was soaking wet or had mud piled up, but if we could dry it out and the audience could sit out there, then we'd do the show with the mud.

If you did it in the elementary school gym, was there a stage there?

There was, and we always did a couple of practices of what we would do for a rain show. Everybody had their assignment of who would carry what up the hill. There were certain props we had to have up there, and certain things we left, but everybody had a job, and it would be spread out through the cast, who was carrying what to get it moved to the high school as quickly as possible. Certain people were responsible for the costumes, or wigs, or a rocking chair or a stump or the guns or whatever it was. So we would practice that as part of the rehearsal schedule before the show opened in July, but we always hoped never to have to do that. I remember at least once, maybe twice, having to move up because of rain.[28]

Mike Murphy recalled a rough indoor show.

It only rained one time that I remember, so we only did the play one time inside, in the local school, and I remember it was just a nightmare. Everything went wrong—Murphy's Law, you know, everything that could possibly go wrong went wrong. It was just a disaster. And I remember—I believe the editor for the *Tribune* had come up there for that night to do a story on it. And I talked to him one time later and he was just kind of laughing at it. He gave them a little bit of leeway, as far as not being too critical of it. We were trying to get the costumes and everything over to the school. I don't even remember what kind of background we had; it was just really bad. But it was amazing that for the whole summer, you would only have one rain event when you had to do it inside. It was hard to do inside.[29]

That summer, director John Lee Welton was finishing his doctoral work and preparing for classes in the fall. Grayson recalls that after the play was running for a few weeks, Welton was often absent from the production and trusted his cast to know what to do.

The play ran on Thursday, Friday, and Saturday evenings, so the cast members

---

[28] Grayson interview.
[29] Murphy interview.

from Carson-Newman had a lot of free time. Some had other part-time jobs that occupied their offstage time; others would go back to Jefferson City or to their respective hometowns. On weekends, cast members would be back in Hancock County, but they still had most of each day free. Grayson recalls enjoying outdoor activities.

> I know there were some days when we had outings of tubing, where they'd all get inner tubes and hook 'em together and go—I don't remember the name of whatever river or creek or stream they would find…A lot of reading, a lot of kind of exploring. I think I told you we went spelunking in a cave on a Friday or Saturday afternoon. (laughs) If something had happened to us in the middle of that cave—we were crazy enough not to be thinking anything could happen to us. We were just crazy, I guess. I think there were some moments when we were thinking, "Oh my goodness, what are we doing, what were we thinking?" But our guide was one of the locals and he kept assuring us we had plenty of time, and he was in the show himself, so (laughs) we were trying to make sure we got back. And we did, so we must have done something right.[30]

Mike Murphy has several memories of his summer in Hancock County.

> One thing I remember about the town was that restaurant; I guess it was the Green Top Inn? I remember the food there was so good, and I remember the older fellows sitting in front of the courthouse, hand-rolling their cigarettes. I've never seen that since. Anyway, that was interesting, those old wrinkled hands—I guess they just did it with two fingers, basically, and rolled that tobacco. I remember getting a parking ticket—in Sneedville, Tennessee, of all places—for fifty cents. I'd parked in front of that restaurant! It's strange what comes to mind when you're trying to bring your memories back. I remember I paid it with fifty pennies; I remember doing that…. And I remember the beauty of the place. We went to Elrod Falls; we went swimming there…. We went to Vardy one time; they had—I guess it was a thrift shop; maybe the church had a thrift shop over there. I got a pair of blue jeans for ten cents; I remember that…. You know, one of the cast members was from New York, and she'd been all over the world, and she said that was the most beautiful—that road, and the one that goes along the river and comes out at Rogersville, and the one that goes out through Kyles Ford and crosses over [Clinch Mountain]—she said those roads were the most beautiful scenery she's ever seen in the world. She was being sincere. It's incredible—the beauty and the people are the two things that stick in my mind even today.

Murphy became very familiar with the notorious Highway 31, which crossed Clinch Mountain between Sneedville and Mooresburg.

---

[30] Grayson interview.

I lived in Dr. Pierce's cabin up on the Ridge for the first few weeks, and then, because I was in Morristown and had a part-time job, they let me live at home that summer, so I would drive to the play and when it was over I would drive back home…. And I remember one night I was driving back to Morristown and my uncle had let me borrow his Sunbeam—a sports car, convertible, something like an MG, I think—and it had a Thunderbird engine in it. You could just barely keep the car facing forward when you went around a curve because it had so much power. So on the way back I was just driving slow, probably around 10:30 at night, with a full moon. And I had noticed before that I hadn't met anybody on that road between Sneedville and Morristown until you got over the mountain to Mooresburg and hit 11-W. And I thought, well, what if I just turn the lights off? It was a full moon; it was like a spotlight. So I did it for about five minutes and I thought, well, I never meet anybody—I'm gonna see how this goes. And I drove from Sneedville all the way over to Mooresburg in that sports car with no lights on, under a full moon. That's one of the things I didn't advertise to anybody; that's the kind of thing you could never do anywhere else, and you couldn't do it now, probably, over there. The place was so isolated you never saw anybody. I drove home all summer, three or four nights a week, and after about 10:30 you'd never meet anybody going out of Sneedville or coming into Sneedville; the road was just abandoned.

One of the goals of Mayor Charles Turner was to get that road improved. But coming from Galax, that road probably wasn't much of a challenge to you.

But that road was pretty crooked! Even growing up in Galax, we didn't have roads that crooked. It was like hairpin turns every few seconds, practically. That road was not something to be messed with. Right after the play, one of the cast members from the community was killed over there.[31]

As summer 1973 progressed, the members of the Hancock County Drama Association had ample reason to feel good about *Walk Toward the Sunset*. The negativity engendered by the uncomfortable 1971 season, and the cancellation of the 1972 season, was beginning to feel like a mere bump in the road, rather than an omen of failure. The people of Sneedville were becoming accustomed to seeing lots of cars with out-of-town license plates every weekend. The rough log benches of the amphitheater may not have been filled to capacity every night, but there usually weren't an awful lot of empty seats, either. The weather—always a concern for outdoor dramas—was cooperative, and most nights the play was performed under clear summer skies.

---

[31] Murphy interview.

When Saundra Keyes Ivey began doing her fieldwork in Hancock County in 1973, "the drama seemed to be regarded positively by at least the majority of the community at the time of my research…. While I remain convinced that the drama has a wide base of popular support—its survival with volunteer labor from the community certainly proves this—I came to realize that this support was not total."[32] As she questioned local residents about opposition to the drama, she found a variety of reasons for that opposition.

> *Ivey*: One thing I've heard is that there have been some people here who have been against the drama. Is that your impression?
> *Informant*: Oh [laughs]. We'd have people against Jesus Christ. [laughs] The first year we even had a bomb threat. Yea, some people's against it, I suppose.
> *Ivey*: Why would you say they are? I've heard some people say they didn't like the idea of the drama, but when I'd ask why—
> *Informant*: [interrupts] They couldn't give a reason?
> *Ivey*: Right. Maybe it's just cause they didn't know me. Anyway, why would you say they are?
> *Informant*: You know, we have a unique situation here in Hancock County. It's predominantly Republican. There's very few Democrats, so instead of Republicans and Democrats we have political factions, one side and the other side, and a lot of times this has a whole lot to do with it, just the political aspect.

One informant complained that the drama was not helping the people about whom it was written.

> Now that's the thing. The only people that we are helping with the drama are people who do not need the help in essence…. Now the poor people in that valley over there, that has not helped them at all monetarily you might say. But it…and I don't guess it's helped them culturally either, really. I bet they haven't even seen it. I'd just like to have a little survey about that valley and see how many have seen the drama.[33]

Ivey was quick to explain that this informant did not believe the situation he described was the result of any deliberate action or desire on anyone's part, but rather caused by a series of circumstances that prevented the play from accomplishing what the informant assumed was the original intent of the drama, which was benefiting the entire community financially as well as spiritually. Some of

---

[32] Ivey, "Oral, Printed, and Popular Culture Traditions," 337.
[33] Ibid., 349.

the more cynical people in the county, however, assumed a lot of money was being made from the drama, and questioned where that money was going. As one informant told Ivey,

> Um, you get rumors started, and tales. And some people felt that since the drama association made a little money the first year, some of the board of directors pocketed some of the money, you know. And that cut some people off from taking part in it. They had bad feelings about it. I've even had people say that I made a lot of money working the drama up here, buy all kinds of things, you know. Sure, I've really gotten rich up here. Anyway, that hurt the drama.

As Ivey pointed out, "county residents working for the drama are almost without exception unsalaried, and since those who do receive salaries are paid minimal amounts, such rumors seem totally unfounded."[34]

When Ivey did her fieldwork, *Walk Toward the Sunset* had been performed four out of the past five summers. The plot and the tone of the play should have been well-known to all county residents; even those who had not seen the play had heard about if from neighbors and friends. Despite this, there were still some—including some Melungeons—who believed the play made fun of the Melungeons.

> Well, now, I've got a brother-in-law by marriage; he's bad against it. He's...I don't know; don't seem like he wants anything to do with it. But I think it's a good idea.
> *Ivey*: What do people mostly have against it?
> *Informant*: Well, some of them think that they're making fun or some-thing. I don't think they are.[35]

Decades later, when Laura Tugman, a Ph.D. candidate in psychology study-ing ethnic identity among the Melungeons, collected oral histories from Me-lungeons, one subject expressed the same concern about the way Melungeons were portrayed. "Yeah, I knew it [the outdoor drama] was about my people but they were making fun of us.... They made fun of us in the play. Really! That's the reason it didn't go over."[36]

Others in the county may have been concerned that the play poked fun not at the Melungeons only, but at the county as a whole. This attitude recalled the county-wide negative reaction to the 1947 *Saturday Evening Post* article. One

---

[34] Ibid., 341.
[35] Ibid., 342.
[36] Tugman-Gabriel, "Seeking Roots in Shifting Ground," 131.

informant told Ivey that had been the case early in the run of the play, but that attitude had dissipated by 1973.

> A lot of people were against it because they thought we were going to make fun of the Melungeons, make fun of our remoteness…They thought we'd be focusing attention on a poor county that had these poor Melungeons, and that we'd be making fun of them.
>
> *Ivey*: Would these have been people who felt kindly toward the Melungeons and wanted to protect them from ridicule, or would they be people who ridiculed the Melungeons themselves and didn't think the county should point out that there were Melungeons here?
>
> *Informant*: I think the second more. Because some of them would say, "People know us, and they know we live good lives." They didn't want to be classed with the Melungeons. And now I don't hear that. You know, it seems that they have found out it's not that bad, being associated with the Melungeons.[37]

Ivey acknowledged that it was difficult to gauge the reaction of Melungeons to the play in large part due to the difficulty in ascertaining who was and who was not a Melungeon. She notes that several Melungeon families attended the play during her fieldwork; some of the townspeople she had met would discreetly tell her, "There are some Melungeons over there." Ivey assumed that other visitors were also informed about the presence of Melungeons and speculated that such attention might have been a reason for some Melungeons to stay away.[38] However, one woman who identified as a Melungeon (and was identified as a Melungeon by others) felt the play was beneficial to the county, that it was not only a positive portrayal of the Melungeons but a historically accurate one as well.

> I think it [the drama] is helping the county…Seems like there's more people comes through; there's more to see since the drama started. I think it's a good idea, myself…. And part of it is true about the Melungeons.
>
> *Ivey*: Part of the drama is true?
>
> *Informant*: Yea. Yea. [At this point, another woman who is visiting the informant interjects "I'm one myself." I try to express surprise, since she obviously thought this would be an announcement; she is, however, one of the few unmistakable Melungeons I have seen.]
>
> *Ivey*: Oh, really?

---

[37] Ivey, "Oral, Printed, and Popular Culture Traditions," 340.
[38] Ibid., 344–44.

Informant: Me and her both is. [Visiting lady laughs loudly.]

Ivey: Well, that's another thing I'm interested—if people think the drama is true or...

Informant: Yea. Cause they've...the Melungeon people was pushed out. [long pause][39]

It's not surprising that the play would be accepted as fact by Melungeons and non-Melungeons alike. Early writings about the Melungeons, including Will Allen Dromgoole's articles, speculated about Melungeon history without offering any concrete evidence. More recent researchers, including William Gilbert, Calvin Beale, Edward Price, and Brewton Berry, dealt with the Melungeons' status in the mid-twentieth century without delving into their history at all. For many in the county, *Walk Toward the Sunset* was the only history they knew about the Melungeons.

Except, of course, *Walk Toward the Sunset* wasn't history; it was the product of the imagination of playwright Kermit Hunter, who had scant historical information on which to base his play. John Lee Welton acknowledged that the play was not historically accurate; he believed historical accuracy would have been detrimental to the drama.

> Well, I think there's a certain fallacy there in that people come to the theatre like this and go away thinking that this is the truth. Obviously it is not. You cannot take the actual historical facts and put them on stage...they'd be dull as all get out. The two leads in our play, I'm sure never existed. Now their names are real, because we've found graves around here with those names on them. Kermit has taken historical names from the county and used them but as far as actual events....
>
> And of course Daniel Boone is in this story. Daniel Boone I'm sure met some Melungeons, but I doubt if he ever went to Colonel Sevier. Boone in this play represents the pioneer man who saw injustices being done to the Melungeons. He's a person we can identify with because we know him as the good guy—the champion of the underdog and so on, so he fits into this show...[40]

Given the choice between historical accuracy and dramatic presentation, Welton, as director of the play, would choose the latter every time. Believing that outdoor drama required "as much splendor as possible," he included "square

[39] Ibid., 341–42.
[40] Ibid., 359.

dancing, fireworks, and an animated Indian dance which culminates in the waving of lighted torches from the top of a wooden tower." (Welton said, "I must take all the blame for the choreography.") When Ivey asked if he had attempted authenticity in the Indian dance, Welton replied,

> None whatsoever. It's one of those show business schmaltz things you throw in to add a little pageantry to the whole show. As a matter of fact, the costuming is totally inauthentic. I have always been afraid, however, that if we went into turbans and robes in this particular show, it would throw the audience. In "Unto These Hills" [an outdoor drama concerning the Cherokee Indians, also written by Kermit Hunter] we accept that as Indian style, but here in this setting, we think of Indian as…INDIAN, rather than the very cultured people that the Cherokee were. I think the first question would be "Why are they wearing turbans?" The square dances are reasonably authentic, but other than that it's just theatre.[41]

Welton did not see the play as an authentic, accurate representation of the actual history of the Melungeons, but rather a story with a moral. "Our play is very frankly a play about prejudice. The first act is a historical prejudice; well, they're both historical prejudices, but the second act is more pulling into the current prejudices against any minority."[42]

The actual history of the Melungeons was sketchy, with yet-undiscovered records and documents in forgotten file drawers in courthouses, in the census records, in libraries, and in the pages of family Bibles, waiting for future researchers to find them and piece together at least a partial history. Until then, the play was all the Melungeons of Hancock County had to help them understand who they were. Anthropologist Melissa Schrift questioned the value of "destigmatizing an identity that existed almost, if not entirely, through media construction."[43] The identity created through media construction was all they had in 1973; it was all they had ever had. The material poverty of Hancock County as a whole could be measured through per capita income and employment figures, but how does one measure the poverty of a people who had no known history except for what had been written about them by mostly hostile outsiders?

Unfortunately, nearly all of the media construction about the Melungeons prior to the 1960s had been negative. *Walk Toward the Sunset* presented the Melungeons in a positive light. So what if Kermit Hunter made up a history for the

---

[41] Ibid., 358–59.
[42] Ibid., 359.
[43] Schrift, *Becoming Melungeon*, 85.

Melungeons? Plenty of writers before Hunter had done just that, and the results had been far less complimentary toward the Melungeons.

Of course, most of the Melungeons knew that the play wasn't based on historical fact. What was important was that the Melungeons were presented as people—as human beings trying to make their way in the world. And they *were* reviled and faced discrimination; Hunter's presentation of that fact might have been fictionalized, but it was still, in essence, true. And while the play might have provided a flimsy foundation for a people's identity, it was a start—just a start.

Sneedville residents had the experience of visitors in their remote town. A town official told Ivey, "In 1969 when we got it [the drama] underway and people began to come to our town and compliment these people, and compliment our town, I think it gave us a sense, a feeling of importance that we hadn't had before." Another informant told Ivey that the town's attitude toward strangers had improved.

> I've told you before that we're all Melungeons, actually, in a way. We're cautious. I think we've all that helped in the drama realized that there are people in the world outside of Hancock County that are interested in us as people. They're not trying to sell us out or anything like that, and they can help us, and if we treat them that way, we can learn from them and they can learn from us.
>
> And I think that's one of the biggest things the drama's done for all of us. Back as a boy, we didn't have anything to do, because we were shut in here. And when a stranger came in, if he talked to us—we just didn't want anything to do with him! Until we found out who he was! But today, this has changed You've found that out. I don't know, if you'd come in here ten years ago and went down and talked to people, I don't know how people would have—I shudder to think of the reception you probably would have gotten.[44]

Everyone concerned with *Walk Toward the Sunset* felt good about the 1973 season. Working with John Lee Welton and the students from Carson-Newman felt right. The audiences had come, the rains held off, and the season felt like a success. And, financially, it was.

Proceeds from ticket sales amounted to $8,697.51. That was $83.44 less than in 1971, but in 1973 the drama had introduced "County Nights." During previous seasons, "Hancock County Nights" had offered reduced admission to local residents. The idea was expanded to include neighboring counties. On one weekend, ticket prices were reduced for attendees from, say, Claiborne County,

---

[44] Ivey, "Oral, Printed, and Popular Culture Traditions," 350.

and on another weekend, discounts were offered for residents of Hawkins County, and so on. That well-publicized promotion might have meant fewer dollars in the till, but it put more people in the seats.

The total income for the play was $17,488.08, the lowest it had ever been, but, because Carson-Newman College paid the salaries of the director and the cast, expenses were also lower than they had ever been, totaling $13,139.89—a little more than half of the total expenses for 1971. As a result, the play was in the black for the first time since its debut season, showing a profit of $4,308.19.[45]

Everyone now realized that the changes they hoped for—new job opportunities, improvements to Highway 31, etc.—wouldn't happen overnight. But the play was on firm footing now, and that was a place from which to build the future.

Six thousand miles away from Sneedville, players in a much longer-running drama were about to introduce a new chapter in their story. And when that new chapter was played out, the world—including remote Sneedville—would never be the same.

---

[45] HCDA, report, 21 October 1975.

14

SETBACKS AND NEW BEGINNINGS

Yom Kippur, the Day of Atonement, the holiest day in Judaism, fell on Saturday, 6 October 1973. That date also fell within the Muslim holy month of Ramadan. On that day, a coalition of Arab military forces led by Egypt and Syria launched an attack on Israeli positions in the Sinai Peninsula and the Golan Heights, areas that Israel had occupied since the Six Day War in June 1967. The offensive took Israeli and American intelligence agencies by surprise, but the Israelis rallied after three days and began pushing the Arabs back. The situation led to tensions between the United States and the Soviet Union, both of whom put their military forces on alert, fearing that the fighting in the Middle East might ignite a global confrontation between the superpowers.

Tensions eased as the fighting subsided, but the Arab members of the Organization of Petroleum Exporting Countries (OPEC), reacting to American support for Israel, decided to reduce oil production by 25 percent per month. When President Nixon authorized increases in military and financial aid to Israel, Saudi Arabia declared an embargo on oil to the United States. This embargo was joined by other OPEC members, leading to an energy crisis in the United States. The price of oil increased from $3 a barrel in October 1973 to $12 a barrel in March 1974.

The stock market began falling in January 1974, and the oil embargo and price increase only exacerbated that fall. The country was mired in a recession and inflation climbed to 11.5 percent. Gasoline prices continued to rise, and shortages became increasingly common. Gas stations in some areas began allowing customers whose license plate ended in an odd number to buy fuel only on odd numbered days, and cars with even-numbered plates to buy on even-numbered days. Even so, there were often long lines of motorists hoping to buy gas, and stations sometimes ran out.

Northeast Tennessee experienced particularly acute shortages, especially in rural areas and small towns like Sneedville. In February, federal "energy czar" William Simon announced that twenty states, including Virginia, would receive emergency allocations of gasoline. Congressman Jimmy Quillen, representing the First District in the northeastern corner of Tennessee, complained to Simon that

> lines forming at gasoline stations in the First District are just as great as they are in Virginia. It is unfair to deny the people of the First District the same consideration your office is giving people in other areas. Many cities and areas in my District are completely out of gasoline and I am not going to stand idly by and see the people suffer while other cities of the nation are enjoying a greater distribution.[1]

The fuel situation in northeast Tennessee was exacerbated by the fact that the distribution of any emergency allocations of gasoline by the federal government would be controlled by Governor Winfield Dunn. The Republican governor was feuding with the Republican First District congressman over the establishment of a medical school in Quillen's district, a school Dunn had wanted for his hometown of Memphis. Tennessee's Democrat-controlled legislature had sided with Quillen, overriding the governor's veto of a bill that would establish the medical school at East Tennessee State University in Johnson City. When Simon allocated an additional 11 million gallons of gasoline to Tennessee, Quillen was concerned that little or none of it would reach his district. "The governor has discriminated against Upper East Tennesseans in the distribution of emergency allocations because of the medical school thing," Quillen complained. "I hope he will respond and give the First District of Tennessee its fair share of the 11 million gallons of additional gasoline which I have worked out through Simon in Washington." Quillen added that "there are hundreds of cars lined up to empty gas tanks in all areas of the First District, and it's obvious they have not been receiving a fair share."[2]

The few gas stations in Hancock County had run out of gas on occasion, as had stations in the surrounding counties. When the stations did have gas, the prices were alarmingly high. That spring, experts were predicting that many families would forego summer vacations. The members of the Drama Association were concerned about the impact the fuel shortages would have on attendance at their play. Those who did travel were less likely to venture into an area that, according to its own Congressman, was suffering more shortages than other areas. And Hancock County could offer scant hospitality to vacationers who might find themselves stranded there; motels rooms and restaurants were almost as scarce as gasoline. The situation might be better by summer—but then again, it might not.

---

[1] Rep. James H. Quillen, press release, 22 February 1974, Quillen papers.
[2] Ibid.

And, inexplicably, a sort of malaise had set in among the members of the HCDA. One of the key members, Elmer Turner, had died in February, the victim of a heart attack. His widow, Hazel, took the loss hard and withdrew from working with the HCDA. That meant the Drama Association would have to find a new ticket manager and a new concessions manager. It was more than just the loss of two members that soured the mood of the HCDA. Most of the members had assumed that, after five years, the play would be self-supporting. Carson-Newman College was covering the salaries of the director and the actors, but there was still no money to pay the locals who devoted countless hours to the outdoor drama.

The material benefits the play's backers had hoped Sneedville would enjoy had not materialized. Since the county had almost no tourist facilities, most tourists only bought tickets and snacks at the drama site. And some county residents were having second thoughts about whether it was even desirable to build up the county's tourist infrastructure. Saundra Keyes Ivey asked one supporter of the play what positive results had come from the project.

> Well, our original purpose was to upgrade the economy of the county in terms of bringing people in, and money. I don't think that we have done that, and in a way—well, I don't mind people having money, but I have changed as far as having a lot of people in. There are so few places left like this that I'd just as soon leave it like this. I like the remoteness. I know a lot of people don't, and they'd still like to have a lot of industry and so on.... I'd just like to keep it sort of like it is now.... I think we've already accomplished the purpose of making the Melungeon name respected.... We've accomplished that purpose, and I think we were wrong in that other purpose.

Another resident told Ivey, "I don't know why anyone would want to see a big campground and factories and big smokestacks and a lot of trains running through the county, and all that junk." The fear that tourism might lead to industrialism was expressed by another person, who said, "As far as industry is concerned, I'd like enough industry to take care of the people that are here and that's all."

Others saw the influx of tourists in a positive light; as one said, "If we can get more people coming into Hancock County the state is going to take notice and hopefully will build some good roads into the county, which we don't have, as you know." And another felt that expanded tourist facilities would serve the county well. "If we had a motel, and more restaurant facilities—now we do have one new restaurant, but if we had more facilities, this would be an ideal place. If that land up on this ridge was developed and we had cabins or something like that where people could come in and stay a week, it would be amazing how many people would come here just to go get where it's quiet."[3]

Clearly, there were differing opinions on the desirability of making Hancock County into a tourist destination. In retrospect, one could speculate that a fear of success might have played a role in the decision whether to stage *Walk Toward the Sunset* in 1974. But the Hancock County Drama Association in spring 1974 was more influenced by the images on television of long lines at gas pumps and of the panic that ensued when stations put up signs reading "No Gas."

It was impossible to predict that spring what the fuel situation might be in the summer, but the Drama Association had to make an immediate decision. Dr. Welton would soon be lining up student actors to commit their summers to performing in Hancock County, and local actors and workers would be planning their summer around the play. Once the wheels began turning, they wouldn't really be able to stop.

The Hancock County Drama Association made the difficult decision not to stage *Walk Toward the Sunset* in summer 1974. The success of the 1973 season made the 1972 non-season seem like a mere stumble in the growth of the play, a blip on the chart of the project's progress. But not staging the play in 1974 gave the project an air of failure, like a restaurant whose operating hours become unpredictable—are they going to be open or not?

As it turned out, the oil embargo was lifted in March and gas supplies became more stable by summer 1974. The threat of shortages still loomed, and Americans did tend to vacation closer to home that summer. It's impossible to tell whether attendance at the play would have been significantly affected by the threat of fuel shortages. More people in the region might have opted to explore nearby attractions like *Walk Toward the Sunset* rather than take vacations far away. Or they might have avoided Sneedville out of fear of being stranded with no gas and no bed for the night. The Hancock County Drama Association was not inclined to gamble; they knew they couldn't afford another bad season and made the best decision they could with the information they had at the time. Skipping the 1974 season would hurt the play; staging it unsuccessfully that summer might hurt it even more.

In spring 1975, gasoline prices were still high, but supplies seemed stable, and tryouts for *Walk Toward the Sunset* were held at Carson-Newman College and at the Hancock County Elementary School. For the first time, professional actors would be used in the cast, and live music would replace recorded music

---

[3] Ivey, "Oral, Printed, and Popular Culture Traditions," 346–47.

for the dance numbers. George Scutt, a sixty-eight-year-old actor and accordion-ist, would provide the music. A veteran of the Chautaugua circuit and the re-nowned children's theater company, the Clair Tree Major Players, Scutt was touring the South with a one-man children's show when he heard about tryouts for *Walk Toward the Sunset*. He was cast as Preacher Givens and Governor Senter.

The female lead for 1975, Kay Crews, was a native of Lake Jackson, Texas. She had been touring the country with the Alpha Omega Players production of *Saint Joan*, in which Crews had the title role. When the Alpha Omega Players performed at Carson-Newman College, Crews learned of the tryouts for *Walk Toward the Sunset* and requested an audition. She won the roles of Alisee Collins and Alisee Gibson.

The male lead, Phillip Dorr, had been one of Welton's students when he performed in *Walk Toward the Sunset* in 1970. The son of missionaries, Dorr had grown up in the Gaza Strip, a much-disputed piece of territory controlled alternately by Egypt and Israel. Dorr had gained further theatrical experience after performing in *Sunset*, playing Judas for two years in *The Smoky Mountain Passion Play* in Townsend, Tennessee.

The fourth professional in the cast was Deborah Kintzing, a recent graduate of the University of Tennessee, who had toured with a road show company of *The Odd Couple* and with the children's show *Aladdin and His Magic Lamp*. Kintzing had also performed in U-T productions and at Hunter Hills Theatre. In addition to portraying Mrs. Farley, Kintzing would serve as wardrobe mistress and said she "became a seamstress real fast" after arriving in Sneedville.

Rose Grayson, who played the female lead roles in 1973 (then under the name Rose Williams), was back. In 1975, she was Rose Crane, the wife of. Jerry Crane, a fellow Carson-Newman graduate and member of the cast. Rose would serve as assistant director and play the role of Mrs. Johnson. Local actors return-ing to the cast included Martha Collins, Annette Turner, and Roy Garland.

Carson-Newman junior Dave Brown, a native of Manassas, Virginia, would play Daniel Boone and Old Pat Gibson. Also from Carson-Newman was Myrtle Beach, South Carolina, native Randy Hardin, who would make his acting debut as John Netherland and would also be one of the dancers. Pete Emery, a Lincoln Memorial University graduate from Bellefonte, Pennsylvania, took the roles of Attakullakulla and one of the lumbermen. LMU drama student Ron Workman of Dayton, Ohio, would play Tom Robertson.

Two siblings from Jacksonville, Florida, joined the cast. Robert Dickerson was working as an elementary school teacher in Lee County, Virginia. He had performed in several shows at Carson-Newman and had worked two seasons with *The Smoky Mountain Passion Play*. Robert would appear as John Sevier and would assist with the choreography. His sister, Bettye Dickerson, was a senior psychology major at Carson-Newman; she had also performed in *The Smoky Mountain Passion Play* and in several Carson-Newman productions. She would be one of the dancers and an understudy along with lighting director Scott Collins. Scott and Bettye would soon form a relationship that was personal as well as professional.

Locals who made up crowd scenes as Sneedville villagers included Wayne Walters, Harry Hopkins, Libby Davis, Roger Hopkins, Alicia Walko, and Benjamin Hopkins. Portraying Melungeons were John Trent, Mike Reed, Mike Mullins, Ray Collins, Greg Wellen, Beatrice Collins, Lila Hopkins, Louise Avery, and Lonnie Bowlin.[4]

The show went on during summer 1975, but for the members of the Hancock County Drama Association, it didn't feel the same as before. It was harder to get volunteers, and the volunteers they got didn't work as hard or for as long as they had previously.

Revenue from ticket sales was up slightly from 1973: $10,206.50, an increase of slightly more than $1,500. The increase in ticket revenue, however, was due to a slight increase in the price of tickets rather than an increase in attendance. Attendance had actually dropped. It's possible potential attendees thought the drama had closed for good in 1974; after all, there wasn't nearly as much press coverage as there had been in previous years. Perhaps interest in the subject of the play was waning; while there were still occasional articles about the mysterious people of Hancock County, those articles merely recycled information from earlier articles. There was nothing new to report.

Income for the play fell to a new low in 1975; only $14,692.25 was brought in. On the other hand, inflation helped boost expenditures to $18,289.12. The season ended with a deficit of $3,601.87.[5]

Some members of the HCDA thought that combining the outdoor drama with another attraction might boost attendance. Discussions were held about moving the drama to Elrod Falls, located in an area known as Thorn Hill, about ten miles outside Sneedville on Highway 31. It was actually three waterfalls cascading off a steep ridge, but only the lower falls were easily accessible.

---

[4] Glenn, "Melungeon Drama to Reopen," 1; *Walk Toward the Sunset* souvenir program, 1975.

[5] HCDA, report, 21 October 1975.

Director John Lee Welton was keenly aware of the malaise affecting the Drama Association. He was still committed to presenting *Walk Toward the Sunset*—but only with the full support of the Drama Association and the town. After the 1975 season closed, he wrote a series of recommendations for the play and presented them to the Drama Association.

> The following recommendations are made due to the changing picture of our society and due to the constantly declining audience attendance over the past few years.
>
> 1. Because of the above problem, I recommend that a larger budget be given to promotion and if possible a person be procured to do publicity on a full-time basis beginning in April or May and running through the summer.
>
> 2. Because of the changing face of our society, I feel the present script has become dated. When the show opened in 1969, the racial issue was of major importance and foremost in the American mind. This is no longer true and has caused the show to look more mellodramatic [sic] and contrived than it did during its first years. I suggest, therefore, that the script be rewritten, or a new script obtained that will still give the Melungeon story, but with a different emphasis from the racial prejudice theme.
>
> 3. In considering the move to Elrod Falls, I recommend that a careful study be made of the needs for water, restrooms, camping facilities, access roads, parking areas, food services and any other auxillary [sic] facilities that will be needed in addition to the theatre itself. Perhaps TVA or some other governmental agency can be persuaded to do this study.
>
> 4. Most importantly, I recommend that a careful survey of the community be made to find out if there is enough *active* interest to continue the show for another year. This means people who are willing to give time and work in keeping the show going. This includes enough people to act in the show, enough people who will work more than an hour or two on getting the theatre ready, and keeping it in repair and clean, and are willing to take on jobs that will demand their spare time for the *entire season*, not just a few days before the show opens. I further recommend that pledge cards be given to these people asking them to commit themselves to this project and only if enough pledges are signed and returned should the show be considered for another season. Each pledge should know, as far as possible, what his job is and commit himself to that job to its completion.[6]

Clearly, Welton thought moving the drama to Elrod Falls would be a bone-headed idea. That area was completely undeveloped; there was an unnamed

---

[6] Welton, "Recommendations for the Hancock County Drama Association," undated report.

gravel road off Highway 31 that led to a small, unpaved area where cars could park. From there, a hike of about one-tenth of a mile brought visitors to the lower falls. There was talk of turning the area into a park, but even so, building an amphitheater and the other necessary facilities there would be a massive undertaking—assuming the necessary property could be obtained. Welton didn't even mention electricity that would be needed, not just to light the stage, but to light the parking area, box office, concession stand, and seating area. There were many other obstacles Welton didn't bother to mention, but he was far too diplomatic to flat-out say the idea was crazy; he simply suggested having some outside agency study the idea.

Welton's recommendations were all sound, and one could infer that if the HCDA ignored them, he would likely not be interested in directing the play in 1976. Welton was concerned about the budget for the production, publicity, and the outdated script, but his major concern was the malaise that had infected the Drama Association members and the people of the county. Enthusiasm and high hopes had gotten the play off the ground in 1969, but those qualities were sorely lacking in 1975.

One person who still had enthusiasm and high hopes was the agricultural extension agent for Hancock County, Roger D. Brooks. In summer 1975, Brooks was looking into the possibility of building an airport in Hancock County. He began corresponding with Congressman Jimmy Quillen about possible federal funding for the project through the Airport Development Aid Program. Quillen made inquiries and reported back to Brooks that prospects for funding weren't good. The Airport Development Aid Program had expired in June; Congress was considering legislation to create a new program for airport development, but that had not yet come to pass.

Furthermore, the director of airport service for the Federal Aviation Administration, William Vitale, pointed out that one of the requirements for federal funding of airport projects was that the location had to be included in the National Airport System Plan (NASP)—and Hancock County was not included in that plan.

The U.S. Department of Commerce could offer no help. David Rally of the Economic Development Administration explained that the Commerce Department could only provide supplementary funds after a primary grant had been awarded by the FAA. A few weeks later, Congressman Quillen forwarded a letter from Phillip Swatek, the director of the Southern Region office of the FAA, reiterating that Congress had not yet renewed the Airport Development Aid Program, and that Hancock County was not included in the National Airport System Plan. Swatek suggested that Hancock County officials should contact the

Tennessee Bureau of Aeronautics for technical advice and information on the availability of state funding for the project. No one had given Roger Brooks a definitive "no," but it was obviously going to be difficult to get a "yes" to the airport project.[7]

Well, if nobody was going to be flying in and out of Hancock County any time soon, perhaps the state could make it easier for people to drive there. In October, Brooks sent a letter to Tennessee Governor Ray Blanton:

> Hancock County is a very clean and scenic area with its many hills and valleys and the Clinch and Powell River, but relatively few tourists come to the Sneedville area because there are no major highways going through the county. Poor roads hinder our farmers when they travel to market, discourage potential new business and industry and prove a handicap to many young people who must travel long distances for jobs. Most of these young people eventually leave the county. While the population of the state and nation has increased, the population of Hancock County has decreased.
>
> During a recent conversation with Mr. Charles Turner of Sneedville, he gave me a copy of a 1970 study showing the proposed Appalachian Highway with Corridor S (25 E) going through Morristown and Tazewell and Corridor B (23) going through Kingsport and Clinchport, Virginia. In this proposal a 4-lane highway would link the two corridors by going through Sneedville and Kyles Ford. I feel that such a highway system would greatly benefit Hancock County. I would also like to see Highway 31 from Mooresburg improved all the way to Sneedville and extended north to the Ewing, Virginia, or Rose Hill, Virginia, area. This would be a very scenic highway across Newman's Ridge and would be a tremendous help to people in the north part of the county.
>
> In a Rural Development Problem Identification Survey conducted by the University of Tennessee in Hancock County last year, one hundred county residents ranked the conditions of the roads as the second most important of 29 community needs.
>
> I and the people of Hancock County would appreciate any state and federal highway aid you can send our way.[8]

[7] James H. Quillen to Roger D. Brooks, 22 August 1975; William Vitale to James H. Quillen, 20 August 1975; David Rally to James H. Quillen, 22 August 1975; James H. Quillen to Roger D. Brooks, 16 September 1975; Phillip Swatek to James H. Quillen, 15 September 1975, all in Quillen papers.

[8] Roger D. Brooks to Governor Ray Blanton, 17 October 1975.

Brooks was finding the same obstacles that Charlie Turner had discovered a decade earlier. Hancock County simply wasn't on anyone's list of places deserving of help, and no one seemed interested in or capable of getting the county placed on one of those lists.

On 16 September, new officers and directors were elected to the newly-restructured Hancock County Drama Association. Dora Bowlin would again serve as president. Claude Collins was first vice-president, with Nell Green as second vice-president and Ray Lawson third vice-president. Faye Rhea was secretary, and Martha Collins was treasurer. The board of directors was named to one-year, two-year, or three-year terms. Twenty directors would serve one-year terms, including Dora Bowlin and her husband, Kyle; Scott Collins; Kyle Greene; Kyle Lawson; and Sonny Turner. Claude Collins was one of five directors appointed to two-year terms; directors appointed to three-year terms included former mayor Charlie Turner, current mayor Truett "Doc" Pierce, Martha Collins, Faye Rhea, and Orban Horton. Five individuals served as honorary members, including Vardy historian Bill Grohse and T.J. Harrison, Jr.

In a letter dated 29 September, Dora Bowlin addressed the newly-elected and re-elected directors.

> Perhaps some of you are aware that a proposal has been put forth for the Drama Association to change the site of our production from its present location to Elrod Falls, which will be developed in the near future into a park. It is necessary for us to discuss this matter and to decide whether this move should be made.
>
> Because a decision needs to be made right away, it will be necessary for us to have a called meeting to put this matter to a vote. We will, therefore, meet on Tuesday, October 7, at 7:30 p.m., at the Community Center Building. I urge each of you to be present for this important meeting.[9]

The board decided not to move the production to Elrod Falls, but the debate left some hard feelings among some of the board members. And there were questions. Some of the board members wanted a year-by-year breakdown of ticket sales, expenditures, and total income. Others were curious to learn how the expenses for *Walk Toward the Sunset* compared with those of other outdoor dramas.

On 21 October, a report was presented to the board members which compared the expenditures for various budget items planned for the 1976 season to the average expenditures of seven other outdoor dramas, based on figures from

---

[9] Dora Bowlin to HCDA board members, 29 September 1975.

1968. The comparisons were made using percentages of total expenditures; for example, office supplies made up 0.27 percent of the expenditures for *Walk Toward the Sunset*, compared with 0.79 percent as the average for the other seven dramas. Figures weren't available for all budget items, but *Walk Toward the Sunset* spent less on many of the items for which comparative numbers were available, and more on others. Some examples:

	Walk Toward the Sunset	Other dramas
Scenery and props	2.3	2.61
Costumes and makeup	1.85	2.39
Maintenance and repairs	4.4	3.24
Utilities	0.62	0.87
Postage	0.36	0.61
Telephone	0.89	1.14
Insurance	4.0	1.8
Lighting and sound	2.3	2.0
Promotion	11.6	12.19

The most dramatic differences were in three areas: administration, theater operations, and salaries.

	Walk Toward the Sunset	Other dramas
Administration	3.44	20.88
Theater operation	5.8	14.54
Salaries for director, actors, stage managers, technical people	55.56	39.3

Costs for administration and theater operation for *Walk Toward the Sunset* were considerably lower than the average of seven other dramas because *WTTS* had no paid positions in either of those areas. On the other hand, salaries for the director, actors, stage managers, and technical people such as lighting and sound directors were higher for *WTTS*, probably because some, if not most, of the other dramas relied more on local volunteer actors in the main roles, whereas the main actors in *WTTS* came from out of town and were paid. However, for *WTTS*, those salaries were paid, not by the Drama Association, but by Carson-Newman College.

The report also listed total income, expenditures, and ticket sales for each of the five seasons *Walk Toward the Sunset* had been performed. Only two of those seasons, 1969 and 1973, had been profitable. The total income for all five seasons was $95,135.29; expenditures for those five seasons had been $100,117.45. The total deficit for the five seasons was $4,982.16.[10]

It was not a huge deficit, amounting to less than $1,000 per season overall. Outdoor dramas often operated at a loss. In many cases, state governments provided assistance, either through grants or in-kind contributions, such as constructing an amphitheater, maintaining the site, or providing promotional literature. Those states recognized the value of outdoor drama in attracting tourists or celebrating historical events or places. However, the state of Tennessee provided no assistance beyond a one-time grant from the Tennessee Arts Commission several years earlier.

The board members of the Hancock County Drama Association realized that without a subsidy of some kind, the future of the play looked bleak. They might have called it quits then and there, but there were two beacons of hope for the coming season that just might buy them some time to work out a permanent source of funding.

The first was a $25,000 grant from the Department of Commerce, under the Job Opportunities Program (Title X). This grant would cover many of the production expenses for the 1976 season.

The second was the upcoming American Bicentennial, the commemoration the two-hundredth anniversary of the signing of the Declaration of Independence. American history would be in the spotlight for the entire year, and historical sites were preparing for a record number of visitors. Outdoor dramas commemorating aspects of American history were also expected to draw larger-than-usual audiences.

"A Bicentennial surge is overtaking the major plays," according to Mark Sumner, the director of the Institute for Outdoor Drama in Chapel Hill, North Carolina, and one of the participants at the initial conference in January 1968 that got *Walk Toward the Sunset* started. "We expect this may be the best year in spite of politics, economics and environmental problems. Reservations are up everywhere." The Institute reported that fifty-four outdoor dramas would be staged during summer 1976, including thirteen new productions, the largest number ever started in a single season.

William Glover, the drama reporter for the Associated Press, wrote,

Outdoor drama spectacles in record number are scheduled this summer from coast to coast. Aimed at the vacationing family trade, the al fresco events

[10] HCDA, report, 21 October 1975.

range from folksy history to classic drama, from religious pageant to boister-
ous romp.... Performed mostly by college actors for spectators in a holiday
mood, the shows rarely come up to professional thespic standards. Nobody,
however, any longer doubts the popular appeal and economic impact of what
supporters regard as America's most original dramatic form. Summer-long
attendance is expected to be well over the two-million mark.[11]

Forty of the fifty-four productions scheduled for the Bicentennial summer
focused on legends or events associated with the areas in which the dramas were
to be performed. Ten of those productions, including three new ones, were written by Kermit Hunter, the author of *Walk Toward the Sunset*.[12]

The script had undergone minor revisions during previous seasons, and
Kermit Hunter agreed to make further revisions for the 1976 season to make the
story more bicentennial-friendly. These revisions would more fully reflect the
participation of the Melungeons in the American Revolution, particularly in the
Battle of King's Mountain.[13] That battle took place on 7 October 1780 on a
mountain that straddled the North Carolina-South Carolina border west of
Charlotte. There, Patriot militias defeated Loyalist militias led by British Major
Patrick Ferguson. One of the Patriot militia groups that participated in the battle
was the Overmountain Men, a group made up of men from west of—or
"over"—the Appalachian Mountains in North Carolina, Virginia, and present-
day Kentucky and Tennessee. These men were especially interested in gaining
independence from England because English treaties with various Indian tribes
prohibited settlement west of the Appalachian Mountains; since the Overmountain Men were already in violation of those treaties, they sought to legitimize
their claims to land by overthrowing English rule and setting up a new government.

The 1976 production of *Walk Toward the Sunset* was designated an official
Bicentennial event by the national American Bicentennial Commission and the
Tennessee Bicentennial Commission. The Hancock County Drama Association
hoped that heightened interest in the Revolutionary era of American history
would draw large audiences to the play.

Dr. John Lee Welton was again directing the drama. Rose Crane served as
assistant director and played the role of Mrs. Johnson. She had received her B.A.
in English and speech from Carson-Newman College. Her husband, Jerry Crane,

[11] Glover, "Outdoor Drama Increase in Popularity," 15-C.
[12] Ibid.
[13] Hancock County Drama Association, National Endowment for the Arts application
(rough draft), 1976.

was stage manager. A member of the 1975 cast, he would also portray Cantrell and Governor Senter in the play. David Behan of Tusculum College, who had helped get the drama started in its first season, was back as technical director.

The choreographer, Jo Kelly, was born in Sydney, Australia, and came to the United States at the age of ten. At that time, she had already been taking dancing lessons for seven years and went on to study dance in Chicago and perform professionally with the Dorothy Hild Dancers and the Miriam Sage Dancers. After living in Puerto Rico with her husband and three daughters, she and her family moved to Morristown, Tennessee, where she worked with the Morristown Theatre Guild and taught dance at the Morristown Girls Club.

Scott Collins was on board for his sixth season with the drama as lighting director and understudy actor. He was now the Circuit Court Clerk for Hancock County. Barbara Burchett had started sewing as a little girl on Newman's Ridge. She was the seamstress for *Walk Toward the Sunset*; she also served as the unofficial seamstress for the community, creating wedding dresses, men's clothing, and costumes for local plays. Ralph Smith was the costume designer, and Zella Mills and Sara Alice Green were costume assistants.

One of the lead female roles had undergone a change of name. There had always been a bit of confusion because the main female character in the first act was named Alisee Collins, and the main female character in the second act was Alisee Gibson. Both roles were Melungeon women, and both roles were always played by the same actress. In the first act, set in 1782, Alisee Collins married Pat Gibson, and in the second act, set in 1868, the same actress played Alisee Gibson, giving some audience members the impression that this was the same woman, who had apparently aged 86 years but still appeared to be in her early twenties. To allay the confusion, the character in the second act was now named Cora Gibson; she was still portrayed as a descendant of Alisee Collins and Pat Gibson from the first act. For the 1976 production, both roles were played by Bettye Dickerson, a veteran of the 1975 season and now a Carson-Newman graduate with a degree in psychology.

The lead male roles of Pat Gibson and Vance Johnson were played by Paul Kersey of Atlanta, Georgia, who had played both those roles in the 1973 production. He was a senior English major at Carson-Newman and had performed in *Medea*, *Cat on a Hot Tin Roof*, and *Who's Afraid of Virginia Woolf?* In summer 1975, he had worked for the University of South Carolina Repertorie Company as an equity apprentice.

Dave Brown, now a junior at Carson-Newman, was back for his second season with *WTTS*, playing Daniel Boone and John Sylvester. He was named "Best Actor of the Year" at Carson-Newman and had major roles in *The Cave*

Dwellers, Skin of Our Teeth, Mrs. Lincoln, A Man for All Seasons, Medea, The Puppetmaster, and *Bye Bye Birdie.* Robert Dickerson, the brother of Bettye, portrayed John Sevier and John Netherland. George Scutt, who had joined the cast in 1975, would play Cherokee chief Attakullakulla. Charles Rickards, a senior business major at Carson-Newman, played Uncle Ben and Tom Robertson. Rickards had performed in a number of plays, including *Carnival, Portrait of America, Interview, Dr. Faustus,* and *The Lion, The Witch, and the Wardrobe,* among others. Rickards had also written and produced two religious dramas presented in Florida and Michigan, and he had toured as a member of the Creative Youth Ministry.

Miller Lyons of Morristown appeared as Preacher Givens in the first act. He had been the editor of the college newspaper at Tusculum College in Greeneville, Tennessee, and had played a major role in Tusculum's production of *The Pursuit of Happiness.*

Ron Vannoy was a junior at Lincoln Memorial University in his hometown of Harrogate, Tennessee, where he majored in fine arts and secondary education. He had been voted "Best Actor" at LMU for his role as Jesus in *Godspell*; he had also performed in *A Midsummer Night's Dream, A China-Handled Knife,* and *Li'l Abner.* Vannoy portrayed the Medicine Man and Carson in *Walk Toward the Sunset.* Roger Hopkins, a junior at Hancock County High School, was the only member of the cast who had performed in each of the six seasons of *WTTS.* For the 1976 season, he portrayed Dragging Canoe and served as understudy for the male lead. Lindalee Fortney, a senior speech and philosophy major at Carson-Newman, appeared as Aunt Lizzie, and also served as property master for *WTTS.* Her previous credits included *Skin of Our Teeth, The Miracle Worker, Sorry, Wrong Number,* and *Mrs. Lincoln.*

The supporting cast was a mix of locals and major cast members who filled out crowd scenes when their characters weren't onstage. They included Lonnie Bowlin, Cheryl Corley, Libby Davis, Gerald Fleenor, Mike Fleenor, Ricky Powell Greene, Sara Alice Greene, Benjamin Hopkins, Harry Hopkins, Lila Hopkins, Oppie Johnson, Bethel Lawson, Juanita Mabe, Laura Mabe, Zella Mills, Mike Mullins, David Trent, Kitty Trent, William Trent, Janet Tuten, Alicia Walko, Kathy Walko, Wayne Walters, James Williams, and Debbie Wolfe.

Indians were portrayed by Ron Vannoy, Rose Crane, Libby Davis, Lila Hopkins, Roger Hopkins, Ricky Powell Greene, Gerald Fleenor, Wayne Walters, Harry Hopkins, Juanita Mabe, David Trent, Mike Mullins, and Cheryl Corley. Dancers included Ron Vannoy, Roger Hopkins, Wayne Walters, Miller Lyons, Lila Hopkins, Lindalee Fortney, Juanita Mabe, Paul Kersey, Dave Brown, Bettye Dickerson, and Rose Crane. Gerald Fleenor played the Messenger, with

Wayne Walters serving as alternate. Janet Tuten portrayed Cindy, and Christine was played by Libby Davis.[14]

In previous years, the out-of-town cast members stayed in basements, spare bedrooms, rented houses, or Doc Pierce's cabins on Newman's Ridge. But this year, there was another option for the actors. "In '76 we were in some new apartments that had been built," Rose (Crane, at that time) Grayson recalled. "We were the first tenants in one section of it. It was like a couple of separate buildings, and girls were in one and guys in the other. But I was married then, and [my husband] Jerry and I were in one."

As opening night approached, the Hancock County Drama Association had reason for celebration. The Appalachian Regional Commission approved a $100,000 grant for repair and renovation of the amphitheater. All renovations were to have a rustic appearance to conform to the motif of the existing facility. The Farmers Home Administration provided an additional $25,000 in loans.

HCDA members were also pleased about a new book that would certainly generate more interest in *Walk Toward the Sunset*. Jean Patterson Bible published *Melungeons: Yesterday and Today* late in 1975, and by summer 1976, the book was being profiled in newspapers. Ms. Bible was an educator in nearby Jefferson County, where she taught history, modern language, and English. She was a prolific history, travel, and feature writer whose articles appeared the *New York Times, Baltimore Sun, Atlanta Journal and Constitution Magazine, The American Home, Historical Review and Antique Digest, The Southern Observer*, and elsewhere. She wrote a weekly column for the *Standard Banner* in Jefferson City, Tennessee, and eventually served for thirty years as Jefferson County historian.

Despite some initial resistance, Ms. Bible found people in Hancock County and elsewhere who were happy to cooperate with her project, people who felt it was important that the Melungeon story be documented before it was too late. Already, outmigration from rural areas and intermarriage with "outsiders" was taking a toll on the various tri-racial communities across the eastern United States. Throughout *Melungeons Yesterday and Today*, Ms. Bible frequently remarks that the Melungeons are fast disappearing as a distinct people, and that soon, only an occasional dark-skinned descendent will appear to remind us of who the Melungeons once were. Thus, her work was motivated by a sense of urgency: the older people who remembered the bits and pieces of their scant history would soon be gone, and their memories gone with them.

Ms. Bible was guided in large part by the work of her friend Bonnie Ball, who had known Melungeons in southwest Virginia all her life and had written

---

[14] *Walk Toward the Sunset* souvenir program, 1976.

about them since the 1940s. Bible also studied the most recent research by Edward Price, Brewton Berry, Calvin Beale, Henry Price, William Pollitzer, and others. She befriended Bill Grohse, a "transplanted Yankee" who compiled genealogical histories of the early families on Newman's Ridge and Vardy Valley. Most importantly, she began methodically searching and compiling all the available historical records on the Melungeons.

As she writes,

> Busy university professors took time to write thoughtful, detailed answers to my questions on history, genetics and anthropology. County historians have dug up facts about Melungeons in their counties. Faded newspaper clippings from historical collections, articles in professional journals, unpublished mimeographed writings, microfilms of long-ago censuses whose original print had sometimes faded almost beyond recognition, valuable old public records such as the Hawkins County *Will Book I* and the early *Tennessee Supreme Court Reports* whose yellowed pages fairly crackled with age, family letters, graduate theses, a doctoral dissertation, numerous bits of correspondence and clippings from kind people who were willing to share their knowledge with me—all played a part.[15]

Ms. Bible recounted the various legends and theories of the Melungeons' origin and presented the major theses chapter by chapter. As she writes, "If some of the chapters sound like research on a thesis or dissertation while others seem more like feature articles in a popular magazine or newspaper, that is the way the Melungeon story reads to me. It is a 'mixed bag,' ranging from hard fact to what is almost fiction."[16]

The final chapter of *Melungeons: Yesterday and Today* was devoted to the outdoor drama. Ms. Bible was optimistic about the future of *WTTS*. She was not as optimistic about the future of the Melungeons as a distinct group of people, feeling—as did nearly all researchers—that the Melungeons were assimilating into the general population and would soon be only a memory. She concludes, "So if the few remaining descendants of the original Melungeons disappear into the country's melting pot, 'Walk Toward the Sunset' has at least provided a happy rendition of the Melungeon swan song. It is a fitting memorial to a vanishing race."[17]

---

[15] Bible, *Melungeons: Yesterday and Today*, ix.
[16] Ibid., x.
[17] Ibid., 117.

The Bicentennial season of *Walk Toward the Sunset* opened on Thursday night, 1 July. Kermit Hunter's revisions emphasized the Melungeons' participation in the Battle of King's Mountain. The script called for a great deal of activity on the stage before the play began.

In the revised opening, actors would gradually take the stage, some stirring off sorghum while two women operated a spinning wheel. A blacksmith would set up his anvil, while a woman churned butter. While these activities were underway, the character of Preacher Givens would appear and address the audience. "Before we start the show, you folks come down here and visit us a while. Git down here where you can see all this. Maybe you can show us better how to make a cane-bottom chair, how to make apple-butter, or put a handle on a broken shovel. This is what our ancestors were doing in the Tennessee Valley two hundred years ago, Come on down, ever'body!"[18]

After about twenty minutes, Preacher Givens was to suggest that the audience members take their seats on the rough-hewn logs that served as benches, while the actors removed the sorghum trough, anvil, churn, and spinning wheel from the stage. Then the play itself would begin.

However, "To the best of my memory the written opening…was never used," John Lee Welton recalled decades later. "If my memory serves me right, the 1976 version was started with a recorded voice-over as the people came onstage. It said something about the origin of these people was lost in the mists of time. Then the play started with a messenger running on stage saying 'Hey, everybody! Hey! Come on out here, everybody! Hey, Preacher Givens!'"[19]

Villagers come from all sides to gather at center stage as Preacher Givens—played by Ron Brannan—appears. "All right, all right! Stop yer hollerin'! Never hyerd such carryin' on! Whaddya want, anyway?"

"They're comin' back—all the Watauga men!"

The people all cheer. The Watauga men, also known as the Overmountain men, were the militiamen from the Holston River area and beyond who gathered at Fort Watauga to march to North Carolina and fight the British in the Battle of King's Mountain. The battle was a victory for the Americans.

From stage right, a column of eight men enter singing "Lincolnshire Poacher." Some of the men are white, but most are dark-skinned. Pat Gibson, played by Paul Kersey, tells Preacher Givens about the battle, including the death of one of their community members, John Sylvester. Alisee Gibson, portrayed

---

[18] Script quotations in this chapter are from the 1976 version of *Walk Toward the Sunset*, Kermit Hunter's unpublished script.

[19] Welton, email to author, 3 January 2018.

by Bettye Dickerson, pushes into Pat's arms; she is clearly his sweetheart and overjoyed by his return. And, despite the loss of one of their neighbors, a feeling of celebration overtakes the village and they begin dancing. As the dance ends and the villagers break into small groups to chat and drink cider, frontiersman Daniel Boone (Dave Brown) and future Tennessee governor John Sevier (Robert Dickerson) enter the village engaged in a spirited debate.

> BOONE: Well, you don't have to get mad about it!
> SEVIER: I'm not getting mad! I'm simply telling you that we have to start some kind of organized government!
> BOONE: John Sevier, you led these people off to King's Mountain and risked your life to get *rid* of government!
> SEVIER: No! To get rid of kings and empires across the ocean! To get rid of taxation without representation! We have to have laws, courts, some kind of social contract. We have to levy taxes, support some kind of government. Leave people alone and they turn into barbarians!
> BOONE: You're not foolin' me any, John Sevier! I've known you too long. You have claims on two hundred thousand acres of land here in this Tennessee country, and you want to sell it for a profit. To do that you have to have an organized government, 'cause North Carolina don't recognize your claims.

In this revision of the script, the war is not yet concluded, and the British treaty with the Indians, including the Cherokee, still prohibited white settlement west of the Appalachians, even though several communities had already formed in the eastern part of what would become Tennessee. Sevier wants Boone's help in bringing more settlers into the new territory. "I'll set up a government, and you get the people to move out here."

> BOONE: *That's* no problem; hundreds of families waitin' for a chance to own a piece of land. But what about the British Crown and the Indians? We're still fightin' a war!
> SEVIER: The war's not coming out here. Besides, this victory at King's Mountain stops the Indians. The British *lost*, and the Indians will back off.
> BOONE: I wouldn't depend too much on Chief Atakullakulla!

Boone and Sevier enter the village, and Sevier explains that with new settlers moving in soon, those already settled will have to put in claims for their land and make a down payment on it. Pat Gibson speaks up for the Melungeon community: "We claim twenty thousand acres of bottom land." But a white man in the crowd objects, saying the Melungeons have no legal right to own land because "a black man can't own land." Preacher Givens points out that a dozen or more Melungeons fought with Sevier at King's Mountain, and "anybody that fought for the American cause ought to have a right to *live* here!"

In the ensuing debate, the uncertain racial status of the Melungeons comes to the fore. Pat Gibson is at a loss to explain his ancestry,

> PAT: Part of my ancestors, and part of Alisee's, are Scottish. The other part, we can't be sure. (Musing) My father said he could remember his grandfather talking about a village near the ocean: southeast…perhaps South Carolina, Florida…
>
> SEVIER: That would have been…when?
>
> PAT: (a shrug) Sixteen-fifty, I suppose. They were driven away from the coast by new settlers, so they came out here to this valley. They've been *here* at least a hundred years.
>
> SEVIER: But I mean before that: where did they come from? Why the dark skin?
>
> PREACHER: John, I've seen people from North Africa, and they are darker than any of these. Besides, these people have straight noses, thin lips straight hair, like you an' me. I reckon they *could* be North African, mixed with white, but I don't think so. Also, I figger each new generation is a little lighter in color than the one before.

There are more variations from the original script in the second act. After the fight in which Tom Robertson is killed, Cora—the character who was previously named Alisee—tells Vance she is going back to the Ridge to talk to the people there, to explain that Vance wasn't to blame for Tom's death. Ezra Johnson acknowledges that the party is over.

> VANCE: You folks got no business collecting in crowds like this anyway. On my way here I heard there's a fever runnin' through this valley. About a mile down the river two families real sick.
>
> JOHNSON: Well, fever or not, those Melungeons are gonna come back here with rifles and shoot up the town.
>
> VANCE: (hotly) What do you expect? …After two hundred years of being treated like mad dogs?
>
> JOHNSON: Oh, hush, Vance! Keep outa this! You men come over here and let's make some plans. You women go on home.

The scene shifts to Newman's Ridge, three days later. Pat Gibson is sitting on a rock as Cora paces nervously.

PAT: Cora, I've told you over and over, our people are mad and hurt! Tom Robertson was their friend! He was one of us! Why should we do anything for them down there?

CORA: Tom is dead and buried. We have a bigger problem now. That fever's hittin' lots of people down in the valley. They think maybe it's smallpox.

PAT: Serves them right! The Lord has a way of evening things up.

CORA: Is that what you want? Revenge? Would you feel better if everyone in Sneedville died of smallpox?

PAT: Vance is the only one I give a hoot about. We can't be friends with *them*! They *despise* us! All they want is to cut our timber and pay us about half of what it's worth!

CORA: That's not what you taught me all these years...

PAT: Maybe I've been a fool, Alisee. Maybe I've been blind to the real facts.

CORA: And maybe you've just all of a sudden *gone* blind to the real facts! *I am going to marry Vance Johnson!* He is going to be your *son-in-law*! These are his people. Vance and I are going to stop this ridiculous feuding if it takes the rest of our lives! Do you understand?

PAT: Well, I reckon you're old enough to go your own way,

CORA: I'm asking you for the last time: will you help me get everybody to go down in the valley and try to stop this fever?

Pat is clearly reluctant, but unsure what he should do. He is fond of Vance and knows him to be a friend of the Melungeons, but has little sympathy for the people of Sneedville.

PAT: They have a doctor in Kingsport.

CORA: You know good and well doctors can't cure smallpox! Nobody can! All they can do is try to keep the fever down. We still have the herb mix that was used by the Cherokee Indians years ago! Many a time we've broken a fever with herb medicine. Maybe we can do something good for a change.

PAT: The herbs don't always work. We had lots of our folks die a few years ago when the smallpox hit us up here. There's nothing we can do.

CORA: Not if you sit here like a toad frog on Newman's Ridge. A lot of us are immune to the pox from the last time, but the young ones are not. What if the fever spreads up here?

PAT: All right, all right! Dang it, I'm tired of this nagging and fussing! It won't do a lick of good, they'll still hate us, but if nothing else is going to satisfy you...you watch, the minute the smallpox is over, we'll be right back where we always were! (Alisee kisses him). What do you want to do first?

CORA: Get about thirty of the women…those that already had the pox. Tell all the men to stay up here on the Ridge. Have them dig roots and get all the mixtures ready. We ought to go down there this afternoon…two or three women to each house. I'll send word down to Vance that we're comin'. Now hurry!

As music plays, the lights dim on center stage and rise on the side stages, where women pantomime working over the beds of sick people. Director Welton takes advantage of the amphitheater site. Lights come up on the hillside behind the amphitheater, and the audience sees men digging roots and passing them in baskets to others waiting below. Cora moves among the women on stage, giving directions. Then Cora goes to the bed of Mrs. Johnson and gives her medicine. Mrs. Johnson relaxes and falls asleep. As Cora sits back in her chair exhausted, the lights go down as the music continues to play. The Melungeons have saved the people of Sneedville.

As the lights come up for the next scene, Vance instructs his father to gather all the townspeople, making sure none of them have guns. He also wants the lumbermen from Knoxville present. Meanwhile, Vance has sent word by way of Cora that he wants the Melungeons to be present. Everyone has gathered on Sneedville's main street. Vance turns first to the Melungeons, and Cora's father opens the conversation.

PAT: All right, boy. We all came down here because Cora said you had something big to tell us. Better be pretty important…

VANCE: You people have been kicked around for two hundred years. Now, things have changed. The State of Tennessee has voted equal rights to all citizens regardless of color. That means you now have a legal right to own land. You hear me? *You have a right to own land.*

The people exchange glances at this momentous news.

VANCE: First thing we're going to get a surveyor to run some lines and mark off every foot of property on Newman's Ridge, all over Powell Mountain. Then we'll go to the courthouse and establish ownership, file deeds.

PAT: (skeptically) That takes money, and it takes a lawyer.

VANCE: I'm a lawyer, and it won't cost you anything. Monday morning we'll get a surveyor from Kingsport.

MAN IN CROWD: Who's gonna pay the surveyor?

VANCE: You are.

MAN: With what?

VANCE: With the money you're going to make from the sale of timber.

PAT: Who says we're sellin' our timber?

VANCE: You let me handle it, and you'll get the right price. And plenty of jobs for the young men.

MAN: What are *you* gettin' out of it?

VANCE: A lot more than I deserve. (People mutter and exchange glances.) All right, make up your minds. I'll get you a good price for the timber.

PAT: And you want nothing in return?

VANCE: One thing: you're going to start a school on Newman's Ridge, and you're going to send all your children to school. Will you promise?

MAN: You sell 'at timber for a good price and we'll send the kids to school.

VANCE: It's a deal.

Vance then turns to the whites of Sneedville, along with the two lumbermen from Knoxville. The Melungeons take a step back as the villagers come onto the stage, and the two sides gaze at each other with a degree of suspicion on both sides. Vance begins speaking to the lumbermen.

VANCE: You all remember we had a big hassle some time back about timbering in this county, and you men here, along with my father, tried to sell a bill of goods about public duty and civic pride and all that stuff, and it all added up to a slick way to get the Melungeons to sell their timber for about half the regular price!

LUMBERMAN: Now, wait a minute…

VANCE: Do you want to cut timber here or not?

LUMBERMAN: Well, er…

VANCE: How much do we want? I'll tell you how much: the Melungeons on Newman's Ridge will cut their timber under careful supervision and log it out to the road, but it will cost you just exactly twice what you were offering!

LUMBERMAN: (hotly) *Twice* as much? You must be crazy!

VANCE: You can't pay one price in Rogersville and another in Sneedville!

LUMBERMAN: We can't pay that much.

VANCE: Very well. The conversation is finished.

LUMBERMAN: Now wait a minute! Dang it, you move too fast!

VANCE: Just say yes or no!

LUMBERMAN: But…

JOHNSON: Just shut up and agree with the boy. You know he's right.

LUMBERMAN: All right, all right, we'll do it. But it's highway robbery!

VANCE: Any time you think the price is too high, go right over to Rogersville and get all the lumber you want. Of course, it isn't as good a grade. If you want this lumber, you make up a list of what you need…

LUMBERMAN: Oh no, nosiree! We'll do the cuttin' ourselves!

VANCE: You don't cut one tree, you hear? Not one sapling! The lumber will be cut and logged down to the road by the Melungeons and others on Newman's Ridge! You give me that list and I'll see that you get what you want…cash on delivery on the road.

LUMBERMAN: You'll get the list, and the timber better be right.

VANCE: It'll be right. These are Melungeon farmers and they'll make it right. Get your mind accustomed to that. And now, I think my father has something to say.

JOHNSON: (surprised) I do? Oh, er…I reckon I do. (He looks over the crowd and hesitates.) We've got…'bout twenty families here in the valley that might not be alive today if it hadn't been for you Melungeon folks workin' and slavin' and tendin' the sick. I jist ask you to forgive us for bein' a bunch o' big-headed fools… I thought I was tryin' to build, when all the time I was tearin' down. Mr. Gibson, on behalf of the people here in the valley I want to shake your hand.

Ezra Johnson and Pat Gibson shake hands. Many of the whites in the crowd move to shake hands with the Melungeons. Then Vance Johnson calls for the crowd's attention.

VANCE: Folks! Folks! I brought a young lady in here a month or so ago and tried to introduce her to all of you, but every last one of you turned your back on her. She's the one who organized those Melungeon women and put an end to the smallpox epidemic. Now, if she'll still have me, I'm gonna make her my wife and you're all invited to the wedding.

MAN IN CROWD: Me and my wife and fourteen young'uns? That'll be quite a crowd! (laughter from the crowd)

VANCE: Kids and all, you're all invited.

MRS. JOHNSON: (moving toward Cora) Cora, I…I had a speech all figured out…I knew what I was going to say…wakin' up those nights and having you sitting there smiling at me and coolin' my forehead…

Vance's mother takes Alisee by the hand, and the two women embrace. Pat is jubilant: "By dang it, there's going to be a wedding, and I'll provide enough Hancock County corn liquor to make everybody forget about the smallpox and everything else!" Clearly, Pat believes corn liquor is the appropriate beverage at all significant occasions; he got a laugh at this line and at his earlier offer of whiskey to the governor.

As a sense of reconciliation and brotherhood sweeps over the townspeople and the Melungeons, Ezra Johnson and the lumbermen offer Pat Gibson a job overseeing the lumber operation. Music begins, and the cast breaks into a dance. As the dance ends in a flourish, the lights go down to end the play. The audience rose in a standing ovation as the cast returned to the stage to take their bows.

The cast quickly fell into the routine. With Rose Crane, a three-season veteran, serving as assistant director, along with David Behan as technical director and Jerry Crane as stage manager, Dr. Welton didn't have to be in attendance every night. Rose Crane appreciated that level of trust.

> I think for the first month of the run or the first several weeks of the run, Dr. Welton would come up—he stayed up there until we opened, and then he would come back up to check on the show. He'd take notes, and depending on his notes, he'd decide whether something needed rehearsing or going over. But usually, once we got running and into the routine, the schedule was usually to get there and check props and check sets and sound and lights and costuming. Then we would meet at a certain time to do some warm-ups, then maybe we would run the songs for some vocal warm-ups. Then we'd be calling places, getting into position and ready to go. I don't think after the first couple of times of him taking notes and checking that it was really running the way he wanted it to run, that we went back and rehearsed scenes; by then we knew the lines and knew what we were doing and would come in and do it. That's the time when it would cut down on our contact with the town people, who weren't there the whole time to rehearse. They'd come in in time for the show, and we'd see them, but then you're running the show.
>
> [Dr. Welton] pretty much left it to us to keep it on track, and he would spot check, you know. If he came up for a Thursday, the next week he would come up on Friday, and maybe stay for Saturday, but he wouldn't be there every Thursday, Friday, Saturday. I think he tried to catch as many as he could, but he was getting ready to start teaching in the fall semester and had other obligations. Once he was satisfied that we all knew what we were doing, and the show was working every night the way it was supposed to, he left it in our hands, which was a lot of trust on his part. We tried to live up to that and make sure the show ran well every night. I don't remember any major guffaws, somebody forgetting something or messing a scene up; by that time, it was rolling and we rolled with it. There were crazy things, like costumes breaking, or silly things like that, but I don't remember, scene-wise, like ever being in the middle of a scene and not remembering, or somebody totally dropping a chunk of the lines. And you were far enough away from the audience that you could get away with whispering a line to somebody if they seemed to momentarily forget something; you could cue each other and the audience wouldn't hear it.

On fair nights, the audience enjoyed the setting of the theater almost as much as the play itself. John Lee Welton has worked in many outdoor venues over the course of his career but recalls the amphitheater in Sneedville as unique. "It was probably one of the most unusual theaters I've ever worked in," he recalls, "because we had some mules up behind the theater that made comments on some of the lines every once in a while, and we had a family that would come up and sit behind the theater and watch the actors changing clothes as well as watching the show. They just became part of the set more than anything else."[20]

For the 1976 season, the Hancock County Drama Association paid a total of $16,637.89 in salaries and housing allowances to the actors and crew. Dr. Welton received $2,200.00 for the summer's directing work, while technical director David Behan made $1,500.00. Assistant director Rose Crane and her husband, stage manager Jerry Crane, each made $960.00. Lighting director Scott Collins earned $720.00 for the season; his assistant made $600. Costumer Barbara Burchett was paid $190 for the season, and choreographer Jo Kelly made $100. For the first time, the Hancock County residents who played minor roles and filled out the crowd scenes were paid—not much, but it was significant, anyway.

Other production costs included $12,889.28 for maintenance and repairs to the amphitheater, $1,013.79 for lighting and sound reinforcement, $584.39 for costumes and makeup, and $383.85 for royalties. Altogether, production costs for the 1976 season totaled $27,763.60.

The Hancock County Drama Association paid a total of $1,768.78 in administrative costs, including $1,104.00 for a secretary. Utilities, insurance, and special printing came under the heading of "Theatre Operation," and amounted to $1,295.33.

Many of Dr. Welton's earlier recommendations had been adopted, and promotional costs for *Walk Toward the Sunset* included salaries for a publicity director ($770.00) and an assistant ($225.00), $665.00 for brochures, $502.25 for materials, $1,490.00 for souvenir programs, and only $85.00 for advertising. Clearly, the HCDA was counting heavily on newspaper and television stories to spread the word about the drama, but relatively few stories were generated about the drama, despite the work of a publicity director. Most of the stories relating to Melungeons that appeared in the press concerned Jean Patterson Bible's book.

Overall, total expenditures for the 1976 season were $34,564.96. It was the most expensive season yet, costing more than $16,000 above the expenditures for the 1975 season, and more than $9,000 above the cost of the 1971 season,

---

[20] Welton interview (2002).

which had been the most expensive season prior to the Bicentennial summer. However, $22,414.16 in Title X funds made the outlay by HCDA only $12,159.80, less than any of the previous seasons.[21]

No figures have been found for ticket sales or other income from the 1976 season, but attendance seems to have been disappointing. The actors didn't pay much attention to how many of the seats in the amphitheater were filled; if there was an audience, they performed. Still, Rose Grayson recalls, "I think there was a sense of less audience."[22] It is probable that, even with the Title X funding, the end of the 1976 season found the Hancock County Drama Association again in deficit.

The Hancock County Drama Association wasn't ready to throw in the towel, but they knew the play would have to be subsidized in some way for it to continue. They had funding from the Appalachian Regional Commission to renovate the amphitheater. The next step was to find funding to keep the production going.

---

[21] Hancock County Drama Association, expenditure report for 1976.
[22] Grayson interview.

15

"A THOROUGH AND BUSINESSLIKE PLAN"

As summer 1976 drew to a close, the Drama Association looked to the National Endowment for the Arts as a possible source of funding. Specifically, they were interested in Federal Program No. 45.001—"Promotion of the Arts—Special Projects."

> The Office of Special Projects enables the Arts Endowment to explore certain *special program activities* and to support a variety of ongoing *interdisciplinary programs*, including Folk Arts, Art Centers and Festivals and service organizations. The purposes of the Office are achieved through contractual agreements, technical assistance arrangements and grants-in-aid.
>
> *Special Program Activities* are designed to:
> • explore areas of potential programming for the Endowment to enable the agency to meet the ever-evolving needs of its cultural constituency.
> • support special projects or programs recommended by the National Council on the Arts, the Advisory Panels, or other Endowment programs.
> • assist special projects proposed from the field.
> Because of limited funds, the Endowment will consider funding proposals from the field only if they are multi-disciplined, maintain professional standards, are unique and prototypical, do not fit other Endowment guidelines and have the potential of regional or national application.
>
> Those wishing to make inquiry should submit a narrative description of the proposed project together with a summary budget for review. Invitations to make formal application may be issued after the preliminary review has been completed. Inquiries must be received at least six months before the project is scheduled to begin...[1]

The guidelines specified projects that involved two or more art forms or program areas. That didn't seem to fit an outdoor drama, unless you counted the music in the play as a second art form. Grants were also available for the presentation of "American folk arts." This included festivals and exhibits. Grants were

---

[1] National Endowment for the Arts, Office of Special Projects, guidelines for project grants, August 1976.

also available for media dissemination of folk arts on local, regional, or national television, or through radio sound recordings, film, or videotape. Again, none of this seemed applicable to *Walk Toward the Sunset.*

The projects also had to meet professional standards. Only a few outdoor dramas could meet that requirement. The members of the Drama Association considered *Walk Toward the Sunset* a well-done outdoor drama, but whether its cast of college actors and local volunteers, its rustic stage, and its enthusiastic but relatively inexperienced organizers could be compared to a Broadway production, or even a professional touring company, was pretty doubtful. However, with funding, they could come a lot closer to that standard.

There were two areas under which *WTTS* might qualify. The guidelines included projects that "have potential national or regional significance." The HCDA could make a strong argument that the Melungeon story had regional significance as a previously overlooked aspect of Appalachian history. In the light of the ongoing American struggle with race relations, an argument for the play's national significance could be made as well.

Even more importantly, the guidelines specifically mentioned projects that were "justifiable on the basis of geographic isolation from other quality arts activity." Few towns in the eastern United States were as isolated as Sneedville. That isolation might just be the ticket for funding. And the craft shop, which was part of the planning for the outdoor drama from the very beginning, might well qualify as "presentation of American folk arts."

While the HCDA began working on a proposal for the National Endowment for the Arts, the University of Tennessee Extension Office, whose leadership classes in 1967 had been the genesis of the outdoor drama, presented HCDA with a summary of a survey they had conducted. At the request of the Hancock County Drama Association, the U-T Extension Office had prepared a questionnaire that was available at the box office during most of the 1976 season, from 2 July and until 21 August.

Most of those attending the drama were in groups—families, groups of friends, civic groups, social clubs, etc. The survey summary explains:

> One member of each group attending the drama was invited to voluntarily complete the questionnaire. Questionnaires were thus completed by interested members of the audience rather than by a scientifically drawn sample designed to be representative of the 1976 drama audience. It would have to be assumed that the people who voluntarily completed a questionnaire were representative of the entire audience to project the results of this study to include the 1976 audience. This assumption is questionable but the results

provide information on about 1/3 of the 1976 audience and offer some useful insights on at least this portion of the audience.

With 278 completed questionnaires, the authors of the survey estimated that 1,288 people were in the groups that returned a questionnaire. Audience members came from as far away as California, Wisconsin, and Florida. However, nearly 60 percent of those completing questionnaires were from Tennessee, and about 22 percent were from Virginia. Forty percent of the respondents were from Hancock or adjoining counties. Two nearby metropolitan areas contributed a significant number of attendees; 14 percent came from Knoxville, while 9 percent came from Johnson City.

The audience for *Walk Toward the Sunset*, according to the survey, was relatively well-educated, with white collar jobs and good incomes; the median annual family income was in the $10,000 to $15,000 range, and more than 16 percent had incomes over $25,000. It was an older audience; only 17 percent were under eighteen years old, while 52 percent were forty-one or older.

Groups of friends or relatives made up 92.7 percent of the respondents, while 2.6 percent came with a club or organization, and 4.6 percent came alone. Slightly over one-fifth of those filling out questionnaires had seen the play before; almost 80 percent were seeing it for the first time. However, nearly 73 percent had seen an outdoor drama at some earlier date.

The Hancock County Drama Association was particularly interested in how respondents heard about *WTTS*. Almost 30 percent heard about the play from newspapers. Others learned of the play from television, radio, magazines, posters, and brochures, but more than half answered "other"—indicating word-of-mouth. Of those, almost 80 percent learned of the play from friends. Information booths accounted for 15.7 percent; few learned of the play from travel agencies or from motel or restaurant personnel.

More than three-quarters of the respondents were in Sneedville specifically to see the play, while just under 10 percent were in the area to visit friends or relatives. More than 81 percent said they would stay in Sneedville only long enough to see the drama. The vast majority of respondents made the decision to see the play in 1976, and of those, 66.9 percent had made the decision to attend in July; 13.4 percent decided in June, and 12.2 percent in August. Of those who came to Sneedville from out-of-state, 63.7 percent made the trip specifically to see the drama; 27.4 percent were there to visit relatives or friends.

Private homes in the area housed 19.1 percent of the respondents on their visit; only 8.3 percent were staying in a motel or hotel, 5.9 percent in a camping area, and 66.7 percent answered "none of the above," presumably returning to their own homes. The survey also wanted to know where respondents had eaten in the area; 21 percent had eaten in a restaurant, 7.3 percent at a drive-in, and 5.5 percent had cooked out. "None of the above" was the answer given by 66.2 percent of the visitors.

When asked "What have you liked most about your evening at *Walk Toward the Sunset?*," 45.4 percent said it was the play itself. The drama surroundings—the atmosphere, music, concessions, sound, etc. were mentioned by 11.6 percent, while the local people were mentioned by 5.8 percent. The local area—the scenery and the river—were mentioned by only 1.7 percent, and 35.5 percent answered "Other."

Respondents were given another chance to answer an open-ended question about what they liked best. Thirty-four respondents mentioned the play itself, while twelve liked the people. The music was mentioned by seven people, as were tradition and local history. Others mentioned the dancing, good sound, the night air, the folksy atmosphere, the portrayal of injustice imposed on a minority group, the usherettes, and the cleanliness of the area.

Likewise, respondents were given seven categories to describe what they liked the least. Roads and travel were chosen by 19.2 percent, while 17.9 percent picked weather conditions. The drama surroundings—the sound, the log seats, the limited number of items available at the concession booth, cigarette smoke, etc.—were chosen by 16.7 percent, and the lack of facilities in the area by 6.4 percent. Directions to the play were disliked by 3.8 percent, the play itself by 2.6 percent, and 33.3 percent chose "Other."

Given an open-ended version of the same question, ten respondents indicated unhappiness with the roads, and three bemoaned the lack of highway directions. Helicopter traffic was mentioned by five people; four mentioned the rain and four mentioned the hard seats. Four people felt that more overnight accommodations and restaurants were needed, and four complained about the long wait before the start of the play. Three respondents indicated that the weather was too cold, but two were unhappy about the heat and humidity. Three respondents complained about the lack of peanuts and popcorn in the concession area, three others were bothered by cigarette smoke, two disliked "the person beside me," and one had to leave because of a baby crying. Also mentioned as negative factors were the Southern accents in the audience and difficulty in understanding words—whether spoken by the actors or by the audience is unclear. Others mentioned the inference that the Melungeons lived by making liquor, a lack of knowledge about the origin of these people, inadequate explanation of history, and "the local people, especially those involved with the play, should be better informed."[2]

The members of the HCDA were happy to see that the play itself was generally well received. Complaints about the weather were to be expected in any outdoor drama. The demographic information about the audience—age, income and educational levels, distances traveled, etc.—would need to be compared with similar information from other outdoor dramas in order to be useful. But the survey pointed out several problems that were particular to *Walk Toward the Sunset*: distances traveled, bad roads, and the lack of lodging and dining opportunities. These were serious problems that could doom the play's chances of drawing larger audiences.

With help from the University of Tennessee Extension Service, the Drama Association prepared their proposal to the National Endowment the Arts. In the end, the Special Projects grants seemed ill-suited to the needs of *Walk Toward the Sunset*. Instead, a proposal was made to the NEA's Theatre Program, with a cover letter from HCDA President Dora Bowlin.

> The enclosed represents a joint effort on the part of the Hancock County Drama Association and the Extension Department of the University of Tennessee to obtain operating funds for the 1977 production of Kermit Hunter's outdoor drama, *Walk Toward the Sunset*, which is staged in Sneedville, Hancock County, Tennessee each Thursday, Friday and Saturday during July and August. *Walk Toward the Sunset* is about the Melungeons, a small group of people whose origin is unknown and whose traditional home is on Newman's Ridge in Hancock County.
>
> The drama idea was originally instituted for the dual purposes of achieving a means of economic growth in this low-income, isolated section of Appalachia and of preserving the heritage of the Melungeon people. The results have been gratifying and we have had the additional benefit of giving all the people of Hancock County a source of pride and satisfaction.
>
> Since it is difficult for an outdoor drama, using professionals, to operate with no outside help, we are asking for funds to help stage the production. Any funds we might receive will be used for salaries to pay the professionals necessary to the quality of the drama.[3]

---

[2] University of Tennessee Agricultural Extension Service, *Characteristics of Persons Attending the Outdoor Drama "Walk Toward the Sunset," 1976.*

[3] D. Bowlin, cover letter to the National Endowment for the Arts Theatre Program, 22 October 1976.

The proposal opened with a request for $20,610 in grant funds to supplement the salaries of the production staff and cast and to expand promotional efforts. It went on to present a brief explanation about the Melungeons, recounted the formation of the Hancock County Drama Association, provided a description of the play itself, which was followed by a section titled "The Current Situation."

> *Walk Toward the Sunset* was created almost entirely from local resources and local participation continues to be significant. The Drama Association is governed by a 30-member Board of Directors; this broad involvement, together with a policy of actively seeking local donations and in-kind contributions, have maintained a feeling that this is a community endeavor.
>
> On a more pragmatic level, this involvement has translated itself into substantial donations of time and materials. Attachment I presents an estimate of the value of the local contributions made in the 1976 season, While these estimates may appear inflated, a conscious effort to be conservative was made and they were in all probability underestimated. Further, this was the first season that the local people who play minor roles and fill out crowd scenes have been paid. For each of the past five seasons, then, donations have included approximately 3,000 hours of time from approximately 20 individuals.
>
> The impact of these contributions may be seen in Attachment II, which compares the percentage of expenditures by budget categories for the 1976 production with the average of seven outdoor dramas in 1968 as reported by the Institute of Outdoor Drama. The use of donations whenever possible has allowed the dedication of available funds to the production itself to present a professional production of the highest possible quality.
>
> Further, the City of Sneedville obtained a total of $125,000 in loans and grants from the Farmers Home Administration and The Appalachian Regional Commission to repair and improve the amphitheater in 1976. This work is currently underway and will be completed before the start of the 1977 season. These funds are for site renovation and cannot be used for production purposes.
>
> *Walk Toward the Sunset* was designated as an official bicentennial event by the National and Tennessee American Bicentennial Commissions in 1976.

Under the heading "The Need for Funds," the HCDA explains that few outdoor dramas are self-sustaining and that many, if not most, operate at a loss. However, state governments often subsidize dramas within their state by providing funds for production costs, underwriting production losses, or providing in-

kind contributions such as constructing and/or maintaining the outdoor theaters. Tennessee, however, provided no support at all for the two outdoor dramas
within the state, *Walk Toward the Sunset* and *The Smoky Mountain Passion Play*
in Townsend. Because the state had only two outdoor dramas, legislative action
to support the plays has been "weak and ineffective," although efforts to obtain
state funding were ongoing.

After reiterating that the funds would be used to pay the salaries of the director, technical director, and actors, the proposal lists the benefits arising from
the outdoor drama, benefits the HCDA felt justified its continuation.

> 1. *Walk Toward the Sunset* is the only cultural activity of this nature in
> the upper East Tennessee area.
> 2. The trained actors are recruited from area Colleges and through the
> Institute of Outdoor Drama. The drama offers these people as well as aspiring
> local actors an opportunity to perform in a unique production and in a setting
> quite different from the customary drama productions.
> 3. Hancock County is relatively isolated and still maintains much of the
> Appalachian folk lifestyle. The visitor, drawn to this rural county to see the
> drama, can also observe and experience a culture that has already disappeared
> from most of America.
> 4. A farmers market is being constructed on a site adjacent to the amphi-
> theater and will be completed by the 1977 season. Stalls will be available for
> the sale of our native crafts and art works. This market was created on the
> strength of the drama and most of the sales will be dependent on the drama
> audience.
> 5. In addition to handicrafts, the money spent by the drama audience in
> local businesses has aided the area economy.
> 6. Finally, the drama is the best means available to preserve and keep alive
> the story of a small group of people who are different—the Melungeons.

To conclude the narrative portion of the proposal, the HCDA expresses its
hopes for the future of *Walk Toward the Sunset*.

> Objectively, it may be questionable if the drama will ever be entirely self-
> supporting; however, a polished professional performance made possible by a
> grant from National Endowment funds together with the enhanced amphi-
> theater facilities are expected to increase audience numbers. In addition to the
> added income which this represents, this may be expected to provide greater
> support for permanent funding from the State.

The next section of the proposal was a proposed budget for the 1977 season.
The HCDA requested no NEA funding for administrative costs, which would

be covered by local donations and associated funds—primarily from sale of tickets, souvenir programs, concessions, etc. These costs included a general manager, a business manager, office supplies, postage, telephone, FICA taxes, secretaries, and travel. These were modest expenses; the general manager was to be paid $2,500, while the business manager would receive only $50. Donations were expected to cover $4,225.00 of the administrative costs, with associated funds providing $1,325.00. The cost of maintenance and repairs would be paid from the Appalachian Regional Commission/Farmers Home Administration grants, which would also cover all but $100 of the cost of lights and sound. Royalties, costumes, makeup, and contingencies would be paid with associated funds.

NEA funding would be matched dollar for dollar from associated funds to pay salaries for the director ($3,000 total), theater designer ($2,000), stage manager ($1,000), assistant director/choreographer ($1,400), music director ($840), costumer ($840), lighting director ($720), and lighting assistant ($600). Twelve primary actors would receive $70 per week for 12 weeks, for a total of $10,080. Twenty-five supporting actors would receive $30 for 12 weeks for a total of $9,000. In addition, local donations would include housing for all of these positions except the supporting actors, lighting director, and lighting assistant, who were local and would not need housing. The NEA was asked for $14,740 toward production costs, to be matched with $16,540 from associated funds.

National Endowment funds were also requested for theater operation, excepting utilities, insurance, and special printing, which would be paid through associated funds, and ground maintenance, which would be donated. The HCDA requested NEA funding for half the cost of a house manager (totaling $600), a ticket manager ($240), three assistants for ticket sales ($600), three parking attendants ($500), and two ushers ($200).

Some of the promotion costs were to be paid entirely with NEA funds, including a publicity director ($2,000), an assistant/secretary ($600), and advertising ($2,000). NEA and associated funds would split the cost of materials, totaling $400. The cost of brochures would be covered by associated funds ($700), while $200 for the advertising sales manager would come from donations. The souvenir program was self-sustaining, and a $1,000 contingency fund, along with the first-year payment of $2,139 on the construction loan, would be covered by associated funds.

Enclosed with the proposal was a copy of the *Melungeons: The Vanishing Colony of Newman's Ridge*, a printed version of a 1966 presentation by Rogersville attorney Henry Price, a 1976 souvenir program, a promotional brochure, an estimate of the value of materials and labor donated to the 1976 production, and a summary of the comparison of costs between *WTTS* and seven other outdoor dramas.

All told, the $20,610 requested from the National Endowment for the Arts would be matched with $23,654 from associated funds and $5,895 in donations.[4]

It was a thorough and businesslike plan. The Drama Association had calculated the costs of production to the dollar. No one was to be paid extravagantly; $3,000 for a summer's work was not a lot of money for an experienced director with a Ph.D., and $70 per week for each of the principal actors was a low wage, even in 1976. Furthermore, the HCDA was only asking for funding for one year and was ready to shoulder more than half the financial burden for the 1977 season. They felt that a one-time grant from the National Endowment for the Arts, along with a renovated amphitheater, would bump the quality and professionalism of the production up a notch or two, which would result in greater ticket sales and improve the drama's argument for a state subsidy.

The board members waited anxiously for a reply from the NEA. They didn't have to wait long. The proposal was rejected. The NEA said the project did not fit funding priorities made necessary by budget limitations.

Sometimes it is impossible to tell why one project receives funding and another doesn't. One project reviewer might look at the HCDA proposal and think, "What a spunky, 'can-do' group of people! With a little bit of help, they could really make a go of this play!" Another reviewer might think, "Those poor folks will never make a go of this; they're too isolated to draw an audience. We'd be wasting our money to fund this project." When Charlie Turner was trying to get federal funding in the 1960s, he was told, in essence, that there was nothing the government could do that would help Sneedville.

One thing that might—*might*—have helped the proposal was to elaborate a bit more about the Melungeons. The proposal seems to shy away from dealing with the racial ambiguity associated with them. The Melungeons are described as "physically distinct from their Anglo-Saxon neighbors…. Their origins are unknown even among themselves." No mention is made of the discrimination they faced because of the likelihood of their African ancestry, even though that is touched upon in the play. Nor was any mention made of the fact that Melungeons were involved in the development of the play and its current operation. These issues might have been discussed by the HCDA board and not included for one reason or another. The National Endowment for the Arts might have

---

[4] Hancock County Drama Association, National Endowment for the Arts application, 1976.

leaned toward funding the play if they understood the racial ambiguity that surrounded the Melungeons. Then again, perhaps it would have made no difference.

The rejection was a blow to the Drama Association. They hadn't asked for
much, just a year's worth of funding, enough to make the production a little
more professional, a little more likely to warrant a permanent subsidy from the
State of Tennessee. After all the hard work they'd put in for seven years with very
little outside help, didn't they deserve a chance to succeed?

George Smith, an assistant professor of Resource Development in the University of Tennessee Extension Service, wrote to the National Rural Information
Center. This was division of the United States Department of Agriculture's National Agriculture Library. Its purpose was to provide services for rural
communities, local officials, organizations, businesses, and rural citizens working
to maintain the vitality of America's rural areas. Smith asked for assistance in
identifying possible sources of financial aid for the outdoor drama, explaining
that their request for funding from the NEA had been rejected.[5]

Smith received a prompt reply from Betty Vinson, the director of the
Information Clearinghouse.

> Our staff is working to find the assistance you need to help resolve your
> problem related to sources of financial aid for your outdoor drama
> production. Our goal is to have an interim response to you within ten days
> of having received your request. It may take longer, but we will report back
> to you as soon as we possibly can. We are utilizing the resources of our library,
> computer information retrieval and agency contacts in developing the
> response. If we need more details about your request, a staff member will be
> in touch by telephone.[6]

Smith received another letter from the National Rural Center nearly two
weeks later, sent by rural program adviser Lawrence Newlin. "I am afraid that I
cannot offer you much encouragement in regard to possible federal sources of
funding for the production of *Walk Toward the Sunset*," he wrote. The only
relevant source of federal funds he could think was the American Revolution
Bicentennial Administration, which would make a grant to each state
bicentennial commission before closing its operations. The state commission
would then choose and fund one project ranging from $12,000 to $15,000 on a
matching dollar-for-dollar basis. Newlin was uncertain whether the state
commission was looking for new projects or whether an outdoor drama would

---

[5] George R. Smith to the National Rural Information Center, 6 December 1976.
[6] Betty A. Vinson to George R. Smith, 7 December 1976.

qualify, but he provided contact information for the Tennessee Bicentennial Commission. Newlin continued,

> Perhaps the best potential source of funding is local foundations. I am enclosing a section on Tennessee foundations from *The Foundation Directory, Edition 5*. The most promising possibilities appear to be the Benwood Foundation, the Massey Foundation, the Memorial Welfare Foundation, and the Plough Foundation. Other possibilities include: the Hamilton National Bank which gives to civic, charitable and educational projects located in the bank's trading area…and the National Life and Accident Insurance Company which puts 1.6% of its funds into cultural programs…I recently spoke with the Vice President of a major foundation who feels that corporate givers are not prodded enough by potential grantees. Most major corporations have a grantsmaking vehicle, and I have a large list of such companies and would be happy to check out possibilities for your region if you would provide me with a list of major employers in the area…Please keep us posted on your progress.[7]

A couple of weeks later, Newlin wrote back to Smith with a few more suggestions for foundations which might be willing to fund *Walk Toward the Sunset*. These were foundations with a record of funding theater and performing arts projects.

> You may already know of the American Revolutionary Road Company based in Johnson City. According to the Foundation News (July/August) the Robert Sterling Clark Foundation granted $10,000 to this drama group to tour Appalachia and present original theater based on actual episodes from American history. The Clark Foundation has broad purposes and gives to educational, cultural, and community support. In 1972 it made some 145 grants ranging from $500 to $50,000 totaling about $1.4 million…. Other foundations include The Schubert Foundation, Inc…. For year ending 5/31/75, assets were $62,468,730 with 229 grants ranging from $500 to $200,000. Seeks to build and perpetuate the live and performing arts, particularly the professional theater…. Support both of theatrical institutions and of those other elements of the performing arts and related institutions necessary to maintain and support the theater…. High Winds Fund, Inc…. For year ending 12/31/75, assets were $16,070,813 with 52 grants ranging from $500 to $1.2 million. Seeks to preserve and maintain places of beauty including buildings of historical interest, art museums, sanctuaries; grants for music, music education, performing arts, and conservation and recreational activities. Funds largely committed. The Charles Merrill Trust…. For year ending 9/30/74, assets were $14,114,355 with 164 grants ranging from $800 to $203,676. Broad support for a number of programs including the

---

[7] Lawrence M. Newlin to George R. Smith, 20 December 1977.

performing arts with sixty percent to be spent at the discretion of the trustees within stated proportions to given types of institutions and forty percent to specified institutions. I hope this information is helpful in obtaining assistance for *Walk Toward the Sunset.*[8]

It is unclear how many, if any, of these foundations were contacted. What is clear is that the Hancock County Drama Association did not receive any further outside funding. A few die-hards were willing to tough it out for another season, to keep the play going in the hope that funding would materialize, but the majority of the board had had enough. Sadly, without fanfare, the members of the Hancock County Drama Association decided that there would not be a 1977 season of *Walk Toward the Sunset.* It was over.

---

[8] Newlin to George R. Smith, 11 January 1977.

16

THE NEXT ACT:
FARMERS MARKET AND FALL FESTIVAL

A few years after the drama closed, anthropologist Anthony Cavender would write that a contributing factor in the demise of *Walk Toward the Sunset* was "bickering between members of the elites," the "merchants, educators, and well-to-do farmers" who had organized the Hancock County Drama Association in order to "maximize the commercialization of the strong and growing interest in the Melungeons."[1]

Cavender's use of the term "bickering" suggests that the Drama Association members fell out with one another over relatively petty issues. Claude Collins attached more importance to the fact that, aside from a few technicians and, during the last season, a token payment to the local "extras" in the play, none of the Hancock County people who had worked for years had ever been paid. "That's really why we had to quit," Collins recalled. "Carson-Newman students were getting paid to come over here. We were boarding them, and also they were getting some sort of a little salary. Our people decided they wanted to be paid or they wouldn't be in it. Elmer Turner and I worked every night…we never got a penny."

The declining attendance was also discouraging to people who had put so much work into keeping the play going. "What happened was, the attendance would drop a little every year," said Collins, "until we would have maybe, for the whole season, a thousand. And that was not enough people."[2]

Scott Collins, who was a member of the HCDA, recalls the effort put forth by all the Drama Association members.

> They worked at it, there's no doubt about it. They really worked at it, and they didn't want it to end—none of us wanted it to end. I mean, it was just a bad time, because we all enjoyed the play, enjoyed working with it, enjoyed the camaraderie with everybody, especially with Carson-Newman…. Dora (Bowlin) worked very hard at it—she and Kyle both. They worked very hard

---

[1] Cavender, "The Melungeons of Upper East Tennessee," 33–34.
[2] Claude Collins interview (2002).

at doing everything they could to make it work. I'll say about Kyle, he didn't care what kind of work he had to do—physical labor, he was ready to put forth whatever he had to do.[3]

Despite any disagreements that might have arisen among the board members, they continued to work together on a project that was originally intended to enhance the outdoor drama: the farmers market. Between the courthouse and the drama site, a small hollow seemed to be a prime location to develop a farmers market. The idea was included in the proposal to the National Endowment for the Arts. Once the HCDA board accepted the idea that the outdoor drama was not going to continue, they developed ideas for the farmers market.

One idea was to use the site as an assembly point for county vegetable farmers. A vegetable buyer had set up operations in Rose Hill, Virginia, just across Newman's Ridge and Powell Mountain from Sneedville. Rather than hauling their loads individually across the narrow, twisting road, local farmers could assemble their crops at the farmers market and reduce the need for individual transportation.

Other ideas included moving existing cannery equipment in the county to the farmers market to be operated; holding auctions of consigned items for a fee; holding "trade days" on certain days of each month, where farmers could sell produce and other items sold in a flea market-style arrangement; and holding craft fairs for local artisans.[4]

Before the idea of a farmers market could be fully developed, the HCDA members put another project in motion. "When the drama stopped," says Scott Collins, "the Association kind of folded, and from that came the Fall Festival. It was a festival that was going to continue with some Melungeon heritage, and that's kind of the way it's been."

The first Fall Festival was held on the weekend of 14–16 October 1977. The idea was to attract visitors to come into the county to enjoy the beautiful fall foliage, and to see—and purchase—locally-grown produce and locally-made crafts. Visitors would also be drawn, it was hoped, by the prospect of seeing real Melungeons, rather than actors portraying Melungeons.

"The first one they had was at the old high school up on the hill here," recalls Collins. "And then—I guess they did it two years up there, and then that third year…they had an opportunity to help the farmers in the county and build a farmers market, where farmers could bring their produce, vegetables, whatever

---

[3] Scott Collins interview.

[4] Hancock County Drama Association, "Possible Uses for the Farmers Market in Sneedville," undated memo.

they had, and sell at the farmers market. That never did go over very well either, but the building is still there, and the building was eventually set up and used for the Fall Festival. It's an excellent place for that."[5]

The Fall Festival continues to this day, its date moved to the first weekend in October. Among the traditional crafts and skills on display are the making of molasses, hominy, apple butter, lye soap, cane chair seats, wood shingles, spinning and carding wool, cording cotton, cornshuck dolls, and quilts. A working still, confiscated by the Hancock County Sheriff's Office, is set up and operated, and visitors are offered a sample of "ethanol," celebrating yet another aspect of Hancock County history and culture. Music is also featured, with local and regional bluegrass, country, and gospel groups performing.

The Hancock County Drama Association gradually morphed into the Sneedville/Hancock Community Partners, the organization that now runs the festival. Most of the $100,000 grant to renovate the amphitheater was presumably returned to the Appalachian Regional Commission, since most of the renovations never took place. The amphitheater sat unused for years and was finally removed. A new elementary school took the place of the old building, which had been the county's high school before becoming the elementary school. The amphitheater has been replaced by a playground, and the hillside that once held log benches and graveled aisles is now covered with grass. The buildings that once housed the box office, concession booth, and craft shop were repurposed for use in the farmers market.

In late March and early April 1977, as the members of the Drama Association were discussing ways of using the plot of land that would be the site of the farmers market, steady rains fell on Hancock County and the surrounding area. On the night of Monday, 4 April, the Clinch River overflowed its banks. The flood inundated nearly a third of Sneedville, and vast portions of Hancock County were underwater. The elementary school was on high ground at the foot of Newman's Ridge, and the gymnasium where *Walk Toward the Sunset* was performed on rainy summer nights became an emergency shelter for people who were forced from their homes.

Hancock County judge Jimmy Roberts was so busy with rescue efforts that he didn't have time to check on his own home. "My farm is under water," he told a reporter, "and I'm afraid my barn has washed away." Roberts said the

---

county had not seen a flood like this one since the 1860s, and markers showed the floodwaters reached a point eight feet higher than that previous flood.

Electricity and telephone service were gone in most of the county, and the four state highways leading in and out of Sneedville were underwater. National Guard helicopters were used to airlift county residents who were cut off by flood waters, and take them to shelters, or to the homes of friends or relatives, in Sneedville.

By the time floodwaters began receding on Wednesday, seven people had died, including two men in Sneedville. Twenty-four counties were affected by the flood, but Hancock and Claiborne Counties fared the worst, suffering an estimated $7.5 million in damages.

Former mayor Charlie Turner was one of the lucky ones whose property was not damaged. "I'm glad I live on high ground," he said.[6]

Turner was no longer mayor of Sneedville, but he was still fighting for his town and his county. In 1982, when the Reagan administration argued that the work of the Appalachian Regional Commission would be better left to the private sector, Turner testified at a congressional subcommittee meeting and recalled the days before the ARC was formed. "Everything was drying up," Turner testified. "People felt they'd been forgotten. There was a hopelessness and a loneliness in them that's hard to describe." He acknowledged that the ARC hadn't turned the situation around completely but insisted that it had helped a great deal.[7]

In the 1960s and 1970s, federal funding had helped Hancock County build an industrial park, a community center, a city hall, a sewage system, and low-cost housing, among other things. The county continued to get funding from the ARC in the 1980s, but at a lower rate than it had previously. And Highway 31 between Sneedville and Morristown was still had a treacherous section over Clinch Mountain that discouraged employers in Morristown from hiring workers who lived in Hancock County. In 1986, the 6,887 people who still lived in the county had a per capita annual income of $4,665, about a third of the national average. Forty percent of the county's residents lived below the poverty line. Jimmy Roberts, now the county's executive officer, said, "Our unemployment rate would be 49.5%, not 9.8%, if you counted the underemployed."[8]

In 1987, Charles Turner was part of a movement by business leaders in nine of the poorest, most remote counties in Tennessee, Kentucky, and southwest

---

[6] Nolan, "Sneedville Loses Property, But Few Lives," 4.

[7] Douthat, "Appalachian Commission Awaits Budget Axe," 4.

[8] Ibid; Associated Press, "Hancock County Struggle to Make Ends Meet," B2–B3.

Virginia to form a new state, the State of Cumberland. David Hartley, the general manager of radio station WSWV in Pennington Gap, Virginia, said, "We have more in common with each other than we do with our states. We're all isolated to some degree. We lack interstates. We have the same economic problems. We're a tongue-in-cheek outfit with a gimmick." The counties were Knox, Bell, and Harlan in Kentucky; Lee, Scott, and Wise in Virginia; and Hancock, Hawkins, and Claiborne in Tennessee. Although they designed a flag, wrote a state song and poem, planned elections in the fall, and had written to President Reagan to inform him of their plans, the representatives of the new State of Cumberland really had one major goal, a goal that was familiar to Charlie Turner. "It's tourism. That's the main objective of it all," Turner said. "They're all distressed areas. We're not aggressive enough is the main problem."[9]

Charlie Turner never gave up on getting Highway 31 improved, and in spring 1987, he finally saw a reason to be hopeful. Tennessee governor Ned McWherter was supposed to visit Sneedville, but fog grounded his helicopter. He had to make the trip by car over Highway 31, and by the time he arrived in Sneedville, he had seen the light. By June, Turner had a letter from the state Department of Transportation promising that bid would be accepted on a project to improve the highway in September. "That fog got us the bid," Turner remarked.[10]

Fog—and the persistence of Charlie Turner. Not to mention the support of the governor. Scott Collins asserts, "McWherter was a real friend to Hancock County."

> He was here more often than any governor that I recall. He wanted to put a four-lane highway—or a piece of four-lane highway—in every county in the state of Tennessee, and he did that; over here on this road that he built there's probably, I don't know, 500 yards, I guess, of four-lane highway, just north of the zinc mines over there. But ingress and egress to this town is easier now than it's ever been. What I would do, when I was elected in '74, I'd leave the office here in the courthouse and I'd drive to Bean Station to do income tax, and it took me at least 40 minutes to get over there because of poor roads, people were driving slow and you couldn't get up through there—you know how it was. It was just tough driving. But then as time went on, the roads got better. You can make it to Bean Station now in about 30 minutes or less. Charles was very instrumental in that road, and in anything else when it came to economic development. There's no way industry was going to locate here, and we still don't have a lot of industry, and it was because of the roads. We

---

[9] Associated Press, "Nine Counties Band Together to Form New State," B-1.
[10] Associated Press, "Hancock County Struggles to Make Ends Meet," B-2.

just didn't have a good way of ingress and egress—there just was no good way; it was either across the mountain or you didn't go.... And coming across the mountain is no big deal anymore because it's just a good, decent road for people to travel.[11]

It took a while, but the road was finally improved. It was widened, the sharpest curves were gentled, and guardrails were installed. It's still a white-knuckle drive for motorists more accustomed to flatlands, but those who remember how it used to be appreciate the changes.

Unfortunately, by the time the road was finished, jobs in Morristown were drying up. The small factories that had once employed unskilled and semiskilled workers from "Overhome" were closing, a trend that continued into the twenty-first century. Manufacturing jobs within Hancock County became almost non-existent. In 1997, there were five hundred manufacturing jobs in the county. Ten years later, there were fewer than fifty.

In 1968, Wayne Morrill of Electric Motors and Specialties explained that the plant his company was building in Sneedville would not replace workers the company already had in Indiana. "[W]e are not moving a plant to Sneedville because that would mean we would have to discharge people working in some other plant," he wrote, "and because most of these people are old friends, some of them friends for 20 years or more, we would not think of doing that. Even if they were not friends, we would not feel it would be fair to take away the jobs of people we already have and give these jobs to new people in another community."[12] What was unthinkable for company executives in 1968 was now just good business; the electric motor plant, after more than three decades in Hancock County, moved to China, taking most of the county's manufacturing jobs with it. Times certainly had changed.

Another manufacturer, Volunteer Fabricators, closed in 2009, ending 115 jobs. The largest manufacturer left in the county is Kiefer Built, Inc., which makes aluminum horse and livestock trailers. Kiefer Built once employed 60 people; by 2010, the workforce was down to 18.[13]

About 90 percent of the county's residents now receive some form of federal assistance, from school lunches to health care.[14] Today, Highway 31 is an escape route for only those few among Hancock County's young people who graduate high school and are going on to college. The factory jobs that drew so many of

---

[11] Scott Collins interview.
[12] Morrill, "To the people of Hancock County," 1.
[13] Marcum, "Hope in Hancock."
[14] Reston and Jones, "Appalachia Needs Big Government."

Hancock County's young people to Morristown, or to Kokomo, Akron, or Detroit, no longer exist. For those looking for better economic opportunities, it's now easier to get out of Hancock County—there's just nowhere to go.

Other forms of escape beckoned. Like many small, rural Appalachian communities, Sneedville and Hancock County fell victim to a plague of drugs—particularly methamphetamine and OxyContin, or "hillbilly heroin." Overdose deaths became all too common. In 2008, the minister of Sneedville's Methodist church told this author he was afraid to let his young son play outside because of the drug trade taking place in the Hardee's parking lot next door.

Hancock County may be on the ropes, but it's not ready to be counted out just yet. There is still a strong sense of community and concern for neighbors. As one person commented on an online real estate site, "It is the only county I have lived in where strangers will nod or wave at you when driving around. A very friendly place."

17

DRAMATIS PERSONAE

Two of the young people who took part in the outdoor drama remained in Hancock County, using their educations for the betterment of the county. Greg Marion, who, as a child "extra" in the play, enjoyed helping the college-aged actresses with their makeup, earned a doctoral degree, served for twelve years as the county mayor, and now teaches science at Hancock County High School. Scott Collins, the lighting director and understudy actor for the duration of the drama, earned a Ph.D. in education leadership and policy from East Tennessee State University, and was appointed clerk and master of Hancock County Court by Chancellor Dennis Inman in 1985. He spent thirty-two years as a court administrator; the day after he retired, he became vice-president for commercial lending at Civis Bank in Sneedville.[1]

Charles W. Turner passed away in 2003 at the age of eighty-seven. Most of the other founders of the Hancock County Drama Association have passed away as well.

Alvin York "Sonny" Turner died in 2009. His wife, Annette, died in 2011. Dora Bowlin, former president of HCDA, died in 2015. Her husband, Kyle, died in 2012. Their daughter, Corrine, also a former president of HCDA, died in 2007.

As noted earlier, Elmer Turner, who managed the box office for *Walk Toward the Sunset*, died in 1974. His wife, Hazel Winkler Turner, who was concessions manager, retired from the Hancock County school system, where she had taught fifth grade at the elementary school above the drama site. She died in 2008. Kyle Lawson, the hardware merchant who played Daniel Boone during the first season of the drama, died in 1976, as the final season was getting underway.

Mollie Bowlin, who played dulcimer in front of the box office before performances, died in 2005. Her husband, Lonnie Bowlin, who acted in the play, died in 1980. Hancock County historian and genealogist Bill Grohse died in 1989.

---

[1] Scott Collins interview.

Ann Haralson, the Canadian VISTA who had written many news articles about the drama for the *Hancock County Post* and who had performed in the drama's first season, never returned to the United States after witnessing her colleagues at the Morristown newspaper celebrating the shooting death of four student protesters at Kent State University in Ohio. She married Don Piper, raised a family, worked for the *Lake Williams Tribune* in British Columbia and later for the *Yellowhead Star*, which became the *North Thompson Star Journal.* She retired as editor of the *Star Journal* in 2004 and died in 2015.[2]

Bettye Dickerson, who played Alisee Collins and Cora Gibson during the final season, remained in Hancock County. She married Scott Collins and became a teacher. She and Scott had two daughters. Bettye Dickerson Collins died in 2016.

Jean Patterson Bible, author of *Melungeons: Yesterday and Today*, died in 2005. Mark Sumner of the Institute for Outdoor Theatre died in June of 2017. Demographer and writer Calvin Beale died in 2008. And playwright Kermit Hunter, whose many outdoor dramas included *Walk Toward the Sunset*, died in 2001.

Few of the actors who performed in *Walk Toward the Sunset* have been back to Sneedville. Some of them are dismissive of the play itself, as they are of the outdoor drama genre overall, but nearly all of them have fond memories of their time in Sneedville.

Mary Bowler, a VISTA in 1968–1969, was in the first season of *Walk Toward the Sunset*, playing an Indian dancer in the first act and a villager in the second. She married fellow VISTA Bob Van Nest, whose article, "Birds and Trees of Hancock County," was reprinted in subsequent souvenir programs until the end of the drama's run.

> We went back to New Jersey. We got married in November [1969] and rented a house in a rural area for two years while I went back to teaching special ed, and Bob did adult education. He had his masters and almost his doctorate from Columbia in history, but he never used that. And then we bought a farm in Maine. We wanted to live in the north country; we both love snow. We wanted to buy a farm and we couldn't afford one in New Jersey, so we came here and bought a farm. We taught school and farmed, and now we're both retired.

---

[2] Smith, "Ann Piper 1946–2015."

Though, looking back, Mary Van Nest was not particularly impressed with the dramatic qualities of *Walk Toward the Sunset*, she has fond memories of her time in Hancock County, and especially its people.

> [F]or some reason, we all felt an instant connection with them, I think. We really—I mean, we knew we were different, but we really built up some close relationships very quickly. And I don't know if it was our idealism at the time, or—I don't know. I had been working with poor people for a long time in Newark, so it wasn't that alien to me. And I also had relatives in New York State, and some of them were quite poor. But as far as the other VISTAs—I don't know. We all—I don't think we ever looked down on them, by any means. We just really respected them, and really got very close to them in a very short time. To this day, I think about them a lot, with such fond, fond memories. I just feel really fortunate that we had that opportunity.[3]

Bob and Mary Van Nest founded the Western Foothills Land Trust in 1987. By December 2017, the WFLT held thirty-two conservation easements covering 4,190 acres and owns nineteen parcels that make up about 3,100 acres. The trust encourages agricultural and recreational uses, such as community gardening, hiking and hunting, while slowing the spread of commercial and residential development.[4]

Steve Nichandros, the VISTA who was in the original 1969 cast and returned to perform in the 1970 cast, started with mixed feelings about the drama but then came to appreciate it.

> I think, intellectually, I thought very highly of it. But I think I thought less of it after we'd been rehearsing for a while. It was going on and on, and I thought, "My gosh, what is this thing?" I think that was just immaturity; I think that had to do with how young I was. I wasn't able to see the positive side of it. I think I'm probably giving you a reaction I had about halfway through, I think…. We did this thing three times a week, so it would get old. But when the rehearsals were over and it finally came to pass, I remember being proud that I was in it, and that this was a great story being told, although I never got clear from the confusion over whether there is a Melungeon race or there isn't.[5]

Ray Buffington, a Carson-Newman student who performed in the 1969 cast, retained an interest in outdoor drama. While a member of the *Walk Toward*

---

[3] Van Nest interview.
[4] Brown, "Dassler, Van Nests honored as Land Trust celebrates 30 years."
[5] Nichandros interview.

the Sunset cast, he journeyed to Pineville, Kentucky, to see *The Book of Job*. Buffington went on to perform in *The Smoky Mountain Passion Play*. He returned to Sneedville in 1975 to watch a performance of *Walk Toward the Sunset*. Of the genre of outdoor drama, he said,

> I think it certainly has its place. You get a completely different kind of experience, I think. It's a little more audience-involved because you're in the same climatic conditions the actors are in. You know, if the wind blows, you feel it, and the actors feel it, too. If there's humidity in the air, or if it sprinkles rain, you feel it and they feel it too. In a lot of ways, it's a heightened sensory experience. It depends on the play, of course. Most of these plays are staged in appropriate settings; *Walk Toward the Sunset* was, and *Unto These Hills*. *The Lost Colony* certainly was. That's why *The Book of Job* was such an oddball; the look of the actors, the costuming and the makeup was sort of Byzantine, stained glass kind of thing—an odd thing to find in the mountains of Kentucky. Although it was very famous....

Buffington eventually became a third grade teacher in southern New Jersey but retained an interest in the Melungeons.

> Some time ago, I don't remember how long ago this was actually, I found a little pamphlet, a little booklet by a guy named Henry Price, and as I was looking through the things I had, I found that too. It's copyright 1971: *Melungeons: The Vanishing Colony of Newman's Ridge*. And it usually comes up this way, too: If I meet somebody, and over the course of conversation it comes up, "well, what have you done, what have *you* done," you know, interesting stories of your life. I tell them about this, and it gets me off on another little period of research or something, looking for information. It was very interesting, this past week, to look online and see what's in the wind now, you know?... When I first started at Carson-Newman, I thought I was going to be a sociologist, so I enrolled in some sociology courses and then quickly found out that theater was a lot more fun, so I got out of that. But I'd never come across the term "tri-racial isolate" before just recently, when I was looking online. It was interesting to see what kind of research has been done since, DNA studies and those kind of things.... You know, I think, at the time—because we were very curious; we were playing Melungeons, the play was about the Melungeons—we were always on the lookout for Melungeons and we never knew if we actually saw a Melungeon, so I'm not sure if we had any preconceived notions that were confirmed or disproved or what, you know? My general sense was that they were poor country people who had been there longer than I had and that it was their land, their territory, their turf, and I was an outsider.... That was it, end of story. I learned a lot from the script

and from the information that was available at the time—I mean, people are people, Melungeons or not.[6]

Nancy Johnston, who played Alisee Collins in the 1969 cast, went on to a career as a professional actress. She appeared in the original Broadway productions of *The Secret Garden* and *Elf—The Musical*, as well as the Broadway revival of *The Music Man*, the first national touring company of *The Producers*, and numerous off-Broadway and regional productions such as *Grey Gardens, Into The Woods, Souvenir, The Baker's Wife*, and others.[7]

Mike Murphy, from the 1975 cast, became a lawyer and practices in Morristown, and so continues to have ties "Overhome" in Hancock County.

> Of course, as a lawyer, I go to Sneedville once in a while, to the courthouse over there. When Jack Stapleton was the clerk, I used to run into him all the time, and Scott Collins when he was the clerk. So I've kind of kept contact in that respect. Then I was city judge here in Morristown from '96 to 2000, and sometimes when someone would come in front of me for a ticket, I'd think about driving back from Sneedville to Mooresburg with no lights, and I'd think, well, you've gotta pass judgment on this poor person. But I've stayed close to Hancock County, and I've represented clients from Bean Station and Hancock County, so I've still kept in touch with folks from Overhome. A lot of folks in Morristown are from Overhome.
>
> *Who are some of the people that stand out in your memory from that time when you were acting in the play?*
> I've kind of kept track of some of them, and I don't think some of them have had a real good life; it really bothers me. And, of course, right now, I think, drugs are a problem in that area just like everywhere else. It's kind of sad; there's not a lot of jobs and people tend to get into trouble. I've just kept track of some of them vaguely when I've run into somebody, and I've never gotten many good responses when I would say, "well, whatever happened to so-and-so" that was in the play, and they'd say, "Well, she's had a rough life" or "He's had a rough life." It's kind of sad…it's a shame [the play] didn't continue, but the benefit—I guess the benefit was to Carson-Newman, as far as the actors go; it was a once-in-a-lifetime experience. And there was a benefit to the community, the ones that were in the play. Honestly, the interaction between the college-educated kids and the teenagers that were in the play, 12 to 17 years old, I think we were a good [influence] on them. We tried to be, and we got a lot from them—just fine, fine folks. And it brought some pride in the town itself, you know, you could just feel it.…I think that was good for those folks. There was nothing negative about the play being over there

---

[6] Buffington interview.

[7] "Johnston, Nancy," Internet Broadway Database.

that whole time; it was all positive, as far as I know. But, economically, you're absolutely right; they probably were aware for a long time that it wasn't going to pan out. It just wasn't. I admire those people for just going ahead, just keeping the thing going even though it wasn't doing what they hoped it would. Because there were other reasons for keeping it going....[8]

Rose Williams (now Grayson) was in the 1973 cast, playing the lead female roles of Alisee Collins and Alisee Gibson. After the 1974 hiatus, she was back in the cast for both the 1975 and 1976 seasons. She was unaware of any of the financial difficulties facing the drama during that final season.

I think there was a sense of less audience. But I don't think at the end of the season, we had a feeling that this was the last. I don't remember thinking, "Well, this is the last time they'll ever do it," or "They're not gonna do this again." I thought they'd go on with other people doing it. I don't remember any feeling like doom and gloom, end of the show; it felt like the end of the season, the end of a run, see you next time, for some of them. I had graduated and I was moving on, going to grad school, so I was looking at a different phase of my life....

What are your thoughts on the play itself?
Well—I always felt a flaw with the play was that there was more drama, more conflict in the second act than the first act. The first act seemed to serve as a set-up; give the information, which dramatically is never as interesting as conflict, and a guy coming in with a knife, and a knife fight, you know? In the second act there was a little bit more dramatic interest.

In the first act they're avoiding conflict.
Right. They're trying to present some conflict—they can't have their land. But if you're totally unfamiliar with script, trying to figure out who Sevier is, and why they have a white preacher—who is he in relation to the Melungeons?—all that was kind of giving exposition, giving information, and script-wise, it was not as strong as the second act. I think we always felt that way, but that was the way it was written, and that was the way it was done. I think there was a feeling that sometimes Kermit Hunter's scripts were a little—(pauses)—past their time, that they were kind of dated in the way they were written, maybe. He was known for his outdoor dramas, and sometimes—I don't know, when you've got college students who are majoring in theater and looking for great drama, plays like that—you couldn't really evaluate them in the same breath as a Tennessee Williams show or a Shakespeare play or something like that. It was a different style; it was designed to be over-acted, which made it seem kind of hokey or corny sometimes, but that we

[8] Murphy interview.

had to project bigger so we could get it to the top of the hill. So what we were doing as actors felt unreal; we always tried to be real and believable, and you can't when you have to get your lines loud enough. This was a different style, a different kind of drama.

> *Did you have a sense of what this play meant to the Melungeons, and to everyone in the community?*

Yes, I think there was a real sense of connection with the aim to bring recognition to the area. I know there were a lot of outdoor dramas done in other areas that seemed to just be a summer job, and we found that there was a little bit more purpose, a need for the show to be done and done well. We either got that through communication from the [Drama Association], or from Dr. Welton, or from other cast members who were townspeople, but I think we got that kind of feeling, that there was more to that drama than others.

Today, Rose Williams (later married to Jerry Crane), is Rose Grayson, a youth services librarian in Lexington, South Carolina. She looks back on her experiences in Hancock County fondly, but with some regret.

The people that were dealing with the show, the Drama Association people, they were *so* gracious and welcoming to the cast. I've often regretted I didn't take more time at that time in my life to get to know them. Because now, as a storyteller trying to learn mountain stories, I've thought "Maybe if I'd only taken the opportunity when I was there to seek out, sort of like the Ray Hicks of that era…if I had only done that." But when you're young and silly and thinking about on your off time, going to see movies or going to Knoxville, or going to Gatlinburg…. We weren't appreciating a culture that, now, looking back on it, I wish I had taken the opportunity…. I'm really glad for the experience of being part of it. Dramatically, I wouldn't say they were my favorite roles, but for a lasting impact, I think it gave me an appreciation for Appalachian stories, and the area, and the people. I told my husband on the way back from a conference a couple weekends ago, "Those people were really celebrating their heritage. We really don't have that." It wasn't my background. It's my children's, because their father was from Grundy, Virginia, and that's his background. But my people, farming in the midlands of South Carolina—it's different than that kind of recognition in that area. I felt like, "Gee, I really wish I had that connection to that area." So I'm glad that *Walk Toward the Sunset* was a part of that, and that I got a taste of it.[9]

---

[9] Grayson interview.

Scott Collins remembers the play fondly and would like to see it revived in Hancock County.

> Having not been involved in theater before in my life, it was fascinating to me just to work with it, because it gave me some experience I hadn't had, and it gave me the ability to maybe communicate with people a little better. It gave me some training to develop an ability I didn't know I had. I'm not saying I was a great actor or anything like that, but I had to do some acting, had to learn how to speak and how to project. Overall, it was a great plus for me, and I think it was a great plus for everyone who was involved in the play locally, and I think it was a big thing for the Carson-Newman people. Dr. Welton selected the people he thought would fit in over here. He was able to select the people that would best be a fit for this area. It was just a big family; everybody just loved one another, and everybody was involved. I couldn't give it anything but an A-plus, to be honest with you. I just wish that we were able to do something like that again. Of course, we would want it to be local; we don't want it to be located, say, over toward where the county park is (Elrod Falls), because that's before you get to Sneedville, that's in the Treadway area. But we would like it to be at least where the tourists would have to come into town or through town in order to get to the outdoor drama. And I'd like to see that happen again one day—and it might. There may be a different slant from someone writing the script. I think we're ready for something like that again. Dr. Hunter's script is really good, and I like it, but maybe because of some more recent research may need to be re-written. I think for tourism purposes it would be a great thing. Our roads are better, and we have the potential to do a little better with that. I think it would be a real plus for Hancock County.[10]

After directing *Walk Toward the Sunset* during the 1971 season, Ben Harville taught acting for a year, then founded a summer theater company at Fontana Village in the mountains of western North Carolina. After that, he toured the country with a company he founded, The Play Group. This group appeared at experimental theater festivals in places such as Ann Arbor, Michigan, and Baltimore, Maryland. Harville went on to study at a theater institute in Poland. In 1981, Harville received his MFA in theater from the University of Tennessee. He began teaching theater at the college level and has taught theater for the past several years as an adjunct instructor at a community college in Knoxville.

Summing up what he gained from his experience in Hancock County, Harville says, "It taught me how to head up a production as the only director for a

---

[10] Scott Collins interview.

long-running show…from casting to managing to working with designers and with the producers—all of that."[11]

Dr. John Lee Welton, the director of *Walk Toward the Sunset*, taught at Carson-Newman College—now Carson-Newman University—until his retirement in 1997. He continues to appreciate the genre of outdoor drama, as he told Saundra Keyes Ivey in 1973, because he believed more people saw outdoor drama than any other type of theater. "It's the magic of going out, like going out camping and being in God's great outdoors. And then seeing the passionate experience of a part of our history happening."[12] But he acknowledges that outdoor dramas are not as popular as they once were.

> I think probably what has happened—you know, these things sort of cycle. Paul Green, who started this with *The Lost Colony* in North Carolina—there was a real resurgence of this kind of thing over the years, especially around 1976 as [people] were thinking about the heritage of the country; it was sort of the thing to go to these historical dramas. Indeed, they have gotten fewer and fewer because it's economically very, very difficult to support these things. I think the life of most of the outdoor dramas was like five years. So these projects like *Unto These Hills* and *The Lost Colony* that have been going for years and years are very unusual.… The first year [of *Walk Toward the Sunset*], of course, people were curious. People from the area, I think, attended a great deal. And then as they were "used up," as far as attendance goes, we had to reach out further and further and further to try to bring people in. Because of that, I think, over the years, attendance tended to become less and less. I tried to stay away as much as possible from the business end of it because the folks there had a very strong organization and they were the ones that managed the thing. My end of it was strictly from the artistic standpoint.

> *What are your views on the play itself, as a work of drama?*
> I think it hit at a very strong time because of the racial prejudice situation. I'm not sure the play would play today, because of the change of attitudes at the time. It would have to be re-written a great deal, I think, from that standpoint. It had a great deal of the typical aspects of outdoor drama, from spectacle—lots of people on the stage—special effects—the church building burning and that sort of thing. So I think it was a fairly good production, a good script, in that they brought in all the elements that are essential to the outdoor dramas.… I had mixed feelings [about the drama closing]. Number one, I hated to see it end because we had put a lot of years into it and I had seen

---

[11] Harville interview.
[12] Ivey, "'Walk Toward the Sunset' Tells Melungeon Story."

what it had done for the community. I also had another project going; I was directing another outdoor drama, so I sort of moved from one place to another. I was glad I was able to do that at that point. But, yeah, I hated to see it close because of what I had seen happen to the community—not necessarily economically, which was the original thrust; it was supposed to help the economy. I think it did over that period of time; after it closed, that was gone. But what happened to the people themselves because of the play.

Over the course of the play, Dr. Welton got to know the people of Hancock County, and his memories are filled with respect and affection.

I'd like to point out one thing about the people of Hancock County and my reaction about them. Although this was an economically deprived community, I found a lot of very inventive and innovative people there. They had had to do for themselves for so long—an example of that: one day I mentioned to one of the workmen there that was working on the theater. I said, "I need a really rough-hewn chair to go in John Sevier's office. Do you have any idea where I could find one?" And he though a minute and says, "Well, I don't reckon I do, but I might could make you one." Well, we took a lunch break and came back, and he had built a chair. He had gone out in the woods, cut down a tree, chopped it up and nailed it together and made us a chair during that lunch break. So very inventive people like that—if they didn't have something they would make do. And that was something I learned to admire a great deal about these folks.

Hancock County, I think, has a charm that is fast fading, unfortunately. The people there are very honest, hard-working people. I was amazed at how the people survived there. I remember when we lived up on the mountain, we would come down and pass a little three-room cabin. An old black man was out front, and we would pick him up and take him to the post office in Sneedville to get his mail. This gentleman and his wife lived on this little rocky farm there and they raised twenty children in that little cabin, and some of them, I understand, turned out to be doctors and lawyers. And yet this old man could not read or write; we would read his letters to him. The tremendous drive that these people had, the ingenuity they had—and also the language fascinates me, because it's almost the old Elizabethan language. It's been preserved up here for all these years. For instance, one day at the theater, I got in the car and was going to go downtown for something, and I asked one of the workers if he wanted to go with me, and he says, "I don't reckon I'd care to." And he got in the car with me. And I said, "I though you said you didn't want to." And he said, "Well, I told you I didn't reckon I'd care to." That meant "I didn't mind if I did." It's a whole language. Recently I was having an X-ray made at U-T hospital, just a general checkup, and the lady said, "Would you care to put your feet up on the table," and I said, "You're from Sneedville, aren't you?" And she looked at me like I was a mind reader or something. Simply because of, "would you care to"—that term has stayed there. It has a language and an atmosphere all its own. There were some people there that I talked with that had never been more than twenty miles away from their home. And yet other people who had been around the world. So it was an interesting mixture of the old and the new. And it was sort of vital at that time, and may still be, about hanging on to the heritage of the area and the people, and still wanting to reach out and become a part of the world.[13]

---

[13] Welton interview (2002).

18

MELUNGEON SUNSET

Walk Toward the Sunset was created and staged to bring economic development to Hancock County, one of the poorest counties in the United States. The outdoor drama failed in that mission; Hancock County is still one of the poorest counties in the United States, and in many ways its prospects are bleaker today than they were in 1967, when the idea of an outdoor drama first came up.

The primary beneficiaries of the outdoor drama have been the Melungeons themselves and those who study and write about them. Prior to the outdoor drama, "Melungeon" was an epithet, denoting not only an uncertain mixed ethnic heritage (with a presumed African lineage), but also a low socioeconomic status. The socioeconomic aspect of the word began to change even before the drama's opening night, as educated and prominent members of the community like Claude Collins and Corinne Bowlin proudly identified themselves in the press as "Melungeons." As John Lee Welton noted, several of the men working on the amphitheater prior to the opening of the drama, men who had used the term "Melungeon" as a jesting insult to their co-workers, eventually acknowledged their own Melungeon backgrounds. As many Hancock Countians said at the time, "It used to be nobody ever said the word 'Melungeon'; now everybody wants to be one."

Indeed, the attitude of the county as a whole was transformed. In 1947, when William Worden's article "Sons of the Legend" was published in the *Saturday Evening Post*, the prevailing attitude in Hancock County was that a dirty little secret had been exposed. At first, the idea of not only acknowledging, but *celebrating* the Melungeons by staging an outdoor drama about them was inconceivable to most of the county's leaders. They quickly realized that the Melungeons made Hancock County unique; they made the county noted for something other than poverty. And curiosity about the Melungeons brought visitors into the county.

Soon after the outdoor drama opened, Hancock County deputies sported shoulder patches that read, "Hancock County—Home of the Melungeons." Visitors entering the county saw signs saying "Welcome to Hancock County— Home of the Melungeons." When the fall festival began in 1977, Melungeons were a significant attraction. In a 1979 newspaper article, a member of the festival committee declared, "This time we guarantee every visitor will meet a Melungeon."[1] In the early years of the festival, guided tours were offered in which visitors could meet Melungeons.

Prior to the outdoor drama, talking about Melungeons was taboo, especially to outsiders. The Rev. Chester Leonard, who spent his career educating and caring for Melungeons at the Presbyterian mission in Vardy, never used the term "Melungeon." The idea of instilling pride of heritage in his students seems not to have occurred to him or his mission staff; rather, students were taught that they could achieve a better life in spite of their ethnic background. When questioned about his Melungeon students for Worden's *Saturday Evening Post* article, Leonard hedged, saying the Melungeons were so intermixed with their neighbors "that one cannot be sure of a typical specimen."[2]

After the drama closed, Hancock Countians were more willing to talk about the Melungeons, even to refer to their own familial connections to the mysterious people. There were those who still refused to discuss the subject, or who expressed negative opinions of the Melungeons, but the topic was no longer taboo. Occasional newspaper and magazine articles, including a few scholarly works, appeared from time to time for the next couple of decades. But interest in the Melungeons exploded with the publication of a book in 1994.

Brent Kennedy, a native of Wise, Virginia, with a Ph.D. in marketing and communications, was a fundraiser for nonprofit institutions and lived in Atlanta. When he was diagnosed with sarcoidosis in the 1980s, he noticed that most of the other patients at the clinic where he received treatment were African-American. Many researchers believe that those afflicted have a genetic predisposition to the disease. Though it occurs worldwide, the disease is most common among Scandinavians; in the United States, African Americans are affected more than other ethnic groups. Kennedy was curious as to why a southwest Virginian like himself, with a Scots-Irish heritage, would fall victim to this disease. Of course, diseases do not strictly follow ethnic lines, but curiosity about this disease set Kennedy on a search for his ethnic roots.

Kennedy knew of Melungeons, of course. Wise County, like Lee and Scott Counties in southwest Virginia, had a significant Melungeon population. Many lived on Stone Mountain, where they were often referred to as "Ramps," possibly a reference to *Allium tricoccum*, a species of wild leek with a flavor—and odor—that suggests a cross between onions and garlic. After some genealogical research,

[1] Yarbrough, "Hancock County's Fair Provides Journey into Past with Melungeons," C-1.
[2] Worden, "Sons of the Legend."

Kennedy discovered several familial connections to the Melungeons. He moved back to Wise, took a job with Clinch Valley College (later renamed the University of Virginia at Wise), and organized the Melungeon Research Committee, made up of a number of dedicated amateur researchers who had written about or otherwise studied Melungeons.

The members of the Melungeon Research Committee couldn't come to any agreement about the origins of the Melungeons, so Kennedy struck out on his own, writing a book titled *The Melungeons: The Resurrection of a Proud People: An Untold Story of Ethnic Cleansing in America.*

Kennedy described his book, published in 1994 by Mercer University Press, as a "manifesto." The book is a combination of historical fact and speculation, integrating many of the common theories and folklore about the origins of the Melungeons. Kennedy was an unconventional researcher and sometimes leapt to conclusions based on scanty factual information. However, he knew there was more to the Melungeon story than had been reported so far, and he hoped his book would inspire more thorough research. "If every one of my ideas is proved wrong," he said, "I'll be happy because I inspired someone to do the work to find out the truth."[3]

Kennedy contended that the Melungeons were a much larger group than anyone had suggested previously, that there were connections between the Melungeons and the other "tri-racial" groups of the southeastern United States, and that generations of Appalachians had hidden their Melungeon ancestry to avoid the discrimination, both social and legal, that accompanied such ancestry.

Kennedy had a unique take on the origins of the Melungeons. "You have to go back to the 1500s, I think," Kennedy maintained, "to get to the primary origin of the Melungeons."[4] As he wrote:

> I contend that the remnants of Joao ("Juan") Pardo's forts, joined by Portuguese refugees from Santa Elena, and possibly a few stray Dominicans and Jesuits, exiled Moorish French Huguenots, and escaped Acadians, along with [Sir Francis] Drake's and perhaps other freed Turkish, Moorish and Iberian captives, survived on these shores, combined forces over the ensuing years, moved to the hinterlands, intermarried with various Carolina and Virginia Native Americans, and eventually became the reclusive Melungeons.[5]

Significant by its absence is any mention of Africans, whether free or enslaved, in Kennedy's origin theory. Although elsewhere in his book, and in

---

[3] Kennedy interview.
[4] Ibid.
[5] Kennedy and Kennedy, *The Melungeons.*

dozens of subsequent interviews and articles, Kennedy acknowledged an African component in the Melungeon ancestry, the relative lack of emphasis on African ancestry may have contributed to some readers' empathy for, and identification with, the Melungeons. Many of those attracted to the book had Appalachian roots and had always identified as "white," but were willing—even eager—to adopt a more "exotic" identity. "Melungeon" seemed to fit the bill perfectly, assuming that "Melungeon" meant "Portuguese" or "Turkish"; many of those who bought Kennedy's book were unaware of the stigma of African ancestry that had always attached to the Melungeons.

The publication of *The Melungeons* coincided with the first widespread use of the Internet among ordinary, non-scholarly people. Internet groups studying Appalachian genealogy picked up Kennedy's book and discovered that it seemed to explain many of the mysteries of their own individual genealogies.

Kennedy promoted his book by speaking to civic clubs, historical societies, and any other organization that invited him. He was a charismatic speaker, worked without notes, and usually talked well past the time allotted to him. The effect on audiences was described by Bill Fields, who attended one of Kennedy's lectures. "I went to the lecture sure that I was not a Melungeon," he said. "I left convinced that I was."[6]

By spring 1997, a website hosted by Darlene Wilson featured historical and contemporary articles about the Melungeons, and a Melungeon email group had formed. The members of the email group organized a gathering to be held in on the campus of Clinch Valley College in Wise, Virginia, where Kennedy now served as a vice-president. Organizers likened the gathering to a family reunion, but since most of the participants had never met in person, they began referring to the event as "First Union." They expected about fifty participants.

On Saturday, 26 July 1997, nearly 1,000 people attended First Union. The participants reflected several aspects of the theories Kennedy had expressed in his book and in subsequent articles and lectures. Kennedy had begun emphasizing a possible Turkish background for the original Melungeons, suggesting that the term "Melungeon" came from the Arabic—and later Turkish—term "melun jinn," meaning "cursed soul" or "one who has been abandoned by God." By this time, Kennedy had made a couple of trips to Turkey, sponsored by the Turkic World Research Foundation, and the town of Wise had entered into a sister city relationship with Çesme, on the Aegean coast of Turkey near Izmir. The mayor of Çesme, Nuri Ertan, attended First Union.

---

[6] Winkler, *The Melungeons: Sons and Daughters of the Legend.*

Others at First Union were interested in health issues. Besides sarcoidosis, Brent Kennedy had also been diagnosed with familial Mediterranean fever, a hereditary inflammatory disorder. Although members of all ethnic groups are susceptible to this disease, it is most common among Mediterranean people, including Turks, Arabs, Greeks, Italians, and Sephardic Jews. Soon, a list of ailments would be considered by some to be "Melungeon diseases," including FMF, Bechet's syndrome, thalassemia, Machado-Joseph disease, and others. Other conditions, such as polydactilism, or six fingers on each hand, and the "Anatolian bump," a prominent bump or ridge at the back of the skull, were soon considered by some to be signs of Melungeon ancestry, even though none of these traits had been mentioned by earlier researchers, including Dr. Truett Pierce of Sneedville, who had treated Melungeon patients for decades.

Most of these notions would be discredited within a few years, and Kennedy himself abandoned the Turkish origin theory after no documenting evidence could be found. But by the time of Second Union, 9–12 July 1998, in Wise, dozens of amateur and professional researchers had come forward to present a variety of theories to an audience that numbered nearly 2,000. Soon after Second Union, the Melungeon Heritage Association was formally incorporated to facilitate the presentation of research relating to the Melungeons.

Few Hancock Countians were present at First and Second Unions, and the Melungeon Heritage Association, with a post office box in Wise, was dominated at first by Virginians. That began to change in 1999 when Claude Collins joined MHA.

Collins and other alumni of the Presbyterian mission school in Vardy had organized the Vardy Community Historical Society. The Presbyterians had ended their missionary work in Hancock County in the 1950s, and the school operated for a time under the direction of the Hancock County school system. By the 1970s, the depopulation of Vardy Valley, combined with the improvement of the road over Newman's Ridge into Sneedville, led to the closing of the Vardy School. The Vardy Community Historical Society created a museum of the old Presbyterian Church building. They also dismantled Mahala Mullins's cabin on Newman's Ridge and rebuilt it across the road from the church museum. The school, already in poor condition, was damaged beyond restoration by a windstorm in 2000.

Hancock Countians began to take a more active role in what was termed by some as the "Melungeon Movement." Third Union took place in June 1999 at Vardy, symbolizing an informal alliance between MHA and VCHS. In 2000, Claude Collins received the first-ever Lifetime Achievement Award from MHA in recognition of his role as the first spokesman for the Melungeons, going back to his dealings with the press prior to the opening of *Walk Toward the Sunset*.

Once again, Hancock County was the focus of attention whenever anyone wanted to know anything about the Melungeons. Now, however, the subject was not taboo; Melungeons and non-Melungeons alike were willing to talk to outsiders, including film crews and reporters from Turkey, Portugal, England, and all over the United States. Hancock Countians were adding to the growing volume of books about Melungeons. Mattie Ruth Johnson, who grew up on Newman's Ridge, published *My Melungeon Heritage* in 1997. Jack Goins, who grew up in the Carter's Valley section of Hancock County, published *Melungeons and other Pioneer Families* in 2000 and *Melungeons: Footprints from the Past* in 2010. And DruAnna Williams Overbay, who was a direct descendent of Vardemon Collins and whose parents both taught at the Vardy School, self-published a book about the school, *Windows on the Past*, in 2002; a revised version of the book was published by Mercer University Press in 2005. A century and a half after outsiders began telling the world about these mysterious people, Melungeons were telling their own stories.

Interest in the Melungeons seemed to decline somewhat in the first decade of the twenty-first century, at least as measured by attendance at the MHA Unions. Many of those who attended the first few Unions believed that they were Melungeons but found it difficult to find documentation to verify that belief. Prior to the 1960s, "Melungeon" was something other people called you, not something you called yourself, and the term was almost never used in any official documents, such as census reports. There was also a division in online conversations between "insiders"—those who knew of and could establish their Melungeon ancestry through kinship with "known" Melungeons, and outsiders—those who could not.[7] Online arguments over varying theories about Melungeons drove many people away from the topic. Brent Kennedy suffered a disabling stroke in December 2005, removing him from a visible position in the "Melungeon Movement." But interest in the Melungeons remains strong today.

People who first learned about the Melungeons in the 1990s (or later) were unaware of *Walk Toward the Sunset* and its impact on the attitudes of Melungeons and non-Melungeons alike. That impact was demonstrated when the play was

---

[7] Vande Brake, *Through the Back Door*, 261–94.

resurrected for one weekend in 2011 at the first annual Mildred Haun Conference. Held at Walters State Community College in Morristown, the conference
was described as a celebration of Appalachian literature, scholarship, and culture
for Appalachians and non-Appalachians.

The conference named for Mildred E. Haun, who was born in Hamblen
County in 1911 but grew up in Haun Hollow, a piece of family land in the rural
and mountainous Hoot Owl District of neighboring Cocke County. She attended Vanderbilt University in Nashville where she enrolled in a writing class
taught by John Crowe Ransom. There, she began writing a series of short stories
based on stories she'd heard growing up. The stories were published in 1940 in
a collection titled *The Hawk's Done Gone*. The tales are strung together through
the narration of the main character, Mary Dorthula White, a "granny woman,"
or midwife, whose life and stories spanned from the Civil War to 1940.[8]

The stories in *The Hawk's Done Gone* might be described as "Appalachian
Gothic," combining modern realism with traditional superstition and mountain
herbal medicine to tell stories of cruelty, incest, racism, and murder, as well as
the resilience of its narrator. Several of the stories feature Melungeon characters.
In one of the stories, "Melungeon-Colored," Mary Dorthula White tries to keep
her granddaughter Cordia from marrying; unbeknownst to Cordia or anyone
else in the community, Cordia's father was a Melungeon. Cordia doesn't have
the physical characteristics of Melungeons, but Mary subscribes to the traditional
belief that the dark features of the Melungeons can skip a generation or two to
produce a child that is "Melungeon colored." Despite Mary's precautions, Cordia elopes with a man in the community, Mos Arwood. Mary plans to use her
knowledge of herbal medicine to abort any potential children. However, by the
time Mary learns of Cordia's pregnancy, it is too late for Mary to do anything
but hope the baby would be a girl, since she believes a boy would be more likely
to have Melungeon features. When Cordia is ready to deliver, her husband sends
for Mary to help with the birth. The child is a boy with dark skin, and Mos
immediately assumes his wife has been unfaithful with a Melungeon. As Mary
watches helplessly, Mos kills Cordia with a stick of firewood, then builds a rough
coffin. He places the still-living baby in the coffin with Cordia and nails it shut.[9]

Dr. Viki Rouse, associate professor of English at Walters State, is considered
one of the leading authorities on Mildred Haun and organized the conference.
Early in the planning of the conference, she talked with her colleague Jerry
Maloy, associate professor of music and theater, about staging an appropriate

---

[8] Lyday-Lee, "Mildred Eunice Haun."
[9] Haun, "Melungeon-Colored," 97–111.

play during the conference. Maloy suggested *Walk Toward the Sunset*. "There was quite a bit of local interest in that play," according to Maloy. "Every once in a while somebody would call me up and say something like, 'Do you think they might do that play again?' So I knew some people had a great fondness and interest in it."

As a high school student, Maloy had seen the 1970 production as part of a Sunday school trip from his hometown of Newport, Tennessee. Prior to seeing the play, he had never heard of the Melungeons. "It really did spark an interest," Maloy recalled. "I remember writing a research paper on Melungeons in high school, so it must have affected me quite a bit at that time."

Maloy was already familiar with the genre of outdoor drama.

> This may be sounding rather nerdish, but I was a great fan of going to Hunter Hills Theatre in Gatlinburg, where they would do three rotating plays during the summer. Some plays up there, like *Dark of the Moon* and *The Sound of Music* fit beautifully, and some plays just probably shouldn't have been presented there. And I remember thinking, in a 16-year-old's mind, that this was the perfect way to present [*Walk Toward the Sunset*]. You had more of a real idea of the Appalachian rural life, the scope, maybe—not only the individual story, but the whole setting lent an air of underpinning to the story, I thought.

Maloy attended Carson-Newman College, where he studied music, while some of his classmates, including Rose Williams, were performing *Walk Toward the Sunset* in Sneedville during the summer. Maloy staged the play in the Inman Humanities Complex Theatre at Walters State and tried to re-create the opening activities described in the 1976 script—unaware that those activities were not actually done onstage in Sneedville.

> The first thing we had to adapt was that opening thing, where you have all the horseshoe making and such and such going on. What we tried to do was to establish that in the lobby of the theatre. We had a loom; we had shape note singers. We had more plans, but they didn't all work out. That was the first thing, to sort of condition the audience outside the theatre. The quilts that were up there on the wall were from the production I directed of *Shenandoah*, and I [introduced the quilts] in various points in the play. The Star Quilt, for example, came out when the girl (Alisee) was falling in love with the soldier (Pat, in the first act)…Inside, I tried to use that Elizabethan principal of just having a base stage and not worrying so much about trying to have things look like the whole interior of a building or the whole village or the whole Indian encampment—to more or less suggest it with the characters and a few props and maybe different lighting schemes…and use that as an adjunct to adapt. As Shakespeare said in *Henry V*, "I wish I could present the whole battle of Agincourt here on the stage for you, but I can't." You know,

to try to symbolically present it rather than as literally as they did in the outdoor drama because they had a lot more space, and they also had those two side stages, as I remember.

Maloy began adapting the play in September 2010, and in late October, he began holding auditions for the parts. Prospective actors received a brief background of the play and its subject matter before the auditions, but "The more they rehearsed it," Maloy said, "the more they realized the responsibility that they had in telling the story."[10]

One major change was the addition of more music than in the original Sneedville production, performed live by a student band. Adele McDonald, a professor of music at Walters State, arranged the music, led the band, and played the fiddle. The musicians performed songs such as "Soldier's Joy," "The Water Is Wide," "Wayfaring Stranger," "Garry Owen," "Dark Woman of the Mountains," and "Bonaparte's Retreat" on fiddles, banjo, gourd banjo, pennywhistle, flute, drums, and other percussion instruments.

The cast in the original Sneedville productions of *Walk Toward the Sunset* was small (not counting the local people who filled out crowd scenes) since the actors had to commit for the entire summer and had to be paid and housed. Therefore, the actors played dual roles, one role in the first act and another role in the second. The Walters State production was performed only for one weekend, with actors who attended the college and lived nearby, so there was a much larger cast, with each actor playing only one role. Emily Myers portrayed Alisee Collins in the first act and was in crowd scenes in the second act. Born in Knoxville, Myers lived in Virginia for several years but moved back to Tennessee to attend Walters State. She had acted in high school performances, but *Walk Toward the Sunset* was her first college production. She had never heard of the Melungeons before but found out she had a connection to the subject.

> I actually had never heard of them until I heard about the tryouts, but before I went to the first tryout I told my dad, and he had lived in Sneedville and knew who they were—and he saw the play.... He saw it when he was younger and he didn't remember everything about it, but he remembered it was done in Sneedville when he was living there.... He told me at that time they were getting ready to put it on for the first time, and the Melungeons there didn't really want to come out and say, "I'm a Melungeon." They were really nervous, and [the subject] wasn't as well known as it is today. And he remembered

---

[10] Maloy interview.

that [after the play opened], more people started coming out and saying, "Yes, I'm of Melungeon descent."[11]

Having seen *Unto These Hills*, she was already familiar with playwright Kermit Hunter. As rehearsals progressed, she was moved by the script and the story of the Melungeons, but when the play was finally performed, she learned how important the play had been to many of those who had seen it in Sneedville.

There were three performances, on Thursday evening, 3 February 2011; Saturday evening, 5 February; and a matinee on Sunday, 6 February. All three performances were well attended, but the theater was filled to overflowing for the Saturday night show, which was preceded by a panel discussion about the play. Many folks from "Overhome" attended the Saturday night performance, traveling not only across Clinch Mountain, but back in time, to the seasons when the play was performed in the rough amphitheater behind the elementary school in Sneedville. Emily Myers recalls that several people, some of whom identified themselves as Melungeons, told various cast members how much the re-staging of the play meant to them.

> Some of them had seen the original play, and they talked about how it brought back memories to them. They thought the play did them justice. I had an experience on Saturday night when one of the original cast members who had played Alisee [Rose Williams Grayson] came up to me and we talked for a while. It meant a lot, hearing what they used to do and what it was like when they did it outside. And several conference members told me how much it meant to them. It was really a blessing; I honestly never expected it to become so big for me. When I first tried out, I just thought it would be a meaningful play, but it meant a lot more than that.[12]

Even though the Walters State production of *Walk Toward the Sunset* was performed indoors, it was still written as an outdoor drama, a genre for which Maloy, like John Lee Welton, has a great deal of fondness.

> The first play I remember seeing was *Unto These Hills* [also written by Kermit Hunter] when I was about five. We didn't have theater in Newport at that time; that just wasn't done. They might have had a high school play, *Here Come the Hillbillies* or something like that. I remember the first time that I went to Hunter Hills and saw *Oklahoma*; I was twelve, maybe. I was just completely bowled over by this concept of having theater out under the stars, in a larger-than-Cinemascope setting. I think it's very important; I think it's

---

[11] Myers interview.
[12] Ibid.

kind of a shame that it's not as important as it once was. Everybody has financial woes, and I think that's one of the things that happens to outdoor theater. I really loved it; I really did. It was just one of the things I looked forward to in the summer, to get to go to the ones that were around us. I can remember clear as a bell seeing *The Book of Job* for the first time. And there's a certain amount of energy, I think, that they had at that time, because they didn't have the body mics—an energy I think our students are lacking today; they're relying too much on the electronic amplification rather than the "Richard Burton shouting against the wind," and I think that outdoor theater is the vehicle for experiencing that. My parents would not go to the theater to see a play, but they would enjoy going to something like that, and they took me, and therefore fostered the initial love for theater.[13]

The popularity of outdoor drama has declined since its peak in the 1970s. Several remain in production, however, including *Unto These Hills, Horn in The West, Trail of the Lonesome Pine,* and the original outdoor drama, *The Lost Colony.* In addition, dozens of outdoor Shakespeare festivals are held across the nation; the works of the Bard of Avon seem to thrive under the stars. Most outdoor dramas still in production are subsidized by government or private entities. The Institute for Outdoor Theatre, formerly the Institute for Outdoor Drama has moved to Eastern Carolina University in Greenville, North Carolina, and continues to provide support for outdoor productions both large and small.

Walk Toward the Sunset had a very brief run, with only six seasons between 1969 and 1976. However, few theatrical productions have had a comparable impact on the people about whom those plays were written.

Although many had predicted the imminent disappearance of the Melungeons in the mid-twentieth century, those predictions were made at a time when Melungeons did not acknowledge their heritage, did not use the term "Melungeon" to describe themselves and their ancestors, and did not acknowledge they were different from their white neighbors. By the early twenty-first century, there were dozens of people in Hancock County who were willing to discuss their Melungeon heritage, as well as people who had grown up in Hancock County and had moved elsewhere, or people with ancestral roots in Hancock County. Dr. Laura Tugman-Gabriel interviewed fourteen self-identified Melungeons about their ethnic identity and what information their parents had passed on to them about their identity. One participant recalled, "I

---

[13] Maloy interview.

wasn't allowed to say that word [Melungeon]. And my mother would…we had a huge maple tree here. She would send me out there for a switch if I said that word…. I don't hold it against her because she might have known more of the discrimination of being Melungeon than I did. But she'd say, 'You don't ever say that word in this house again!'"

Another remembered the use of a common euphemism, one which, like "Portuguese," was often used to hide African ancestry. "[W]hen we were kids, the only thing I ever heard mentioned about my dad's people was they were Black Dutch. And that was a good code name for a whole lot of folks who had no reason to go to the Bahamas [laughs]."[14]

As Tugman-Gabriel noted, several of the Melungeons she interviewed had had DNA tests performed. Most did not shy away from acknowledging their African ancestry. "If the Melungeons are basically tri-racial then I've got the Cherokee Indian blood in me…. I've got the English white and German white and Welsh. Because I had the DNA study done and I kept looking and looking. [I thought] 'Where's all this other?' And I had some African in me, too. So we probably are the first melting pot."[15]

One interview subject regularly attended the Melungeon Heritage Association Unions, not to learn more about her heritage from the many presentations offered, but for the sense of community she found there. "[At the Unions] I don't listen to none of the talks. I got my own talking to do! Somebody asked me why I go and I said, 'To see my friends,' cause that's the only reason I go. A man and woman came from Kansas City and took me over to [a Melungeon gathering] and she said, 'Every time I looked you were hugging somebody!' I said, 'That's what I go for.'"[16]

That feeling of belonging was all the more special for some who recalled the trauma of leaving the secure environment of the Vardy mission school to attend public high school in Hancock County. As one study participant recalled,

> We weren't the slick kids that go to high school. Most of us hadn't been to town before. You what I mean? And uh, of course we only had one high school and the teachers—not all of them— but they kind of thought that they didn't need to be bothered with us. I kind of realized why, you know, why everybody else quit. And I really don't know how I made it. I really don't. But I knew that was the gateway to getting out of here.

---

[14] Tugman-Gabriel, "Seeking Roots in Shifting Ground," 92.
[15] Ibid., 97.
[16] Ibid., 101.

It wasn't easy, you know, I had to fight and scratch. I had a confrontation just about every day. It was hard…we were shunned by the people who lived just across the mountain because that's the [school] bus we rode…. They wouldn't let us sit down. I'll tell you how tough it was. I started with six or eight other boys in high school. I was the only one who graduated out of the group, and the majority of them didn't make it the first year. [17]

Several of the people Tugman-Gabriel interviewed recalled the 1947 *Saturday Evening Post* article as a watershed moment. One person told the story as an amusing anecdote, another grew tearful at the memory, and another recalled resenting the publicity the article brought to the Melungeons, but all remembered it clearly as the moment they learned that they were Melungeons.

Whenever the magazine came out…the *Saturday Evening Post*…in October of 1947. I was 5 years old going to [the Vardy] school up on the hill, here. And I'd been sent down to pick up the mail and bring it back up during recess. And I came back up the school steps and was sitting down on the front looking at the magazine because I felt like I could read. Of course, I probably was reading pictures [laughs]. But whenever I saw the article in the magazine, I saw people in the pictures that I knew. I started yelling, "Come quick!" to all the other kids. I said, "Look! There's a picture of A.C. Paul," who…was one of the tenants that lived on our farm. And I said, "Here's a picture of A.C. Paul and here's a picture of Ralph and a picture of Laura and R.C.!" People that I knew! And all the other kids came and gathered around and my mother was in the classroom because someone else was watching the kids on the playground on that particular day. She came rushing out of the room and said, "Give me that dirty, filthy magazine!" And she took it out of my hands and did not show it to me again [for years].

I went to the University of Tennessee for the first time in 1947. And I had never heard the word, "Melungeon" before that time…. I went to the library one day to do some research and there was the *Saturday Evening Post*…. There was an article in there and it had pictures and it talked about Melungeons. And the pictures were my relatives. It was my aunt. She was one of them [in the pictures]. And I read this article, and it talked about people here… and how [Hancock County] was a place with Melungeons. So, I thought, "What in the world is this?" So I couldn't bring the magazine home. So I finally got home and I told my mother the story that was in there in the magazine. And

---

[17] Ibid., 105.

she listened to me very tentatively and when I finished, she said, "Don't you name that word [Melungeon] anymore!"

[I realized I was Melungeon] in 1947 when the *Saturday Evening Post* did a story and that's when I read it…. I was about 8 years old and what really got my attention was my best buddy was [pauses] there was a picture of him with his mother and sister in there [article] and they lived in Mahala Mullins' cabin. So of course, all of us, we all talked about that. After that article a lot of people came in here. People from New York came in buses wanting to see us and everything. Mom, she dared us to even speak to them! My older brother would get really hot about it. He would say, "If you see any Melungeons come get me because I want to see them, too!" People were really upset, so I think something—there was somewhere in our past they were treated terribly…. I wasn't allowed to say that word [Melungeon].[18]

Some of the study participants acknowledged the role of the outdoor drama *Walk Toward the Sunset* in changing the attitudes of Melungeons and non-Melungeons alike.

[A]t that time, at the beginning of the drama—I've always felt that this was very true—nobody wanted to be a Melungeon. That was a bad, bad word. But when we had the drama here for seven years and it depicted the Melungeon people as being honest, hardworking, good-looking people, everybody wanted to be one at the end…. It changed, yes, but now still today there's some people who don't want to be classified as Melungeons or even talk about it.

There was a time if you'd come around here asking about Melungeons I'd have told you to, uh, hit the road, but it's different now. People want to be Melungeons now.[19]

People want to be Melungeons now—now that the discrimination has ended, now that their children can go to school like everyone else's children, now that the law allows Melungeons the same rights as everyone else, now that the

---

[18] Ibid., 125–26.
[19] Ibid., 118.

very word "Melungeon" doesn't brand them as shiftless, ignorant, and malicious. Being a Melungeon is a good thing now. Of course, many of those with the closest ties to that heritage call themselves "Melungeon descendants," acknowledging that they, unlike their parents or grandparents, never had to contend with what that word once meant. It's a good heritage, one that reflects the ethnic melting pot that was eighteenth- and nineteenth-century America, and one that celebrates the resiliency of people who were scorned and reviled but who survived to pass on that distinctive "Melungeon look" and that mysterious legacy to their descendants.

Claude Collins not only saw the remarkable change in attitude about Melungeons, he played a large part in bringing it about. He acknowledged his ancestry at a time when few others would, and he did it in the most public way possible, in the pages of major newspapers and magazines, on television, and in documentary films. He continued to work to build a positive image for his people until his death on 15 February 2017 at the age of 89.

Though *Walk Toward the Sunset* did not achieve its primary goal of bringing economic development to Hancock County, no one could have predicted the effect it would have on the people who were the subject of the play. Those simple words, spoken by a "Happy Pappy" laborer building the amphitheater, or by Claude Collins talking to a reporter—"I am a Melungeon"—were unthinkable before a group of determined people set out to improve their home county by telling a story no one wanted to tell before.

The predictions of the disappearance of the Melungeons will eventually come true, of course. The Melungeons never were a completely distinct group of people and have become less so with each generation, as assimilation into the larger population of Appalachians and Appalachian descendants makes their heritage ever more remote. The Melungeons are, indeed, walking toward the sunset. But they have cast a shadow that will not be forgotten.

ACKNOWLEDGMENTS

A lot of people gave of their time, memories, and expertise, and provided support to make this book possible. I want to thank, in no particular order:

Mary Van Nest, Raymond Buffington, Steve Nichandros, Mike Murphy, Larry Clifton, Jerry Maloy, Emily Myers, Rose Grayson, Bruce Shine, Greg Marion, Jack Goins, Melanie Teegarden, Fred Sauceman, Joe Smith, Michelle Freeze, Mattie Ruth Johnson, Richard Kennedy, Calvin Beale, Haley Richardson, Scott Collins, DruAnna Williams Overbay, Sandy Ray, S. J. Arthur, Amy K. Guinn, Darlene Wilson, Connie Clark, Pete Dykes, Monica Thomas, R. C. Mullins, the Melungeon Heritage Association, The Vardy Community Historical Society, Ric LaRue and the Charles C. Sherrod Library at East Tennessee State University, the Archives of Appalachia at East Tennessee State University, Viki Dasher Rouse and the Mildred Haun Conference at Walters State Community College, and Marc Jolley and Marsha Luttrell at Mercer University Press.

I want to especially thank Ken Smith of the Smith-Turner Drug Store in Sneedville, Tennessee, and Bonnie Manning and the Hancock County Historical and Genealogical Society, for their assistance in obtaining materials for this book.

I'd also like to express special thanks to W. C. "Claude" Collins, who was a major part of this story; Dr. John Lee Welton, whose information and guidance have been priceless; Brent Kennedy, who opened many doors for me; Dr. Laura Tugman, for research assistance and much more; and the staff at the University of Tennessee Institute of Agriculture Extension Office in Sneedville, Tennessee, for never throwing out the old material in the bottom drawer of that file cabinet. I also want to take a moment to remember Charles Turner, Dora Bowlin, Corinne Bowlin, Dr. Truett Pierce, and the other members of the Hancock County Drama Association. This story would not have happened without them.

This book is dedicated to the memory of my own Mclungeons who have passed on: my aunt, Hazel Winkler Turner and her husband, Elmer Turner, who gave me my first collection of articles and documents and turned me into a Melungeon researcher; my uncle, Shields Winkler, who often surprised me, sometimes in very good ways; my cousin Larry Turner, who was in the cast of the play; my uncle, Earl Winkler, and his wife, Lucille Hatfield Winkler, who showed how far you can move from your roots without ever really leaving; my grandmother, Mattie Givens Winkler, whose devotion to her children allowed them to exceed anyone's expectations; and my father, Willis Winkler, who often thought I wasn't listening, but I heard every word.

I also dedicate this book to the living, whose inspiration, encouragement, support, and love have made it all possible: my mother and first mentor, Wanda Barker; my brother, Wade Winkler, with whom I shared many Hancock County adventures; and, especially, my daughter, Claire, and my son, Josef, who were patient with their father during the writing of this book, and who make it all worthwhile.

BIBLIOGRAPHY

"A History of the Drama." *Hancock County Post*, 7 August 1969, 2.

Alther, Lisa. *Kinfolks: Falling off the Family Tree*. New York: Arcade Publishing Company, 2007.

"Around the State." *The Dispatch* (Lexington, NC), 30 June 1969, 16.

"Arts Commission Commends Local Drama." *Hancock County Post*, 22 January 1970, 1.

Associated Press. "Hancock County Struggles to Make Ends Meet." *Kingsport Daily News*, 3 July 1987, B-2, B-3.

———. "Outdoor Dramas Aid Economies." *Reading (PA) Eagle*, 11 June 1970.

———. "Nine Counties Band Together to Form New State." *Times Daily* (Florence, AL), 19 June 1987, B-1.

Atkin, Carolyn. "VISTA Won't Go back to Hancock." *Kingsport Times-News*, 8 March 1970, 11-A.

Aswell, James. *God Bless the Devil*. Federal Writers' Project. Chapel Hill: University of North Carolina Press, 1940.207-208.

Baird, Dan W. "A Backward Glance." *Nashville Daily American*, 15 September 1890, 2.

Banker, Mark T. "Missionaries and Mountain Peoples: Presbyterian Responses to Southern Appalachia & Hispanic New Mexico." Paper presented at the 16th Appalachian Studies Conference, East Tennessee State University, Johnson City, TN, March 1993. Available at https://files.eric.ed.gov/fulltext/ED375987.pdf.

Beale, Calvin L. "American Triracial Isolates: Their Status and Pertinence to Genetic Research." *Eugenics Quarterly* 4/4 (December 1957): 187–96.

———. "An Overview of the of the Phenomenon of Mixed Racial Isolates in the United States." *American Anthropologist* 74 (1972): 704–10.

———. "Notes on a Visit to Hancock County, Tennessee." In Beale, *A Taste of the Country*, 42–52.

———. *A Taste of the Country: A Collection of Calvin Beale's Writings*. Edited by Peter Morrison. University Park, PA: Pennsylvania State University Press, 1990.

"Ben Harville to Direct Hancock Play." *Rogersville (TN) Review*, 8 April 1971, 12.

Berry, Brewton. *Almost White*. New York: Macmillan, 1963.

Bible, Jean. "A People with an Unknown Past." *Baltimore Sun Magazine*, 13 June 1971, 14–15, 17, 19.

Bible, Jean Patterson. *Melungeons Yesterday and Today*. Rogersville, TN: East Tennessee Printing Company, 1975.

Bowler, Mary. "Retardation Group Formed." *Hancock County Post*, 27 March 1969, 8.

Bowlin, Corinne. "Drama Committee Meets." *Hancock County Post*, 1 January 1968, 1.

Bowlin, Dora. Letter to the National Endowment for the Arts Theatre Program, 22 October 1976. University of Tennessee Institute of Agriculture, Hancock County Extension, Sneedville, TN.

———. "Drama News." *Hancock County Post*, 27 March 1969, 1.

———. "Drama News." *Hancock County Post*, 3 April 1969, 6.

———. "Drama News." *Hancock County Post*, 10 April 1969, 1.

———. "Drama News." *Hancock County Post*, 17 April 1969, 5.

———. "Drama News." *Hancock County Post*, 1 May 1969, 8.

———. "Drama News," *Hancock County Post*, 5 June 1969, 1.

———. "Drama News." *Hancock County Post*, 26 June 1969, 1.

———. "Drama Season Highly Successful." *Hancock County Post*, 28 August 1969, 4.

———. "Drama Still Needs Funds." *Hancock County Post*, 8 May 1969, 1.

———. "Drama Try-Outs Re-Set." *Hancock County Post*, 22 May 1969, 1.

———. "Hancock County Can Be Proud: *Walk Toward the Sunset* Successful and Rewarding." *Hancock County Post*, 21 August 1969, 1.

———. Letter to HCDA board members, 29 September 1975. University of Tennessee Extension, Hancock County office.

Breeding, Josephine Stone. "A Letter and an Article." *Hancock County Post*, 11 September 1969, 4.

"Brenda Carter at Tazewell This Saturday." *Hancock County Post*, 17 July 1969, 1.

Brooks, Roger D. Letter to Governor Ray Blanton, 17 October 1975. University of Tennessee Extension, Hancock County office.

Brown, Adam. "Dassler, Van Nests honored as Land Trust celebrates 30 years." *Sun Journal* (Lewiston, ME), 25 December 2017, http://www.sunjournal.com/dassler-van-nests-honored-as-land-trust-celebrates-30-years/.

Brownlow's Whig (Jonesborough, TN), 7 October 1840, 3.

"Bruce Shine Announces as First District Congressional Candidate." *Hancock County Post*, 4 June 1970, 5.

"Bruce Shine to Speak on Importance of Drama." *Hancock County Post*, 9 April 1970, 1.

"Budget shortfall may force schools to close in Hancock." *Rome (GA) News-Tribune*, 23 January 1992, 5-A.

Buttrey, Gary. "A History of the Hunter Hills Theatre, 1956–1977." Master's thesis, University of Tennessee-Knoxville, 1979.

Carter, Edna Ann. "Educational Resources and Needs in Hancock County, Tennessee." Report to the Clinch and Powell River Valley Association, Inc., September 1965. University of Tennessee Extension, Hancock County office.

Cavender, Anthony P. "The Melungeons of Upper East Tennessee: Persisting Social Identity." *Tennessee Anthropologist* 6/1 (Spring 1981): 27–36.

Code, Doris N. Customer review of *Daughter of the Legend* by Jesse Stewart. https://www.amazon.com/Daughter-legend-Jesse-Stuart-ebook/dp/B01AX5YACA/ref=sr_1_1?keywords=daughter+of+the+legend&qid=1556656398&s=gateway&sr=8-1#customerReviews, 13 September 2013.

Cohen, Henry. "Here and There in Hawkins County." *Kingsport Post*, 8 July 1976, 4.

Connor, R.B. "Why Have a Drama About the Melungeons in Hancock County?" *Hancock County Post*, 8 February 1968, 1.

"County Outdoor Historical Drama." *Hancock County Post*, 4 July 1968, B1.

Davis, Louise. "The Mystery of the Melungeons." *Nashville Tennessean Sunday Magazine*, 29 September 1963.

———. "Why Are They Vanishing?" *Nashville Tennessean Sunday Magazine*, 29 September 1963.

Douthat, Strat. "Appalachian Commission Awaits Budget Axe." *Pittsburgh Post Gazette*, 8 February 1982, 4.

"Drama Group Makes Plans." *Hancock County Post*, 26 September 1968, 1.

"Drama Meeting Set." *Hancock County Post*, 4 January 1968, 1.

"Drama off to a Good Start. *Hancock County Post*, 17 July 1969, 1.

Dromgoole, Will Allen. "Land of the Malungeons." *Nashville Sunday American*, 31 August 1890, 10.

———. "A Strange People." *Nashville Sunday American*, 15 September 1890, 10.

———. "The Malungeons." *The Arena* 3 (March 1891): 470–79.

———. "The Malungeon Tree and Its Four Branches." *The Arena* 3 (May 1891): 745–51. Also available at https://babel.ha-thitrust.org/cgi/pt?id=nc01.ark:/13960/t3nw0dx6f;view=1up;seq=5.

"EDA Approves $98,000 Grant." *Hancock County Post*, 21 March 1968, 1.

"Ellington Announces Industry for Hancock." *Hancock County Post*, 7 December 1967.

"Ernie Ford Is Drama Campaign Chairman." *Kingsport Post*, 11 February 1971, 4.

Everett, C. S. "Melungeon History and Myth." *Appalachian Journal* 26/4 (Summer 1999): 358–404.

"Factory Opening Due Soon, Production to Begin in April." *Hancock County Post*, 13 March 1969, 1.

Farley, Gary, and Joe Mack High. "Social Systems and Economic Development in a Rural Environment: Hancock County, Tennessee." Report to the Office of Tributary Area Development, Tennessee Valley Authority, 1966.

Fetterman, John. "The Melungeons." *Louisville Courier-Journal Magazine*, 30 March 1969, reprinted in *Walk Toward the Sunset souvenir program,* 1971.

"Fire Destroys Cash N' Tote." *Hancock County Post*, 20 February 1969, 1.

"Ford Heads 'Sunset' Drama Drive." *Kingsport Times-News*, 31 January 1971, 33.

Haston, Robert Jr. Letter. September 1966.

"Former Hancock County Youth Dies: Victim of Vietnam War." *Hancock County Post*, 31 August 1967, 1.

Gallegos, Eloy J. *The Melungeons: The Pioneers of the Interior Southeastern United States, 1526–1997*. Knoxville: Villagra Press, 1997.

Gamble, John. "Melungeon Line Almost Extinct." *Kingsport Times*, 26 November 1964, 9-C.

Gilbert, William Harlan, Jr. "Memorandum concerning the Characteristics of the Larger Mixed-Blood Racial Islands in the Eastern United States." *Social Forces* 21/4 (May 1946): 438–77.

Glenn, Juanita. "Hancock Countians Prepare for Drama about Melungeons." *Knoxville Journal*, 1 May 1969, 5.

———. "Hancock Countians Aiding Dream with Drama." *Knoxville Sentinel*, 11 March 1971.

———. "Melungeon Drama to Reopen." *Knoxville Journal*, 30 June 1975, 1, 10.

———. "The Melungeons have left, but their heritage remains." *Knoxville Journal*, 5 September 1975, 17, 21.

Glover, William. "Outdoor Drama Increases in Popularity." *High Point (NC) Enterprise*, 9 May 1976, 15-C.

Goins, Jack. *Melungeons and Other Pioneer Families*. Rogersville, TN: Privately printed, 2000.

———. *Melungeons: Footprints from the Past*. Rogersville, TN: Privately printed, 2010.

———. "Newman's Ridge Goins Families," Jack Goins' Melungeon and Appalachian Research, http://jackgoins.blogspot.com/2013/12/newman-ridge-goins-families.html, accessed 15 October 2017.

———. "The First Melungeon Community," Jack Goins' Melungeon and Appalachian Research, http://jackgoins.blogspot.com/2013/08/the-first-melungeon-community_26.html, accessed 15 October 2017.

———. "History of the Melungeons." http://www.historical-melungeons.com/history.html, accessed 15 October 2017.

Grohse, William P. "H.R.D.A. Meets." *Hancock County Post*, 20 February 1969, 1.

———. "Hancock County—'Land of Mystery.'" *Hancock County Post*, 4 July 1968, 10–12.

———. "Leadership Classes Underway." *Hancock County Post*, 27 April 1967, 2.

———. "Leadership Classes Underway." *Hancock County Post*, 4 May 1967, 9.

———. "Leadership Classes Underway." *Hancock County Post*, 11 May 1967, 8.

———. "Leadership Classes Underway." *Hancock County Post*, 18 May 1967, 5.

———. Papers. Microfilm Roll # 7. East Tennessee State University, Johnson City, TN.

———. "Support the Drama," *Hancock County Post*, 10 April 1969, 6.

Hancock County Comprehensive Overall Economic Development Program Association. Report, 4 February 1963.

Hancock County Drama Association. Budget worksheet for Tennessee Arts Commission proposal, 1970.

———. Proposal for Aid from the Tennessee Arts Commission for the Outdoor Drama *Walk Toward the Sunset*, 1970 season. James H. Quillen papers, Archives of Appalachia, East Tennessee State University, Johnson City, TN. Cited as Quillen papers.

———. National Endowment for the Arts application, 1976.

———. "Possible Uses for the Farmers Market in Sneedville," undated memo.

————. Report, 21 October 1975.

————. Expenditure report for 1976.

"Hancock County Drama is Hoped." *Middlesboro (KY) Daily News*, 9 January 1968.

"Hancock County Night Thursday." *Hancock County Post*, 7 August 1969, 1.

"Hancock County Struggles to Make Ends Meet." *Kingsport Daily News*, 3 July 1987, B2-B3.

"Hancock Drama Association Honorary Directors Named." *Hancock County Post*, 4 June 1970, 7.

"Hancock Drama Set Again." *Kingsport Times-News*, 25 April 1971, 22.

"Hancock Votes 98.6 'For the Bonds.'" *Hancock County Post*, 21 December 1967, 2.

Haralson, Ann. "Alex Stewart." *Walk Toward the Sunset* souvenir program (reprinted from the *Hancock County Post*). Rogersville, TN: East Tennessee Printing Company, 1973.

————. "Construction Underway at County Drama Site." *Hancock County Post*, 12 December 1968, 1.

————. "Craft News." *Hancock County Post*, 26 June 1969, 1.

————. "Dr. Hunter Discusses Drama." *Hancock County Post*, 5 December 1968, 1.

————. "Drama Group on the Move." *Hancock County Post*, 28 November 1968, 1.

————. "Drama Plans Announced." *Hancock County Post*, 23 January 1969, 1.

Haun, Mildred. "Melungeon-Colored." In *The Hawk's Done Gone and Other Stories*. Edited by Herschel Gower. Nashville: Vanderbilt University Press, 1968

Hess, Earl J. *Lincoln Memorial University and the Shaping of Appalachia*. Knoxville: University of Tennessee Press), 2011.

High, Joe Mack, to Dora Bowlin. 16 January 1968. University of Tennessee Extension, Hancock County office.

————. Letter to Earl Hobson Smith. 23 February 1968, University of Tennessee Extension, Hancock County office.

————. Letter to Norman Worrell, 17 January 1970, James H. Quillen papers, Archives of Appalachia, East Tennessee State University, Johnson City, TN.

Hughes, Michael. Letter to James H, Quillen, 19 February 1970, James H Quillen papers, Archives of Appalachia, East Tennessee State University, Johnson City, TN.

Hunter, Kermit. *Walk Toward the Sunset*. Unpublished script for the Melungeon outdoor drama held in Sneedville, TN, 1969 season.

————. *Walk Toward the Sunset*. Unpublished script for the Melungeon outdoor drama held in Sneedville, TN, 1976 season.

Ivey, Saundra Keyes. "Aunt Mahala Mullins in Folklore, Fakelore, and Literature." *Tennessee Folklore Society Bulletin* 41/1 (1975): 1–8.

————. "Oral, Printed, and Popular Culture Traditions Related to the Melungeons of Hancock County, Tennessee." Ph.D. dissertation, Indiana University, 1976.

————. "'Walk Toward the Sunset' Tells Melungeon Story." *Nashville Tennessean*, 19 August 1973, 6-E.

Jarvis, Lewis. "The Melungeons." *Hancock County Times*, 17 April 1903, 1. In William Grohse papers, Archives of Appalachia, East Tennessee State University.

"John Lee Welton Will Direct Summer Drama." *Hancock County Post*, 16 April 1970, 1.

Johnson, Mattie Ruth. *My Melungeon Heritage*. Johnson City, TN: The Overmountain Press, 1997.

"Johnston, Nancy." Internet Broadway Database. https://www.ibdb.com/broadway-cast-staff/nancy-johnston-76730, accessed 8 May 2019.

Jumper, Robert. "Editorial: What a Year This Has Been." *Cherokee One Feather*, 19 December 2017, https://theonefeather.com/2017/12/editorial-what-a-year-this-has-been/.

Kennedy, N. Brent, with Robyn Vaughn Kennedy. *The Melungeons: The Resurrection of a Proud People; An Untold Story of Ethnic Cleansing in America*. Macon, GA: Mercer University Press, 1994, rev. 1997.

Kirkus Reviews. Unsigned review of *Daughter of the Legend*, by Jesse Stuart, https://www.kirkusreviews.com/book-reviews/jesse-stuart-13/daughter-of-the-legend/.

Larue, Ric. "Sneedville Drama is Product of History and Hard Work." *Morristown Citizen-Tribune*, 17 June 1973, D-1.

"Legislature to Hear Story of the Melungeons." *Kingsport Times*, 17 March 1971, 39.

"Local Civic Leader Ross Hopkins Dies." *Hancock County Post*, 24 April 1969, 1.

Lyday-Lee, Kathy. "Mildred Eunice Haun." *The Tennessee Encyclopedia of History and Culture*, 8 October 2017, http://tennesseeencyclopedia.net/entry.php?rec=610.

Magnussen, Paul. "Appalachia scrapes bottom of pork barrel." *Detroit Free Press*, 4 May 1986, 1-B. 7-B.

"Man Dies, 110 Years Old." *Middlesboro Daily News*, 23 August 1972.

Marcum, Ed. "Hope in Hancock: Economically strapped county gets boost from stimulus funds." *Knoxville News Sentinel*, 6 March 2010, online edition, http://archive.knoxnews.com/business/hope-in-hancock-economically-strapped-county-gets-boost-from-stimulus-funds-ep-408881390-358877661.html, accessed 6 August 2018

Matheison, David E. "New VISTA Workers Ready." *Hancock County Post*, 8 August 1968, 3.

Mathis, Eugene. "An Open Letter of Introduction." Autumn 1970.

McElfresh, Tom. "Theatre for Vacationers." *Cincinnati Enquirer*, 20 July 1973, 1-G.

"Meeting Set." *Hancock County Post*, 15 May 1969, 12.

"The Malungens." *Littell's Living Age* 20 (January–March 1849): 618–19. Available at https://archive.org/details/livingage32projgoog/page/n622.

"Melungeon Drama Goes on Despite Money Problems." *Kingsport News*, 20 April 1972, 27.

"Melungeon Drama to Be Staged Again." *Kingsport Post*, 20 April 1972, 4.

"Melungeon Play Director Sought." *Middlesboro (KY) Daily News*, 10 May 1972, 5.

"The Malungeons." *The Courier-Journal* (Louisville, KY), 26 September 1897, 15.

"Miscellaneous information regarding assassination of President John Fitzgerald Kennedy." Airtel and memos to J. Edgar Hoover, Director of the FBI, from Special

Agent in Charge, Dallas, TX, 4 December 1967, Collection at Hood College, Frederick, MD, http://jfk.hood.edu/Collection/FBI%20Records%20Files/62–109060/62–109060%20Section%20146/146B.pdf, accessed on 20 March 2016.

Montgomery, John. "Applications Now Being Taken." *Hancock County Post*, 20 March 1969, 1.

———. "C.P.C. Votes to Discontinue Future Hancock VISTA Programs." *Hancock County Post*, 19 June 1969, 1, 3.

———. "Early Settlement of 'Walkout' Seen." *Hancock County Post*, 20 April 1967, 1.

Morrill, Wayne J. "To the people of Hancock County." *Hancock County Post*, 28 March 1968, 1.

National Endowment for the Arts, Office of Special Projects. Guidelines for project grants, August 1976.

Neal, Dale. "Melungeons explore mysterious mixed-race origins." *Asheville (N.C.) Citizen Times* (online edition), 25 June 2015. Also available at https://www.usatoday.com/story/news/nation/2015/06/24/melungeon-mountaineers-mixed-race/29252839/.

Newlin, Lawrence M. Letter to George R. Smith, 20 December 1976. University of Tennessee Extension, Hancock County office.

———, to George R. Smith, 11 January 1977. University of Tennessee Extension, Hancock County office.

Nichols, Jim. "VISTA Puts Community on Its Own Feet." *Daily Kent Stater* (Kent State University, Kent, OH), 21 May 1969, 6.

"No Cast, No Crowd—Another Drama Fails." *Kingsport Times-News*, 28 September 1972, 22.

Nolan, John. "Sneedville Loses Property, but Few Lives." *Jackson (TN) Sun*, 7 April 1977, 4.

Nordheimer, Jon. "Mysterious Hill Folk Vanishing." *New York Times*, 10 August 1971, 33, 38. Available at https://www.nytimes.com/1971/08/10/archives/mysterious-hill-folk-vanishing-mysterious-mountain-folk-are.html.

Olson, Ted. Liner notes from *Tennessee Ernie Ford: Portrait of an American Singer* (CD box set), Bear Family Records, 2015.

"Outdoor Drama Conference Concludes." University of Tennessee Extension, Hancock County office.

Overbay, DruAnna Williams. *Windows on the Past*. Macon, GA: Mercer University Press, 2005.

"Parking Meters." Announcement in the *Hancock County News*, 4 April 1962, 2.

Peters, Mouzon. "Melungeons Steeped in Mystery: Many Theories of Their Origin." *Chattanooga Times*, 29 November 1970.

Pollitzer, William, and William Brown. "Survey of Demography, Anthropometry, and Genetics in the Melungeons of Tennessee: An Isolate of Hybrid Origin in Process of Dissolution." *Human Biology* 41/3 (September 1969): 388–400.

Price, Edward. "The Melungeons: A Mixed-Blood Strain of the Southern Appalachians." *Geographical Review* 41/2 (1951): 256–71.

Price, Edward T. "A Geographical Analysis of White-Negro-Indian Racial Mixtures in the Eastern United States." Association of American Geographers, *Annals* 43 (June 1953): 138–55.

Price, Shirley. "The Melungeons Are Coming out in the Open." *Kingsport Times-News*, 28 January 1968, 4.

"Pvt. Douglas Seal Wounded in Vietnam." *Hancock County Post*, 8 June 1967, 1.

Quillen, James H. Letter to Dora Bowlin, 20 October 1969. James H. Quillen papers, Archives of Appalachia, East Tennessee State University, Johnson City, TN.

———. Letter to Norman Worrell, 20 October 1969, James H, Quillen papers, Archives of Appalachia, East Tennessee State University, Johnson City, TN.

———. Letter to Roger D. Brooks, 22 August 1975. University of Tennessee Extension, Hancock County office.

———. Letter to Roger D. Brooks, 16 September 1975. University of Tennessee Extension, Hancock County office.

———. Press release, 22 February 1974. James H. Quillen papers, Archives of Appalachia, East Tennessee State University, Johnson City, TN.

———. Press release, 23 February 1974. James H. Quillen papers, Archives of Appalachia, East Tennessee State University, Johnson City, TN.

Rally, David, to Rep. James H. Quillen, 26 August 1975. University of Tennessee Extension, Hancock County office.

Razor X. "Album Review: Porter Wagoner & Dolly Parton—'Always, Always.'" My Kind of Country, 9 August 201. Available at https://mykindofcountry.word-press.com/tag/brenda-carter/.

———. "Classic Rewind: George Jones & Tammy Wynette—'Milwaukee, Here I Come.'" My Kind of Country, 28 June 2009. Available at https://mykindofcoun-try.wordpress.com/2009/06/28/classic-rewind-george-jones-tammy-wynette-mil-waukee-here-i-come/

"Road Projects on Move." *Hancock County Post*, 7 November 1968, 1.

Reed, John Shelton. "Mixing in the Mountains." *Southern Cultures* 3/4 (Winter 1997): 25.

Reston, Laura, and Sarah Jones. "Appalachia Needs Big Government." *New Republic*, 17 April 2017, https://newrepublic.com/article/142074/appalachia-needs-big-gov-ernment.

Schrift, Melissa. *Becoming Melungeon: Making an Ethnic Identity in the Appalachian South*. Lincoln: University of Nebraska Press, 2013.

Seely, Mike. "They're 'Working Up' A Drama." *Kingsport Times-News*, 23 May 1973, 22.

———. "The Lady Wears a Star." *Kingsport Times-News*, 3 June 1973, B-1.

"Sexton 'Proud' of Childhood Training." *Hancock County Post*, 3 August 1967, 3.

"Sgt. Harris Awarded Medal for Heroism." *Hancock County Post*, 21 December 1967, 2.

Shepherd, S. L. *Memoirs of Judge Lewis Shepherd*. Chattanooga, TN, 1915.

Shine, Bruce. Letter to J. M. High and Dr. Thomas Slaughter, 18 December 1969, James H. Quillen papers, Archives of Appalachia, East Tennessee State University, Johnson City, TN.

Smith, Drake. "Ann Piper 1946–2015." https://www.norththompsonfuneral.com/ann-piper-1946-2015/, accessed 1 October 2017.

Smith, George R., to the National Rural Information Center, 6 December 1976.

"Sneedville Man Dies, 110-Years-Old." *Kingsport Daily News*, 23 August 1972.

"Sneedville Mayor Heads Citizens for Shrine [*sic*] Campaign." *Kingsport Post*, 3 September 1970, A-6.

"Sneedville Mayor Named 'Mayor of the Year.'" *Hancock County Post*, 26 June 1969, 1.

"Sneedville Sets an Example for Other Areas in the State." *Hancock County Post*, 18 September 1969, 1.

"Sneedville Wins Progress Award in State Competition." *Hancock County News*, 5 December 1963, 1.

Social Security Administration. National Average Wage Index. National average wage indexing series, 1951–2017. Available at https://www.ssa.gov/oact/cola/AWI.html.

Stuart, Jesse. *Daughter of the Legend*. New York: McGraw-Hill, 1965.

Swatek, Phillip M., to James H. Quillen, 15 September 1975, University of Tennessee Extension, Hancock County office.

"Taps for Jesse Stuart." *Daytona Beach Sunday News-Journal*, 9 January 1966.

Tennessee Arts Commission. Uniform Proposal Form for Hancock County Drama Association, James H. Quillen Papers, Archives of Appalachia, East Tennessee State University, Johnson City, TN.

Tennessee Secretary of State. Business Services, Business Entity Details. Hancock County Drama Association, Inc. https://tnbear.tn.gov/Ecommerce/FilingDetail.aspx?CN=0412250271302551761800340161872251030311141082086, accessed 30 April 2019.

"Then the Floods Came." *Hancock County Post*, 8 January 1970, 1.

"Title 1 Funds Approved for Hancock High School." *Hancock County Post*, 28 March 1968, 1.

Todd, Roxy, and Jessica Lilly. "What Happened When VISTAs Came to a W.Va. Mining Town in the 1960's?" *Inside Appalachia*, West Virginia Public Radio, 17 April 2015, https://www.wvpublic.org/post/inside-appalachia-what-happened-when-vistas-came-wva-mining-town-1960s#stream/0.

Tugman-Gabriel, Laura Dawn. "Seeking Roots in Shifting Ground: Ethnic Identity Development and Melungeons of Southern Appalachia." Ph.D. dissertation, Fielding Graduate University, 2011.

Turner, Charles, "This Is YOUR Town," *Hancock County Post*, 19 September 1968, 2.

———. "This is YOUR Town." *Hancock County Post*, 31 July 1969, 1.

———. "This Is YOUR Town," *Hancock County Post*, 22 January 1970, 1.

———. "This Is YOUR Town," *Hancock County Post*, 30 April 1970, 1.

———. "This Is YOUR Town," *Hancock County Post*, 16 July 1970, 1.

———. "This Is YOUR Town: Do You Care?" *Hancock County Post*, 22 June 1967, 1.

———. "This Is YOUR Town: Our Interesting People." *Hancock County Post*, 8 February 1968, 1.

———. "This Is YOUR Town: Roads." *Hancock County Post*, 7 March 1968, 1.

———. "This Is YOUR Town: Roads." *Hancock County Post*, 19 September 1968, 2.

———. "This Is YOUR Town: The Magic Circle." *Hancock County Post*, 28 August 1969, 1.

Turner, A. Y. "Sonny, "Clean Up-Fix Up-Paint Up." *Hancock County Post*, 2 May 1968, 1.

"United States House of Representatives elections, 1970," Wikipedia. Available at https://en.wikipedia.org/wiki/1970_United_States_House_of_Representatives_elections#Tennessee.

University of Tennessee Agricultural Extension Service. *Characteristics of Persons Attending the Outdoor Drama "Walk Toward the Sunset,"* 1976.

Vande Brake, Katherine. *How They Shine: Melungeon Characters in the Fiction of Appalachia*. Macon, GA: Mercer University Press, 2001.

———. *Through the Back Door: Melungeon Literacies and Twenty-first Century Technologies*. Macon, GA: Mercer University Press, 2009.

Vinson, Betty A, to George R. Smith, 7 December 1976.

"VISTA to Seek Recruits Among Collegians Here." *Daytona Beach Sunday News Journal*, 7 April 1968, 5-A.

"VISTAs Announce Wedding Plans." *Hancock County Post*, 12 June 1969, 5.

"VISTA Question." *Hancock County Post*, 26 June 1969, 1, 2, 6.

Vitale, William V., to James H. Quillen, 22 August 1975. Quillen papers.

"Volunteers in Service to America (VISTA)." The Encyclopedia of Arkansas History and Culture. 10 September 2014. http://www.encyclopediaofarkansas.net/encyclopedia/entry-detail.aspx?entryID=4257.

Walk Toward the Sunset souvenir programs, 1969 (mimeographed sheet), 1970, 1971, 1973, 1975, 1976. Rogersville, TN: East Tennessee Printing Company.

Walko, Stephen. "May Lose Community Center Project." *Hancock County Post*, 4 December 1969, 2.

Wanniski, Jude. "Mayor Turner: 'Sorry to Jump on You Fellows': The Appalachia Act in Action." *The National Observer*, 27 December 1965.

Waxman, Leanne. "Counties Come Together to Form New State." *Times-News* (Hendersonville, NC), 12 July 1987, 2-D.

Wells, Ryan. "Volunteers in Service to America." *Encyclopædia Britannica*, Brittanica.com, http://www.britannica.com/topic/Volunteers-in-Service-to-America (accessed 24 March 2016).

"Welton Again Named to Head Local Drama." *Hancock County Post*, 19 February 1970, 1.

Welton, John Lee. "A Promise of Greater Things to Come." *Hancock County Post*, 4 September 1969, 1.

———. "Drama Try-Outs Saturday at Elementary School." *Hancock County Post*, 15 May 1969, 5.

———. "Drama in Sneedville? You're Kidding." *The Student*, October 1970, 44–48.

———. "Recommendations for the Hancock County Drama Association." Undated report found in the University of Tennessee Institute of Agriculture, Hancock County Extension, Sneedville, TN.

Winkler, Wayne. *Walking Toward the Sunset: The Melungeons of Appalachia*. Macon, GA: Mercer University Press, 2004.

———. "Mahala Mullins: The Facts behind a Tennessee Folk Legend." *Now & Then* 26/1 (Summer 2010): 51–54.

———. "'Mulungeons and Eboshins': Ethnic and Political Epithets," http://historical-melungeons.com/eboshins.htm, accessed 29 February 2016.

———. *The Melungeons: Sons and Daughters of the Legend*. Radio documentary, WETS-FM, January 1999.

Worden, W.L. "Sons of the Legend." *Saturday Evening Post*, 18 October 1947.

Worrell, Norman. Letter to Rep. James H. Quillen, 30 October 1969, James H. Quillen papers, Archives of Appalachia, East Tennessee State University, Johnson City, TN.

Yarbrough, Willard, "Maligned Mountain Folk May Be Topic of Drama." *Knoxville News-Sentinel*, 8 January 1968, 1.

———. "Come Enjoy A Piece of History with Melungeons." *Knoxville News-Sentinel*, 28 June 1969, 1.

———. "Melungeon Ways Are Passing." *Knoxville News-Sentinel*, 26 April 1972, 33.

———. "Trippers Take Melungeon Tour." *Knoxville News-Sentinel*. 2 July 1969, 21.

———. "Hancock County's Fair Provides Journey into Past with Melungeons," *Knoxville News-Sentinel*, 30 September 1979, C-1.

Interviews and Presentations

Beale, Calvin. Interview by author, Kingsport, TN, 21 June 2002.

Beale, Calvin. "Researching Triracial Communities," presentation at Melungeon Heritage Association gathering, Kingsport, TN, 18 June 2004.

Buffington, Raymond. Telephone interview by author, 3 March 2011.

Clifton, Larry. Panel discussion, Mildred Haun Conference Morristown, TN, 5 February 2011.

Collins, Scott. Telephone interview by author, 22 May 2018.

Collins, W.C. "Claude." Interview by author, Sneedville, TN, 19 January 2002; Big Stone Gap, VA, 25 June 2016.

DeMarce, Virginia Easley. Interview by author, Williamsburg, KY, September 1998.

Dykes, Pete. Telephone interview by author, 15 November 2016.

Ford, Jeffrey Buckner. Telephone interview by author, 15 October 2015.

Gallegos, Eloy J. Interview by author, Knoxville, TN, September 1998.

Grayson, Rose. Telephone interview by author, 18 February 2011.

Kennedy, Brent. Interview by author, Wise, VA, 26 July 1997.

Maloy, Jerry. Telephone interview by author, 19 February 2011.

Marion, Greg. Interview by author, Sneedville, TN, 19 April 2010.

Mullins, R.C. "The Vardy School," presentation at Fourth Union, Kingsport, TN, 21 June 2002.

Murphy, Mike. Telephone interview by author, 22 February 2011.

Myers, Emily. Telephone interview by author, 14 February 2011.

Nichandros, Steve. Telephone interview by author, 20 March 2011.

Overbay, DruAnna Williams. "The Vardy School," presentation at Fourth Union, Kingsport, TN, 21 June 2002.

———. Presentation to tour group, Vardy, TN, 13 August 2016.

Shine, Bruce. Interview by author, Kingsport, TN, 23 February 2010.

Van Nest, Mary Bowler. Telephone interview by author, 1 April 2011.

Vande Brake, Katherine. Interview by author, Johnson City, TN, May 2001.

———. "Melungeon Literacies and 21st Century Technologies." Presentation to Melungeon Historical Society, Rogersville, TN, 12 June 2008.

Welton, John Lee. Interview by author, Jefferson City, TN, March 2002.

———. Panel discussion, Morristown, TN, 5 February 2011.

———. Interview by author, Morristown, TN, 24 June 2017.

INDEX